The Expansion of
International Society

THE EXPANSION OF INTERNATIONAL SOCIETY

Edited by
HEDLEY BULL
and
ADAM WATSON

CLARENDON PRESS · OXFORD

Oxford University Press, Walton Street, Oxford OX2 6DP
Oxford New York Toronto
Delhi Bombay Calcutta Madras Karachi
Petaling Jaya Singapore Hong Kong Tokyo
Nairobi Dar es Salaam Cape Town
Melbourne Auckland
and associated companies in
Berlin Ibadan

Oxford is a trade mark of Oxford University Press

Published in the United States
by Oxford University Press, New York

First published new as paperback 1985
Reprinted 1989, 1992

British Library Cataloguing in Publication Data
The expansion of international society.
1. International relations—History
I. Bull, Hedley II. Watson, Adam. 1914–
303.4'82 JX1395
ISBN 0–19–821997–0

Printed in Great Britain by
Butler & Tanner Ltd, Frome, Somerset

PREFACE

The present work originated in a series of discussions of a group known as the British Committee on the Theory of International Politics, which for some years has interested itself in the history and working of the modern international system. We decided to turn our attention to the broad issue of the transition from the European international system that grew up in early modern times and was still predominantly European in our own lifetimes to the worldwide international system of today.

Most of the chapters in the present volume were written by members of the Committee and discussed and modified at meetings of it. We also invited a number of other scholars to contribute chapters on lines which we suggested, and we gratefully acknowledge their willingness to take the time and trouble involved and to agree to the revisions for which we asked.

This book was planned from the beginning as a coherent whole. We have aimed not at a collection of separate essays but at a systematic analysis of the subject under four main headings: the nature and expansion of European international society; the entry of non-European states into it; the reaction against the European international order; and the nature of the new global society of states. Of course, a survey of such a broad and complex transformation cannot treat every aspect in detail. We have aimed at setting out the broad outlines, and at supplementing this general picture with some illustrative detail. The book can only be a statement of the position as we see it. We have tried to look at the scene from many sides, and to obtain contributions and advice from scholars with many different backgrounds. But there are certainly many aspects of the subject which we have not been able to cover. The responsibility for the over-all shape of the book as it stands, and more particularly for the introduction and the conclusion, is ours alone.

The essay by Elie Kedourie first appeared in *Commentary*, December 1980, and we are grateful to the editor for permission to reprint it. We wish to acknowledge the help we have received from a grant by the Ford Foundation to Hedley Bull to pursue work in this field.

Hedley Bull
Balliol College
Oxford

Adam Watson
Center for Advanced Studies
University of Virginia

PREFATORY NOTE

FOR THE PAPERBACK EDITION

The contributors to this volume and I deeply regret to announce that Professor Hedley Bull died on 18 May 1985.

Adam Watson

CONTENTS

Part III: The Challenge to Western Dominance

Part IV: The New International Society

THE CONTRIBUTORS

Christopher M. Andrew is Fellow and Senior Tutor of Corpus Christi College, Cambridge and Editor of *The Historical Journal*. His works include *France Overseas: The Great War and the Climax of French Overseas Expansion* (1981, with A. S. Kanya-Forstner).

Coral Bell is Senior Research Fellow at the Australian National University and was formerly Professor of International Relations at the University of Sussex. She is the author of *Negotiation from Strength: A Study in the Politics of Power* (1962), *The Debatable Alliance* (1965), *The Conventions of Crisis* (1971), and *The Diplomacy of Détente* (1977).

Adda Bozeman is a Barrister-at-Law of the Middle Temple and former Professor at Sarah Lawrence College. Her works include *Politics and Culture in International History* (1960), *The Future of Law in a Multicultural World* (1971), and *Conflict in Africa: Concepts and Realities* (1976).

Ian Brownlie, QC, DCL, FBA is Chichele Professor of Public International Law at Oxford University and a Fellow of All Souls College, and is Joint Editor of *The British Yearbook of International Law*. His works include *International Law and the Use of Force by States* (Clarendon Press, 1963) and *Principles of Public International Law* (Clarendon Press, 1966).

Hedley Bull is Montague Burton Professor of International Relations at Oxford University and Fellow of Balliol College. His works include *The Control of the Arms Race* (1961) and *The Anarchical Society. A Study of Order in World Politics* (1977).

Michael Donelan is Senior Lecturer in International Relations at the London School of Economics and Political Science. He edited *The Reason of States* (1978), and has contributed to James Mayall, ed., *The Community of States* (1983) and various scholarly journals.

Ronald Dore of the Technical Change Centre, London, has spent most of his academic career in the study of Japan and the light its history throws on the problems of Third World development. His recent works include *The Diploma Disease* (1976), *Shinohata: Portrait of a Japanese Village* (1978), and *British Factory: Japanese Factory* (1973).

David Gillard is Senior Lecturer in Modern History in the University of Glasgow, and area editor for the Middle East of the *British Foreign Relations* series. His works include *The Struggle for Asia 1828–1914* (1977).

Gerrit W. Gong is Fellow in Sino-Soviet Affairs at the Georgetown Center for Strategic and International Studies at Washington DC. He is a graduate of Brigham Young University and a former Rhodes Scholar at Wadham College, Oxford, and the author of *The Standard of 'Civilization' in International Society* (Clarendon Press, 1984).

Michael Howard, CBE, MC, D.Litt, FBA is Regius Professor of Modern History in the University of Oxford and Vice-President of the International Institute for Strategic Studies. He was formerly Chichele Professor of the History of War in the University of Oxford and Professor of War Studies in the University of London.

Elie Kedourie, FBA is Professor of Politics in the University of London and Editor of *Middle Eastern Studies*. His works include *Nationalism* (1961) and *Nationalism in Asia and Africa* (1971).

Gopal Krishna is Senior Fellow of the Centre for the Study of Developing Societies in Delhi, and a former Research Fellow of Wolfson College, Oxford. He is a specialist in modern history and political sociology and has held visiting academic appointments at McGill University and the University of California.

Wm. Roger Louis, D.Litt. is Professor of History at the University of Texas. His books include *Imperialism at Bay* (Clarendon Press, 1978), (with Professor Gifford) *The Transfer of Power in Africa* (1982), and *The British Empire in the Middle East 1945–1951* (Clarendon Press, 1984).

Richard Löwenthal is Emeritus Professor of International Relations at the Free University, Berlin. He has worked extensively on the Soviet Union and the impact of communism on world affairs, concerning which his latest work is *Model or Ally?: The Communist Powers and the Developing Countries* (1977).

Peter Lyon is Reader in International Relations and Secretary of the Institute of Commonwealth Studies in the University of London, and is Editor of *The Round Table*. His works include *Neutralism* (1963) and *War and Peace in South East Asia* (1969).

Ali Mazrui is Research Professor at the University of Jos in Nigeria and Professor of Political Science and Afroamerican Studies at the University of Michigan. His works include *Towards a Pax Africana* (1967), *Cultural Engineering and Nation-Building* (1972), *A World Federation of Cultures: An African Perspective* (1976), and *Africa's International Relations* (1977).

Thomas Naff is Director of the Middle East Center and the Middle East Research Institute of the University of Pennsylvania. He received his Ph.D. degree from the University of London, School of Oriental and African Studies and has taught and conducted research extensively in the Middle East.

Patrick O'Brien is University Lecturer in Economic History at Oxford University and a Fellow of St. Antony's College. He is the author of *The Revolution in Egypt's Economic System* (1966), *The New Economic History of the Railways* (1977), and *Economic Growth in Britain and France 1780–1914* (1978).

Sir Michael Palliser, GCMG was Permanent Under-Secretary of State and Head of HM Diplomatic Service 1975–82. He had earlier been Head of Planning Staff of the Foreign and Commonwealth Office, a Private Secretary to the Prime Minister, and Permanent Representative to the European Communities.

James P. Piscatori is Research Fellow at the Royal Institute of International Affairs and was formerly Assistant Professor of Government and Foreign Affairs at the University of Virginia. He is the editor of *Islam in the Political Process* (1983).

Hidemi Suganami is Lecturer in International Relations at Keele University, and studied in Tokyo, Aberystwyth, and London. He is the author of a number of articles on international relations and law.

R. J. Vincent is Lecturer in International Relations at Keele University. He is the author of *Non-intervention and World Politics* (1974) and various articles on the theory of world politics.

Adam Watson, CMG is Professor in the Center for Advanced Studies, University of Virginia, and a former member of HM Diplomatic Service and British Ambassador in West Africa and Cuba. His works include *The Nature and Problems of the Third World* (1970), and *Diplomacy: The Dialogue Between States* (1982).

INTRODUCTION

THE EDITORS

The purpose of this book is to explore the expansion of the international society of European states across the rest of the globe, and its transformation from a society fashioned in Europe and dominated by Europeans into the global international society of today, with its nearly two hundred states, the great majority of which are not European.

By an international society we mean a group of states (or, more generally, a group of independent political communities) which not merely form a system, in the sense that the behaviour of each is a necessary factor in the calculations of the others, but also have established by dialogue and consent common rules and institutions for the conduct of their relations, and recognize their common interest in maintaining these arrangements. Such was the international system that emerged in Europe in early modern times, which Voltaire called 'a commonwealth divided into several states' and Burke 'the diplomatic republick of Europe', which was exclusively European until the time of the American Revolution and remained predominantly so until the Second World War. Such an international society also, it seems to us, is the worldwide system of today, with its vast and complex array of international institutions and its long catalogue of laws and conventions, which most of its members habitually obey. We are concerned to see how, by the flood-tide of European dominance over the world and its subsequent ebb, the one became transformed into the other.

When European expansion began in the late fifteenth century the world was not organized into any single international system or society, but comprised several regional international systems (or what we choose to call international systems, with some danger of anachronism), each with its own distinctive rules and institutions, reflecting a dominant regional culture. The global international society of today is in large part the consequence of Europe's impact on the rest of the world over the last five centuries. Europeans, of course, have never had any monopoly of knowledge or experience of international relations. The rules and institutions of contemporary international society have been shaped by North and South Americans of European stock or assimilation and also by Asians, Africans, and Oceanians, as well as by the European powers in their period of dominance. Indeed, in the last few decades there has been a massive revision of international rules and conventions carried out by African, Asian, and Latin American states. But it was the expansion of Europe that first brought about the economic and technological unification of the globe, just as it was the European-dominated international society of the nineteenth and early twentieth centuries that first expressed its political unification. Moreover, with the decline of European dominance and the achievement or recovery of political independence by the societies of America, Asia, Africa, and Oceania, it was the rules and institutions of European international society which they accepted as the basis of their international relations, even while seeking in some respects to modify them. The present international political structure of the world – founded upon the division of mankind and of the earth into separate states, their acceptance of one another's sovereignty, of principles of law regulating their coexistence and co-operation, and of diplomatic conventions facilitating their intercourse – is, at least in its most basic features, the legacy of Europe's now vanished ascendancy. Because it was in fact Europe and not America, Asia, or Africa that first dominated and, in so doing, unified the world, it is not our perspective but the historical record itself that can be called Eurocentric.

In the centuries immediately preceding Europe's expansion the most important regional international systems, alongside medieval Latin Christendom from which the modern European states-system developed, were the Arab-Islamic system, which stretched from Spain to Persia; the international system of the Indian subcontinent and its extensions eastward, founded upon a traditional Hindu culture but with predominant power in the hands of Muslim rulers; the Mongol-Tartar dominion of the Eurasian steppes, which had also become Muslim; and the Chinese system, long under Mongol domination.

All these regional international systems were built upon elaborate civilizations, including complex religions, governments, law, commerce, written records, and financial accounts. Outside them lay areas of less developed culture, usually pre-literate and sometimes without awareness of the techniques of smelting metal, but organized as a rule into recognizable political entities which had contacts and relations with their neighbours without achieving a general system. The largest and most significant of these areas was sub-Saharan Africa, which the Arab-Islamic world was beginning to penetrate, but they also included most of the Americas and Australasia, which before their discovery by the Europeans were quite unknown to the Old World. In the Americas two empires similar to those of the Old World had developed in Mexico and Peru, each administered by a small ruling group that dominated subject peoples; outside these restricted realms there lay an enormous area of pre-literate peoples. Here as in Australasia there were no highly organized empires, and political communities were often stateless. Peoples dealt with their neighbours according to established codes of conduct, which were often elaborate, but their geographical awareness did not extend very far; and there was nothing that could plausibly be called an international system, such as had existed for millenia in the Middle East, India, and China.

These regional international systems were, of course, very different from one another: the Arab-Islamic and Indian systems, for example, were in practice composed of a number of independent political entities, whereas the Mongol-Tartar and Chinese systems were more effectively centralized. But they had one feature in common: they were all, at least in the theory that underlay them, hegemonial or imperial. At the centre of each was a suzerain Supreme Ruler – the Khalifa or Commander of the Faithful, the Emperor in Delhi, the Mongol Great Khan, the Chinese Son of Heaven – who exercised direct authority over the Heartland; and around this empire extended a periphery of locally autonomous realms that acknowledged the suzerain's overlordship and paid him tribute. Many peripheral states were able to maintain a complete independence in spite of the nominal claims of the Supreme Ruler. Beyond each fluctuating periphery there lay kingdoms and principalities which were recognized, even by the Supreme Ruler, as independent, although not as his equal – for example, the reduced state of Byzantium before its final collapse in 1453, the kingdoms of the Deccan and Java, some Russian principalities, and Japan.

Within each of the suzerain-state systems, different as they were, relations among political authorities were regulated by specific treaties as well as by traditional codes of conduct, governing such matters as the movement of envoys who came and went, the payment of tribute, commercial exchanges, and the waging of war. States of the periphery maintained relations with each other as well as with the Supreme Ruler. But they did not combine to overthrow the central authority. They might disobey it or rebel aginst it, and sometimes a powerful king might aspire to take it over; but they all assumed that some hegemonial focus would continue to exist, to lay down the rules and determine the nature of relations among the members of the system. There was no attempt, within these major, extra-European international systems, to question the underlying hegemonial concept.

Contacts among these regional international systems (and with the different world of medieval Latin Christendom) were much more limited than contacts within them. There was trade, especially by sea across the Mediterranean and the Indian Ocean. There was some diplomatic communication and military conflict, in some cases severe, as between Latin Christendom and the Arab-Islamic system. The Arab-Islamic system, to a limited extent, provided brokers and middlemen between the other systems; Islamic geographers, for example, had a much more accurate concept of the Old World than either the medieval Europeans or the Chinese, Marco Polo notwithstanding. But not even the three Islamic systems (Arab-Islamic, Mongol-Tartar, and Indian) may be said to have formed among themselves a single international system or international society, in the sense in which we use these terms; much less did any such system embrace the world as a whole.

In this era preceding the emergence of a universal international society, what assumptions were made about the relations between states or rulers that belonged to different regional international systems, as opposed to the much more intimate and continuous relations among states or rulers within the same system? This question has an important bearing on our study. We do not know enough to be able to provide a comprehensive answer to it, but certain things can be said. It is clear that states or rulers have commonly enough entered into agreements with states or rulers – and indeed with merchants and other individuals and groups – outside their own regional international system and the civilization with which it is associated. Societies which recognize that *pacta sunt servanda* among their own members, do not find it difficult to recognize the advantages of fulfilling obligations and contracts in dealings with individuals and groups in different societies. The fact that all societies appear to recognize that there is an obligation to fulfil contracts, along with prudential advantage in fulfilling them (just as, it is often argued, they all recognize rules that limit violence among their members and enjoin respect for rights of property) provides a basis for the extension of the principle of the sanctity of contracts beyond the bounds of particular societies.

It has been said that the advantages of implementing contracts become apparent first in economic transactions between buyers and sellers, and that the spread of agreements between members of different societies and civilizations first occurs in the area of commercial exchanges. It is pertinent to our inquiry that the relations between the Chinese and the Indian worlds, and even among the Islamicized systems, were largely economic in nature, just as the activities of the Europeans in the Indian Ocean and beyond were almost entirely concerned with trade until the nineteenth century. We have also to note, however, that states or rulers belonging to different regional international systems and civilizations have not found it impossible to enter into agreements about war, peace, and alliances: one has only to think of the role played by such agreements in the history or relations between Latin Christian and Arab-Islamic powers.

It is also clear that such agreements reached, as it were, across the boundaries of international systems and civilizations are often written in a form intelligible to both sides. A celebrated example is the series of agreements between the Pharaoh of Egypt and the Great King of the Hittites in the fourteenth century BC, preserved in the Tell el Amarna tablets; these agreemnents were written down in cuneiform Aramaic, a mercantile Semitic language used by neither imperial government domestically, and there is extensive diplomatic correspondence about their implementation. So too Muslim and Hindu rulers in India, whose beliefs about the ordering of society perhaps showed more differences than those between any other great civilizations of Asia, found no great difficulty in negotiating written agreements, often with texts in more than one language, or in arguing about their implementation. From the historic moment when Vasco da Gama dropped his anchor in Calicut harbour, Asian rulers applied these principles also to Europeans, who were of course equally familiar with them.

When the Europeans embarked upon their historic expansion they did so with a set of assumptions about relations with non-European and non-Christian peoples inherited from medieval Latin Christendom and ultimately from the Ancient World. They had a conception of what they called the law of nations, meaning the law common to all nations, that could be used to regulate relations among nations and applied beyond the bounds of Christendom or Europe just as it was within them, at least in cases where there was acceptance on both sides of the principles and practices connected with it. They also had a conception of the law of nature, the law binding upon all human beings and made apparent to them by the faculty of reason, that provided a normative basis for regulating relations among nations and with private traders throughout the world as a whole and not merely within the European or Christian community. Indeed, in the three centuries from 1500 to 1800, as European involvement in Asian politics persisted and grew, and with it the armed rivalry of the European powers in Asia, a loose Eurasian system or quasi-system grew up in which European states sought to deal with Asian states on the basis of moral and legal equality, until in the nineteenth century this gave place to notions of European superiority.

However, it was never the case, before Europe unified the globe, that relations between states or rulers that were members of different regional international systems could be conducted on the same moral and legal basis as relations within the same system, for this basis was provided in part by principles that were culturally particular and exclusive: the unity of Christendom, the community of the faithful in Islam, the conception of the Chinese Empire as the Middle Kingdom. In the European tradition ideas of a universal law of nations or law of nature were contested by doctrines of a fundamental division of humanity between Greeks and barbarians, Christians and infidels, Europeans and non-Europeans. Most importantly, there was no single, agreed body of rules and institutions operating across the boundaries of any two regional international systems, let alone throughout the world as a whole, such as we imply when we speak of an international society.

Among the regional international systems into which the world was divided that which evolved in Europe was distinctive in that it came to repudiate any hegemonial principle and regard itself as a society of states that were sovereign or independent. This non-hegemonial society was not without historical precedent: the city states of classical Greece, the Hellenistic Kingdoms between the death of Alexander and the Roman conquest, perhaps the 'period of warring states' in ancient China, may all be thought to provide examples. Nor should it be overlooked that the European states, as they evolved this non-hegemonial system in their relations with one another, at the same time established a number of empires which, while they were rival and competing, taken together amounted to a European hegemony over the rest of the world, which in the nineteenth century became an immense periphery looking to a European centre. Moreover, the non-hegemonial system among the Europeans themselves was evolved only slowly, and with great difficulty, after 1500. Medieval Latin Christendom, which gave birth to the modern European states-system, while it did not have a Supreme Ruler, had not itself recognized the independence of its various parts, and the model of the Roman suzerain-state system remained an inspiration to the Catholic Church and to a series of lay imitators such as Charles V, Louis XIV, Napoleon, and Hitler, who were restrained only by coalitions seeking to maintain a balance of power. Only in the eighteenth century was the idea firmly implanted among European states that an attempt by any one of them to establish hegemony over the others was a violation of the rules of their international society.

This European international society, it should be noted, did not first evolve its own rules and institutions and then export them to the rest of the world. The evolution of the European system of interstate relations and the expansion of Europe across the globe were simultaneous processes, which influenced and affected each other. Both began at the end of the fifteenth century, and both were concluded by the end of the Second World War, by which time European dominance was clearly at an end and the global international system, while still evolving, was being shaped less by Europeans than by others. When the Spanish conquistadors first encountered the Aztecs and Incas, European states were far from having repudiated the hegemonial principle even in their relations with one another; they had not begun to embrace the idea that relations between independent political communities should be conducted on a secular rather than a religious basis; the doctrines of the internal and external sovereignty of states had not yet been clearly formulated; and although the principle that there should be a balance of power was known among the renaissance Italian states, the great European powers north of the Alps were only beginning to grope towards it. The idea that states, even within the European system, were equal in rights did not emerge until the middle of the eighteenth century, and only then to receive a setback in the nineteenth when the great powers in forming the European Concert put forward claims to special responsibilities for maintaining order, and corresponding rights that small powers did not have. Resident embassies, that distinctively European contribution to diplomatic practice, spread among the European states after, not before, the beginning of European expansion, and diplomatic precedent up to the time of the Congress of Vienna in 1815 was determined by status in the ancient hierarchy of kingdoms and republics, not by the principle of equal rights. The development of international organizations, although it may be said to have begun towards the end of the period of European ascendancy with the founding of technical international organizations late in the nineteenth century, and of the League of Nations after the First World War, has been more remarkable since the end of European dominance than it ever was before.

Part I of our book, *European International Society and the Outside World*, describes the floodtide of expansion that established the domination of one of the several regional international systems that existed in the fifteenth century over the others, and over the less developed parts of the world as well – a domination that united the whole world into a single economic, strategic, and political system for the first time.

Part II, *The Entry of Non-European States into International Society*, examines the process whereby non-European states came to take their place alongside European states not merely as participants in a single international system, but as members of the same international society accepting its rules and institutions – some of them old-established polities like the Ottoman Empire, China, and Japan, others former colonies or dependencies that gained their independence for the first time. The international society that emerged from this process, while it was no longer exclusively European, was still one in which the Europeans had a dominant position. An underlying issue here is the conflict between the view of this entry of non-European states taken by the European powers at the time, that it was a process of admission to an exclusive club with rigorous qualifications for membership drawn up by the original or founding members, and the view taken later by many Third World states that it was not so much an admission as a re-admission to a general international society of states or peoples whose independence had been wrongfully denied.

Part III, *The Challenge to Western Dominance*, describes the repudiation of European (and by extension of American and Russian) domination by the non-European, and more particularly Asian, African, and Latin American states and peoples, which together make up the coalition we call the Third World. This part is concerned with the transition from a universal international system based upon European hegemony to one that is not, even if it may be argued that new hegemonies and new forms of hegemony have replaced old ones. The revolt against the individual European empires first manifested itself among the European settlers in the Americas, who wished nonetheless to retain their European civilization and culture and to be recognized as independent members of European international society. The European powers accepted this independence of the trans-Atlantic Europeans before they had established effective government over any considerable parts of Asia or Africa. But as European empires and hegemonial claims spread over those continents, the non-European peoples too began to resist European dominance.

Part IV, *The New International Society*, is concerned with the international order that has emerged from the ebb tide of European dominance. Has the geographical expansion of international society led to a contraction of the consensus about common interests, rules, and institutions, on which an international society properly so-called, as distinct from a mere international system, must rest? Or can we say that the framework of the old European society of states has been modified, adapted, and developed in such a way that a genuinely universal and non-hegemonial structure of rules and institutions has taken root?

We address these issues from a particular standpoint. Our contributors, although not all European, are for the most part Western in outlook. We have no illusion that our treatment of this large subject is comprehensive or definitive. We believe that international political life, including its normative or institutional dimension, has its own logic and is not to be understood simply as the reflection of economic interests or productive processes. We are inclined to take seriously the cultural differences between modern societies, as against those who hold either that these are disappearing under the impact of modernity or that they have no bearing upon international relations. We have been concerned with the moral questions raised by our subject, but have not interested ourselves in questions of policy and have no thought of offering advice to governments as to what they should so. We certainly hold that our subject can be understood only in historical perspective, and that without an awareness of the past that generated it, the universal international society of the present can have no meaning.

Part I

European International Society and the Outside World

1

EUROPEAN INTERNATIONAL SOCIETY AND ITS EXPANSION

Adam Watson

The society of Medieval Latin Christendom was not divided into separate states each encompassed within a geographical perimeter; it was organized horizontally across the whole of Christendom according to function. Alongside the universal administrative structure of the Latin church – religious, administrative, educational, charitable – were the lay authorities, drawn from the noble class which fought, governed, and dispensed justice, and which was organized in a complicated net of vassalage and feudal obligation that was often unenforceable. The townsmen and merchants, many of them Jewish, were in practice largely autonomous, especially in Italy and Germany. The peasantry were more directly subject to the nobility and the church. The two governing orders provided a framework of society that, in spite of many deficiencies, enabled the peasants and townspeople to improve their own standards of living and to multiply in numbers as well as to support the governing orders and their creative achievements.

Latin Christendom, lacking the regulating hand of a centralized or co-ordinating government, proved to be exceptionally turbulent, dynamic, and enterprising. It was far from being a closed world largely sealed off from other cultures and societies, as some Asian cultures have been. Innovative and expansionary, it filled out the uncultivated spaces within its boundaries and began to push back its geographic limits in many directions. The expansion was animated by the church and led by rulers and knights, and appealed also to merchants in the towns and to many humbler folk. The more adventurous members of all classes of society looked eagerly outward: to spread the Faith, and in pursuit of trade, warfare, land, and even new techniques and ideas.

The medieval expansionary thrust developed in three main directions. The first and most permanent was to the south and west, the reconquest of the territories which had been part of Latin Christendom before their conquest by Islam. The Muslims were slowly driven back from Iberia and Sicily; and the recovered kingdoms, from their thrones and sees to their fields and fisheries, received throngs of settlers from all over Christendom. This thrust proved to be the most important of the three for the theme of this book. It did not stop at the water's edge, but continued overseas, to become the great maritime expansion of Western Europe. The second thrust was south-eastwards, towards the lands which had once been Christian but not Latin. The Holy Land of Palestine was the supreme objective of the crusaders; but Syria and Egypt and the Byzantine Empire also lured them with wealth and opportunities. 'Outremer', the memorable name given to the Latin settlements in the Levant, endured for some centuries. But the Muslims, under the leadership of Turkish peoples who were also newcomers to the area, succeeded in driving the Latins out. The Ottoman Turks went on to conquer the Byzantine Empire and to extend their dominion over nearly a quarter of Europe as far as Budapest and Kiev. The third thrust was eastward, from Scandinavia and Germany and also Latinized Poland, into the non-Christian areas round the south and east of the Baltic. Over the centuries this thrust moved the frontier of Latin Christendom some hundreds of miles to the east, until it pressed up against the Orthodox Christianity which the Russians had inherited from Byzantium.

The motives which lay behind this first medieval expansion of Europe were complex. They continued in different guises in subsequent expansions which took the Europeans all over the globe. In particular it is necessary to understand the crusading motive along with the more mundane ones. A crusade was a religious, legal, and military enterprise that had to be proclaimed by the Pope, preached by the Church, open to volunteers from all Christendom, and justified by reference to the interests of the whole. 'To present these wars as . . . matters of interest disguised as matters of conscience . . . is too easy', says Eric Christiansen. 'It avoids the unavoidable question of why men who were never reluctant to wage war for profit, fame, vengeance or merely to pass the time, without any disguise or pretext, nevertheless chose to claim that certain wars were fought for God's honour and the redemption of mankind.'[1] God's honour was uppermost in the minds of the clergy, who also provided the administrative cadres of the newly won lands and were the forerunners of dedicated bodies of colonial administrators with an equal sense of higher purpose, such as the British Indian Civil Service. Knights and princes were impelled to join a crusade for God's honour too, but especially for their own. Richard Coeur de Lion did not campaign in Palestine, or the Black Douglas in Spain, or Henry Bolingbroke in Prussia, to extend their own dominions or for material gain. 'I am not covetous for gold', Shakespeare makes Bolingbroke's son say, 'But if it be a sin to covet honour I am the most offending soul alive.'[2] Of course material advantages – trade, booty, and above all land – always played their part in the expansion of Europe, from the earliest crusade to the final brief extension in this century of British and French authority in the Middle East and the Italian conquest of Ethiopia. The medieval expansion of Europe was by no means all military, or confined to crusading. By and large, it was the Latins who sought trade outside the bounds of Christendom, and their merchants who conducted it. The same was true with treaties and alliances. Following the precedent set by Charlemagne's alliance with Harun al Rashid, Latin princes and trading cities took the initiative in making agreements with non-Christian rulers. All those who pushed beyond the geographic limits of their world, both in war and in peace, were held in especial esteem in Latin Christendom. The error of our age is that, too preoccupied with the economic basis of society and the element of commercial profit in European expansion, we are apt to underestimate the other motives which in varying degrees have always been present as well.

Medieval Christendom was not yet a society of politically distinct states. But at first in Italy, and then throughout the area, the complex horizontal structure of feudal society crystallized into a vertical pattern of territorial states, each with increasing authority inside defined geographic borders. The Renaissance turned men's minds towards classical models of independent statehood. The Reformation broke the authority of the universal church, which came to depend on the lay power of the new rulers even where it remained Catholic. In the sixteenth century there was, in Herbert Butterfield's phrase, a wind blowing in favour of kings. It also blew in favour of any smaller prince or military commander or city or league of peasant cantons that could maintain its independence in practice. North of the Alps princes whose authority was legitimate but shadowy learnt Italian techniques and turned their realms into states. Latin was replaced as the administrative language by official and increasingly standardized vernaculars. In religion as in other matters the decision of these new sovereign states was final. The principle of *cujus regio ejus religio* applied formally only to the Holy Roman Empire, but the practice quickly extended throughout the Christian commonwealth of Europe. It carried, as a corollary, another principle which rulers readily acknowledged and proclaimed though they did not always scrupulously observe it: non-interference by one state in the affairs of another. This doctrine of the separateness of the new states into which Christendom was now divided suited their sovereigns great and small, hereditary and elective, who all wanted to exclude outside interference from complicating their relations with their own subjects. The concept of the legitimacy of absolute sovereignty involved the formal rejection of a hegemonial order.

The resolution of medieval Christendom into sovereign states, each within the hide of a separate Leviathan, enabled rulers and governments to concentrate great powers into their hands. The growing resources and ambitions of princes and merchants, and the new forms of wealth and strength which were continually being generated by the highly inventive and dynamic civilization of Europe, combined to produce a society of states which increasingly pressed and jostled against one another and competed in the arts of war and peace. Wariness, and an eye for economic and military threats from outside, were important for survival and necessary for success. Europe, as Latin Christendom came to be called, did not have room enough for the power of all its active thrusting communities.

A states system in recognizably modern form, where at least the major states interact with one another on a regular basis so that each feels obliged to take the actions of the others into account, had developed in Italy in the fourteenth and fifteenth centuries, while the medieval reconquest of Iberia and the Scandinavian-German expansion round the Baltic were still in process of achievement. Within two years of the completion of the Spanish reconquest and Columbus's discovery of America in 1492 the French invaded Italy and incorporated it into the wider states system that was then beginning to develop in southern and western Europe.

The dominant states of the western part of that system in the century and a half from the French invasion of Italy in 1494 to the Westphalian settlement of 1648 included the five great maritime colonial powers from which the expansion of Europe overseas was almost entirely conducted. These were newly united Spain; Portugal; France, which at the beginning and again at the end of the period was the most powerful state in Europe; England; and the Netherlands. All five had a substantial seaboard on the Atlantic, which thus became the home sea linking Western Europe to its colonial *ultra mar*, a new mediterranean. The two great imperial structures of Europe, the now largely German Holy Roman Empire and the Turkish Ottoman Sultanate, also occupied major positions in what was called the southern system. Through the Habsburg dynasty Spain was linked with the Empire and after 1580 with Portugal, while France was allied to the Ottomans. The French encouraged the independence of principalities in the Empire – especially the Netherlands which were thus enabled to make a separate and highly significant contribution to the expansion of Europe overseas.

To the north and east of this closely interacting pattern of relations in

Western Europe was another system, focused on the Baltic and the area between it and the Black Sea. In the sixteenth century there was an unstable balance in which the Habsburg Empire and the Ottoman Turks played major parts, along with the two crusading kingdoms of Sweden and Poland-Lithuania and also the expanding realm of Muscovy which in 1480 had thrown off the Tartar yoke. The struggle between the Ottomans and the Habsburgs linked the two European systems in practice throughout the sixteenth century, and their policies in each system are comprehensible only in the light of their involvement at the same time in the other. Nevertheless the two systems remained distinct, and only became effectively merged into one in the first half of the seventeenth century as a result of the Thirty Years War in the west and the alliance of France and Sweden.

The first westward overseas expansion of Europe was Iberian, and followed the traditions and experience of the two states that conducted the operations, Portugal and Castile. In 1493, the year after Columbus discovered what was later found to be a new continent, Pope Alexander Borgia divided the non-European world down the Atlantic as he and his experts supposed, assigning to Spain what lay to the west and Portugal what lay to the east, in order to direct the colonizing efforts of the two Iberian powers along separate channels, and to keep them from wasting their energies *ultra mar* in fighting each other. The Pope's decision was a development of the medieval practice of papally authorized crusades by which the reconquest of Iberia had been greatly assisted. It also recognized that expansion must be left in the hands of individual states, as had already increasingly happened in Iberia, and could no longer be organized as a joint venture of all Christendom. This orderly division of opportunity was eminently successful. The Spaniards and Portuguese did not compete overseas, even though the dividing line gave a large part of South America to Portugal, which became Brazil.

The Spanish or more correctly Castilian acquisition of an immense land empire in the Americas was the first and perhaps the most spectacular colonial achievement by a single European state. The principalities established *outre mer* by the crusaders in Syria and Palestine were collective enterprises, and territorially limited: the crusaders did not come anywhere near to overthrowing Muslim rule and replacing it with a Latin empire, as Alexander the Great replaced the Persian Empire with a Macedonian one. The Muslim world, and particularly its Turkish champions, were the heirs of previously highly developed civilizations and were in active intercourse with a wider range of foreign peoples than any other society of that time. Their inheritance, and contacts, and pressures from outside had made them at least the technological and military equals of the crusaders. Moreover, Islam enjoyed wide and fervent popular support in the Levant, and its doctrines of racial and social egalitarianism even when diluted in practice offered the Faithful unusual social mobility and individual opportunity. The empires of the Aztecs and Incas were by contrast isolated from outside pressures. They were imperial structures with an advanced civilization based on a stone age technology and governed by a small ruling race whose subject peoples accepted their dominion without loyalty and in the Aztec case only after a long period of warfare. It would not have been difficult for any expedition trained in the military arts of Europe or Asia to substitute its own authority for that of the ruling group; and in the logic of events this was fairly likely to happen sooner or later across either the Atlantic or the Pacific. The two 'aristolithic' empires occupied only a small part of the hemisphere. All the rest, including the large areas accidentally assigned to Portugal, was inhabited by much more primitive and usually nomadic peoples whom the Europeans called wild men (*bravos, sauvages*).

The Spaniards treated the civilized societies of Mexico and Peru in essentially the same way as they were used to treating the inhabitants of the lands reconquered from the Muslims in Spain. The territories belonged to the crown of Castile by right of conquest following Papal designation. They were given names like New Spain and New Granada; and as in Granada itself, Castilian law and language were enforced, the Church made strenuous and successful efforts to convert the Crown's new subjects, and the Viceroys encouraged settlers from Spain. Elsewhere in America the Spanish authorities, and the Portuguese in Brazil, considered the territories sparsely peopled by 'wild men' as equally theirs by Papal award, discovery, and conquest. They might find it expedient to make agreements with savage tribes, but did not regard them as moral equals with a legitimate right to territory except as designated by the Castilian or Portuguese Crowns – which in 1580 were merged in one Habsburg monarch.

The Europeans thus incorporated the New World from the beginning into their system of administration and government. It became an extension of Christendom, as the Iberian peninsula and the eastern Baltic lands had been.

This imperial incorporation was in marked contrast to Portuguese practice in the East, round the shores of the Indian Ocean. The Portuguese expansion there was maritime and predominantly commercial, designed to transact with the Indies directly the trade which had been carried on for centuries through Muslim intermediaries. It was an attempt to rearrange an existing pattern of intercourse rather than to europeanize a hitherto unknown world. More laudable purposes like spreading Christianity and combating the Turkish enemy were also present, and gave Portuguese operations a degree of respectability in many European eyes. The Portuguese commanders were the representatives of their king and of the Portuguese state. They treated Asian authorities, and especially Hindu ones, much as European rulers dealt with each other. From Vasco da Gama's first arrival at the great Indian trading port of Calicut in 1498 the Portuguese were prepared to accept a client relationship with local rulers. Though they found it necessary to fortify their coastal trading stations and sometimes to acquire small areas of land round them, the Portuguese kept in mind the advice of their first Viceroy in the Indian Ocean: 'The greater the number of fortresses you hold, the weaker will be your power. Let all your forces be on the sea.' Soon they became allies and enemies of Asian states other than the Ottomans – with whom the Habsburgs were already at war – and occasionally even reduced a minor Asian ruler to vassalage or annexed small areas of territory as Iberian sovereigns had done during the centuries of the reconquest. The Portuguese maritime dominion in the East was very lucrative while it lasted. But its economic purpose was complicated by an aggressive hostility to Muslims inherited from the reconquest of Portugal itself and reinforced by Portuguese involvement in the southern European system on the side opposed to the Ottoman Turks.

The conceptually hegemonic or suzerain state structure of India was in abeyance when the Portuguese found their way there. A multitude of Hindu and Muslim rulers governed independently: many of the small principalities with whom the Portuguese dealt were much smaller than Portugal itself, but independent in practice and usually engaged in a struggle with at least one neighbour. Hindu rulers especially welcomed the newcomers as valuable trading partners who were able to offer better terms than the Arab middlemen. They also found the Portuguese to be effective allies and enemies in local conflicts, for in spite of their limited numbers the Portuguese controlled the sea. East of India, in Java and the Spice Islands, the Portuguese were accepted on the same basis as the Arab and Chinese merchants who also traded there. In short, the Portuguese became marginal members of the strategic play of forces round the Indian Ocean, and important members of the commercial pattern. We might say in modern phraseology that the Asian powers concerned recognized the Portuguese as members of their system without seriously modifying their concepts and their practices to suit the newcomers.

This orderly pattern was disrupted by the overseas activities of the

Dutch. After the Habsburg acquisition of Portugal the Dutch, who were fighting to secede from the Habsburgs, could no longer obtain the wares of the East from Portugal and resolved to import them directly and more cheaply. Commercial enterprise and the struggle for independence took the form of systematic attacks on Portuguese positions overseas, both in the Indian Ocean and in Brazil where the Dutch tried to found a colonial state. They left the solidly entrenched Spanish empire on the American mainland prudently alone. Dutch operations in the Indies were conducted not by Viceroys on behalf of the Crown but by companies of private merchants which became consolidated into the united East India Company. They concentrated their activities in Java and the Spice Islands, providing armed protection to local rulers in return for a trade monopoly. Gradually in the course of the seventeenth century the Company's Governors on the spot gained control over most of Java. The Company took over the existing structures of authority and government, merely replacing the Muslim rulers at the apex of each administration. The purpose of the Company remained commercial; and its involvement in government arose from the local situation as the Dutch in the Indies understood it, rather than from any design in the Netherlands.

Dutch activities in the Indian Ocean, and in Brazil, inflicted severe and intentional damage on Portuguese interests, and were thus of indirect benefit to the Ottomans and other associates of the Dutch against the Habsburgs, and also to Muslim powers in Asia generally whom the Portuguese treated as actual or potential enemies. In addition, by offering an alternative market and proclaiming the principle of freedom of the seas for trade, the Dutch presence was useful to many Asian rulers and communities. The Dutch played a major part in shaping the international society which was evolving in Europe in the seventeenth century, particularly its anti-hegemonial assumptions and its emphasis on international law. They were also largely responsible for carrying this outlook and the new European rules with them beyond Europe to the East and the Americas, and for breaking up the older Iberian approach based on Papal authority, hemispheres of influence, and avoidance of conflict and competition.

On the heels of the Dutch came the two other west European peoples to play a major part in the expansion of Europe overseas, the English and the French. Both founded extensive colonies of settlement in North America and the West Indies. These settlements were under the general authority and protection of the Crown; but royal authority was delegated much more than in the Spanish viceroyalties to the actual emigrants and chartered companies who colonized, traded, and pushed back the frontiers of European settlement. Religious motives were prominent in the founding of many British colonies; but the production of goods like sugar, tobacco, and furs that found a ready market 'at home' was the main incentive, and led to the massive importation of African slave labour into areas where manual work was difficult for Europeans. The forms of government were also imported from the mother country, and soon developed a life of their own. In the seventeenth century the French seemed to be more enterprising than their English rivals; but in the second half of the eighteenth century the English settlers established a dominant position, and Napoleon sold to them what remained of French possessions on the North American mainland.

In the East both the English and the French followed the maritime pattern pioneered by the Dutch and the Portuguese. On the coasts of the Indian Ocean and on the route round Africa leading to it their companies established trading centres and ports of call for their ships. They fortified and garrisoned their stations principally against European rivals and only secondarily against Asian rulers, who derived considerable advantages from their presence. These mercantile operations were supported by ambassadors who conveyed assurances of friendship from the sovereigns of England and France and requests for permission to trade. In the seventeenth century neither the English nor the French aimed at anything more in the East. The English saw themselves as commercial rivals of the Dutch, and were inclined to support and benefit from the waning maritime position of their traditional Portuguese allies. The English East India Company acquired at an early stage an awareness of the advantages of orderly monopoly as opposed to a dangerous and expensive naval and commercial free-for-all. Other merchants also saw these advantages. Much of the dialogue of all the Europeans with Asian rulers was concerned with excluding each other from trade and even diplomatic contacts with their Asian hosts.

The inducements and pressures that involved the Dutch in local government took another form in India. The spectacular Mogul Empire began to take shape there in 1556. By the end of the century it had proclaimed the re-establishment of the former suzerainty of Delhi, and by the end of the seventeenth century it made that suzerainty substantially effective. Local potentates now ruled once more as vassals of the Emperor, with varying degrees of independence. The Portuguese, and the French and English who succeeded them in India, now had to find their place within this suzerain system. They did so in the same way as the local Indian rulers, by accepting subordinate positions within the government of the empire. The Moguls, says Alexandrowicz, 'allowed the English and French companies to rise to the status of Grand Officers or vassals of the empire and ultimately negotiated with them within its constitutional framework'.[3]

So the Asian rulers, by design or weakness, progressively involved the Europeans not only in their alliances and quarrels, but also in the administration of their realms. Gradually also the large-scale production of commodities for sale to European traders supplemented the export to Europe of products intended for the local market, and further enriched rulers and state treasuries. The activities of competing European traders strengthened Muslim and Hindu states round the Indian Ocean economically and administratively. Informed Muslims surveying the scene round the year 1700 would see that the long Portuguese crusade against Islam in the Indian Ocean had failed, and that Islam had continued its military and religious expansion to bring almost all that great area under Muslim influence.

However, during the eighteenth century the Moguls lost their tenuous control of most of India, and the subcontinent reverted to the pattern found by the Europeans when they first arrived on the scene. A large number of warring states asserted their independence in practice, thought they usually acknowledged a nominal Mogul sovereignty. The unstable political equilibrium of Europe and commercial rivalry made Britain and France particularly anxious that neither should steal a march on the other. European maritime technology had made such tremendous strides that no Asian power could even consider matching the British or the French in the Indian ocean, and all these two powers had to fear at sea was each other. On land it was still a different story. Indian rulers had learnt to respect European military techniques, and were eager to enlist their services. The leading powers – the Mahrattas, Mysore, Hyderabad – imported French instructors and equipment. But the results were disappointing. Wellington reporting on his Mahratta campaign said that he could expect to beat European-trained troops, but that when the Mahrattas used their own methods of warfare, based especially on light cavalry, they were a match for the Company's forces. The English and French thought in terms of a balance of power in the subcontinent, with particular regard to each other, and of carefully worded alliances with Indian powers. In 1798 Wellesley reported to his Company that 'the balance of power in India no longer rests on the same footing on which it was placed by the peace of Seringapatam. The question therefore must arise how best it may be brought back.' There was in India at that time a new and transitional international order, a hybrid between Indian custom and the irruption of the Europeans into the area. In one sense the Europeans, by their trade, their diplomacy and alliances, and their involvement in Indian wars, brought the subcontinent and the Indian Ocean marginally into the European states system. In another sense the Indians, who had often in the past involved non-Indian powers in their calculations – from Darius the Persian to the Ottoman Sultans – now did so again.

In the Pacific the Philippines were colonized and Christianized by Spain in the same way as Spanish America, as a far western extension of Mexico. But this was an exception. North of it European activities in the Far East remained until the end of the eighteenth century very tentative and mainly concerned with commerce and Christianity. When the first Portuguese trading ship reached China in 1513 the powerful Ming dynasty dominated the area. In the next century the Ming dynasty weakened, much as the Mogul dynasty did in India in the eighteenth. But in contrast to India the Manchus quickly re-established a suzerain regime all over China in 1644, styled the Ch'ing dynasty. They kept themselves aloof from their Chinese subjects but took over the traditional Chinese administrative system. The Ch'ing dynasty was a period of firm authority, prosperity, and cultural conservatism, which concentrated on defence of the land frontiers. European states, including Russia which had expanded tenuously to the Pacific by land, treated the Manchu Empire with respect, and European merchants traded as clients on the restrictive terms laid down by the Manchus. The European impact on China remained slight in spite of intensive missionary efforts. But Chinese culture made a profound impression on educated eighteenth-century Europeans, who were attracted by the exquisite rococo works of art which the Chinese exported. Liberal intellectuals pictured China as a civilization which had achieved what they advocated, such as government open to talent on the basis of examinations, and no revealed dogma in religion. Japan too, after seeming to open itself to Portuguese and other navigators, in the seventeenth century closed its door to foreigners. In 1638 the Japanese government prohibited sea voyages by its subjects. The Europeans were obliged to accept their exclusion.

While Europe was expanding outward overseas and across the steppes, the states of the European system were also working out, by trial and error, an elaborate and remarkably successful international society. Two fundamental principles which determined the rules and institutions of that society were that all member states were to be regarded as juridically equal and that their sovereignty was absolute. Time, war-weariness, expediency and a certain legal cast of mind were needed to win general acceptance for these principles. But once established they applied logically to any new members of the society, and so proved eminently exportable. When towards the end of the eighteenth century the European settler colonies of the Americas began to demand independence, absolute sovereignty and juridical equality were the only formula which they put forward. These principles assumed that the member states of the evolving 'diplomatic republic' of Europe could ensure a sufficient degree of domestic law and order and of administrative integrity and continuity to observe the rules and operate the institutions of their international society. By the middle of the seventeenth century this was indeed usually the case in Europe. The question of whether a state which was unable to meet the standards of conduct required by European society could nevertheless be admitted to full and equal membership did not arise.

However, the new European society of juridically equal states did not disregard the great differences of power between its members. Four principal institutions served as techniques for managing order and, particularly important in such a dynamic and expanding society, for managing change.

The first of these was the balance of power, the systematic practice of anti-hegemonialism. By the eighteenth century the balance of power came to be viewed as analogous to the Newtonian solar system. Its basic premiss was that as a member state grew more powerful relative to its fellows, so their policies should shift away from it and towards each other in order to maintain an equilibrium and prevent any one state from 'laying down the law' to the society of states. Neither dynastic right, nor religious affinity, nor any other loyalty should stand in the way of preserving the independence of the member states, and if a judicious use of force was necessary to uphold the balance, then independence was more important than peace. The overseas involvement of several states led European statesmen to calculate the balance of power on a global basis.

The second institution was the codification of the practices of the system into a set of regulatory rules of war and peace, which became international law. International law ensured that in most cases the conduct of the independent states was predictable, in place of the uncertainty and chaos which had prevailed. It was not infallible or enforceable, and in any case only codified what princes in the European system actually and habitually did. But it gradually acquired overtones of obligation, indicating what states ought to do not merely in Europe but all round the world.

The third institution was the practice of settling the affairs of the

European society by means of congresses of interested sovereigns or their delegates, at which treaties to conclude wars were supplemented by agreements on general rules and institutions. The three principal congresses were those concluded in Westphalia in 1648, in Utrecht in 1713, and in Vienna in 1815; and a number of lesser congresses were also held. Non-European states were not invited. Even the great congress of Vienna, the climax of the European society, was attended only by Christian European powers.

The fourth institution, which spanned the others and enabled them to function, was a continuous diplomatic dialogue between the statesmen of Europe, conducted mainly through two imaginative innovations: a network of resident embassies and other missions, and the interchange of their personnel with organized ministries in the capital of each government. By means of this dialogue the modalities of the balance of power, of international law and of the periodic congresses were elaborated and applied, and some sort of consensus about European society gradually emerged. In the eighteenth century Europe came to be regarded as a single diplomatic commonwealth made up of a number of independent states 'resembling each other in their manners, religion and degree of social improvement',[4] or in other words operating within the framework of a common culture. During all this period European states also of course conducted a more distant dialogue with Asian powers.

Outside Europe the rules were recognized as being rather different in practice. Both states and privateers continued to operate against one another in the Americas and Asia in ways that were no longer permissible in Europe between states not formally at war. Nor could the rules and institutions of European society govern relations with states that were not members. But as their European commonwealth developed, and particularly in the eighteenth century, Dutch and other European statesmen tended increasingly to see how far the rules and the experience of their society could be applied beyond its limits.

The Ottoman Empire, which during much of the period stretched over a quarter of Europe, was reluctant to accept the institutions of the Europeans, who therefore dealt with it largely according to arrangements formulated by the Ottomans. The Europeans were also content to deal with more distant civilized Asian states, most notably the Persian, Mogul, and Chinese Empires, according to practices which, for all their individual particularities, bear a family resemblance to the arrangements which have developed at various times and places to regulate intermittent relations between different civilizations. Within this framework European traders and representatives took account of the particular stipulations laid down by individual Asian rulers as well as European rules and precepts.

During the three centuries from Columbus to Napoleon the attention of European statesmen and rulers remained concentrated in Europe. However, as the military and economic capacities of the European states increased, and as the practice of the balance of power brought them more into equilibrium, it became clear that a given expenditure of effort produced ever less advantage within Europe compared with what could be achieved outside it. The states on the geographical periphery of Europe therefore encouraged their expansive forces to push outward along the lines of less resistance and greater advantage when it seemed safe to do so. The five principal Atlantic states expanded overseas, the Russians by land. The states locked geographically in the centre of the system were virtually unable to participate in this expansion, though the Austrians were later able to pursue a policy of reconquest down the Danube at the expense of the Ottomans. But the maintenance of a competitive edge in Europe was what mattered, and it was from other states in Europe that the threats were perceived. Therefore the quest overseas of governments, and the efforts of subjects sponsored by governments, was for economic and territorial gains which would enhance the position of their state in the struggle for power and independence in Europe. The expansion of European society now consisted of a number of parallel and competitive enterprises by European states and trading companies in which the main enemy was not an overseas power but a European rival. Each European state wanted the advantage of trade, bases, and settlement to be exclusive extensions of its own domain. The language, religion, law, and culture which the European states spread were their own particular versions. The economic development of the European colonies and trading points was designed to cater exclusively to the needs and interests of the individual imperial power. The complex mosaic of interspersed European settlements – Spanish, English, French, Dutch, Portuguese, Danish – in the West Indies, down to the partition of some small islands, remains today a vivid illustration of the colonial rivalry engendered by the European states system, which the Papal partition was intended to forestall.

The wealth brought back to Europe, and European military operations against each other overseas became important elements in the European system. How far European overseas trade created a world economy, or amassed enough capital to fuel significantly the industrial revolution, is a matter of controversy, discussed later in this book. Certainly the overseas operations of the Europeans materially affected the balance of power between them. In the sixteenth century this overseas advantage increased the power of the Habsburgs who ruled Spain and Portugal, and so helped what was at the time the hegemonial side. But in the seventeenth and eighteenth centuries the overseas advantage – which as always depended on the upper hand at sea – chiefly strengthened the anti-hegemonial maritime powers, the Dutch and the English. So it became a makeweight which helped to ensure the anti-hegemonial character of the European society of states formulated in the settlements of Westphalia, Utrecht, and Vienna.

The nineteenth century saw a decisive change, both in the organization of European society and in its relation to the rest of the world. In Europe itself the leading states, dismayed by the wilful domination of Napoleon and the dangers of unbridled sovereignty, agreed that their society should no longer be left to the mechanistic adjustments of the balance of power, but should be directed by a diffused and balanced hegemony of the five great powers who would act in concert to manage order and change. Other states, while juridically independent, were relegated to a secondary role. At the same time the industrial revolution enormously increased the economic and military power of the Europeans. Looking outside Europe they became increasingly convinced of the superiority of their capacities, which was manifestly the case, and also of their institutions and their moral values. Europeans and Asians alike had long regarded preliterate peoples as primitive but redeemable if civilized; now many Europeans came to regard civilized Asians as decadent. In their eyes modern civilization was synonymous with European ways and standards, which it was their duty and their interest to spread in order to make the world a better and safer place. For two centuries European expansion had been concerned mainly with European settlement, trade, and a balance of power. In the nineteenth century the Europeans, and particularly the three colonizing great powers of the day, Britain, Russia, and France, became involved in imposing their administration and civilization on almost all of Asia and Africa. They did so more reluctantly and less deliberately than was later supposed, and usually in the interests of what they called order and security. Destiny only became manifest in retrospect. The non-European states which remained theoretically independent were expected and induced to conform to the rules and institutions of European international society. In carrying out this expansion the great powers recognized the same need to curb their rivalries and act in concert as in Europe itself.

The European settler states of the Americas were easily admitted as sovereign and juridically equal members of European society. The

Europeans regarded them all, even the United States, as somewhat separate. They too were determined to stay apart from European power politics and from any supervision of their affairs by either the Concert of Europe or individual European states. Otherwise the American states were in much the same position as the lesser European powers. Both groups played minor but real parts in the elaboration of the society's rules, institutions, and codes of conduct. The United States also played an active part in the expansion of 'European' or 'Western' dominance. Landbased expansion steadily increased its size and power until by the end of the period 'the flag outran the constitution.' The originally anti-imperial United States acquired dependent territories of its own in the Caribbean and the Pacific, and the European powers co-opted it as a quasi-equal partner in formulating agreed policies towards Eastern Asia.

The incorporation of the non-European world in the new global society presented greater problems. Still geographically present in Europe, a much weaker Ottoman Empire was progressively obliged to deal with the Europeans on their terms rather than its own, and to conform to European rules and standards. Similarly Persia, which in the eighteenth century had been able to embark on a career of military conquest, during the nineteenth century came increasingly under British and Russian pressures. It and neighbouring Afghanistan were saved as juridically sovereign states by the rivalry in Asia of the two greatest European imperial powers. But the northern Muslim states of Central Asia were beyond Britain's maritime reach, and were easily brought under Russian dominion. In the same way and more importantly the hybrid international order which had developed in India in the eighteenth century had depended on the competitive presence of at least two European states. Therefore the collapse of French power overseas during the Napoleonic wars laid the way open for British dominance. The idea of replacing the Moguls as the suzerain authority in India was far from the minds of the British Government in the first half of the century, and the East India Company in London was also opposed to the assumption of further administrative responsibility. But the frontier of European expansion and the endemic warfare beyond it possessed their own momentum. By 1830 the Mahratta Confederacy had disintegrated, and Indian rulers, perhaps recognizing that a new form of the traditional Indian suzerainty was in the making, were unwilling to form an anti-hegemonial coalition against rising British power. The British replaced alliances on an equal footing with subsidiary ones that recognized British paramountcy, so that Indian states ceased to be independent actors on the international scene. At the same time the British greatly extended their direct administration. In 1877 the shadow of the Mogul Empire was abolished and Queen Victoria was proclaimed Empress of India in its stead. The Dutch, who had advanced further along these lines than the British in the eighteenth century, now extended their direct administration over Indonesia. The French, later arrivals after the interruption of their power in the East, followed a similar path in Indo-China.

Beyond the great area of individual European dominances in Asia, China and Japan were able to retain their independence at the price of Westernization. China remained fully independent under Manchu rule, and until as late as 1842 set its own conditions for limited contacts with Europeans. Then, following war with Britain over trading rights, the Treaty of Nanking and corollary agreements opened certain Chinese ports to European traders and the British acquired the island of Hong Kong as a trading depot. This was little more than the Portuguese and others had acquired in India many centuries before. But Chinese confidence in their superiority was shaken, and the grip of the Manchus weakened. Internal unheavals made the position of foreign traders insecure and led to progressive interventions by Europeans and Americans, joined later by the Japanese. The arrangements imposed by the foreigners in China took a collective form, and were joint operations of international society. They included the international settlement at Shanghai, the shared facilities at other ports designated by treaty, the provisions for extraterritoriality and for joint extraterritorial courts, shared river patrols, combined military intervention, and the increasing co-ordination of the continuous diplomatic negotiation with the Chinese Imperial Government. China was too large and valuable a market for the rival trading powers to allow others to establish a colonial monopoly; and the great powers were becoming more accustomed to collaboration on overseas issues. The result was the policy of the 'open door'. Slowly and reluctantly the Chinese found themselves obliged to conform to European rules and standards.

Black Africa between the Sahara and the Dutch settlements of the extreme south was the last large area to be brought under European government and the jurisdiction of international society. Most of the continent remained unsubjected and much of it unvisited by Europeans until about 1870. In the last decades of the century the rival European ports of call and trading stations round the coast were expanded into colonial control of their commercial hinterlands. The partition of Africa was achieved in an atmosphere of rivalry between European states, but with the colonial boundaries and certain provisions for freedom of trade agreed in Europe. The immeasurable technical superiority of the

Europeans ensured that any military encounters with Africans were short and sharp. A patchwork quilt of colonial territories came into being, which became wholly new dependent states on the European model. At the same time the long-established Arab states along the Mediterranean coast of Africa were brought under European domination. The British established themselves intermittently from the Cape to Cairo, and the French from Morocco to Madagascar; and many other states were also represented.

The flood-tide of European expansion over the globe, and the various responses to it, are discussed at length in subsequent chapters of this book, so it is necessary here to give only a brief indication of some of its general characteristics.

First, it was not to be expected that the loose but effective hegemony of the great powers, which relegated the smaller European members of the system to a subordinate role in a more closely regulated society, would assign a higher place to those outside. In practice non-European voices carried even less weight. But the accordance of a regional great power status to the United States and Japan shows that by the end of the nineteenth century the management of international society was no longer limited to European states.

Secondly, the tide of European control over the settler states of the Americas (and more slowly Australasia) had already turned before the flood of nineteenth-century expansion brought most of Asia and Africa under European administration. The word colony, which had hitherto meant a settlement of immigrants hived off from their parent country like a new swarm of bees, now came to mean primarily the rule by 'white men' over 'coloured' Asians and Africans. Trade and alliances based on bargains between independent parties gave way to the authority of alien government and a plantation economy run by European managers and 'native' labour.

Thirdly, the final stages of European expansion, while still competitive, proceeded by mutual agreement or acquiescence, and avoided war between the European members of international society. This was a remarkable enough achievement in itself, which the incessant armed conflict of the European states *ultra mar* during the previous two centuries had given no reason to expect. In particular the consensus achieved by the Europeans over the partition of Africa takes us back to the orderly spheres of expansion agreed between Spain and Portugal, with the Concert of Europe playing the part played by the Pope.

The case of China is even more striking. Many actions of individual 'foreign devils' and even of governments in China from the Opium War in 1839 to the invasion in 1900 seem to us outrageous. But the degree of collaboration between the great powers of international society, including the United States and Japan, in establishing the standards which that society considered necessary in the vast and increasingly chaotic Chinese Empire stands out in retrospect as the most impressive overseas achievement of the international Concert: a sustained and developing collective action on behalf of international society as a whole. Such co-operation has proved to be beyond the reach of the twentieth century in troubled areas like the Middle East.

Fourthly, the almost exclusive concentration of the Europeans in the East in the seventeenth and eighteenth centuries on economic interest and a mercantilist view of competition was mitigated by a return to the more mixed motives of earlier times. Exploitation of non-Europeans was intensified. The propagation of Christian civilization acquired a renewed prominence. Indeed the new ordering of international society was itself related to the revival of Christianity and an increased respect for the Middle Ages. Devout and selfless missionaries spread various forms of the Chiristian religion. Parallel with this largely non-governmental endeavour the other responsibilities of the medieval church were carried out by educators, doctors, and administrators who usually without thought of personal gain dedicated themselves to diffusing the values and achievements of western civilization and to opposing the grosser forms of exploitation by their own countrymen as well as to strengthening European authority. First the slave trade and then slavery itself were banned by international society under British leadership, and effectively ended where its writ ran. Worthy successors to the scholars of the Middle Ages and the Renaissance who had sought out Arabic and classical learning and diffused them through Christendom appeared in the form of great numbers of western savants who studied every aspect of non-European civilizations and unearthed many forgotten civilizations of the past.

Fifthly, the ninteenth century is notable for the creation throughout Asia, Africa, and Oceania of Europeanized or Westernized élites. The Europeans and the Americans offered the instruction, and usually met with an enthusiastic response, both in independent countries (the King of Siam is a familiar example) and in areas under European rule. Some genuinely accepted the superiority of Western institutions and techniques, while others saw personal advantage in adapting themselves to the ways of the conqueror. The mastery of Western governmental practice and military technology enabled these élites to run a modern state, while the assimilation of Western ideas like freedom of speech, the rule of impersonal law, independence, nationalism, democracy, and Marxism prepared the way for the drive by the élites towards separate and independent statehood in this century. A comparison of this process with the development of independence in the settler states shows that Westernized élites played the same role and voiced the same aspirations as the settlers, and were the essential element that brought the non-European states formed by Europeans to their logical climax of independent membership of the international society that had been elaborated in Europe and had become world-wide. The dilemma of the non-European élites was not over statehood and international status, but over the nature of their domestic societies. How could they best reconcile the imported ideas and methods which they admired or at least recognized as effective, and to which they owed their superior position, with the traditional ways and values of the great unwesternized majority of their own people?

The expansion of Europe was neither uniform nor systematic. It occurred over several centuries, for a number of reasons, and assumed many different forms. Chronologically we can distinguish in retrospect four main phases. First came the medieval crusades into Iberia and round the Baltic. The second phase covered three centuries of competitive maritime exploration and expansion and the parallel evolution of a European international society. Thirdly in the nineteenth century the industrial revolution enabled the European Concert to encompass the entire globe and to administer most of it. Lastly in our own century the tide of European dominion ebbed, and was replaced by a world-wide society based on the European model but in which Europeans now play only a modest role. Geographically the settlement of the Americas and Australasia by Europeans stands in contrast to the trading and administrative policies of European states in Asia and Africa. Among motives Christianity, commerce, land hunger, and the rivalry of European powers were the most prominent. But while these distinctions may help us to understand the long series of events which has done so much to shape the modern world, they do not describe the bewildering complexity of the events themselves. We must remember that what we have called the characteristics of one century or one area of the world or one European power were also present to some degree in all the others, from Portugal to Russia and from the crusades to the decolonization committee of the United Nations.

2

THE MILITARY FACTOR IN EUROPEAN EXPANSION

Michael Howard

In this post-imperial age the era of the expansion of European power between 1450 and 1900 is now generally regarded as one for which amends must be made rather than in which pride should be taken.* That expansion is considered, not improperly, to have been the result of greed and arrogance. Even its more benign manifestations, the genuine desire to bring first Christianity and then the more general 'benefits of Western civilization' to the extra-European world, are today condemned as cultural imperialism. Even the most traditionally-minded of imperial historians are reluctant to endorse the belief that was not only universally held in nineteenth-century Europe but was for a time accepted among most of the societies subjugated by the Europeans; that European societies asserted dominion over non-European because they were *superior*; because Europeans were better organized, healthier, more ingenious, more energetic, and more self-confident than anyone else, and in any contact with other cultures these qualities would have rapidly gained them dominance, whether they had to fight for it or not. But if that was not the case, it is difficult to understand why it should have been Europeans that did the colonizing rather than being subjected to it; why they were the active and not the passive partners in the process. It is unlikely that they were more avaricious than anyone else. European merchants met their match in Arabs and Indians. They were certainly no more arrogant than the Chinese. They were no more, if no less, given to religious proselytization than were the peoples of Islam. They were no more martial than the Ottoman Turks, the Ashanti, the Zulus, or some of the indigenous tribes of North America. Why was it, then, that in conflict with non-European communities, conflicts usually fought under conditions of great disadvantage at the end of supply lines reaching half-way round the world, the Europeans gradually developed an ascendancy over the rest of mankind which was, by the end of the nineteenth century, to become global and absolute?

The answer of course lies in a whole complex of cultural and economic factors that this chapter cannot even attempt to examine. But one way in which the ascendancy of European culture was manifested, and by no means the least important, was through military confrontation and conquest; and a study of that process, something today almost taboo among historians of European expansion, may at least contribute to our understanding of how the European Empires grew. Such a study, of course, takes us back to a kind of imperial history now regarded as too alien and remote to be taken seriously into account at all. Books written between 1880 and 1914 on 'Deeds that Won the Empire' are indeed now being reprinted as a kind of historical 'high camp', the equivalent of Art Nouveau. But the Empires *were* won; and they were won, in the overwhelming majority of cases, by small groups of men exceptional in their energy, intelligence, endurance, and physical courage, even if they had all the power of an industrialized civilization behind them. And it must be remembered that it was only during the last fifty or sixty years of imperial expansion that that industry gave them a massive technological advantage to counterbalance the quantitative and other disadvantages under which they normally fought.

The first artefacts that made expansive imperialism possible were developed by techniques that were at the disposal not only of Europeans but of, among others, Turks, Indians, Arabs, and Chinese, had they cared to use them. The expansion of the Portuguese and Spanish Empires, with the Dutch, British, and French hard on their heels, was brought about by the combination of the ocean-going sailing ship and the heavy gun: what has been well described as 'the floating castle enveloped by all-round batteries of quick-firing guns'.[1] These vessels were developed to deal with the peculiar problems of navigation in the North Atlantic, but a ship that could navigate in the North Atlantic could, unlike one built for, say, the Indian Ocean, sail anywhere, and take its guns with it. The guns gave it at least parity with other vessels it encountered and superiority over most, and they enabled it to defend its anchorage against land as well as sea attack. But that was all. The naval gun did not enable Europeans to project power inland. It was too heavy, too slow in its fire, and once its initial moral effect had worn off, too easily overwhelmed. But it enabled Europeans to establish entrepôts throughout the Indian Ocean and the China seas, and, a little later, small footholds of settlement in North America; where they were accepted by the indigenous comnmunities on a basis of equality as useful trading partners. Everywhere they treated their hosts with wary politeness. Their numbers were too small and they were too far from home to do anything else. The only other firearm they had available was the clumsy matchlock, and that they found at least as useful as an object of trade as a weapon of defence. In North America in particular the dependence of the indigenous inhabitants on the settlers for a continuing supply of power and shot for their own use gave the latter valuable leverage in their diplomacy.

Only in one region did the Europeans extend their dominion inland before the eighteenth century, and that was in Mexico and Peru. But the purely technical advantages enjoyed by the conquistadors over the native communities were negligible. Cortes took some cannon from his ships, but, points out Professor Parry, 'They must have been small and not very effective pieces, though no doubt their noise and smoke made a great impression. Apart from the cannon Cortes had 13 muskets.' More importance has been attached to the horses that the *conquistadores* brought with them, to the amazement of the natives; but as Parry again points out, 'Cortes had only sixteen horses when he landed and some of those were soon killed in battle. Most of his men fought on foot with sword, pike and crossbow.'[2] The Spaniards had a further advantage in that they fought with metal weapons against stone, but basically they owed their victories to their single-minded ruthlessness, their desperation, and their fanaticism. Like their forefathers of the *reconquista* in Spain, they were fighting both for land and for Christ; also of course for gold, if they could find any. Acquisitiveness and fanaticism were to characterize subsequent empire-builders as well, but none fought on quite the same basis of technical equality and quantitative inferiority as did the *conquistadores*.

With this sole and notable exception, European settlements overseas remained within range of the protection of the guns of their ships, on coasts or tidal estuaries, until the beginning of the eighteenth century. Then inland expansion began, in North America and the Indian subcontinent. At least one factor in making this possible was the emergence in Europe, during the latter part of the seventeenth century, of professional regular military forces; forces not only disciplined but with a logistical infrastructure that made possible regular pay, administration, and supply. Such forces could be stationed, on a permanent or rotating basis, overseas. The first British troops sent to India were raised to garrison the fortress of Bombay that Catherine of Braganza brought as her dowry to Charles II in 1662, while the first regular units were sent to North America in 1677 to put down a rebellion among settlers in Virginia. Such troops not only had the organization to carry out, if necessary, expeditions into the interior involving the establishment of bases and lines of supply, but by the end of the century they had novel and greatly more effective weapons. Their guns were smaller, more manoeuvrable, and quicker firing, while the infantry's pike and matchlock had been replaced by the composite flintlock and bayonet.

This meant, first, that small groups of men could effectively defend themselves; and secondly that disciplined forces could deliver a quantity of fire capable of overwhelming larger and more inchoate forces armed with cruder weapons.

If the first era of European expansion from 1500 to 1700 had been made possible by the sailing ship with its guns, the second, from 1700 until *circa* 1850, was based on the organization and firepower of the disciplined professional troops developed by European states in the internecine conflicts they fought between 1660 and 1720; not least those of the House of Austria, which, remodelled by Montecucculi and Eugene of Savoy, were to roll the Ottoman Turks back into the Balkan peninsula and establish a European dominance over the Ottoman Empire that was cultural as much as military. Indeed the two elements were indistinguishable. Only sophisticated and wealthy political organisms could produce and sustain regular armies on the eighteenth-century model. Tax-systems to pay for them, the bureaucracy to levy and maintain them, the arsenals to manufacture their weapons, all implied a degree of social organization that was becoming palpably higher in Western Europe than among the other societies with which Europeans were in contact. The speed with which the armies of Charles XII cut into the still semi-barbaric Russian Empire at the beginning of the eighteenth century was a spectacular indicator of this, and the reaction of Peter the Great was to foreshadow that of all subsequent non-European rulers anxious to maintain their independence. The only way to beat the Europeans was to imitate them, and the necessary military reforms would not be forthcoming without a huge social upheaval.

The realization that their greater social efficiency could be translated into the political dimension began to dawn on the European merchants in India at about the same time. In 1687 perception of the disorder into which the Mogul Empire around them had fallen made the East India Company determine to 'establish such a politie of civil and military power and create and secure such a large revenue to maintain both . . . as may be the foundation of a large, well-grounded, sure English dominion for all time to come'.[3] That military power was not to be used for another sixty years, and then it would be the French who showed the way, in the first encounter between regular European troops and an Indian army at the siege of Madras in 1746. Until that moment European troops had served mainly as *condottieri* for Indian rulers. Now, as was the way of *condottieri*, they turned on their masters. The speed and accuracy of their gunfire, in particular, astounded the Indians, who 'with their own clumsy artillery not yet advanced beyond the stage attained by the Europeans in the 16th century . . . thought it good practice if a gun were discharged four times in an hour'.[4] And in a briskly decisive action a force of 230 European troops and 700 Sepoys routed an Indian army 10,000 strong, terrible with cavalry and elephants, with rolling volley fire and disciplined bayonet charges. 'With this action', wrote Sir John Fortescue,

> it may be said that the dominance of a European nation in India was assured. Hitherto the native armies had been treated with respect. Their numbers gave the impression of overwhelming strength; and it had not occurred to Europeans that they could be encountered except with a force of man for man. Consequently all dealings of Europeans with native princes had been conducted in a spirit of humility and awe. . . . Now the spell was broken, and Dupleix from being the courtier had become the master.[5]

A decade later Clive at Plassey confronted an Indian army numbering 50,000 with a force 3,000 strong, only 800 of them European, and routed them (thanks to the indecisiveness of their commander and the treachery of his subordinates) almost without firing a shot.[6] A total moral ascendancy had been attained which the Europeans, particularly the British, were to retain for nearly two centuries. Clive himself saw how this imbalance of social efficiency could be, indeed was bound to be exploited. 'It is scarcely hyperbole to say', he wrote in 1765, 'that tomorrow the whole Moghul Empire is in our power. The inhabitants of the country have no attachment to any obligations; their forces are neither disciplined, commanded or paid as we are.'[7]

Discipline that turned a handful of men into a highly mobile fire machine; *command* by enterprising, bold, and skilful officers; *pay*, to ensure loyalty: the triad was fundamental to military power, and when at the turn of the century British power began to extend over the central plateau and northern plains of the sub-continent a fourth element had to be added: *logistics*, the field in which Arthur Wellesley made his reputation. In this all the mathematical and topographical skills being developed in eighteenth-century Europe were brought into play. These were indeed probably taught in the new officers' schools which were being founded in every major European state (and many minor ones as well) to a higher standard than in any civilian establishments. The 'scientific soldier', mocked both by Clausewitz and by W. S. Gilbert, had appeared on the scene. It was the graduates of the Royal Military Academy at Woolwich, of the École Polytechnique, and of the new school of military science and engineering established by the United States Army at West Point, that were to act as trail-blazers throughout the world, mapping the waste lands (as, simultaneously, the Royal

Navy was charting the oceans), driving roads and building bridges, not simply where no white man had ever penetrated but where no man of any colour had set foot before.

The administrative and scientific developments in European society during the eighteenth century thus made it possible to drive the area of European dominion inland from the coasts even before the beginning of the third great epoch of European expansion which was brought about by the industrial expansions of the nineteenth century. They made possible, in particular, the complete subjugation of the Indian sub-continent, and also the Russian conquest of Turkestan and Central Asia in the mid-nineteenth century. Accounts of these Russian campaigns repeat almost precisely those of the British campaigns in India. 'Superior discipline and modern arms prevailed with telling force against medieval-style opposition . . . lances, ancient flint-lock and crude cannon were no match for the tight formations of the Russians who were trained to stand in the open field and mow down the enemy with a succession of volleys or to shatter his fortifications with well-aimed artillery and rocket fire until he can be overwhelmed with the enthusiastic *Ura*! and the cold steel of a bayonet charge.'[8] And as in India, according to the same authority, 'supply more than manpower was the key to successful operations in Central Asia.'[9] The inhabited areas both of Central Asia and of Northern India had been conquered before the reciprocal apprehensions of growing Russian and British power led the two governments, in the 1880s, to begin to drive railways through the almost impassable and uninhabitable mountain country bordering Afghanistan to make possible, not further colonization, but war with one another.

The third era of European expansion which opened in the mid-nineteenth century was the result of three developments within European society.[10] The first was steam transport and the associated transformation of the metallurgical industries. The second was the introduction of the quick-firing, long-range firearms made possible by the development of high explosive; and the third and perhaps most important of all was the growth of medical knowledge that gradually overcame the greatest enemy of all those that European armies had to contend with in 'savage' countries: disease. About this nothing has been said in the foregoing pages, but it had provided incomparably the most important barrier to European expansion and settlement; and European medical techniques were to do perhaps more than anything else to reconcile colonized populations to their new masters. One can argue endlessly as to the respects, if any, in which the culture of the Europeans was in fact 'superior' to that of the indigenous societies which they subjugated, but the capacity of the colonizing communities to relieve suffering, to cure disease, and prolong life not only among themselves but for everyone willing to associate with them provided an indicator about which it was difficult to disagree.

Steam transport was to open up the interior of all the continental land masses of the world to European armed forces and the culture they brought with them, but for this purpose riverine transport was often more important than rail. Nowhere was it more important than in the opening up of the Chinese Empire to Western military power. In the early 1830s British warships little different from those in which Nelson fought established dominance over the forts guarding the approaches to Canton by the precision and rapidity of their fire; but within a few years steam vessels were available, both as tugs to pull men-of-war upstream, and as armoured gunboats equipped with shell-guns. In 1841 the forts were again attacked and had 'fallen within an hour to superior gunnery and disciplined troops. Most of the Chinese fought with the desperate gallantry of the hopeless . . . but they had had no experience of modern explosives.'[11] The iron steamer *Nemesis*, apparently invulnerable to Chinese fire, threw shell, grape, and canister-shot at her opponents and destroyed eleven warjunks with her rockets; 'thence she moved up a twisting creek, grappling and towing away two more junks without giving or receiving a single shot'.[12] By 1842 British sea power had extended up-river 200 miles to Nanking. By the end of the 1850s it had penetrated a further 400 miles to Hankow. By that time the British were equipping their vessels with Armstrong breech-loading rifled guns calibrated in thousands of yards, whose long-range fire smashed the way through to the walls of Peking. 'I never saw anything more beautiful', wrote the British military commander, Hope Grant, 'than the precision of their fire at long ranges.'[13]

Riverine transport also opened up the interior of Africa, via the Senegal, the Niger, the Congo, and the Nile. But the difficulties of navigating the upper waters of this last river made necessary the use of railways as well, and Kitchener's drive into the Sudan, 1896–8, was made possible by a combination of steam transport by river and rail. The speed of rail construction was astonishing: 216 miles were completed in thirteen months up till May 1897 and another 232 miles in the next five months, bringing into the heart of the Sudan an army equipped with breech-loading rifled guns, magazine-loading rifles, and Maxim machine-guns firing 2,000 rounds a minute; not to mention gunboats in support fitted out by Krupp. 'Our chance of a good show was entirely spoiled by the artillery', complained a disgruntled infantry officer after Omdurman, 'but really they shot so splendidly that one ought not to grumble that they killed them all before they came properly under our fire.'[14]

Everywhere railways completed the task of opening up the rest of the world to European military power, and consolidated that dominion where it had already been established. But by this time the technological imbalance between the Europeans and the indigenous societies into which they were expanding was so great that military power could be kept in reserve, if used at all. The Europeans no longer appeared as tiny bands of pioneers dependent on local good will or savage intimidation for survival, but as closed, sophisticated communities in close communication with their homelands, possessing facilities and opportunities whose advantages, for those who chose to associate with them, were self-evident.

It is possible however that as this technological superiority increased, so the moral dominance created in the earlier stages of European expansion by the sheer vigour, courage, and self-reliance of the pioneers began to diminish. The men who had founded the Empires, from the Spanish in Mexico to the British in India and the French in Africa, were exceptional even within their own societies: restless, dominant, ruthless people who could not be absorbed into their own communities and needed wider challenges. It was not the technical superiority of the flint-lock and bayonet that gave Europeans their ascendancy, but the exceptional qualities of discipline and courage needed to make it an effective weapon against overwhelming odds. The techniques of topography and road-building taught at Woolwich and the *Grandes Écoles* would not by themselves have opened up India and Africa, if they had not been applied by men of unusual vigour, imagination, and pertinacity. These qualities, often reinforced by deep religious convictions, must have made an impression in Africa and India of overwhelming charismatic power. But the virtues needed to run a railway are of a different order from those required to build one, and the skill involved in firing a Maxim or a Nordenfeldt machine-gun is not comparable to the combination of endurance and precision that went to create the infantry led by Clive and by Wellesley. By the beginning of the twentieth century non-European communities were becoming familiar with a different type of European: one whose claim to rule them rested not on charismatic power but on communicable technical and administrative skills.

The final stage in the assertion of European dominance over the rest of the world was marked by the introduction of air bombardment. Initiated by the British as an economical way of 'policing' the remote borders of North-West India and Mesopotamia, it was first used as a means of pacification in British Somaliland in 1920, and fifteen years later by the Italians in Abyssinia, in the last campaign of colonial conquest to be fought by a European power. In both instances it achieved its purpose in terrorizing resistance into rapid submission and so diminishing the requirement for a prolonged land campaign. Thirty years later in Vietnam, however, the outcome was very different. The American War in Vietnam can hardly be described as a deliberate attempt to extend an empire, though neither were many of the wars the British fought in India to protect their client states against their adversaries; whose result, whatever their intention, had always been the extension of imperial power. Yet it does fall into the pattern we have been describing, of an industrially developed State using its technological advantages to impose its will on a more 'backward' society. Its failure was all the more interesting as a result.

The American experience in Vietnam indeed suggests not only that technological superiority had ceased to possess those charismatic qualities associated with it in the nineteenth century, but that this superiority was now morally self-defeating. Logistical problems were brilliantly solved. Firepower was delivered in fantastic quantities against some of the most remote areas in South-East Asia. Half a million service-men were poured into Vietnam and maintained in a life-style far superior to that they were used to in the United States. But the result was not victory, but shame at home, obloquy abroad, and, on the part of the enemy, a passionate determination to survive and win at any cost.

Superior military technology was thus not in itself a sufficient explanation for the European conquest of the world during the centuries of imperial power. The question remains to be answered, why this hegemony should have crumbled so rapidly just at the moment when the technological superiority was at its most absolute. Much of the solution must be sought in the realm of intellectual and moral assumptions. On the part of imperial powers, empires – at least, formal empires – were seen to bring neither political power nor economic advantage commensurate with the effort involved in maintaining them. Within the framework of Western values non-European adversaries could no longer be depicted as barbarians whom it was a moral duty to bring within the pale of civilization. As Mussolini discovered to his chagrin in 1935, there was no longer a tacit 'right to war' on the part of 'civilized' powers against 'uncivilized'. As for the colonial peoples themselves, unopposed bombing from distant bases did not in itself confer charismatic authority on their conquerors; nor did the behaviour of European expatriates in their countries, whether military or civilian, any longer inspire respect. Their technical skills were seen to be transferable, and their military advantages could no longer be easily translated into political power. The effective influence of European upon non-European peoples once again came to depend, as it had in the pre-industrial age, on their political skills, and on the wares they had to sell.

3

EUROPE IN THE WORLD ECONOMY

Patrick O'Brien

I

Before the Age of Revolutions, demographic and economic growth proceeded at slow and comparable rates throughout the world. Everywhere most people worked in agriculture, and the density of urban and industrial activity in regions of Asia and the Islamic Empire seems not markedly different from Iberia, Italy, France, England, and Germany. As late as the second half of the seventeenth century some provinces of China and states of India may have enjoyed standards of living on a par with advanced regions of Western Europe.

The dramatic gap in per capita incomes between Europeans and peoples of what is now called the Third World (of Asia, Africa, the Middle East, and Southern America) probably emerged after 1800. A century later (when Europe's navies ruled the oceans and European Governments had annexed millions of square miles of territory on the mainlands of Africa and Asia) 62 per cent of the world's output was consumed by Europeans, North Americans, and Australasians who formed only 35 per cent of the world's population. By 1914 the Third World had clearly declined economically as well as politically from the position of parity held up to the beginning of the eighteenth century.

Most Western historians remain convinced that Europe's rise to a position of economic hegemony over other continents emanated from the discovery and diffusion of technical innovations behind agricultural and then industrial revolutions which occurred in Western Europe after 1750. That Eurocentric interpretation has provoked a challenge concerned to place the rise of modern industry within a broader international context and to emphasize the importance of commerce with 'periphery' for economic progress achieved by the 'core'. This 'revisionist' historiography sees the economic connections built up between Western Europe and other regions of the world over the three centuries after the discovery of America as a decisive factor in Europe's 'take-off' towards industrial society. Thereafter, from the late eighteenth century to 1914 economic relations with the periphery are perceived to sustain an irreversible trend towards widening differentials in income per capita between Europeans and other peoples. My essay seeks to quantify the relevance of an international context for the explanation of industrial development in Western Europe. It will dispute the proposition that commerce with the periphery contributed significantly to that development before, during, or indeed for several decades after the industrial revolution.

II

Transnational commerce evolved in response to the famous discoveries of the long sixteenth century, to the diffusion of information on possibilities for profitable trade, to a decline in risks and the transaction costs involved of moving merchandise over longer distances by sea. Recent research is, however, not inclined to see the voyages of discovery as a marked discontinuity in the expansion of international commerce. Furthermore, the bulk of that commerce (which I will define to include flows of labour and investible funds, as well as commodities across national boundaries) remained local in character. Throughout the mercantile era (1492–1789) international transactions continued to be exemplified by such movements as the export of grain from Galicia in Northern Spain across the Portuguese border rather than shipments of spices in Dutch vessels from the Indies to Amsterdam. International trade hardly differed from interregional and local trade of which it formed a tiny – if growing – proportion. Like landings on the moon, the voyages of discovery excited contemporaries, continue to fascinate historians, but their economic gains took a very long time to materialize. Portugese, Spanish, Dutch, French, and English marines obviously consolidated the foundations for oceanic trade over the three centuries following the discovery of America. But to describe economic relations across state borders in that era as an 'international economy' or a 'world economic system' may mislead us into supposing these terms refer (as they do in contemporary parlance) to the importance of an international context in determining the growth and economic stability of nominally sovereign states.

Today when all countries participate in and form part of a world economy, their autonomy in economic matters spans a spectrum from potential autarky enjoyed by empires such as the Soviet Union to the purely nominal sovereignty of islands like Mauritius. At the latter end of this spectrum of 'dependency', prices for commodities bought and sold on local markets are to a very large extent determined by conditions of demand and supply in the world at large. Trends and fluctuations in ostensibly 'local' prices, wages, and returns on investments move in line with changes on international markets. So-called national commodity and factor markets then form a subordinate part of a wider regional, continental, or even global market. These dependant economies also rely on inflows of capital for future development. Their stability is vulnerable to flows of foreign loans and credit which is not subject to control by local monetary authorities. Furthermore, key sectors and positions within such open economies may be manned by foreigners whose skills are sold to the highest bidder. Loyalty and commitment to any national economy will be contingent basically upon levels of remuneration offered in a particular locality. This kind of labour mobility across frontiers implies that wage rates are set (like the price of capital) on international markets by factors outside the control of national governments. In these conditions, local workers, skilled and unskilled, competing with mobile immigrants will be compelled to accept wages established by exogenous forces operating beyond the boundaries of their own countries. At the other end of the spectrum independent economies tend to determine local prices, wage rates, and flows of investible funds.

International economic intercourse both enlarges and confines the autonomy of legally sovereign polities and their citizens. It enlarges by creating higher incomes through specialization, by opening markets for new lines of production, and by offering greater variety in consumption. It confines by embedding enterprises, farms, workers, and governments within a matrix of constraints which tighten continuously as firms become ever more sensitive to prospects of gain from moving merchandise and capital across national frontiers.

An integrated international economy might be represented as a system where rather limited profit margins prompt merchants to ship commodities across frontiers, where investors are awake to small national differentials in rates of interest, where labour migrates readily to alien societies in response to prospects for slightly higher earnings. Finally, an international economy is one in which governments recognize the stake their own citizens have in its stability and efficient operation. Political leaders become not only more aware of constraints on their actions but sensitive to the wider implications of their economic policies. National interests are perceived to include some concern for an 'international economic order'. Competition and even retaliation against foreigners are checked to include co-operation over economic matters of mutual concern.

To define an integrated international economy is to expose just how far commerce between nations as late as the last quarter of the twentieth century falls short of anything that might be called a world economic system. Even today that entity operates only in embryo or catches our attention as a theoretical model of how merchandise, capital, and labour (unimpeded by political barriers to the movement of goods and factors of production) might flow around the globe in response to movements in relative prices, interest rates, and wages, and in the costs of transport and information.

Historians of international economic relations respond to the excitement of voyages of discovery in the sixteenth century. Some are no less impressed with the conquest of the Southern Steppes by Russians in the course of the seventeenth and eighteenth centuries. In time these outward movements by Europeans along their sea and land frontiers added the harvest of the oceans (fish and fish oil), the fruits of boreal forests (timber, furs, hides, hemp, salt, and tar), and the luxuries of the tropics (spices, sugar, tobacco, and cotton) to their continent's own abundant resources. In the wake of discovery and conquest came trade, overseas investment, immigration, and settlement but to describe the tenuous economic connections built up between peoples and continents in the course of the mercantile era as an 'international economy' or a 'European economic world system' represents a misplaced appropriation of a contemporary concept. To begin with, transport costs by land remained prohibitive for all but commodities of the highest value in relation to weight and volume. Freight costs certainly fell whenever merchandise could be shipped by water. This had long been the case, and while costs per ton mile by sea and river declined, the percentage decrease in markups for transport and distribution embodied in the selling prices of commodities traded between 1492 and 1789 represented but a fraction of the far sharper fall brought about by canals, railways, and steamships over the following century. An international economy (even a national economy) is predicated upon cheap transport which makes it profitable to move goods from region to region and across frontiers. Pronounced and widespread falls in freight rates only began to provide really strong stimulus to international trade in the second quarter of the nineteenth century.

Flows of commercial intelligence about the risks and legal constraints on conducting business across frontiers also form preconditions for the growth and stability of international commerce. Risks from piracy and arbitrary exactions by political authorities diminished rather slowly. Before the Royal Navy finally established the Pax Britannia at Trafalgar in 1805, frequent resort to armed aggression against the commerce and colonial settlements of rival powers could not be described as conducive either to the rapid expansion of world trade or to the migration of capital and labour overseas. Trade was also restrained by extremely high tariffs on imports and on exports, which provided the aristocratic and military establishments of this age with the bulk of their revenues before states learned how to borrow regularly and to tax income and wealth effectively. Debasement, that other expedient of rulers (too timid or incompetent to tax their subjects effectively) created much uncertainty for international monetary transactions. The frequent debasement of the coinage which marked the mercantile era offset favourable effects on the level of world trade which the international monetary system derived from imports of silver and gold from the Americas.

The preoccupation of rulers with bullion reserves for strategic purposes, their hostility to imports as a 'drain' on national wealth, and their proclivity to reward favourites with monopolies of national markets operated (as Adam Smith observed) to frustrate economic intercourse between nations. Of course they also signed treaties which suggest they occasionally recognized the mutual advantages enjoyed from international markets. Most negotiations over commerce tended, however, to issue in bilateral agreements which traded off concessions one against another, often at the expense of excluded rivals. In that kind of international economy regulated trade within European and Asiatic empires represented a feasible but a decidedly second-rate solution to aggressive national competition for potential gains from commerce and colonization. Given the persistence of high transportation costs, the strictly local horizons of business men, and the barriers erected against foreign commerce by Governments, that international commerce developed at all over the three centuries which succeeded the discovery of America is a remarkable tribute to the mercantile entrepreneurship of that era.

III

By the time political revolution came to France and the industrial revolution took hold in Britain, world trade had certainly expanded well above levels achieved at the time of Columbus and also increased faster than output. European capital, labour, and enterprise established permanent settlements along the seaboard of the Americas. European ships had forcibly transported millions of African slaves to labour on the plantations of the New World. European sea power had established and consolidated commercial relations with India, China, and other parts of the Orient. But did the flows of merchandise, capital, and labour so visible and growing so rapidly after the American Revolution constitute an interconnected and interdependant economic system? How far had the system of nominally sovereign national economies travelled along the road towards an international economy?

On any of the indicators normally used to measure degrees of integration achieved by economic systems, the answer seems to be hardly any distance at all. For the majority of independent states ratios of exports to production and imports to national consumption probably remained in the 1–2 per cent range of significance. Even for maritime powers such as Britain, Portugal, and Holland, seriously engaged in international commerce, the ratios of trade to national income fell below 10 per cent. Only a handful of commodity prices on local and national markets were in any degree influenced by international trade. Gold and silver come immediately to mind. Prices for sugar, tobacco, spices, and cotton fibres were also in large part set by interactions of consumers and producers within the protected imperial trading systems of Portugal, Spain, France, Britain, and Holland. At the margin, smuggling and Dutch sea power from time to time created something akin to international markets, at least for a highly restricted range of goods. But prices paid for the vast majority of commodities and services consumed by mankind at the close of the eighteenth century were established in conditions of demand and supply in segregated and highly localized markets. Producers and traders the world over remained not merely insulated from foreign rivals but protected by transport costs and barriers of many other kinds from competition even within their own national boundaries. Econometric tests for the convergence of prices across national free trade areas serve to reveal how local and regional price structures survived well into the railway age. Given the persistence of impediments to flows of exports and imports across and within frontiers it is not surprising to find that wages and return on capital and land engaged in producing comparable commodities continued to diverge by wide margins from country to country.

Capital, historically a more mobile factor of production than labour, can be observed moving around the globe from the sixteenth century onwards. Such flows not only formed a miniscule percentage of world capital formation but could only be attracted into the international economy by prospects of a quick fortune or by the safety offered to foreigners who invested in the public debts of England and Holland in the second half of the eighteenth century. By and large overseas investment in the mercantile era can be described as 'venture capital' responding to the lure of super-normal profits. The institutional and legal framework to facilitate flows of investible funds across frontiers in response to normal, or rather small, differentials in rates of return hardly existed at the end of the eighteenth century. Even as late as 1900 when sophisticated institutions in international banking and finance engaged in moving millions of pounds of short- and long-term investible funds around the world, the marked divergence of interest rates within as well as across countries continued to impress economists as evidence of abiding and serious imperfections in the international market for capital.

Long before Waterloo millions of workers crossed national boundaries to labour in the Americas and to push the margin of settlement southward on to the Steppes of Russia, but compared to the period 1815–1914 the numbers migrating on a permanent or temporary basis over the mercantile era remained small. Some fraction (perhaps less than 20 per cent) moved to take advantage of opportunities for cheap land available at the 'frontier' or to obtain higher payments offered far away for their skills. In these centuries people in general passed their working lives not simply in their country of origin, but close to their place of birth. Internal mobility proceeded faster than external migration and the majority of those who traversed the seas to work abroad were either forcibly transported to 'New Worlds' as slave or convict labour or compelled to uproot by religious and political repression. Flows of labour across frontiers which depended fundamentally on force could only proceed erratically and on a limited scale. Labour's domain (even the horizons of professional and skilled labour) remained essentially local. No 'brain drains' or international markets for labour operated to disturb local wage structures. That really emerged when the gaps in living standards became known and visible enough to promote the great migrations of European and Asian workers during the age of steam.

To conclude: the so-called world economy became economically significant only when the matrix of connections through flows of merchandise, labour, and capital across frontiers clearly affected local prices and incomes and constrained possibilities for independent policies by nominally sovereign governments. The gradual evolution of an international economy can (in theory) be measured by observing the rise in the ratio of trade to output for individual countries and for the world as a whole. As that nexus of interdependence through trade built up economic historians expect to trace a *convergence* of prices for comparable goods; of wages for similar kinds of labour (particularly skilled labour); and of returns on investment committed anywhere to enterprises of similar risk. They also expect the emergence of an international economic dimension to impinge on the policies of sovereign states. Political leaders might begin to recognize the baneful effects of aggressive competition against foreign enterprise and capital and begin to co-operate to establish an economic order conducive to the development of commerce between nations. Economic connections across frontiers and continents certainly extended and developed over the mercantile era. Nevertheless, the commerce of that era seems to have more in common with its medieval past or with the commerce of ancient empires than with the kind of international economy which stepped rather suddenly into prominence after the Industrial Revolution.

Quantum and qualitative leaps forward in international economic relations occurred over the nineteenth century. For that epoch and particularly for the six decades before the Great War, the growth and integration of a world economy based upon Western Europe can be observed and measured. For example, between 1800 and 1913 world trade per capita probably multiplied by a factor of 20. Ratios of trade to output jumped from 2 to 3 per cent at the beginning of the century to about a third in 1914. Between 1821 and 1915 46 million people crossed the oceans in search of work as part of that continuous shift out of primary production into industry and urban services. The gross value of capital invested beyond national boundaries increased from just under \$1 billion in 1825 to \$44 billion by 1913. In the *belle époque* capitalists invested \$2–3 billion a year outside their countries of origin. These enormous sums represented 40 per cent and sometimes 50 per cent of total savings generated by the economies of Western Europe; particularly Britain and France. All this movement of commodities, migrants, and capital emanated above all from pronounced declines in the real costs of transporting men and merchandise by land and water. In 1913 freight rates by sea had declined to something like a quarter and by land to approximately a tenth of their 1800 levels. Institutional and political factors also forged the tenuous connections built up in the mercantile era into something that might plausibly deserve to be called an international economy. Developments in banking and financial intermediation, the consolidation of an international monetary system based on gold and with stable rates of exchange, the rapid diffusion of economic intelligence, the willingness of governments to stand back and allow foreign sectors of national economies greater autonomy, and finally that extraordinary hegemony over the system exercised by Britain all played a part in making the era of international commerce from 1815 to 1914 qualitatively different in scale and form from anything which the world had witnessed before. What made the contrast with the mercantile era was technical progress and population growth in Western Europe which generated surpluses of manufactured exports and created demands for the primary produce from European settlements in the Americas and Australasia and for the tropical foodstuffs and raw materials of the Third World.

I have argued that quantum jumps in world trade and the emergence of an international economy should be perceived more as the product than the progenitor of industrialization in Western Europe; the opposite view, that Europe's economic growth in the nineteenth century derived strong impetus from the economic connections built up with the periphery over the three centuries before 1950 is now well established and will be analysed point by point.

IV

For most of the mercantile age, technological progress in Europe consisted of the diffusion of techniques of production known in many parts of the world since medieval times. For example, in the critical area of power supplies, energy had been provided for centuries by labour, animals, wind, water, and heat generated by burning wood. Before 1750 the steady application of energy from wind and water to an ever increasing variety of industrial processes increased Europe's non-biological sources of power long before coal and steam pushed its production of energy onto a qualitatively different plateau.

Any list of major innovations introduced into European agriculture, industry, and commerce from the twelfth to fifteenth centuries reveals how significant discoveries had been made by other peoples. Examples are numerous; from the shoulder harness for horses, the spinning wheel, printing, and gunpowder which came out of China, to the Arab compass and the all-important windmill from Persia. Europeans surged ahead of other cultures in the adaptation of technology connected with long-distance trade and military power. Thus it is the compass, naval charts, the stern rudder, artillery, gunpowder, small arms, and, above all, the fully rigged and effectively armed ship which emerged as the technology behind voyages of discovery and the dominance at sea achieved by the marines of Europe over oriental shipping during the sixteenth and seventeenth centuries. 'The gunned ship developed by Atlantic Europe in the course of the 14th and 15th centuries was the contrivance that made possible the European saga.'[1]

That saga began with the voyages of exploration but led in time to a considerable expansion of the trade between Europe and Afro-Asia. Long before the historic journeys of Vasco da Gama, tastes of rich Europeans for oriental spices, Chinese and Persian silks, Indian textiles, and precious stones had been catered for by merchants from Venice, Genoa, and Pisa trading in the Levant and Eastern Mediterranean for wares carried thousands of miles across continents to the edges of the European market. New sea routes (charted by

Portuguese, Spanish, Dutch, and English navigators) shifted freight onto waterborne carriers and transport costs fell to a fraction of overland charges. At the same time, improvements in the design of ships increased their speed, manoeuvrability, and capacity to carry cargo which lowered the cost of capital and labour required per ton mile of freight transported. Innovations in seamanship, improved navigational instruments, and cannon for protection against pirates also helped to bring about the pronounced fall in the costs of moving merchandise from continent to continent. Credit facilities in the form of bills of exchange, promissory notes, paper money, cheques (well known to merchants of Islamic cities and emulated by Italians in the fourteenth and fifteenth centuries) became available in the great commercial ports of northern Europe. Mercantile houses in Antwerp, Hamburg, Amsterdam, and London competed to organize, finance, and insure the growing volume of transcontinental trade. By the middle of the seventeenth century bills of exchange on houses at Amsterdam could be discounted at rates below 4 per cent. Before the end of the sixteenth century, this fall in transaction costs made oceanic voyages frequent. Two centuries later when Europeans had consolidated contact by sea with peoples of other continents oceanic voyages had become regular.

Of course the Mercantile Era seems dominated by the entry of the Americas into international commerce. In time that entry made a profound difference not only to commodity trade but to flows of labour and capital between Europe, Asia, Africa as well as the Americas. But at the beginning of the Era, trade for Europeans meant internal trade or trade across the boundaries of states located mainly on their own continent. Intercontinental trade (inflated in value by silks, spices, jewels, gold, and silver) formed only a small proportion of Europe's exports and imports. Statistics of the imports of sugar, tobacco, coffee, tea, spices, slaves, cotton, as well as the tonnage of ships cleared from Spanish, Dutch, and British ports, indicate that the upsurge in intercontinental trade occurred after 1650. A century later trade with the Americas (North and South) had grown rapidly to supersede 'traditional' trade with Asia, Africa, and the Middle East.

Nevertheless (to reiterate the point) as late as the 1790s the 'periphery', to appropriate a modern term to include South America, Africa, and Asia, together with the plantation economies of Virginia, Maryland, the Carolinas, and Georgia, purchased only 20 per cent of exports and supplied 25 per cent of its imports. Not only was that commerce a small proportion of European trade, it formed a far smaller share of total economic activity. By 1800 something under 1 per cent of Europe's aggregate output was sold to Africa, Asia, Latin America, the

Caribbean, and the slave states of America. Only a tiny percentage of total consumption by Europeans took the form of imports from these same parts of the globe. Even for maritime powers, Portugal, Holland, Britain, and France, these links through trade formed a limited proportion of economic activity.

V

Nevertheless the view suggested by the data that commerce with the periphery was of slight quantitative significance for Europe's long run growth could be superficial. At points in time, European output was the produce of all historical forces which cumulatively over the long run generated capital, a skilled labour force, techniques, and institutions to produce commodities and services year after year. Economic growth takes place at the margin. The problem is to specify and measure the contribution of particular inputs which generated *additions* to output. Commerce between Europe and the periphery may have exercised a special influence on patterns of specialization, on capital formation, technical progress, and institutional reform which promoted economic growth to an extent which is derogated by these statistics.

To discuss specialization, some notion of the type of merchandise traded is required. It is difficult to see how a mix of tropical merchandise which included sugar, tea, coffee, rice, tropical fruit, hardwoods, dyestuffs, gold and silver, increased possibilities for production along lines of comparative advantage. Trade simply allowed wealthy Europeans to consume exotic commodities which could not be grown or mined in their own region. As European incomes went up and when the prices of tropical foodstuffs fell their consumption spread down the social scale. But long run gains in productivity from division of labour and competition originated overwhelmingly in exchanges within Europe and far less from trade with other continents.

Some dynamic benefits certainly accrued. For example, Europeans exchanged manufactured goods for primary products and their governments promoted this tendency by regulating industry within their imperial domains. Europeans also specialized in the sale of shipping and commercial services to other continents basically to obtain the means to pay for a persistently adverse balance of commodity trade with India and China – countries which before the nineteenth century imported only limited quantities of industrial goods. Concentration on these 'invisibles' stimulated shipbuilding and developed banking, insurance, and shipping enterprises to service inter-continental trade. The direction of these effects is not in doubt, but is there any reason to suppose that the statistics of European trade with the periphery underrates its contribution to shipbuilding and to the 'commercial revolution' which promoted industrialization after 1750?

Raw materials, foodstuffs, and industrial commodities imported from Asia, Africa, and Tropical America also reduced constraints on European supplies of agricultural and industrial commodities and exercised 'demonstration effects' which led to the expansion of Europe's manufacturing capacity. Long before Colombus, Europeans successfully transplanted rice, sugar, sorghum, cotton, citrus fruits, and silkworms into Italy, Iberia, and Southern France. From the Americas came a range of new foodstuffs, including maize, potatoes, groundnuts, beans, tobacco, cocoa. Maize did increase grain supplies from Southern Europe – but its real impact came after the mid-nineteenth century. Although the potato certainly helped support population growth in Britain, Ireland, Belgium, and Germany, the additional calories provided by potatoes never made it a critical element in food supplies in the eighteenth or nineteenth centuries. For certain regions of north-western Europe (especially for Ireland), the potato created a Malthusian problem and emigration.

Raw materials imported from the tropics led to development of sugar refining, the processing of tobacco, and, above all, the manufacture of cotton fibres into textiles. By imitating the muslins and nanqueens imported by the East India Company, the English cotton industry followed a classic pattern of import substitution where foreign manufactures pioneered the market, and domestic substitutes gradually replaced imports; assisted, of course, by prohibitions against Indian and Chinese textiles. Such industries seem inconceivable without an assured supply of raw materials from Asia and the Americas. The crux of the matter is, however, to *quantify* the relative importance of industries which depended upon raw materials imported from the periphery, and British figures show that by 1841 cotton textiles accounted for about 7 per cent of gross national product and industries processing imported foodstuffs contributed a further 1 per cent. Since Britain had already passed through an industrial revolution, there is no reason to claim that *if* the European economy had been forced to manage without imported sugar, tobacco, hardwoods, and cotton, its industrial output *would* have fallen by a large percentage. Over time that hypothetical decline could be mitigated by patterns of substitution for tropical foodstuffs and raw materials and by the redeployment of labour into other industries. While cotton was the first industry to be transformed by the factory, tropical foodstuffs and raw materials were by no means indispensable. Industrialization proceeded on too broad a front to be checked by the defeat of an advanced column whose supply lines stretched across the oceans to Asia and the Americas.

VI

Could a far more significant contribution be located, where Adam Smith and Karl Marx first perceived it: within the process of capital accumulation? Definition and measurement of that particular 'input' raises complex problems. Europeans undoubtedly invested some portion of their gains from commerce with Africa, Asia, and the Americas in fixed and circulating capital, and thereby added *something* to the growth of agricultural and industrial output, but how much?

Once again the British example is critical. Not only did Britain pass through an industrial revolution before the rest of Europe, the country also traded with the periphery on a larger scale. As the pioneer industrial economy, it invested more in new technology, paid more for its own mistakes, and could not supplement domestic savings by importing foreign capital. For these reasons, the ratio of capital to output is likely to have been higher in Britain than in some 'follower countries' on the continent who benefited from British experience and finance offered at relatively low rates of interest.

Gross domestic investment rose from 8 per cent of Britain's national income in 1761–70 to 13 per cent by 1791–1800, and then declined slightly through to 1851–60. Most of the increment to national output from 1740 to 1801 must be imputed to additions to supplies of labour and capital. Only a small share came from improvements in the productivity of primary inputs. Only after 1801 did 'technical progress' become a more important source of growth. Although capital accumulation was clearly important in early phases of Britain's industrial revolution, that may be less true elsewhere in Western Europe where there were advantages in being able to learn from Britain's early start. Nevertheless, the role of capital formation should not be exaggerated as 'the motor of European economic development'. In 'modern' sectors of industry (such as textiles, metallurgy, energy supplies, and transport), growth emanated far more from technical progress and organizational changes than from capital accumulation.

Furthermore, a potential source of finance for investment can certainly be located in trading profits received by merchants, shippers, insurance-brokers, factors, and other 'capitalists' who organized Britain's trade with the periphery. Finance was also derived from direct investment in the plantation economies of the Caribbean and the Southern States of America. Overseas assets (land, equipment, and slave labour) not only produced merchandise sold on British markets but generated returns which could be repatriated into the domestic economy. Finally, profits from industries which produced exports sold to the periphery also became available for reinvestment in Britain. But did all these flows of income add up to an investible surplus large enough to finance a significant share of the capital formation which occurred in the British economy between 1750 and 1850? Hard evidence is difficult to find, but my tentative estimates for the 1780s and 1820s suggest that 'commerce with the periphery generated a flow of funds sufficient, or potentially available, to finance about 15 per cent of gross investment expenditures undertaken during the Industrial Revolution.'[2]

And there should be no presumption that *if* the New World had not been discovered until 1892, or *if* Africa and Asia had emulated Japan and refused to trade with the Europeans, resources deployed in these trades would not have been reallocated to some other (albeit less productive) lines of activity. Capital and entrepreneurship utilized to carry on commerce with the periphery were not specific to that form of enterprise. Logically any contribution that they made to the finance of domestic capital accumulation must be circumscribed to include only the 'increment' to the investible surplus which emanated from using capital and labour for that commerce rather than in other sectors of the economy.

Exponents of 'world economic systems analysis' (Wallerstein, Frank, Emmanuel, and Amin, who apply Marx's notion of primitive accumulation to commerce between Western Europe and the periphery during the mercantile era) exaggerate its contribution to industrialization from 1750 to 1873.[3] Their emphasis on that connection is derived from a simplistic perception of the First Industrial Revolution as a paradigm for the rest of Europe. European economies managed to industrialize with far lower ratios of trade to output than Britain.[4] Even for Britain, trade with Africa, Asia, and Tropical America formed a small proportion of total economic activity, and the contrary impression rests upon the assumption that this commerce (based upon 'exploitation', 'unequal exchange', and 'pillage') was an uniquely profitable field of enterprise which must have contributed an enormous surplus for the finance of capital accumulation. Behind this view its proponents have marshalled vivid descriptions of the tropical trades, some selective data on profits, and graphic quotations from Adam Smith, Karl Marx, and Maynard Keynes. But the views of that formidable trio have not been supported with historical evidence required to 'demonstrate' that *average* rates of profit derived by European capitalists from investment and trade with the periphery rose significantly above potential returns on feasible investments at home.

What stands out from the meagre range of statistics collated together by Dutch, French, and English historians is the variance in profits from year to year. Lucrative gains reaped in the favourable circumstances of one voyage could be transformed into losses on another. Recent attempts at measurement come up with *average* rates of return around the 10 per cent mark. And the long run decline in the prices of sugar, pepper, coffee, tobacco, and tea on the commodity markets of Amsterdam, London, and Paris does not suggest that abnormal profits were sustained in these trades. Whatever may have happened during the sixteenth century, the vastly increased volume of tropical imports carried into European ports after 1650 forced down prices to fractions of their original levels when tropical merchandise had constituted luxuries for the rich. Elastic supplies of homogeneous commodities and competition conducted between the Portuguese, English, Dutch, French, and other merchants are not normally congruent with the persistence of monopoly profits. This observation applies even to the infamous slave trade. *A priori*, gains from the exploitation of unfree labour and the sale of luxury produce from tropical America should have been extremely high. Supernormal profits were made by the Portuguese in the sixteenth century. But a century later when the output of sugar, tobacco, and coffee rose dramatically and plantations switched from indentured to unfree labour, the slave trade appears to have become competitive at every stage of its inhumane chain of operations. Two groups reaped gains from slavery: Arab and African entrepreneurs who organized the 'business', and consumers of tropical produce. If Europeans had been compelled to pay a price for their imports which reflected the cost of attracting and maintaining 'free' labour in the New World, then their sugar, tobacco, spices, indigo, coffee, and cotton would have cost far more. By how much more remains to be calculated. But given the tiny ratios of tropical imports to national expenditure and the elastic demand for tropical produce, the fall in real income which would, undoubtedly, have followed from a hypothetical British edict abolishing the slave trade in 1607, rather than 1807, could not have made much difference to levels of output and capital formation achieved in Europe by 1807.

VII

American treasure has been singled out by Gunder Frank as 'the principle functional contribution of the New World regions to the expansion of trade in the world, the accumulation of capital in the

European metropolis and the development of capitalism'.[5] Silver and gold had an impact which transcended the effects of other imports because they formed the basis of Europe's money supply. Money mattered between 1450 and 1750 when the spread of markets and monetary transactions (both within and between states) accompanied economic progress. Precious metals from the Americas relieved a potential monetary constraint on exchange and production, facilitated the expansion of international trade with Asia and the Baltic, and exercised upward pressure on prices which redistributed income between workers and capitalists and encouraged trade to respond to differential rates of inflation within and between countries.

To substantiate claims made for the pervasive effects of imported bullion requires, however, a specification of relevant connections and some attempt to gauge the importance of money in the European development. Spooner and Braudel rejected the notion that the American mines poured their precious metals into a deprived Europe because 'the accumulated stocks in the Old World since early times represented a considerable monetary mass'.[6] On their estimate, as late as 1650 the inflow had added not more than 25 per cent to the existing stock of silver and gold in Europe. Although Europe demanded more money (for increased exchanges, the division of labour, population growth, urbanization, the shift from barter transactions, and the growth of public expenditure) American specie was only one of several means utilized to cope with a potential monetary restraint. Europe's own silver and copper provided some of the money. Merchants and financiers pushed up the velocity of circulation. By debasement European rulers reduced the weight of specie required for each coin of account. There can be no presumption that the silver and gold from South America carried most of the monetary load required for economic expansion after 1500 or that Europeans would have found it excessively difficult and costly to develop either paper substitutes or a fiat coinage if silver from Mexico and Peru and gold from New Granada and Brazil had remained underground. Money was a lubricant not a source of power – oil but not petroleum.

Specie continued to be indispensable for the settlement of adverse balances with the Far East and the Baltic. Apparently the famous 'drain' of bullion to the East diminished over time as the Europeans sold services, especially shipping, to Asians and as the relative costs of goods made in the two continents narrowed. And this trade was of limited significance, even for the maritime countries. 'What Asia provided was luxuries. Now luxuries are not to be sneezed at but they take second place to food . . . also to bullion.'[7] Silver was drained from one part of the periphery (America) to another (Asia) in order to provide rich Europeans with luxuries.

Commerce with the Baltic not only exceeded trade with the East by a large margin but imports from this region (grain, timber, and other intermediate goods for shipbuilding) seem more 'strategic' for the long run development of the core. Not one of these commodities formed a large percentage of total supply consumed in Western Europe. Only about a third of Baltic imports were paid for with specie. Without relatively cheap supplies of American bullion, could European merchants and entrepreneurs have found other commodities to exchange for Polish grain, Russian hemp, and Swedish timber? Demand in the Baltic region was surely not unresponsive to a lowering of export prices?

There is a strong correlation between imports of specie and swings in the general level of prices throughout Europe from 1450 to 1750. Discussion of this issue has centred around the importance to be attributed to monetary or real factors, in *initiating* and *sustaining* the inflation of the long sixteenth century, the deflation of the seventeenth century, and the upswing in prices after 1750. Unfortunately, that debate will remain unsettled until the connection between bullion and prices can be quantified. And discussion on connections between imported silver and capital accumulation has not progressed much beyond Hamilton's famous thesis that wages lagged behind prices and redistributed income from workers to capitalists and landowners, which fostered investment. In several core economies wages did lag, markedly over the long sixteenth century and perceptibly again in the eighteenth century. That lag was more pronounced in primary production than in industry or urban services because the terms of trade shifted in favour of agriculture during the price revolution and again during the eighteenth century. But the rather mild inflations of the mercantile era did not provide favourable conditions for economic growth. *If* industrial profits were a primary source of accumulation then the rapid rise in the prices of primary produce operated to reduce investment. *If* wage earners formed an important segment of the market for manufactured goods the erosion of their real incomes by higher food prices narrowed that market. *If* (as classical economists suspected) landowners and farmers consumed a high share of their 'windfall' gains from inflation, then the over-all rate of investment would not increase very much. Optimal conditions for industrial advance at the core occurred when agriculture delivered a rising volume of food and raw materials to towns at stable or falling prices.

VIII

Recent debates in international history have emerged against the background of the North–South dialogue. The 'South's' challenge is directed at those who regard the contemporary international economic order as benign. That challenge derives support from historians with sympathies for the Third World who have, alas, overestimated the significance of economic relations with the periphery for the long run growth of the core. Even if we agree that contact with Western Europe contributed to underdevelopment in Asia, Africa, and Southern America, that does not imply that the gains which accrued (disproportionately perhaps) to Europeans did much to push their economies onto paths of sustained industrialization after 1750.

Links across the oceans were built up over the three centuries which followed the discovery of America, but to refer to the international commerce of that mercantile age as a 'world economy' is to misapply a contemporary concept which, as argued above, has relevance only for our times. Throughout the pre-industrial era connections between economies (even within states) remained weak, tenuous, and liable to interruption. Except for the economic development of a limited range of famous ports, growth and fluctuations can be explained mainly by reference to endogenous forces. The 'world economy', such as it was, hardly impinged. If my assertions are correct, then for the industrial revolution in Western Europe the periphery was peripheral.

4

RUSSIA AND THE EUROPEAN STATES SYSTEM

Adam Watson

The advent of Russia as a European power occurred comparatively late. Russia was not part of Latin Christendom. During the latter part of the Middle Ages the Russian lands formed part of the Mongol-Tartar dominion, and were separated from the Latin West by pagan Lithuania. The gradual Westernization of Russia in the chaotic seventeenth century and the establishment by Peter the Great of an effective Westernized state gave Russia in the eighteenth and nineteenth centuries – the Petersburg era – the desire and the ability to play a major part both in the management of European international society and the expansion of European government and technology into Asia. In our own century the Bolshevik Revolution, together with the decline of European dominance in the world, has resulted in the dissociation of the Soviet Union from the West, though Russia remains a major power in Europe.

Orderly government of a large area by a single authority – the first step towards statehood – was introduced into Russia by Scandinavians, and the word Rus itself originally referred to them. In the thirteenth century the Tartar Golden Horde swept westwards over the Eurasian plain. Moscow fell in 1238. Soon afterwards the Tartars destroyed Cracow, the spiritual capital of Poland, and pushed on into the heart of Europe. Pope Alexander IV summoned Latin Christendom to a crusade. The Poles took the lead in pushing back the Tartars, confirming themselves as the bulwark of the Latin world against the East. The Tartars were driven out of Poland and western Russia; but they stabilized their immense suzerain empire from the Dniepr to the China Sea (approximately the territory of the Soviet Union), and embraced Islam. Their khans conducted sporadic negotiations with European sovereigns and married into the Byzantine and other royal families; but the subject principalities of their empire were substantially isolated from the rest of the world. Muscovy was quicker than the other Russian principalities to adapt to and profit from Tartar suzerainty. Its princes ingratiated themselves with the Golden Horde, and received their investiture from the Great Khan as Grand Dukes of Muscovy. They learnt Tartar techniques of war and administration, and helped to extract the tribute due to the Khan from other Russian princes. Muscovy thus developed its statehood under the aegis of the Tartar system.

Towards the end of the fifteenth century the grip of Tartar suzerainty waned. In 1480 Muscovy threw off the Tartar allegiance and established itself as a Russian successor state to the empire of the Khans, both in its systematic subjection of other Russian principalities and in expansion eastwards towards Asia. It quickly mobilized the resources and at least the tacit allegiance of the northern and eastern Russians and was soon pushing out along the rivers and trade routes towards the seas. The area of Tartar dominion had become something of a power vacuum. The Muscovites planted their banners on the Caspian in the 1550s and, more tenuously after the immense trek across Siberia, on the Pacific in the 1640s. But in the south and west the Muscovite state found itself still opposed by superior force. The Ottoman Empire and its client khans now controlled all the Black Sea. Poland and Sweden barred the way to the Baltic, and Muscovy lost control of the outlet that Novgorod formerly used on the Gulf of Finland. Western Russia as far as the Dniepr had meanwhile been brought under the rule of the borderland state of Lithuania. The fusion of Poland and Lithuania into a powerful dual Catholic state in 1569 brought about the compulsory Westernization of West Russia including the historic cultural centre of Kiev, up to within 200 miles of Moscow. Polish and Italian cultural influences penetrated beyond Lithuania, as did Baltic commerce. The architecture of palaces and churches adopted visibly western features. At the end of the sixteenth century, Eastern Russia dissolved into chaos. As a result, early in the seventeenth century the Poles pushed eastwards. Twice they conquered Moscow and established puppet tsars there, the second of whom was the King of Poland's son. It was clear that if the Muscovites did not master the new European military techniques, all Russia would be Polonized as Lithuania had been.

During the centuries of Tartar and Mongol dominance the Russian people preserved their sense of identity by looking inward into themselves and cherishing their distinctive customs and language and above all their 'true Slav' Orthodox Christianity. This sense of difference, almost of consecration to their own values, kept the Russians from learning more than a minimum from their Muslim suzerains. Medieval Europe was remote and unappealing. Only Byzantium, the source of Russian religion and of other strands in Russian culture, was an acceptable source of influence until its fall in 1453. But when in the sixteenth century the expansive thrust of Europe really impinged on the Russian world, the Westerners whom the Russians encountered turned out to be, like the Muslims, clearly superior in almost all material abilities; but they were also Christians of a sort and somehow more civilized than the semi-nomadic and radically alien Easterners, in whose shadow the Russians had lived for so long. The challenge was inescapable. The response was deeply divided, ranging from avid acceptance to traditionalist revulsion.

The purpose of the new Romanov dynasty (1613) and their supporters was to restore the independence of the Muscovite state from Poland, and ultimately to liberate western Russia and the Ukraine which was then divided between Poland and Muslim vassals of the Ottomans. They saw that to do this they must learn the military and also the administrative and manufacturing skills of the West, which the Russians disparagingly described as 'khitry', meaning clever and tricky. In their opposition to Polish and Jesuit influences Muscovite governments turned in the seventeenth century to the Protestant north of Europe, the Germanic world. They learnt military and administrative techniques from Poland's enemy Sweden, which under Gustavus Adolphus had perhaps the most effective army and government in Europe. For commerce and other technology they looked further afield, to the trading and maritime powers: the Dutch, the Hansa, and the English. The great English clock which still stands over the principal gate to the Moscow Kremlin, and was a symbol of the Western sense of accurate time, was installed in 1625. By the 1630s most of the officers in the Muscovite army were mercenaries from Protestant Europe. Boris Gudonov started a navy with German ships. A '*nemetskaya sloboda*' or foreigners' free zone, known as the German City, was permitted in a suburb of Moscow to purvey trade and technology. But aesthetically and culturally the court and the outward-looking members of the nobility found Polish ways easier to adopt. Slav Poland was not foreign in the way that the Germanic countries seemed to be, and its aristocratic culture was well adapted to the area. Throughout the century Polish was spoken alongside Russian at the Muscovite court. The acquisition of Polonized Kiev in 1667 increased the influence of Polish culture on the court and government and on the Orthodox Church. But as the borrowing, and especially the cultural aping of the West increased, so did the reaction of the majority of the nobles, the clergy, and the people against western ways. The rejection of Westernizing authority was strongest in the domain of religion, where it was known as the raskol.

By the sixteenth century the horizontal patterns of medieval Latin

Christendom had given way to a number of more or less independent states. As the arts of war and peace developed, these European states impinged increasingly on one another, and two groups or systems of states emerged. The northern system centred on the Baltic, with its attention focused on the area won for Christendom by the northern crusades. Sweden and Poland/Lithuania were the pivotal powers of the northern system, which also closely involved Muscovy, the Ottomans, and the Holy Roman Empire. In the middle of the sixteenth century Ivan the Terrible, the first Grand Duke of Muscovy to call himself Tsar, was able to combine a policy of active expansion eastwards with a bid for a substantial Russian outlet on the Baltic, which in alliance with Denmark he held for some years before losing it to Sweden and Poland. But though Muscovy and the Ottoman sultanate were closely involved in the strategic and economic dealings of the north European system, they regarded themselves, and were regarded by the states that developed out of Latin Christendom, as outside the civilization and traditions of Europe. Ivan's Muscovy was a Byzantine-Tartar state with a population that was predominantly Slav but included substantial Asian minorities. As late as 1689 a provision in the historic treaty of Nerchinsk between the westernizing Regent Sofia and the Manchu Emperor, that boundary posts and other notices should be written in Latin as well as Chinese, Manchu, Russian, and Mongolian, was included not at the request of the Russians but of a Jesuit priest on the Chinese delegation.

The other half of Latin Europe was encompassed by the so-called southern (we would today rather label it western) system of states. The pivot of the system was the struggle of France and the Ottomans against the Spanish and Austrian Habsburgs, a contest that was fought mainly in Italy and Germany and the Mediterranean, and that lasted from the first French invasion of Italy in 1494 to the settlement of Utrecht in 1714. This system was also involved from the beginning in the great overseas expansion conducted by the five Atlantic powers (Spain, Portugal, Holland, England, and France). The most comprehensive and far-ranging diplomacy of the seventeenth century was that of France under Richelieu and later under Louis XIV. The aim of French policy in the northern system was to use the powers on the other side of Germany, and particularly Sweden, Poland, and the Ottomans, to harass the Habsburgs. The practical effect of that policy was to encourage the gradual merger of the two European systems into a single complex interplay of forces and interests.

The Christian states of the southern system also began in the seventeenth century to develop, consciously and explicitly, the rules and institutions of what we would call an international society. The practice preceded the theory. Seventeenth-century statesmen did not implement any theoretical plan or body of doctrine about the nature of their relations. They devised and elaborated responses to the growing pressures of the system. Their expedients solidified into conventions and codes of conduct, and some of these in turn became formulated into laws and institutions ratified by formal treaties. The codification of international law is associated especially with Grotius; the conduct of a continuous multilateral diplomatic dialogue, with Richelieu; and congresses to negotiate general peace settlements, with the pioneer achievement of Westphalia. As the two European systems interacted with each other, those states in the northern system that formed part of Latin Christendom were increasingly drawn into the network of the emerging European society and helped to shape its institutions and conventions. The Swedes, through their alliance with France and their involvement in the Thirty Years War in the southern system, were the first to see clearly that the west European distinction between the two systems was being overtaken by events. Gustavus Adolphus wrote to his Chancellor in 1628 that 'all the wars that are afoot in Europe have become one war.'[1] Two lawyer-statesmen who made an outstanding contribution to the formulation of the rules of the society of states, Grotius himself and Pufendorf who gave currency to the term states systems, were professsional diplomats in Swedish service.

The Swedes and Poles were well aware of the latent strength of Muscovy and its potential impact on the European balance of power. If Muscovy could remain a major independent actor in the northern system – that is, if it could avoid becoming a vassal of Poland or being driven far from the Baltic by Sweden – the fusion of the two systems would involve Muscovy in the affairs of all Europe. There was a latent community of interest between Muscovy and the Habsburgs in opposition to the three associates of France that stretched between them; but the French grand design aimed to concentrate the attention of France's associates westwards and so was also of help to Muscovy. This awareness of Muscovy's military and economic importance did not lead the powers of the northern system to regard it as a candidate for the society of European states which was in process of being formed. Successive Polish-Lithuanian governments in particular had long aimed at keeping their activities in the Russias separate from European politics, and especially at preventing any centre of authority in Russia which was outside Polish control from acquiring western technology or strengthening its military capacity. An often-quoted Polish remonstrance to Queen Elizabeth about English trade with Muscovy via the Gulf of Finland stated:

> We know . . . that the Muscovite is daily growing mighty by the increase of such things as be brought to the Narva . . . . We do foresee, except other princes take this admonition, the Muscovite puffed up in pride with those things that be brought to the Narva, and made more perfect in warlike affairs with engines of war and shippes will make assault in this way on Christendom to slay or make bound all that shall withstand him.[2]

This warning is characteristic of one Western approach to Russia, the total rejection which corresponds to the equally total rejection of the West by some Russians down the ages. In the settled lands of Western Europe little was yet known about Russia. There was some trade, less important to the West than to the Russians, and some travellers' tales. Neither the French nor, more surprisingly, the Austrians were actively aware of the potential impact of Muscovy on Europe. The powers of Western Europe regarded their own dynastic struggles, and the religious conflicts between Catholics and Protestants, as separate from the basically triangular conflict between Poland, Sweden, and Muscovy which was concerned with a different balance of power and different issues. Even in Vienna the struggle in and beyond the Baltic seemed remoter than the threat from the Ottomans who for much of the century operated against the Habsburgs from as near as Buda.

Gradually the military power of the Polish-Lithuanian state weakened. What at the beginning of the seventeenth century was a struggle to establish a Polish protectorate over Muscovy became a struggle for the control of Lithuania between Poland and a somewhat Westernized and Polonized Muscovite regime. In the reign of Peter the Great's father Alexis, Westernization was stimulated by the success which it visibly brought, in the military struggle against the Poles and in other fields too. A further important advance towards the Westernization of the Muscovite court and administration was achieved during the reign of Alexis's daughter the Regent Sofia in the 1680s. She was educated by Polish Jesuit trainees and attracted to Western humanism. Her lover and chief minister Golitsyn was of Lithuanian noble origin. He tried to Westernize more thoroughly the administration and the armed forces, and brought Muscovy as a 'European' power into an alliance with Poland and Austria against the traditional Turkish enemy. The court at Vienna thereby acknowledged the Romanov Russian state as part of the system in the same way as the Ottomans, but not yet as a member of the European Republic. However Golitsyn's reforms were half-hearted and his military efforts against the Muslims ended in failure. Up to this point cultural Westernization had been a fashion at court, but remained superficial and voluntary, while almost all of Muscovy remained at heart as it had been centuries before.

Peter the Great continued the family tradition of Westernization, but in a much more radical manner, with a revolutionary determination that effectively transformed the state but drove the traditionalists to regard him as Antichrist. The young Peter was attracted not by Polish aristocratic graces but by Dutch and other Western traders and artisans. During his sister Sofia's regency the child Tsar spent much time with such people in the *nemetskaya sloboda*. He also had it borne in on him by the violence which Sofia used to maintain her power that military force was the key to the control of the Russian state as well as to defeating the Turks; and this confirmed in him the conclusion derived from long Russian experience that Western techniques must be mastered in the military field above all. He formed and trained a small Western-style army and took over power from Sofia in 1689. Externally he continued the policy of war with Turkey and alliance with Poland, but devoted his efforts to introducing industries and craftsmen from northern and western Europe and to reorganizing the Muscovite army and administration largely on Swedish lines. Peter's personal taste for the Protestant north marked a significant change. Hitherto Russian borrowings from there had been almost exclusively military and administrative, and had shown no interest in the manners and style of life, or attitudes to religion, science, and education of those countries. But these appealed to Peter; and he tried to force an eclectic and Russianized form of them on Russia.

The young Peter was fascinated by technology. He retained a lifelong passionate interest in every machine, every tool, every industrial process which he could acquire or import from the West, for its own sake. From his contacts in the *nemetskaya sloboda* he learnt that Holland and England were the centres of this technology, as well as of the trade which seemed so important to his western friends and therefore to him. Though military technology seemed to him the most important, his main personal interest in the field of war, his real hobby, was ships and the navy, and everything connected with the sea. This further increased his admiration for Holland and England. Peter's famous 'Grand Embassy' or apprentice tour of the West with Menshikov and other companions who also became major actors in the process of Westernizing Russia, took him especially to Holland and England, where he worked as a shipwright and carpenter out of sheer interest in the techniques. He continued in after years to speak a kind of Dutch to Menshikov, to his wife, and other close friends, and to scatter Dutch phrases through his correspondence. The Dutch and English made it clear to him that they wanted peace between the Habsburgs and Turkey, and in 1699 mediated a peace between the two. On his return to Russia Peter, who wanted an alliance with the Maritime Powers, also concluded peace with Turkey and turned his ambitions from the Black Sea to the Baltic, from which Russia was cut off by France's ally Sweden.

There were three main ingredients in Peter's attitude towards the Dutch and northern Europe generally. First, the Dutch were prominent in the *nemetskaya sloboda*: it was there that he 'fell in love with Holland from afar'. Second, Holland then was recognized as the first country in Europe for technology and for the skills of its craftsmen and artisans, especially in shipbuilding. It was a country with little ceremony and etiquette, things which he hated. Third, he saw Holland, England, and Austria as Russia's natural allies in the European states system against her enemies Turkey and Sweden who were the traditional allies of Louis XIV's France.

Though Peter never dropped Russia's traditional hostility to Turkey and his aim to reach the Black Sea, then entirely in Ottoman or client Muslim hands, the commercial importance of the Baltic, and the interest of the Maritime Powers in it, became decisive for him. He conceived of 'Sankt Pietersburg', with its Dutch/German name on non-Russian soil on islands at the mouth of the Neva, as a trading entrepôt, a 'Russian Amsterdam' as he said. Whether or not he really used the phrases 'the window on the West' and 'a new Venice', they describe his attitude. His Baltic fleet was intended both to oppose Sweden and to ensure safe passage for trade between Russia and the high technology of the North Sea.

In the techniques of land warfare Peter particularly studied Swedish methods: partly because he had to fight Charles XII to gain and hold his Baltic outlet, and partly because of traditional Russian respect for Swedish military pre-eminence. After his victory at Poltava he offered the captive Swedish generals the toast 'To our masters in the art of war'. This ambivalent relation to Sweden, along with Peter's military incursions into Poland and his insistence on giving important posts to Russians rather than to foreigners, have led some historians to classify him too as learning Western techniques in order to defeat the West. In fact, Peter never regarded 'the West' as his enemy. On the contrary, he wanted almost desperately to be accepted by the rulers of Europe as a full and equal member of their society, of the 'European Republic'. If you were a member of that club, you had enemies as well as allies, just as you had foreign policy objectives and dynastic connections. Sweden, which was a member of the club, was his enemy as well as Turkey, which was not; but at the end of his reign he experimented with a Swedish alliance. In Poland he allied himself with the Austrian candidate for the throne, Augustus of Saxony, against the Franco-Swedish candidate. One of his proudest moments was when he sailed out of Copenhagen in formal command of a joint Russian-English-Danish fleet against Sweden, precisely because this visibly established him as a major and equal partner in a Western alliance. His writings and recorded statements, like those of his closest associates, are full of Russian national pride and assertiveness, and impatience for the 'fledglings', his élite of Westernized Russians, to take over from foreign hirelings. But there is not in them any hostility to the West or any desire to limit the Westernization of Russia to what was necessary for military success. Peter was equally determined to cut off his subjects' beards, make them wear Western dress, emancipate the women, break the power of the anti-Western church and of the traditionalists among the aristocracy. Peter did not want to lick the West, he wanted to join it. His Chancellor declared, 'we have stepped from the darkness of ignorance onto the stage of fame, and have joined the society of political peoples'.[3]

The opposition to Peter's Westernization of Russia was symbolized by the Tsaryevich, his son by his first wife, led by sections of the clergy and the nobility, and supported by a majority of the people. They wanted to turn their backs on the West: to revert to Muscovy in manners and customs, to abandon bleak western Petersburg and the navy, and stop warfare in the West. If the price of westward expansion was such a degree of Westernization as Peter demanded, they preferred to renounce it.

Viewed as part of the long process of Westernizing and modernizing Russia over the centuries, Peter's reforms in many ways continued those of his predecessors. Billington looks from this perspective: Russia, he says,

> underwent a profound transformation that pointed toward the future. What had been a monolithic and monastic civilization became a multinational secular state. Under Alexis Mihailovich and his son Peter the Great, Russia in effect adopted the aesthetic and philosophic culture of Poland while rejecting its Catholic faith, and the administrative and technical culture of Sweden and Holland.[4]

Westernized Russians stiffened with Western experts had begun to take control of the court and the army a century before Peter; and Alexis's victories over the Poles removed a greater threat than Peter's over the Swedes. The difference between Peter and his predecessors was that at least until Sofia's time Western techniques were adopted by Muscovy in order to preserve Holy Russia against forcible Westernization, and are rightly considered as part of the wider phenomenon of modernization against the West; whereas Peter was what later in Japan was called a West-worshipper, who actively disliked the old Russian civilization and felt that the West was superior not only technically but as a way of life. It was Peter who formulated and partly made good Russia's claim to be accepted as a member of the European society of states.

Peter's policies were continued with varying emphasis by his Westernizing successors. The ultimate guardian of the secular Western Petersburg-based state was the new model army which, as explained above, Peter had built to maintain his system within Russia as much as to expand it abroad. After his death the guards regiments occupied a pretorian position in Russian society. They established in power each of the four Empresses, including his wife and daughter, who consolidated his system. Peter's widow, Catherine I was in the Russian context a Westerner. Of Polish origin, she had been brought up in a German Lutheran pastor's household in Swedish Livonia. In her short reign she pursued a more pacific policy but maintained all Peter's Westernizing programmes, and actively pursued the dynasty's entry into the club of European sovereigns by dynastic marriages in Germany and Scandinavia. Her correspondence in the 1720s with George I, in which she signed herself 'Your affectionate sister', illustrates the acceptance of the new Petersburg-based Russian Empire into European international society. On her premature death the anti-Western elements acquired the upper hand for a while and returned to Moscow and Muscovite ways. But Westernizing autocracy was soon restored, under Anna and more notably under Peter and Catherine's daughter Elizabeth. Anna governed from Petersburg again, through her German favourite Biron with the help of other Westerners, and guards regiments with German officers – a departure from Peter's reliance on Russians where possible. Her foreign policy was based on a close working alliance with Austria. Elizabeth reverted to her father's policies, notably the use of Russians. Her remarkable minister Bestuzhev showed considerable elasticity in dealing with the changing alliances of the European society of sovereigns. He strengthened Russian influence in Poland and Sweden, and opposed the rise of Prussia by alliance first with Vienna and London, and then with France which was at last coming to see Russia as the only effective ally on the other side of the Germans.

Perhaps 1760 may be taken as marking Russia's full acceptance as a great power in the European family. In that year Elizabeth negotiated a secret clause with Maria Theresa about the annexation of East Prussia and also corresponded secretly and separately with Louis XV, in her efforts to hold together the anti-Prussian coalition in the West. Indeed by Elizabeth's time Petersburg was already a 'civilized' Western city;

and the despatches of Western ambassadors show that whatever they thought of the Russian world beyond, the Russian government had established itself as a European great power. Elizabeth's son married a German princess who usurped the throne as Catherine II the Great. She, being a Westerner rather than a Russian bewitched by the West, was able to work out a more thoroughgoing synthesis between Western and Russian elements. Many Western historians underestimate this achievement. Abroad Catherine, benefiting from the temporary weakness of both France and England, was able to make Russia the most influential state in Europe. She recovered extensive Russian territories from the Turks and incorprated most of Russian Lithuania (though not ethnically Polish lands) by the partitions of Poland; but in the rest of Europe she tried to maintain a balance of power and to preserve an approximate status quo. By her correspondence with Western intellectuals she had more personal influence on the development of European thought about statecraft than any European sovereign of her time except Frederick the Great.

It fell to Catherine's grandson Alexander I, a Tsar three-quarters western by blood, to establish Russia as one of the five Great Powers of Europe. He carried the long struggle between Poland and Muscovy through to the annexation of Warsaw. More important, Russia played a major part in the defeat of Napoleon; and Russian troops shared in the occupation of defeated France and the restoration of legitimate government there. Alexander and his ministers were among the principal figures at the Congress of Vienna. The period of Napoleon's ascendancy had shown that England and Russia on the two edges of Europe were the only powers strong enough to offer effective opposition to the organized strength of post-revolutionary France. These two global powers, drawing much of their strength from outside Europe, therefore occupied a dominant position in the formulation of allied policy in the final struggle and the Vienna settlement. The two major German powers, Austria and Prussia, and the restored Kingdom of France were in a sense states delivered by England and Russia from Napoleonic dominance. They owed their equal status at the Vienna negotiations and the emerging Concert of Europe to their diplomatic skill and to the awareness in both England and Russia that a stable directorate for Europe required a broader base than the uneasy polarity of London and Petersburg. Alexander took the lead in determining that the international society of Europe should not be a free-for-all based on the balance of power but a Holy Alliance of European sovereigns who would together lay down the law and who were pledged to defend the spiritual, religious, and social values of their common European civilization against the destructive revolutionary forces which he saw manifesting themselves in Russia as well as in France and other Western countries.

The Vienna settlement and the early period of the Concert of Europe were the apogee of Russian influence in ordering the affairs of Europe. But this influence was considerable throughout the two centuries of the Petersburg era. In the eighteenth century Europe was regarded as a commonwealth divided into several states, of which Russia was one of the most powerful. It was what we call an international society, but not yet a collectivity in whose name great powers presumed to act. The use of the term Europe as a diplomatic entity, in the sense of a group of states having common interests and duties and in whose name member states could take joint decisions, is no older than the nineteenth century. The change which this usage reflected was brought about especially by Alexander and Metternich.

Under Alexander's successors Russia's position in the society of European states remained undisputed. The tsarist governments played a major and on the whole moderating and constructive part in the Concert of Europe and the ordering of the international system. Meanwhile Russia continued to expand into Asia. The Romanov Empire Westernized, modernized, and settled a vast area of Siberia and Central Asia, comparable only to the contemporary and similar westward expansion of the United States, and parallel to the seaborne expansion of England.

During the nineteenth century the native Russian and the Western elements in the Romanov Empire continued to fuse. The Westernized Petersburg-based administration, and those responsible for the Empire's industrial, commercial, and financial management, became more consciously Russian in their beliefs and values, and more in tune with those they governed. The Russian people for their part became subtly Europeanized, and absorbed often almost unawares the ways of thinking and of doing things of those in authority. The quarrel between the Westernizers on the one hand and the Slavophils – the advocates of Pan-Slavism and of revolutionary Russian populism – on the other continued in Russian society. But an increasing number of Russians felt the attraction of both tendencies. The struggle took place inside individuals searching for a synthesis, inspiring among other achievements the unsurpassed Russian literature of that time in which ambivalence to the West is transmuted into the issues confronting every thinking individual man.

The sense continued among the people of Russia until the twentieth century that while the Tsar was still the little father of his people the government in St. Petersburg and the westernized upper classes were somehow alien, and that Moscow remained the heart of the country. The collapse of the Romanov Empire under the strains of war in 1917 owed much to this inchoate feeling. As the Bolshevik Revolution of 1917 recedes into history, and the continuities with the Russian past as well as the ruptures emerge into perspective, it is possible to discern how those tremendous events fit into the pattern of Russian attitudes towards Europe and the West. Lenin and his Communist colleagues who seized power in the confusion of the Revolution were themselves dedicated Westernizers, importing into Russia a Marxist ideology acquired from the West, a belief that their new order could only be achieved in backward Russia if it was also established in the developed industrial countries, and a Petrine conviction of the value of Western technology and the need to industrialize and modernize Russia. But in fact the deep feelings of the Russian soldiers and peasants who had already overthrown the Romanov regime, and who under Lenin's leadership secured the Revolution by force of arms, rejected the West. There were in the popular revolt elements of the earlier raskol and of previous Cossack and other populist rebellions against Westernized authority. Lenin and his associates, in spite of their cosmopolitan intellectual beliefs, were affected by this anti-Western emotion. In George Kennan's words, they 'hated the Western Governments for what they were, regardless of what they did'.[5] The west was once more, as it had been before Peter, officially condemned as khitry, interventionist, and the source of contamination from which Russia, the land of the true faith, must be guarded and insulated. The move back from Petersburg to Moscow was fraught with symbolism deeper than the practical reasons which most Russians imperfectly understood, and confirmed the ambivalent but deep-seated desire to shut the window on the West and to establish an impregnable military and industrial autarchy with its own distinctive salvationist message. This message Lenin and subsequent Soviet governments have addressed to mankind in general, but especially and increasingly to those who for their own reasons wish to throw off the domination of the West.

Russia thus illustrates many of the characteristic features of a non-Western civilization which in the case of Muscovy Westernized and modernized itself by its own decision rather than by conquest, but was induced to do so by the pressure of European expansion. The closest parallel is perhaps Japan. The Japanese Westernized themselves much later than the Russians, and they did so not in order to avoid conquest by a European power as the earlier Romanovs had done, but with a Petrine appreciation of European values as well as technology and in order to 'join the society of political peoples'. There were West-worshippers in Japan who adopted a European form of government, European law, dress, and manners as eagerly and eclectically as Peter and his fledglings, equally convinced of their superiority. And there was a similar religious and popular reaction against the West, which for a short period was able to resume control of the government. Japan's alliance with England and defeat of Russia played the same part in her entry into the expanded European states system as Peter's alliance with England and Holland and his defeat of Sweden. In both cases the defeat of a major European power was not a victory over the West but participation as an equal in the struggle of the European powers and thus the attainment of a new status.

The most characteristic feature of the social pattern called into being by the expansion of Europe beyond its own cultural boundaries is the replacement of a previous culturally monolithic society by a new type of state, copied from European models and controlled by a small – often tiny – Western or Westernized élite, very different from the great majority made up of un-Westernized former nobility, religious figures, and the lower ranks of society. Consequently a great cultural gap opens between the rulers and the ruled – 'entre le peuple et le pouvoir'. This pattern is of course characteristic of all societies imposed by a dominant culture on an alien and subordinated one: it is typical for instance of the Hellenized kingdoms of Asia and Egypt, of Islamic India, and of contemporary black Africa. Romanov Russia is a striking example. And in spite of the popular upheaval of the Revolution this social pattern and the ambivalence towards the West still continue in the Soviet Union.

5

SPAIN AND THE INDIES

Michael Donelan

From time to time over the centuries, the states system is challenged by fideism. This is not the same as faith. Fideism is the conviction that the faith, whether religious creed or secular ideology, is the beginning of truth; and accordingly (in one of fideism's forms) that the faith supplants existing moral and political rules; and that all rights, notably the right to have a separate state and to exercise government, are dependent on possession of the faith. One such challenge to the states system occured at its very beginning. In 1492, great militant religious empires on opposite sides of the Atlantic, as yet unknown to each other, were about to clash.

The Aztecs and the Incas were small bands of conquerors. They erupted against the neighbouring peoples at the beginning of the fifteenth century, subjected them, and lived by tribute. The Aztec Empire, about the size of Spain, was loosely-knit: their city-state, Mexico, kept the others in subjection by military power. The Inca Empire, 2,000 miles to the south and about twice the size of Spain, was tightly-knit: the subject tribesmen were brought into a single elaborate organization culminating in the monarch. Both empires developed civilizations that are among the wonders of the world.

We know a little about the motives of the Aztecs and the Incas for their conquests. They do not appear to have been pushed by economic distress, but we may surmise that they sought wealth from the labour of subjects. They had great systems of honours. They had a further motive which had the crucial quality of being a justification: religion. The Incas believed that their royal house was of divine descent; the expansion of the empire was a sacred mission. For the Aztecs, the purpose of warfare was to capture the prisoners needed for sacrifice to the sun.

These beliefs, probably in some form very old, were shaped into a detailed and fervent creed and proclaimed to the people by the first of the great conquerors, the Inca Viracocha and the Aztec ruler, Itzcoatl. We may guess that among the motives of these leaders for conquest there was, as with all history's great conquerors, a belief in themselves and in a personal right of conquest, justifying what they were doing. It seems likely that they also believed the religion that they taught their peoples. Certainly their successors, Atahuallpa and Montezuma, at the time of the coming of the Spaniards, were men of intense religious faith.

The 600 *conquistadores* who marched with Cortés, the 180 with Pizarro were in some ways amazing to the Aztecs and Incas, whom they called 'Indians'. They themselves were equipped for an encounter with strange civilizations by their knowledge of the Muslims. Nothing had prepared their hosts. A Mexican saw one day 'towers or small mountains floating on the waves of the sea'; these were Cortés's ships.[1] 'To our Indian eyes,' an Inca wrote, 'the Spaniards looked as if they were shrouded like corpses. Their faces were covered with wool, leaving only the eyes visible, and the caps which they wore resembled little red pots on the tops of their heads.'[2]

None the less, between Spaniards and Indians, there were similarities. We know much about the motives that inspired the *conquistadores*. They wanted wealth in the shape of gold, and not just in the way that Europeans had always wanted gold but because of the shortage of the metal at that time in Europe for monetary and other purposes which had already sent the Portuguese exploring down to the Gold Coast of Africa; and wealth in the shape of estates which would enable them to set themselves up like Andalusian gentlemen with peasants to work the land for them. They wanted honour, meaning a higher rank in society and, for those like Cortés who were already gentlemen, glory.

These adventurers had a further motive which in their eyes made what they were doing right. They took the greatest pains at each stage of their exploits to get the endorsement of the Crown, partly no doubt from fear of its long arm and because they needed it as a source of demarcation among them if there was not to be chaos, but partly, it seems clear, from loyalty. Whether this was so or not, their actions at any rate had the effect of extending the territories of their king, and this justified them. At the very beginning, Columbus reported his triumph in these words: 'in thirty-three days, I passed from the Canary Islands to the Indies with the fleet which the most illustrious king and queen, our sovereigns, gave to me. And there I found very many islands filled with people innumerable, and of them I have taken possession for their highnesses, by proclamation made and with the royal standard unfurled, and no opposition was offered to me.'[3]

There was a still greater cause for Columbus. The island of his landfall he named San Salvador. He had been sustained throughout his long frustrating negotiations first with John II of Portugal, then with Ferdinand of Aragon and Isabella of Castile, by conviction of a mission from God. Cortés, the Pizarro brothers, and their companions were fortified by devotion to St. Peter, St. James, the Mother of God, to Christ. Their faith, along with their sense of intellectual superiority over the Indians, gave them the audacity which was the cause of their success. They had the right to do what they were doing because they were extending the realm of the Cross.

The cause of the king and the cause of the Cross were hardly separable in the minds of the *conquistadores*. Because of centuries of hostility to the Muslims, to feel Castilian or Aragonese was at the same time to feel Christian. Ferdinand and Isabella set out to create a new united monarchy of Spain on the basis of religious fervour. They revived the crusade against Islam with the conquest of Granada. They sought to re-animate the religion of the people by the extension of the Inquisition, the expulsion of the Muslims and Jews, and the church reform of Ximénez. The Spanish kings were to be the Catholic kings. The effect may have been that to a Spaniard of the time only a Catholic kingdom was a true kingdom. A Muslim kingdom was just 'a Saracen tyranny'. Similarly, perhaps, the kingdoms of Atahuallpa and Montezuma, as infidel, were not proper kingdoms. There need be no scruples about conquering them and setting up true Christian rule in their stead.

There was some feeling in the conquest of the Indies of driving the idolators from the Promised Land as Joshua drove the Canaanites. Indian wickedness seemed in some ways far darker than Muslim. They permitted incest and sodomy and homicide in breach of the natural law, the last in the shape of human sacrifice to their idols and, in Peru, the burial of servants alive with their dead masters. When Cortés's company were poised to march inland from Vera Cruz in 1519 they wrote a letter to the King and Queen seeking endorsement of their actions. In the course of this they described the Mexican holocausts at length and said:

> Let Your Royal Highnesses consider, therefore, whether they should not put an end to such evil practices, for certainly Our Lord God would be well pleased if by the hand of Your Royal Highnesses these people were initiated and instructed in our Holy Catholic Faith, and the devotion, trust and hope which they have in these their idols, were transferred to the divine power of God.[4]

If the cause of the king and the true Faith justified the *conquistadores* in their own eyes, let us consider what justified the king in his. Thanks to the *conquistadores* and to the royal officials rapidly despatched after them, Ferdinand and Isabella and then Charles V were gaining the royal fifth of all gold and many millions of new vassals. These were vast advances in the rivalry with Portugal. But by what right? Next only to the Faith, the intended foundations of the monarchy were justice and legality. How then did the monarchs justify the wording of their commission of 1492 to Columbus: 'Forasmuch as you, Cristóbal Colón, are going by our command with certain vessels of ours and with our subjects to discover and to gain certain islands and mainland in the Ocean Sea . . .'?[5]

An eminent scholar tells us that the Spanish kings believed that they had a right to the Indies 'by conquest'.[6] Unfortunately, it is not clear what the kings understood by this. In the case of 'the right of discovery', there is some hint of a muddle at the time between a right against other claimants, such as the Portuguese, and the absurd idea of a right against existing occupants, the Indians.[7] Correspondingly, it is very likely that the Spanish monarchs thought that they had a right of conquest of the Indies against the Portuguese; it is possible that by a muddle they persuaded themselves that they had a right against the Indians; but this is improbable. For these were still the ages of belief in 'the just war'; states were not yet credited with the sovereign right to make war at will and to acquire title to territory simply by declaring it annexed; they had to have a just cause. It is true that the tradition of European kingship was that the proper work of a king was to extend the lands and glory of his dynasty. People believed this the more lightly in that before the days of the centralized nation-state, though the warfare caused suffering, the change of ruler usually made little difference. This and the egotism of a great king no doubt gave him a sense of personal right to go out and conquer. None the less, it was necessary to have a legal right, a public justification.

When Charles V, king of Spain from 1516, was elected Holy Roman Emperor in 1519, he became the heir to an old idea that there was an *imperium mundi*, an empire of the world. One of the deepest convictions of medieval people was that the world was in all respects a unity, and accordingly that it must be so in politics. From this, some concluded that the hierarchy of temporal rulers must culminate in a highest ruler, having universal lordship.[8] However, those who concluded this were mostly supporters of the German emperors, few others in Europe had ever believed it, and though Charles V certainly had the highest ambitions, he can hardly have believed (because no one had ever believed) that universal lordship gave a right to dispossess kings of their kingdoms, as he was doing in the Indies.

It seems clear that for Charles V, as for Ferdinand and Isabella, the justification for taking certain islands and mainland in the Ocean Sea, by force if necessary, lay in and only in the spreading of the Faith; but it was a problem for the scrupulous and still is whether this justification really was morally valid. In discussing this, we have to take account of an aspect of the conquest of the Indies on the Spanish side of the Atlantic that had no analogue on the other among the Aztecs and Incas. All that we have said so far about these militant religious empires has been roughly parallel: their motives for conquest, their justification, the contribution to this of faith. The great difference was that the Aztecs and Incas did not belong to a continent-wide society of kings, whereas the Spanish monarchs did. This society still had for a few more years a formal head, the Papacy. In 1493, the year after Columbus's triumph, Pope Alexander VI, at the request of Ferdinand and Isabella, issued the famous bull *Inter Caetera* about events in the Indies.[9]

'Among other works well-pleasing to the Divine Majesty and other things desirable to our heart, certainly the most outstanding is that the Catholic Faith and Christian Religion especially in our times is being exalted and spread and extended everywhere and the salvation of souls procured and barbarian nations subdued and brought under that faith.' The Pope goes on to praise the Spanish monarchs for their recovery of Granada and for their proposal to subject the Indies to the Papacy and the Catholic Faith.

The question is whether the Bull was meant to endorse subjection by force and, if so, how this was compatible with the moral law of which the Church was custodian. According to that law, if a war was to be just there had first to be an offence by the other side. Even the Crusades were not exempt from this requirement. Those aimed at Palestine were thought of as 'the recovery' of the Holy Land, wrongfully seized by the Muslims in that it was Christ's land and inherited from him by the Christians. A similar idea was held to justify the crusade in Spain: it was a 'reconquest'. But none of this could apply to the Indies.

Christians could otherwise only make war on infidels who had attacked them. Warfare with Muslims was endemic from the Balkans to West Africa and much of it could be justified in this way. Recent parallels for *Inter Caetera* had been the bulls *Dum Diversas* of 1452 and *Romanus Pontifex* of 1455, issued in support of the Portuguese advance down the coast of West Africa, praising them for their desire to spread knowledge of the Faith and to make the Saracens and other infidels come into the Church. These bulls plainly envisage warfare but since they describe the Saracens and other infidels as hostile to Christ, it is possible that defensive warfare is intended. Once again, this could not apply to the Indies for it was not alleged that the Indians were guilty of attacking the Christians.

Since the time of Innocent IV in the thirteenth Century, the Church had been concerned not merely with defensive war against the Muslims but with the sending of missions and a general pastoral duty. In this connection, Innocent had taught that there were two other possible grounds for war against them: if they should refuse to admit missionaries, and if their rulers should fail to prevent breaches of the natural moral law. Both these grounds were in principle applicable to the Indians, but in practice neither was, for the Indians did not reject preaching, and not the natural law but the spreading of the Faith was the issue for the Spanish monarchs and the Papacy.

Let us move on to the next stage of the Bull, the purpose of which was to give practical support to the Spanish monarchs in spreading the Faith. 'By the authority of Almighty God granted to us in St. Peter and of the Vicarship of Christ . . . we give, concede and assign' to the Spanish monarchs and their successors all lands west of a line 100 leagues west of the Azores and the Cape Verde Islands. We have here the famous claim by the Pope to give away the American continent; or more exactly to give lordship over the Indies to the Spanish monarchs, demoting the infidel rulers. The qualification should be made, however, that probably this was not the main purpose of the Bull and that all concerned may have had reservations about it.

Doctrinally, it was uncertain whether the temporal powers of the Papacy could be made to stretch so far. From the earliest centuries of the Church, thinkers had sought to reconcile the unity of Christendom with the duality of spiritual and temporal powers, and not just as a matter of theoretical interest but under the hard practical necessity of managing the relations of rulers with the Papacy and of having a highest court of appeal at law. The basic principle arrived at in the days of Innocent III at the end of the twelfth century was that the Pope had the 'fullness of power' (*plenitudo potestatis*). This meant that he could exercise temporal power if need arose for the well-being of Christendom; he could, for example, exercise temporal jurisdiction if the relevant secular judge was negligent or suspect; at the extreme, he could depose a ruler for total incompetence or incorrigible malice.

Seeking a theory to underpin this practical principle, Innocent IV had propounded the notion that, at the Creation, God had the lordship of the world, then Christ, then St. Peter and his successors. However, when discussing relations between Christians and infidels, he taught that infidels had the right of dominion, that is, of ownership and lordship. As to warfare, as we have seen, there had to be specific reasons for attacking them; they could not be attacked just as such. Innocent's pupil, Henry of Susa, Cardinal Bishop of Ostia (Hostiensis), the other leading canonist of the thirteenth century, took a harder line: 'It seems to me that with the coming of Christ every office and leadership and lordship and jurisdiction was taken from every infidel lawfully and with just cause and granted to the faithful through Him who has the supreme power and cannot err.' Correspondingly, he appears to have taken the view that in principle it was justifiable to make war on infidels simply because they refused to recognize the lordship of the Papacy and the Emperor.[10] Over the following centuries some other experts maintained this view, but apparently not most and not the Papacy.[11]

It was on this uncertain ground that one had to stand if one wanted to support the right of the Papacy to grant the Indies to the Spaniards. The Spaniards themselves certainly attached some importance to this aspect of the Bull. They used it as a title to the Indies. They incorporated it henceforth in their proclamations to the Indians, eventually standardized officially as 'The Requirement', and in this way asserted that resistance to them was unlawful and war on their part just. Yet there is a hint of sham about The Requirement. The Inca Atahuallpa is said to have commented on hearing it that 'the Pope of whom you speak must be crazy to talk of giving away countries that do not belong to him'.[12] The Spaniards may have had some inkling of the justice of the remark. Moreover, they always claimed that they had other titles to the Indies besides the papal gift, though they did not specify these. They said this, no doubt, because they did not wish to be beholden to the Papacy for the new lands, but they may also have had reservations about how much weight the idea of a papal gift would bear. We may add that to say that one has other titles to a thing makes nonsense of the idea that it is a gift.

Probably the main purpose of *Inter Caetera* was not to make a gift but to make a demarcation. It was aimed not at the problem of whether it was right to conquer the Indians but at the problem of keeping the peace between the Spaniards and the Portuguese. What was needed was a general line between the two countries that would spare them reliance on piecemeal rights of discovery. Here was a well-grounded use of the papal 'plenitude of power' in the society of states. The Bull made a start in demarcation. After much further diplomacy, the final stage was the Treaty of Tordesillas of the following year in which the Spaniards and the Portuguese adjusted the details for themselves.

Looking back over this discussion of the Spaniards' justification for conquering the Indies, the outcome is that it was morally dubious on their own terms. They were not covered by the ordinary rules of just war. They may not have really believed that they had the Indies by grant of the Pope and that their warfare was just on this ground. The conquest of the Indies is one of those occasions in the history of the states system when faith alone seems justification enough, and a militant creed bursts through traditional bounds, sweeps aside the scrupulous demand for precise rights and justifications, and sets out to establish the reign of truth by heroic violence. Faith inspired herosim in the *conquistadores* but also, being boundless, may have justified in their eyes treachery and torture and the murder of Atahuallpa and Montezuma against the natural rules of hospitality and diplomacy. The *conquistadores* may have thought, as we said, that the infidel states were not proper states, worth scrupling over. If the Spanish monarchs agreed, if they did indeed believe in the opinions of Hostiensis and in the idea that the Papacy could dispose of infidel kingdoms, then the Spanish conquest is not merely a case of fideism but of fideism avowed, as from time to time since, in explicit theory: a state is not legitimate and exists only on sufferance if it does not possess the true faith.

Though founded on faith and carried into conquest by unrestrained faith, the Spanish monarchy was not a tyranny. A debate sprang up in Spain without parallel in later imperialism about the justice of what was being done. The Crown permitted and in some forms encouraged this debate; it had sent Columbus, the results had turned out enormous, and now it wanted to know the justification of what it had done and how policy for the future could be made right as well as practical.

The debate had two aspects. The first was the angry controversy between the Spanish colonials and the missionaries, with the Crown in the middle, over the treatment of the Indians. A big issue here was whether the Indian communities should be direct vassals of the Crown or whether the colonials should be given lordship over them (*encomienda*). The gravest issue was slavery. Seeking a more disposable labour force for their gold and silver mines and the like than came to them by *encomienda*, the colonials used The Requirement to claim that Indians who resisted the conquest were making unjust war and could therefore be enslaved. The leader against oppression of the Indians and in favour of the peaceful spreading of the Faith was the fiery Dominican bishop of Chiapas, Bartolomé de las Casas, eventually given the official status of Protector of the Indians:

> As if the son of God which died for every one of them had commanded in his law where he saith 'Go teach all nations' that there should be ordinances set down unto infidels, being peaceful and quiet and in possession of their proper land, if so they received it not forthwith without any preaching or teaching first had: and if they submitted not themselves to the dominion of a king whom they never saw and whom they never heard speak of and namely such a one as whose messengers and men were so cruel and so debarred from all pity and such horrible tyrants, that they should for it lose their goods and lands, their liberty, their wives and children, with their lives, Which is a thing too absurd and fond, worthy of all reproach and mockery, yea, worthy of hellfire . . .[13]

The quieter aspect of the debate concerned the point with which we have been concerned: did the Spaniards truly have a justification for taking over the Indies at all? The matter first came to a head in 1512–13 as did the question of the treatment of the Indians. King Ferdinand asked the Dominican theologian Matías de Paz and the civil jurist Juan Lopez de Palacios Rubios to write papers for him. They advised that the Indians had complete rights of personal liberty and ownership but that the king was entitled to rule over them because the Pope had universal temporal and spiritual lordship and had granted him this right. The point seems to have aroused little interest among theorists more widely in Europe, but in Paris in 1510 the Scottish Dominican theologian John Mair contributed the argument that the Indians might be an example of Aristotle's 'natural slaves'. The Dominican Juan Ginés de Sepúlveda, editor of the *Politics*, developed this idea in a book *Democrates Alter* into a full statement of the natural superiority of the Spaniards over the Indians and thus of their duty to rule them. The aged Las Casas debated the matter with him before an official panel at Valladolid in 1550. The *imprimatur* for Sepúlveda's book was refused.

Meanwhile, what was to prove the most enduring work to come out of the controversy had already appeared, the lecture *De Indis* (On the Indians) given in January 1539 by the Dominican Francisco de Vitoria, professor of theology at Salamanca and a leader of the revival at that time of the philosophy of Thomas Aquinas.

Vitoria's opening point is that, since the Indians possessed goods and exercised government before the arrival of the Spaniards, it is not enough simply to call them 'natural slaves'; specific arguments have to be produced to show that really they were incapable of these rights: they were not in a state of grace or they were infidels or mad. He refutes these points.

Given, then, that the Indians did have valid rights, Vitoria next discusses one by one seven alleged justifications for taking over their countries. We have mentioned most of them here. All, Vitoria concludes, are invalid: an imperial lordship over the whole world; a papal temporal and spiritual lordship over the whole world; the right of discovery; refusal to accept the Christian faith; offences against the natural law such as incest and sodomy; the argument that the Indians submitted freely; the belief that God had given the Indies to the Spaniards as he gave the Promised Land to the Israelites.

In the final part of his lecture, Vitoria offers eight justifications for Spanish rule over the Indies that are valid provided all the conditions are truly fulfilled. In one of these Vitoria can perhaps be said to rely on the fact that he and his listeners were Christians, namely, the argument that if a large number of the Indians were to become Christians, the Pope might be entitled under certain circumstances to appoint a Christian ruler over them. Otherwise, Vitoria relies, as in his rebuttals of the false justifications, on the idea to be found in Aquinas and in Aristotle and constantly in Western thought and perhaps universally that, irrespective of their faith, the Indians and Spaniards like all men are bound by a natural moral law and as part of it, a *ius gentium*, a law of nations.

Thus, Vitoria argues, men have a right to travel and trade over the whole world. If the Spaniards were to use this right inoffensively and if the Indians were to prevent this maliciously, a situation might arise in which the Spaniards might justifiably go to war against them and perhaps as a result deprive them of goods and liberty and take over the government. Again, the Spaniards have a right to spread the Faith peacefully and the Indians must not try to prevent them. The Spaniards could protect fellow-Christians among the Indians. Though the Spaniards have no right to punish the Indians for offences against the natural law, they can go to the defence of innocent people who are being killed. A state can choose its own ruler, and the Indians might freely choose the Spanish king. There is a right to assist allies in a just war (Vitoria is perhaps thinking of the alliance of Cortés with the oppressed city-state Tlaxcala against the Aztecs), and the acquisition of new territories can legitimately arise from this. Last, uncertain, put forward for discussion, it may be that a primitive people should be taken over for their own good.

The lecture *De Indis* is the main reason for seeing Vitoria as one of the earliest theorists of the states system. His theory is a balanced one. On the one hand, he pictures a world consisting of states that are independent. There is a law between them by which they must respect one another, whether they are Christian or infidel. Historians of international law have drawn attention to the way in which Vitoria silently amends inherited Roman concepts and begins the transformation of the *ius gentium* from a law common to all men into a law between states, that is, a modern international law.[14] However, we should not push this point too far. For, on the other hand, Vitoria is a long way from thinking of states as completely independent, as 'sovereign' in the way asserted in recent centuries. They are parts of a single world-wide natural community, and for this reason have inescapable obligations to one another, to keep their borders open to travel, trade, and the spreading of truth, and to intervene against the killing of the innocent.

Though Vitoria is claimed by the international lawyers, it is worthwhile for two reasons to repeat that he was a moral theologian. His propositions are not rules that will settle what a state must and must not do in foreign policy; they are principles that point towards a certain sort of world and guide the mind in making particular judgements. Second, it is satisfying to recall that the first defender of the states system against fideism was a man of faith.

6

BRITISH AND RUSSIAN RELATIONS WITH ASIAN GOVERNMENTS IN THE NINETEENTH CENTURY

David Gillard

At the end of the eighteenth century Eurasia contained four main 'systems' of states: European, Islamic, Indian, and Chinese. During the nineteenth century power from within the European system, mainly that of the British and Russian governments, was exercised in such a way as to shatter all three Asian systems. This prompts the question as to why these European and Asian governments so often failed to accommodate one another's interests that their conflicts brought catastrophic change.

Although very different from the European system, each of the groups of Asian states may be said to have constituted a system at this time. In the first place, most of the governments in each group were primarily concerned with one another, seeing even outside threats mainly in terms of how these might affect the distribution of power within the group. Secondly, even though their mutual antagonism was often greater than their hostility to outside powers, most of the governments in each group had a sense of being part of a common civilization superior to that of other systems.

Governments in the Islamic system of western and central Asia saw international politics then in terms of almost permanent conflict over the region's unstable and largely undefined frontiers. Iran was normally at odds with its neighbours in western and central Asia over lost territories; in central Asia some of those neighbours such as Bukhara, Khiva, Khokand, and the Afghan principalities were recurrently at war with one another and with nomadic or semi-nomadic tribes; and Arabia was the scene of struggles arising from the expansion of the Wahhabi sect. The Ottoman Empire itself had at the height of its power divided its attention between meeting the challenge of Iran within the Islamic system and extending the domain of Islam at the expense of powers within the European system. It had now entered a period of decline in which its European frontiers shrank and it faced the threat of internal war. After the Crimean War it acquired formal membership of the European system, but this was a diplomatic convenience for Russia's recent enemies rather than a genuine acceptance of the Turks as Europeans. At the same time, it still enjoyed by far the greatest power and prestige within the Islamic system, and its rivalry with Iran persisted. The last of a series of Turkish-Iranian frontier wars was fought in 1821–3, and the frontier was not finally agreed until 1914.

In India a new system of Hindu, Muslim, and Sikh states had emerged out of the break-up of the Mogul Empire in the first half of the eighteenth century. In the ensuing struggles both the Iranians and the Afghans failed in their bids to succeed the Moguls as conquerors of the subcontinent, and none of the native rulers who had carved out states for themselves, notably those of Mysore, of Hyderabad, and the Marathas, seemed powerful enough to dominate the rest. The French and British East India Companies, deprived of the Mogul Empire's secure framework for trading, took part in the struggles as rivals, and, by their conquest of Bengal, the British had become a major power within the system before the end of the eighteenth century.

The Chinese system was, in theory, a world order, in which it was the duty of all other rulers to acknowledge by tribute the supremacy of the emperor in his role of preserving world harmony. In practice, the Chinese system extended to east and south-east Asia and parts of central Asia; even there its control of areas like Tibet and Vietnam was no more than occasional, and Japan did not accept any form of vassal status. But the Chinese emperor presided over a system which was of mutual convenience for the governments of east Asia, even for those like the Siamese and Japanese, which did not concede the Chinese view of international politics. The Japanese, for example, exercised effective but discreet control over the island kingdom of Ryukyu, but they were content to let its kings be invested by the Chinese emperor and to allow its tributary relationship with China to continue so that Ryukyu could serve as the entrepôt for a Sino-Japanese trade that was not supposed to exist.[1] Such ingenious ways of avoiding an open challenge to the region's dominant power, coupled with Chinese restraint in using armed force to assert the emperor's authority, made the Chinese system generally acceptable and stable, even though it constituted a striking imbalance of power.

The Indian system was the first to collapse. Between 1798 and 1818 the British moved from being the strongest of the powers within the system to imperial domination of the whole sub-continent south of the Sutlej. In these years the British destroyed the power of their most dangerous rivals, Mysore and the Marathas, and negotiated with the other Indian rulers treaties which deprived them of power beyond their borders. The Islamic system broke up more gradually in face of both British and Russian attempts to control the policies of the Muslim governments whose territories lay between their empires. By 1914 only Turkey and Afghanistan, among these, survived as states with any real claim to independence. Meanwhile, war waged by the British against China in the eighteen-forties began the process by which its emperor's international pretensions faded, his government's power of independent action was curtailed, and his tributary states came to be mostly under European or Japanese control.

The three systems collapsed, of course, because most of the Asian states were so easily defeated by the Europeans in the numerous wars of the nineteenth century. Why they were so easily defeated has been explained above by Michael Howard. Why the wars were so numerous also requires explanation. Neither the British nor the Russian government welcomed the expense and risks of even minor wars in Asia, and each would have preferred to solve its strategic and commercial problems there by diplomatic means. In India the directors of the East India Company sought security for their commerce with as little military and administrative expenditure as possible. They and the British government would have been content with membership of a stable system of Indian states friendly enough to guarantee a peaceful framework for commercial operations. In central and western Asia British and Russian diplomacy was aimed at stabilizing the turbulent and unpredictable relationships of neighbouring states, like Sind, Panjab, and Afghanistan, on the one hand, and Khiva, Bukhara, and Khokand, on the other, and at establishing closer diplomatic and commercial links than would be available to the rival empire. In the case of China the Russians settled their frontier disputes without direct conflict, while after 1842 the British consistently favoured a stable and territorially intact China as the best framework for their trade; it was only the nature of Sino-British diplomatic and commercial relations that was in dispute. There were occasional instances of war being waged by ambitious and insubordinate frontier commanders, such as Napier against Sind in 1843, Lambert against Burma in 1852, and Chernyayev against Tashkent and Bukhara in 1865–6, but most wars arose out of the failure of a diplomatic offensive rather than from planned and systematic conquest. British and Russian goals in Asia were, therefore, more limited than their achievements. They would have been realized by concessions far more modest than those which many Asian governments made in the aftermath of defeat. All three Asian systems might have survived, if in temporarily weakened form.

Why, then, in view of these relatively moderate aims, was the British and Russian record in Asia so warlike during a period when the behaviour of each in relation to other European states, large and small, was, on the whole, cautious and restrained? Was their belligerence towards neighbouring governments in Asia a sign of impatience with leaders regarded from the start as barbaric and half-civilized, and as such given too little chance to prove themselves capable of 'civilized' diplomatic intercourse? Were the relatively weak governments of Asia treated according to a different code of conduct than that applying to the weaker European governments? Sir Robert Peel implied that they were. 'I am afraid', he said, in answer to complaints in the Commons about the annexation of Sind in 1843, 'there is some great principle at work whenever civilization and refinement come into contact with barbarism, which makes it impossible to apply the rules observed amongst more advanced nations.'[2] Yet there is reason to suppose that Peel was seeking refuge in this 'uncontrollable principle', as he called it, to explain to himself as well as to the House a conquest he had not wanted but had failed to avoid. On the whole, the British and the Russians do not seem to have treated Asian states with any more impatience and violence than that experienced by smaller European countries in time of conflict with more powerful neighbours. For example, the reason, or excuse, given for the partition of Poland was much the same as that given for the annexation of the Panjab and of Khokand – the 'need' to control anarchic conditions in an adjacent state; Metternich's claim to the right of intervention in the smaller states of Italy and Germany, and the German bid to control Belgium and eastern Europe between 1914 and 1918 were based on the same quest for stability and security that the British and Russian governments pursued in Asia.

In Europe and Asia alike great powers believed – as they still believe in every continent – that they had a superior right to security, and, therefore, a right to expect that weaker neighbours should contribute to that security, even at the expense of their own, by accepting limitations on their freedom of action. The only variation was in the ideas of what constituted security, and in this respect the British and the Russians in their Asian roles were, simply because of the greater risks and uncertainties, sometimes less demanding than European states towards smaller neighbours. Lawrence's policy of 'masterly inactivity', which prevailed with regard to Afghanistan in the eighteen-sixties and early eighteen-seventies, was a more thoughtfully argued version of policies urged for central Asia by most British observers in the mid-eighteen-thirties and initially adopted by the Russian government in the late eighteen-fifties.

Based on the assumption that British India's security depended on a friendly Afghanistan, Lawrence's argument was that what the Afghans prized above all was their freedom and independence, that, if the British treated them as equals and proved their determination to abstain completely from Afghan affairs, the Afghans would offer no threat, and that, if the Russians threatened their independence, they would resist and call confidently on British aid. This required more of an iron nerve than most governments could sustain for long, but it showed that there was nothing inevitable about 'forward policies', and that there were alternative conceptions of security which might even be compatible with the genuine independence of weaker neighbours.

Nor was British or Russian diplomacy in Asia normally overbearing or offensive. There were exceptions. European diplomacy in China was outrageous by the standards of the other system, but then Chinese requirements were outrageous by European standards. In Burma, in 1852, a British mission did approach an official residence on horseback instead of shoeless and on foot, but, on the other hand, after the second Anglo-Burmese war the British allowed their representatives, until 1875, to remove their shoes before entering the presence of a Burmese monarch whose survival depended more on British restraint than on his power to resist.[3] Most British and Russian agents adapted themselves as successfully as could be expected to the diplomatic manners and usages of the courts with which they were negotiating, and they were usually men whose diplomatic experience had been Asian rather than European.

The main difference between developments in Europe and Asia was in the behaviour not of the great powers but of some of the weaker governments. In Europe governments of the smaller states did not defy an overwhelmingly stronger neighbour to the point of war unless sure of the support of a strong ally, as was Piedmont in 1859, or in misplaced expectation of such support, as in the case of Denmark in 1864. The facts of relative power were sufficiently understood and accepted, so that restraint by the strong and weak alike made possible, for much of the nineteenth century, stable and friendly relationships between them, as in the Chinese system. In Europe, it was usually the great powers which fought one another, or those seeking recognition as such. In Asia, on the other hand, many of the weaker governments defied the powerful British and Russian Empires to the point of war, and predictably suffered some form of subjugation. Others, with or without fighting, adapted themselves to European intrusion with striking success. Nepal and Siam retained their independence throughout the nineteenth century, Turkey and Afghanistan through much of it, and Japan acquired a degree of power to which its government had not aspired under the Chinese system and became a serious rival to the intruders. Indeed, the preference of the British and the Russians for solutions short of war and annexation – though ready enough for both if those solutions were not forthcoming – meant that weaker governments had a wider range of choices open to them than might appear from the usually vast disparity in military effectiveness. Thus this great variety of relationships which evolved in Asia can, perhaps, be better explained in terms of the attitudes of the weaker governments to their imperial neighbours than the other way round.

In offering a tentative explanation, I have made three assumptions derived from George Kelly's theory of personal constructs: first, that the actors in international politics are not states or peoples, but those individuals and groups – very few in nineteenth-century Asia – actively concerned with political affairs beyond the frontiers of their own country; secondly, that the behaviour of these people can best be understood by examining the ways in which they construed international situations in their efforts to anticipate and control events, rather than by seeing them as primarily beneficiaries or victims of 'historical forces' beyond their control; thirdly, that international politics consists of the attempts by such people to modify the constructs of their counterparts in other states by a wide range of methods from discussion to war.[4] I take it, therefore, that the various relationships in nineteenth-century Asia depended not only on how the imperial leaders construed their needs and opportunities but, even more, perhaps, on how Asian leaders reconstrued their international position and its possibilities in the light of British and Russian advances. They had to assess their capacity to resist, to imagine how that capacity could be enhanced by internal change or outside help or both, and to identify the kind of relationship with the intruders to which it was practicable to aspire and which would preserve as much as possible of their independence.

With the advantage of hindsight, the kind of relationship to which they could aspire with the minimum risk and with the minimum restriction on their freedom of action as rulers seems, to judge from British and Russian actions, fairly clear. Two categories of states may be considered. In the first place, there were states directly adjacent to a military or naval frontier of only one of these two imperial powers: for example, the central Asian khanates on Russia's border, and the immediate neighbours of the British in India. All the Asian states in this position proved to be highly vulnerable in a military sense; even the most successful, the Afghans and the Nepalese, achieved no more through war than the avoidance of actual annexation by giving the British a clear demonstration of what its military cost would be. They and the others might have avoided war altogether by two concessions, whether in the form of a treaty or by making them manifest in their conduct of affairs: the exclusion of any foreigners whose influence might damage imperial interests, and the relinquishment of diplomatic relations with any other European governments. Rulers who accepted these limitations and who did nothing detrimental to the empire's trade or nationals could hope to retain control over the internal affairs of their country and to pursue an independent, if cautious, foreign policy in relation to other Asian governments.

Secondly, there were states adjacent to a military or naval frontier of both imperial powers: Afghanistan after 1885, the Ottoman Empire, Iran, China, and Japan. Whatever their military capacity, these were all in a relatively strong position to play on the rivalry of the British and the Russians and of other adjacent empires. A ruler who construed the position correctly could hope to avoid the most damaging kinds of concession and to retain considerable freedom of manoeuvre in domestic and foreign affairs alike. Any Asian government's survival, therefore, depended on its assessing accurately and in time the minimum it would have to concede to the currently dominant empire or empires. Its degree of independence beyond that would depend on how much diplomatic skill and military strength it could muster to discourage the intruders from demanding more than that minimum.

Of states in the first category, only Nepal and Afghanistan came to think and behave in such a way as to elude foreign control. The others were absorbed into the British and Russian Empires either by annexation or as protectorates. For warlike leaders like Tipu Sultan of Mysore, the Maratha chiefs, and the Burmese kings, all accustomed to a career of conquest and expansion, acceptance of subordination to the British would have required the kind of mental upheaval likely only after decisive defeat. In the case of Mysore and the Marathas the defeat was so decisive that they had no chance to reconsider. The Burmese did. The first two Anglo-Burmese wars left upper Burma intact, and a new king, Mindon (1853–78), felt his way towards a precariously balanced relationship with the British, based on his facilitating British trade. It remained precarious because he kept British anxieties alive by his contacts with other European governments and by his tolerance of other commercial interests, but the risks Mindon took did not extend to challenging British pre-eminence in the region. His successor failed to understand the conditional nature of British restraint or the dangers Mindon was running. His interference with trade and intrigues to substitute French influence for British led to war and annexation in 1885–6. The Panjab offers another example of an intelligent ruler preserving his independence and of his successors misunderstanding its conditional basis. Ranjit Singh remained a loyal ally of the British for thirty years, despite his possession of a far stronger army than most of those who had opposed them, and the British welcomed a powerful and stable border state which could be relied upon not to intrigue with other Europeans. The struggle for power after his death in 1839 took a recklessly anti-British turn, ending in the Panjab's annexation. Similarly, Khudayar Khan, in face of defeat by the Russians, preserved a large measure of independence for a reduced Khokand by conceding Russian commercial demands, but his overthrow brought turbulence and confusion, which the Russians ended by annexation in 1876.

The rulers of Bukhara and Khiva totally misread the new situation in central Asia and failed to see until it was too late that some form of accommodation with the Russians was unavoidable. The Emir of Bukhara believed that he had a choice between using the Russians as allies in his own regional struggles or defying them altogether, and, when Russian victories disillusioned him, his 'clergy' remained unconvinced and successfully demanded war. The khan of Khiva exaggerated the security which difficult desert country had conferred on Khiva in face of previous Russian expeditions. That of 1873 was too successful to leave him time to revise his outlook. What remained of Khiva and Bukhara became submissive protectorates comparable to the princely states of India, their rulers enjoying as much power as the Russians saw fit. Most Indian rulers had accepted this status voluntarily. In contrast to the khans of central Asia, subordination to an imperial power was for them a familiar and acceptable construct. Once the British had established themselves as the strongest power in India, those weaker rulers without pretensions to supremacy themselves accepted them as successors to the Moguls, concluding, perhaps rather too readily, treaties which would have been thought severe in another psychological context.

The success of Afghanistan and Nepal in remaining independent was partly due to their having made the British pay so heavy a price for victory that they were as reluctant as the Afghans and the Nepalese to renew the fighting, and partly due to leaders who learned in the time thus won how to avoid provoking further conflict. The British occupied Afghanistan in 1839 and installed in power an exile, hoping that he would make Afghanistan the same sort of loyal frontier ally that Ranjit Singh had made the Panjab. The war showed how easy it was for the British to depose a ruler in Kabul and how difficult it was to impose an unwanted successor on the Afghans. Each side learned its lesson for the time being. The British abandoned their interference in Afghan affairs, while Dost Muhammad, the ruler whom they had temporarily ejected, chose to become the reliable frontier ally the British had wanted. After his death in 1863 the lessons of mutual accommodation were sufficiently forgotten for war to occur again in 1878–9, a war which once more brought military disasters to both sides and whose outcome left Afghanistan still independent for most practical purposes. The new ruler, Abdur Rahman (1880–1901), went even further than he needed to ensure that his independence would last. Not only did he observe the uneasy compromise by which he received British money and weapons in exchange for abandoning diplomatic contact with other powers, but he prevented nationals of any power, including Britain, from establishing in Afghanistan the kind of economic enterprise whose protection might form a pretext for intervention.

This formula for independence had been anticipated by the Nepalese. After the costly British victory of 1816 they had agreed to exclude other Europeans and to confine their European diplomatic contacts to the British, but the fall from power in 1837 of Bhim, who had initiated the policy, was followed by a turbulent period comparable to that in the Panjab. Representing less immediate danger, Nepal had time to regain its stability and security under Jung Bahadur (1846–77), who carried Bhim's policy a stage further. Impressed by a visit to Britain in 1850, he was convinced that friendly cooperation at government level must be combined with the isolation of his people from all Europeans. He and his successors thereby convinced the British of their reliability as allies, even though it meant excluding British traders as much as those of other European countries.[5] The price of trying to guarantee independence in this way was, for both Nepal and Afghanistan, continued economic backwardness, but even after 1885, when Afghanistan became a state in the second category with frontiers adjacent to both the British and Russian Empires, Abdur Rahman did not experiment to see how far he could play one side off against the other. The opportunity was there in the eighteen-nineties with most British leaders increasingly pessimistic about their power in central Asia and many Russians increasingly restless with the status quo, but, like his counterparts in Nepal, Abdur Rahman can hardly be blamed for over-insuring his position when most of his neighbours had construed theirs too casually to survive.[6]

Among other states of the second category, Turkey and Iran present a contrast. Turkish leaders played a fairly skilful role in nineteenth-century international politics, though not always in the internal politics of their own Empire. Leaders like Mahmud and Abdul Hamid shrewdly exploited the divisions among the powers. But the Turks were not, of course, facing a new situation. They had during the seventeenth and eighteenth centuries suffered a succession of defeats and territorial losses at the hands of European neighbours, but the process had been slow enough and the core of their empire had remained intact long enough for them to adapt themselves to the military superiority and convenient rivalries of the European powers. The Iranians, by contrast, had suffered too little for their interpretation of the world to be undermined. They had enjoyed an imperial revival in the eighteenth century, and until the early nineteenth century the Caucasus mountains had shielded them from Russia. The consequences of defeat by Russia in 1828 and by Britain in 1857 were relatively mild. Perhaps because of this, the shahs persistently misread the international situation. They exaggerated their capacity for resistance and expansion down to the eighteen-sixties, and thereafter exaggerated their capacity to modernize rapidly through European concession-hunters without undermining their independence. Instead of keeping a balance between the British and the Russians, they tended to side with one or the other alternately. The opportunities offered by Iran's military and diplomatic weaknesses became so obvious that the British and the Russians could use its helplessness in settling their own differences. Events had not pressed its rulers hard enough and soon enough to make a radical reconstruing of Iran's position seem inescapable, and its leaders lacked the imagination for an unforced reappraisal.

China and Japan, as states having initially more commercial than strategic importance for European governments, had more room for manoeuvre than other states at risk from both Empires. The reasons for the very different speeds with which they modernized are complex and controversial, but their differing reactions to European threats in the middle of the nineteenth century are readily understandable. China's rulers could easily accommodate the Opium and Arrow wars within their traditional framework of interpretation as barbarian raids, especially as they were a minor problem compared with the Taiping rebellion. They drew comfort from the discovery that neither conquest nor even major cessions of territory were intended, and only slight changes of outlook seemed to them necessary at first. The Japanese, on the other hand, had had no real foreign policy for two centuries. They had no fixed ideas, apart from seclusion, to discard and the American and European challenges occasioned fruitful debates on foreign policy among leading Japanese. The more imaginative and judicious could, more easily than their counterparts in China, adopt whatever new constructs seemed most appropriate for understanding and controlling the new situation. Their samurai scholars had been absorbing knowledge of the rest of the world from the detachment of seclusion for over a century, and after 1868 a group of exceptionally adaptable and well-informed leaders were in control.

Most Asian rulers were faced during the nineteenth century with an unfamiliar international situation, which called for major changes in their personal constructs of the world if their states were to survive as independent units. Such changes required time, the availability of alternative constructs, and a great deal of intellectual flexibility. Much depended on how big a change was needed or on how quickly it had to be implemented, but it is not surprising that rarely were there both enough time and leaders shrewd and imaginative enough to make the adjustment. The result of the failure of most Asian rulers to see how to accommodate the interests of the European intruders without loss of independence was the collapse of the Asian systems and the temporary integration of most Asian states into the European international system.

7

EUROPEAN STATES AND AFRICAN POLITICAL COMMUNITIES

Hedley Bull

I

Africa south of the Sahara was the last major land area of the world to be brought within the expanding European international system: even as late as 1880, on the eve of the scramble in which they were to partition almost the whole of the continent by the end of the century, the European states did not have contact or interaction enough with most African political communities to have brought them within a common international system, let alone a common international society. Apart from Portuguese incursions into Angola and Mozambique, French penetration of Senegal, and the Dutch and British settlements at the southern tip of the continent, European rule was confined to coastal and offshore areas. Nor was there any extensive network of diplomatic and military contacts linking European states with African political communities, such as had grown up in the seventeenth, eighteenth, and early nineteenth centuries between the former and the powers of south and south-east Asia. Pre-partition Africa did, however, have its own distinctive patterns of what we may call international relations among the numerous and very diverse political communities of which it was made up.

II

Among the political communities that existed in the continent before 1880 a basic distinction may be drawn between those whose roots were wholly or partly outside Africa, and which remained linked with one or another part of the outside world, and those that were indigenously black African. Of the former communities, all of which were geographically on the periphery, the first in order of importance are the Muslim societies of North Africa, which represent for Africa south of the Sahara the oldest point of contact with the outside world and one of the deepest sources of external influence. When the Arabs conquered the Maghreb from Byzantine armies and Berber tribes in the seventh century they established what was in effect an Arab colonial outpost, but by the ninth century the societies of that area were strong enough to establish independent Muslim states of their own; in the tenth century the Fatimid dynasty, originating in Tunisia but transferring itself to Egypt, was able to free Africa from Arab dominance and set up a caliphate to rival that of the Abbasids, while in the eleventh and twelfth centuries the Almoravid and Almohad empires founded by Arabic-speaking Berbers from Morocco stretched across vast areas of north-west Africa and Spain. These and other Muslim powers penetrated across the Sahara to exert what was ultimately a commanding influence upon the savannah belt of West Africa – partly through the caravan trade, partly by promotion of Islamic religion and culture, and sometimes by means of military expeditions. This influence, founded as it was on trans-Saharan connections that pre-dated the rise of Islam, was at work in West Africa many centuries before the Europeans crept tentatively around its coast, and was in no way halted when they did. It carried with it conceptions of statecraft and diplomacy radically different from those the Europeans brought when eventually they had their moment of rule.

Secondly, there were the Muslim communities on the periphery of east Africa. Originating in Arab penetration of the coast as early as the ninth century, and growing apace as part of the great wave of Islamic expansion in the thirteenth century that left the whole Indian Ocean trading system in Muslim hands until this came to be disputed by the Portuguese, these communities by the eighteenth century comprised a series of small Arab-ruled states owing allegiance to the Sultan of Oman, then a maritime power that had ejected Portugal from the area. In 1840 the Sultan of Oman transferred his capital to Zanzibar, which in the nineteenth century was the chief commercial entrepôt of the area and base for penetration of the interior. The Arab presence on the east African littoral did not, like the Islamic influence across the Sahara, result in the creation of great Islamic or Islamicized kingdoms. It did, however, produce the Swahili language and culture among the Islamicized Bantu of the coastal plain. It linked east Africa to the Arab slave trade which, while smaller in volume than the Atlantic slave trade, began much earlier and lasted longer. By the nineteenth century it had penetrated to the region of the Great Lakes, where it met the rival influence of the 'Khartoum Arabs' from the Sudan, which had been conquered for Egypt by Mehemet Ali in 1820. The Arab presence made east Africa part of the maritime community of the Indian Ocean, which it remained during the period of British ascendancy, when the east

African littoral, like the Gulf area, became in some respects a westward extension of British India.

A third political community on the periphery of Africa was Ethiopia. Able as it was, like Egypt, to look back on a continuous existence since ancient times, the heir of the empire of Aksum which existed from the second to the seventh centuries, it was one of the oldest of states. Christian since the fourth century but cut off from Christian Europe by the rise of Islam, it was associated by Europeans with the legendary empire of Prester John, the Christian ally at the rear of the Muslim foe, which had been sought since the time of the Crusades, at first in Asia and later in Africa, and in the sixteenth century Ethiopia did in fact become the ally of Portugal against the Turk. Its relations with its Islamic neighbours were not in fact akin to those of Latin Christendom: the ties of the Ethiopian Church were not with Rome but with the Coptic Church of Alexandria, and Aksum, whose Christianity was a form of religious syncretism akin to that of Islam itself, had not been a target of the Arab *jihad*. But isolated by its highland position, pre-occupied by internal conflicts and border wars, and belonging neither to Islam nor to the pre-literate societies of indigenous Africa nor yet to the new world being created by the European colonialists, Ethiopia on the eve of partition was set apart from other African political communities. In the colonial period, the uniqueness of Ethiopia's international position was further accentuated by its military victory over Italy in 1896, its success in surviving the partition of Africa as a formally independent state, its early acceptance as a member of 'the Christian family of nations', and in 1923 as a member of the League of Nations.

Fourthly, there was the black state of Liberia, which had developed from the settlement of freed slaves founded by the American Colonization Society in 1821. This settlement had been preceded by the British settlement of freed slaves at Sierra Leone in 1787, and was followed by the French settlement at Libreville in 1849, but whereas the British and French settlements in due course became part of colonial empires, Liberia became a nominally independent republic; so did the neighbouring freed slave state of Maryland, founded by the Maryland Colonization Society in 1831, which Liberia later absorbed. Liberia, although its inhabitants were black, was a settler state in which an immigrant people, modelling their government upon the United States constitution, faced an alien majority of indigenous peoples rather as white settlers did in other parts of the continent. Liberia's status as a Christian and 'civilized' state helped it to overcome the handicap of being black: its declaration of independence in 1847 was quickly recognized by Great Britain and other European states, although the United States (because Southerners opposed the idea of black ambassadors in Washington) did not recognize it until the time of the Civil War, just as it did not until then recognize the comparable Christian and black state of Haiti. It did, however, provide Liberia with diplomatic support, sometimes needed against the designs of France. Thus Liberia, like Ethiopia, survived the scramble for Africa to serve as a long-standing example of black African independence, to be cited as a model by some, and as a warning by others.

Finally, mention should be made of the Boer republics established after the Great Trek of 1835–7. The independence of the Transvaal, later called the South African Republic, was recognized by the British government, at least as regards its internal affairs, in 1852; in 1877 Britain annexed the Republic, but following a Boer rebellion and the defeat of British forces at Majuba, a qualified independence was again recognized in 1881 and extended in the London Convention of 1884. The independence of the Orange Free State was recognized by Britain in 1854 and maintained until both republics were defeated in the Boer War and subjected to British rule in 1902. These states had little capacity for engaging in international relations except on a local scale: their independence was limited in theory by British claims to paramountcy in the region, and in practice by Britain's success in denying them an outlet to the sea. It might be asked whether their independence was in reality any greater than that of the Cape Colony which, although it was under the Crown, was self-governing in 1872. Nevertheless, the two republics enjoyed international personality in European eyes and their war with the British Empire, which was regarded on all sides as an international conflict arising over an international dispute, projected them briefly onto the stage of world diplomacy.

III

The indigenous communities of black Africa on the eve of partition were radically different from those of the periphery. Except in so far as some of them had by then been influenced by Islam or Europe they were pre-literate, and the absence of written communications imposed limitations on their size and continuity. Like the Germanic peoples of Europe in the age of migrations they were based upon ties of kinship, or belief in the existence of such ties. All of them were deeply shaped by magical or religious belief. They were, however, immensely various, ranging from small bands of nomads in desert areas to polities comparable in size to modern African nation-states that had endured for several centuries. A vital distinction (although it is not one that can be drawn clearly in every case) is between those communities which had a centralized political authority, such as a hereditary or elective king or chief, and those that did not, the so-called stateless societies or 'tribes without rulers'.[1]

The oldest and largest pre-colonial African kingdoms were those of the savannah region of West Africa. Ghana, which existed from the eighth to the eleventh centuries some hundreds of miles to the north and west of the present state of that name, and Kanem-Bornu, a smaller but more enduring empire in the vicinity of Lake Chad, were pre-Islamic, and in common with other so-called 'Sudanic' states, are sometimes thought to have been influenced by dynastic Egyptian traditions of divine kingship and matrilineal succession. They were, however, in touch with Islam across the Sahara, and Almoravid invasions of the eleventh century appear to have brought about the disintegration of Ghana and the conversion of Kanem-Bornu's ruling dynasty. Mali, which existed from the twelfth to the fourteenth century in the upper Niger region, was Islamic from the beginning, as was its successor Songhai, lasting from the fourteenth to the sixteenth centuries. The Islamic impact did not sweep indigenous institutions aside, even where it took root; kinship allegiances, in particular, survived in the Islamicized kingdoms. It did, however, bring written language and along with it the possibility of more complex social organization, and it brought the savannah communities into touch with the most advanced civilization of the time. The fourteenth-century ruler of Mali, Mansa Musa, who on his pilgrimage to Mecca distributed so much gold in Cairo as to inflate the currency, was known in Europe, as a result of which Mali appeared on an early European map of Africa.[2]

Although the seventeenth and eighteenth centuries saw a decline of Islamic influence, the early nineteenth century was a period of Muslim renewal in the Sudan as in other areas of the Islamic world. The *jihad* of Othman dan Fodio led to the Fulani empire, conquering what had been the city-states of Hausaland; further west another *jihad* created the less stable Tukulor empire, whose expansion westwards was checked in the eighteen-fifties by the French on the Senegal. The last of the Muslim African conquerors, Samory, whose empire was created in the eighteen-sixites in the area that was to become French Guinea, resisted the French until his capture in 1898.

In the forested, southern region of West Africa there existed, at least in modern times, the so-called Guinea or forest kingdoms, of which the best known are Oyo, Benin, Dahomey, and Ashanti. These kingdoms were established at a time when they were beyond the reach of Islam, but they were affected by the arrival of the Europeans by sea: the Guinea Coast was also the Slave Coast. The Yoruba kingdom of Oyo and the Edo kingdom of Benin existed before the rise of the slave trade; the latter, according to a fifteenth-century Portuguese description, already stretched 250 miles from east to west and had a great walled city for its capital. Dahomey and Ashanti both arose only in the seventeenth century, as alliances or federations of peoples of common culture for military purposes. The period when the Guinea Coast slave trade reached its height – the seventeenth and eighteenth centuries – was, paradoxically, also the period when these states reached the height of their prosperity and power: the firearms and other Western products they received in exchange for slaves enabled them to expand their dominion at the expense of weaker neighbours.

On the Atlantic coast, south of the Congo river in present-day Angola, there lay the Bantu kingdom of Kongo, founded in the fourteenth century. When the Portuguese arrived there in 1482 they found a kingdom with a centralized government, court officials, and provincial governors, together with a friendly king whom they converted to Christianity. His successor Affonso, a kind of African precursor of Peter the Great, who ruled 1506–43, learnt Portuguese, adopted Portuguese dress, imported Portuguese teachers, military advisers, and craftsmen (including two German printers), sent scholars to Lisbon and an embassy to the Pope, named his capital San Salvador, built a cathedral and churches and corresponded with King Manuel I, who treated Affonso as a king and an ally and drew up a comprehensive programme for the Christianization and Lusitanization of Kongo. The alliance of Affonso and Manuel, however, did not endure; it derived from the personal commitment of these monarchs, and after their deaths, the impetus waned. The Portuguese teachers and technicians sent to Kongo were too few and weakened by disease. Portugal did not rate the kingdom high among its overseas priorities, and in the longer term proved less interested in Lusitanization of Kongo than in the procurement from it of slaves for the American and Caribbean plantations.[3]

In the interior of central Africa, in the savannah land south of the Congo rain forest, there existed the so-called Luba-Lunda empire, which is supposed to have originated in the establishment of Luba supremacy over the stateless Lunda peoples of the region, and which was visited by traders from the Portuguese settlements on the west and east coasts from the seventeenth century. To the south and east, in the region of the lower Zambezi, was the kingdom of the priest-king the Monomotapa, known to the Portuguese in the sixteenth century, and believed to contain King Solomon's Mines; its rulers are sometimes thought to have descended from the people of Great Zimbabwe, whose ruins lie to the south. Between the Great Lakes of east Africa there were the so-called interlacustrine kingdoms, of which the best known is Buganda, visited by Speke in 1862 and by Stanley in 1875. In the south-east, the most striking African kingdom was that of the Zulus. At first a small chiefdom within the Mthethwa empire built up by Dingiswayo in the late eighteenth and early nineteenth centuries, through the military genius of Shaka (who ruled 1816–28) it pursued a policy of military expansion whose effects were felt throughout southern Africa: the Zulu impis of Shaka's successors Dingaan and Cetewayo inflicted defeats on Boer and later British forces in Natal in wars that lasted until the end of the century.

At the other extreme from powerful kingdoms such as those of the Zulus, the Ashanti, or the Baganda were the numerous stateless or decentralized political communities that have been the object of such careful scrutiny by twentieth-century anthropologists. While these communities were without the institutions of government they nevertheless provided order through the strong moral or social sanctions possible in small and culturally homogeneous societies, through religious or supernatural sanctions and through the enforcement of law by decentralized measures of 'self-help'. Students of the modern system of states have noted resemblances between the devices for maintaining order in these anarchical societies of primitive peoples and those that provide a modicum of order among modern states, in the absence of government, while also noting differences (the less self-regarding character of the constituent groups in African stateless societies, by comparison with modern states; the culturally homogeneous nature of the former, in contrast to the culturally heterogeneous nature of modern international society; and the prominent role of religious belief as a form of cohesion in African stateless societies, in contrast to the secular basis of modern interstate relations).[4]

In the pre-colonial period indigenously African political communities maintained their own distinctive institutions for the conduct of relations with one another. In recognizing the existence of these institutions and the validity they had in their own terms it would be wrong to lose sight of the differences between them and the institutions that governed relations among European states, even in the early modern period, when European diplomacy and international law were themselves more rudimentary. Except in areas subject to Islamic influence relations among African communities were conducted without benefit of written records. The political communities engaged in these relations were immensely various. The dealings of communities with one another were largely those of dominant rulers with tributaries or vassals. They were in most cases geographically confined, and indeed conducted against the background of very limited geographical knowledge. There was no African international system or international society extending over the continent as a whole, and it is doubtful whether such terms can be applied even to particular areas.

It is clear, however, that among African as among other pre-literate peoples intercourse was regulated by complex rules and institutions.[5] Oral traditions of diplomatic experience were often systematic. Normative principles that lie at the basis of the international society of modern Europe (the immunity of envoys; *pacta sunt servanda*; respect for boundaries) were deeply respected. Diplomacy was subject to elaborate conventions and protocol, involved extensive messenger services, and sometimes the equivalent of resident ambassadors or consuls. There were marriage alliances, hostages and vassalage. There were institutions for the peaceful settlement of disputes and rules for the limitation of war. There was regulation of trade and the use of 'international' languages such as Hausa in parts of West Africa and Arabic in Islamicized areas. Most notably, there was a strong sense of the subjection of relations among independent communities to customary law – not only within but also between ethnic groups – a customary law that appears to have had some basic elements of similarity throughout the whole of Africa.[6]

IV

Modern European contacts with African political communities south of the Sahara began with the Portuguese voyages of discovery in the fifteenth century, but in the four centuries that followed – centuries in which north and south America, south and south-east Asia, Australasia, and finally China and Japan were brought within the European-centred international system – these contacts were only with the periphery of the continent. The Portuguese, drawn initially by crusading zeal, by the search for Prester John and prospect of a southern belt of Christianized states that would outflank Islam, by the lure of Guinea gold and by the hope of establishing a route to the spice trade of the Indies, established trading posts on island and coastal positions. But while they entered into relations, mainly of a peaceful nature, with local communities, they did not seek to penetrate far inland. Disease often provided an obstacle to their doing so, and as the seaborne trade with Asia developed, offering richer possibilities than any afforded by Africa, the Portuguese possessions came to be valued more as staging-posts on the route to the Indies than as springboards for the exploitation of the interior.

By the end of the sixteenth century the principal interest of the Portuguese in Africa had become the slave trade, and throughout the seventeenth and eighteenth centuries, when the Portugese were joined by the Dutch, the English, and the French among others, manpower remained the African resource to which Europeans were most attracted. It is possible to dispute whether or not the Atlantic slave trade in this period played an essential role in establishing the conditions which led later to the industrial revolution in Europe, but it can scarcely be denied that the export of perhaps as many as twenty million black slaves to the sugar, coffee, tobacco, and cotton plantations in the Americas and the Caribbean made a vital contribution to the development of the New World, or that it brought private fortunes to some Europeans who profited from it, while facilitating the accumulation of capital in European countries. Nor can it be doubted that the slave trade had profound effects within Africa itself, measured not only in terms of depopulation but also in terms of the stimulus provided to conflict among African political communities by the incentive to enslave one another's populations and the firearms provided to them in return for doing so. But if the Atlantic slave trade did ensure that events in Europe and in Africa were now impinging on one another, it still did not bring European states and the African communities of the interior into any direct relationship with one another: it was not European governments but merchants who procured the slaves, and this was by purchase from intermediaries; there was still no need for inland expeditions. The forts which the Europeans built along the coast were primarily for defence against rival European powers and only secondarily for defence against local Africans.

In the course of the nineteenth century the pressures making for European encroachment in Africa became stronger. With the prohibition of the slave trade in the British Empire in 1807 and the United States in 1808, and the international sanction given by the Congress of Vienna to British efforts to stamp it out, the slave trader on the African coast gave place to the anti-slavery patrol. Unlike the slave trade itself, efforts to suppress the slave trade required the imposition of political control, and thus the latter proved more destructive of the independence of African political communities than the former had been: the goal of stamping out the Atlantic slave trade in west Africa, later the Arab slave trade in east Africa, and also slavery itself, whether among the Dutch settlers in southern Africa, the Arabs in Zanzibar, or the emirates of northern Nigeria, formed part of the motivation and rationale of imperial expansion.

The decline of the slave trade was accompanied by the rise of the 'legitimate trade': palm oil in the region of Nigeria, gold on the Gold Coast, groundnuts in Senegal, and later in the century dramatic mineral discoveries in the south. Geographical exploration of the interior of Africa, above all the journeys of Livingstone between 1853 and 1873, promoted knowledge and concern about the continent as never before. The activities of missionaries, especially of the Protestant churches, which since the late eighteenth century had come to challenge the virtual monopoly of missionary work held by Catholics, aroused European public opinion on behalf of an active policy of suppression of the slave trade, control of settlers and traders, and spread of the Christian message. The technological gap between European and African societies widened as in the course of the century the steamboat, quinine, the Maxim gun, and the railway made their appearance on the scene. There was a widening also of the social distance between Europeans and Africans: the former, who in earlier centuries had sometimes been able to deal with black Africans as equals, came increasingly to perceive them as objects either of exploitation, or of curiosity and compassion. In southern Africa the Boer peoples, seeking to escape from British rule, moved into the interior to fight a series of frontier wars with the Bantu, akin to those fought between European colonists and Amerindians in north America. The European powers began to extend the areas of their jurisdiction or influence: the Portuguese in Angola and Mozambique; the French, who had established themselves in Algeria in 1830, in Senegal; the British in the Gold Coast and at Lagos, in Natal, and, through their influence over the Sultan of Zanzibar, in east Africa.

V

The encroachment of the European powers up to 1880 still amounted to no more than a nibbling at the edges of the continent: the external power with by far the largest territorial domain in Africa was not any European state but the Ottoman Empire, whose suzerainty was still acknowledged over Egypt and (apart from Algeria) the Maghreb. The governments in London, Paris, and Lisbon still had no plans for a massive extension of their jurisdictions. If the interior of Africa was bound sooner or later to be brought into touch with the modern world, nothing that had so far happened made it inevitable that this should take the form of a general partition among the colonial powers. But the scramble for Africa arose suddenly. On the one hand it was precipitated by rivalries among the most powerful of the established colonial powers: France, which since its defeat in Europe in 1871 was seeking compensation by imperial expansion, reflected in Africa in the annexationist treaties concluded by the explorer de Brazza; and Britain, whose occupation of Egypt in 1882 gave rise to deep resentment in Europe. On the other hand it was precipitated by the arrival of newcomers: Leopold II and his assistant Stanley, whose International African Association created the Congo Free State in the heart of Africa; and Bismarck's Germany, whose whirlwind annexations of territory in South-West Africa, Togoland, the Cameroons, and East Africa between 1883 and 1885, perhaps designed chiefly to stimulate conflict between France and Britain and thus deflect French pressure on Germany in Europe, presented an unprecedented challenge to existing arrangements.

The process of partition that now got under way was not a mere scramble but was conducted in relation to guidelines laid down by the Concert of Europe. The European powers did indeed engage in an undignified jostling for position, as conferences took place in European capitals at which spheres of influence were drawn on maps that were sometimes imperfect in areas where in some cases Europeans had not yet penetrated. Chartered companies sprang up to take advantage of the economic opportunities that were opening up, following the precedent set by King Leopold in the Congo, as they had done in Holland and England to exploit the Indies trade in the mercantilist era. International tensions were generated which (as between Britain and France at Fashoda in 1898, or between France and Germany over Morocco in 1906 and 1911) even raised the spectre of war. But these tensions were effectively contained; when war eventually broke out in Europe it was not over the imperialist rivalries that Lenin later described, but over European issues. Just as, at the beginning of the process of European expansion, the Pope held the ring between Spain and Portugal, so at the end the European Concert held the ring during the partition of Africa.

This holding of the ring was facilitated by the Berlin Africa Conference of 1884–5, called by Bismarck initially to discuss the Congo. The Berlin Conference, attended by all European states except Switzerland, along with Turkey and the United States, did not itself 'partition Africa', as is sometimes said: the partitioning was effected by bilateral agreements, and by this time was already under way. It did, however, ease the immediate tensions arising over conflicting claims in the Congo. It laid down guidelines for the partitioning powers that served to minimize friction between them. And it provided a collective sanctification or legitimization of the partition process as a whole.

The Final Act that issued from the Berlin Conference upheld free trade in the Congo basin and access to the coast for ships of all flags.[7] Freedom of navigation was to be recognized on the Congo and the Niger and an International Navigation Commission of the Congo was to be set up. The Congo Free State was recognized by the powers in separate agreements. There was to be common commitment to 'preservation of the native tribes, and to care for the improvement of their moral and material well-being',[8] as well as to suppression of the slave trade and slavery. Freedom of conscience and religious toleration were to be guaranteed to the natives. Christian missionaries, scientists, and explorers were to be protected. All powers acquiring new territories on the coast were to notify other signatories. Most importantly, the powers recognized the obligation to insure 'the establishment of authority' in the regions occupied by them – which implied that title to territory was to depend on 'effective occupation', the doctrine that England had used in the reign of James I, as a late-comer to the field of imperial expansion in the Americas, to contest the claims to title of Spain and Portugal, and which Germany now sought to use, so as to place itself on a more equal footing with Britain, France, and Portugal.

It is common to belittle the impact of the Berlin Conference.[9] In place of free trade in the Congo, monopoly was established; in place of improvement of native welfare, there was notorious exploitation; the Congo itself did not remain long a Free State but in 1908 became a Belgian colony. The obligation to notify other signatories about acquisitions of territory referred to notifications after, not before, these acquisitions had taken place. The provision requiring 'effective occupation' applied only to new territories, not existing ones; only to coastal territories, not inland ones; and, as a result of the distinction on which Britain was able to insist between annexation and the declaration of protectorates, did not apply to the latter. The United States, whose representatives sought to uphold the idea that African native chiefs had rights in international law (an idea which the Conference declined to endorse, while not explicitly repudiating it), declined to ratify the Act.

But the settlement of incipient international disputes over the Congo contained a major source of tension among the imperial powers. In the succeeding years the guidelines about notification and 'effective occupation' were given a wider application than had been envisaged in the Final Act itself, embracing the interior as well as the coast, and the Conference itself served to make the point that merely bilateral agreements among the imperial powers, without a wider endorsement by the society of states as a whole, as it then was, were insufficient. The insistence of the international community that colonial powers had international obligations to act as trustees for the welfare and advancement of dependent peoples, first manifest in the Berlin Final Act, was formulated more pointedly by the Brussels Conference of 1889–90, was thence transmitted to the League Mandates system and the UN Trusteeship system, and survives today, in different form, in the idea of the duties of developed towards under-developed countries. It is a shallow view which fails to recognize the significance of the doctrine because the trusteeship was sometimes abused or because it was then defined in the language and in relation to the circumstances of a different era.

VI

How far did European states and African political communities conduct 'normal' relations with one another before the latter were absorbed by the former? In the long period of contact before the final scramble European states displayed a considerable disposition to acknowledge that African political communities had rights of independent existence. There cannot have been anything 'normal' in the experience of European states, or comparable to their relationships within Christendom or Europe, about contacts with societies that were pre-literate, pagan, and in some cases stateless. We need also to remember that in 1444, when the Portuguese first made contact with black African communities, this was more than two centuries before the Peace of Westphalia, when modern notions of what constitutes normal behaviour in international relations had not taken shape.

It is clear, however, that the Europeans in Africa did not put forward any general claim that African land was *territorium nullius*, as they did in Australia and some other sparsely inhabited lands, but chose to recognize the existence of local communities with rights both of political independence and ownership of land,[10] at least until the time came when they were strong enough to overthrow these communities. Even in the course of partition it is notable that European states did not base their actions on any explicit doctrine that African political communities were without rights of independence: title to territory was generally based upon claims that it had been ceded by consent of African rulers or, much less frequently, that it had been acquired by right of conquest; even the many agreements among European powers staking out spheres of influence were not thought *by themselves* to confer rights over African territory.

There is no *a priori* reason to doubt the genuineness of treaties concluded between European states and African political communities in the pre-partition period. As we have seen, the principle of the sanctity of agreements was no less well understood by African than by European societies. Problems of definition and interpretation are not insurmountable, even in the absence of a common language or culture, and African rulers were not ignorant of diplomacy or unskilled in its arts. The uncertain claims of some of the African parties to these treaties, measured by European conceptions of the rights of a sovereign prince, do not appear to have been an obstacle to the conclusion of these agreements, any more than they were in the case of the many treaties concluded in modern times between European powers and the Muslim powers of north Africa, at a time when they were not sovereign states but vassals of the Ottoman Sultan. Treaties facilitating trade, conceding trade monopolies, or ceding territory for trading posts were not necessarily the result of coercion, which Europeans were often in no position to apply, nor did they necessarily confer unequal or disproportionate benefits on the parties.

Even in the case of the many hundreds of treaties concluded between European governments, or sometimes companies, and African rulers, in the era of partition, it would be wrong to assume that these were always bogus.[11] The treaties of cession, or of acceptance of protectorate status, concluded by Stanley, de Brazza, Peters, Lugard, Johnston, and others, to justify extensions of imperial authority, are rightly treated with some scepticism: it is said of some of these treaties that the African parties lacked sovereign personality; that the persons concluding them were without full powers; that the African representatives lacked understanding of their contents; or that they were subject to coercion. But because the claims of a European power to title over a territory depended (given the principle *nemo dat quod non habet*) upon the correct form of such treaties of cession, which was liable to close scrutiny by rival governments, careful attention was often devoted to ensuring that it had been observed: treaties sometimes contained clauses asserting that the African chief concerned did indeed have sovereign powers; witnesses were produced to testify that the substance of the treaty was fully understood; cases of coercion of the African signatory did occur, but it appears that they were rare. It would be wrong also to assume that African rulers were necessarily reluctant to enter into agreements of this sort; from them such rulers might derive prestige, protection against domestic or external enemies, or access to superior technology; indeed, the initiative for some of these agreements facilitating the extension of colonial rule was taken by African rulers themselves. While it would be wrong to accept the imperialist thesis of the time, that African political communities all over the continent voluntarily extinguished themselves, there is also danger in projecting backwards into history the assumption of the present time, that no political community could knowingly prefer colonial status to independence.

It may seem strained to apply the term diplomacy to the various *ad hoc* missions that were sent to and from pre-colonial African communities, but we need to remember that these began when resident diplomacy was not yet general in Europe, and modern diplomatic conventions had not yet evolved. We know that various African kingdoms sent missions to Europe: Benin in the fifteenth century, Benin and Kongo in the sixteenth, Allada and Asebu in the seventeenth, Dahomey in the eighteenth, Shaka the Zulu King in the nineteenth (although his mission got only as far as Cape Town).[12] Portugal sent ambassadors to Kongo in the fifteenth century and to Mali in the sixteenth, and it has been pointed out that European trading posts throughout the early centuries were, in one of their several aspects, resident diplomatic missions.

We have already noted that in pre-partition Africa there did not exist any general system of warfare and alliance, involving European and indigenous powers alongside one another, such as did exist in the East Indies (and also in the struggles involving Britain, France, and Amerindian powers in north America). There were, however, many cases where such alliances existed on a local scale. The Portuguese, for example, in 1570 sent a military expedition to assist Kongo against the Jagas; in the seventeenth and eighteenth centuries forts built on the Slave Coast by Portuguese, Dutch, English, French, Spaniards, Swedes, Brandenburgers, Danes, and others fought with one another in alliance with local powers; and in the nineteenth century Britain formed alliances with the Fante against the Ashanti and the Somalis against Ethiopia. Such alliances were often important to African rulers in maintaining or extending their own power against local rivals.

VII

In the course of the era of partition, however, these elements of co-existence between European states and African political communities were swept away. As European powers reached agreements setting out their spheres of influence, African parties were not consulted. Some African political communities were overthrown by conquest, in some cases (e.g. the French conquest of Madagascar) after their independence had been recognized by European governments. The doctrine of 'constitutive recognition' was invoked by European powers to show that African rulers did not have the rights of sovereign states, while these same European powers argued that it was the sovereign rights of African rulers, voluntarily transferred to them, that provided the title to their colonial territories. Whereas for Europe the solidarity of the imperial powers, symbolized by the conferences of Berlin and Brussels, meant that the partition was orderly and that the peace of Europe was preserved, for Africa it meant that the imperial powers could not be played off one against another but were united in imposing their domination.

A new school of historical interpretation has emphasized the active role taken by African political communities in resisting the imposition of colonial rule and rebelling against it.[13] It is indeed the case that the Zulus, the Ashanti, Samory, Abershiri, and many others, although they were defeated in the end by the Europeans, did not fight in vain: their struggles sometimes served to affect the terms of the rule to which they were made subject, to determine the relationships they were to have with colonial rulers, to preserve their identity throughout the colonial period, and to enhance their status when it came to an end. It is true also that there is not as great a disjunction as was once supposed between these acts of resistance and rebellion in the name of established African political communities and the nationalist movements that in our own times have led Africa to independence: the 'traditional elements' in the latter and the 'modernizing' elements in some of the former have been overlooked. There is evidence enough in African political life today that the African political communities which European states encountered in the pre-colonial or diplomatic phase of their relationship with one another were not wholly submerged in the colonial period, and remain a vital part of the political heritage of the continent. But when Africa emerged from the colonial era it was not these old political communities that took their place in international society but a series of 'new states', their boundaries inherited from the external (and in some cases the internal) boundaries of the colonial territories, their demands for self-determination or national liberation put forward on behalf of the populations defined by these territories rather than on behalf of traditional communities, and the claims of some of them to have inherited the mantle of pre-colonial African empires carrying little conviction.

Part II

The Entry of Non-European States into International Society

8

THE EMERGENCE OF A UNIVERSAL INTERNATIONAL SOCIETY

Hedley Bull

The expansion of Europe from the fifteenth century to the nineteenth, which was discussed in Part I, gradually brought into being an international system linking the various regional systems together, which by the middle of the nineteenth century was nearly universal. This did not mean, however, that there yet existed a universal international society. A pattern of economic, military, and political interaction had grown up in which not only European states and their colonies of settlement but Asian, African, and Amerindian rulers and peoples were involved – in different ways and to different degrees. But they were not united by a perception of common interests, nor by a structure of generally agreed rules setting out their rights and duties in relation to one another, nor did they co-operate in the working of common international institutions.

It is true that in this expanding international system that had not yet become an international society some of the elements were already present out of which a universal international society came later to be constructed. The expanding Europeans, on their part, as they encountered Amerindian and African kings and chiefs, Muslim sultans, khans, and emirs, Hindu princes, and the empires of China and Japan, did not seek always to subjugate or colonize them, which in any case they were not capable of doing on a general scale before the nineteenth century, but rather sought to trade with them, to convert them to Christianity, and in some cases to join them in military alliances. There was thus a disposition on the part of European states to enter into relations of a peaceful and permanent nature with particular non-European powers.

The non-European powers on their part were sometimes able and willing to reciprocate in entering into agreements, in facilitating trade, and in concluding alliances. The Ottoman Empire, geographically a partly European power throughout modern times, had been a participant in the European system of economic and strategic relationships since before that system came to be thought of as European and if it was perceived as an external menace to Christendom or Europe as a whole, it was also sometimes the ally of one Christian or European power against another. East Indian states from the seventeenth century to the nineteeenth made commercial and military agreements with European powers on a basis of mutual acceptance within what we have called the Eurasian international system. Amerindian political communities at the beginning of the historical process of European expansion, like African communities at the end of it, made agreements and entered into alliances with the European intruders in their respective continents which, although they led ultimately to the absorption of the local parties to them by the intruders were not for this reason always unreal at the time they were concluded. Even in the cases of the hermit empires of China and Japan, brought into the European network of commerce and diplomacy by coercion as they were in the nineteenth century, voluntary agreements with European powers had earlier played some role, as the accounts below make clear.

But neither the Europeans nor the non-Europeans in their dealing with one another can be said to have been moved by common interests they perceived in maintaining an enduring structure of coexistence and co-operation among independent political communities over the world as a whole. They were not able to invoke a common and agreed set of rules to this end, such as came later to be assumed as the basis of international intercourse over the world as a whole. They were not able to appeal to established universal international institutions – diplomatic conventions, forms of international law, principles of hierarchy, or customs of war – such as did facilitate exchanges within the various regional international systems. When the Spaniards were engaged in the conquest of Mexico and Peru, the idea of the coexistence of equal sovereign states, so far from being capable of playing any role in relations between Christian and Amerindian rulers and peoples, had not yet established itself in relations among the Christian powers themselves. In the long encounter between European states and the Ottoman Empire the rulers of the latter thought of relations with outsiders in terms of a fundamental division of the world between the faithful and the infidel; their settled relations with outsiders were those of an imperial authority dealing with its subjects or vassals; not until well into the nineteenth century were they accustomed to conceive of international relationships conducted on a secular basis and according to principles of equality and reciprocity.

Up to the point at which European trade and consular and diplomatic missions were imposed upon them, China and Japan in their approaches to what today we call international relations were governed by the idea of the relations between suzerains and vassals; the demand for equality of status with European powers, which assumed so prominent a position in the foreign policies of China and Japan in the late nineteenth and early twentieth centuries, when they were struggling for a rightful place in the European-defined international order, presupposed an abandonment of indigenous conceptions that did not come about until after the cultural and intellectual impact of Europe had been deeply felt. In the case of the dealings between European and south Asian powers within the Eurasian international system there was indeed some approximation to the working of an international society, but its cultural base was slight, its level of institutionalization was not high, and its geographical scope was limited. In the case of relations between the mature industrial powers of Europe at the time of the partition of Africa and the economically primitive, pre-literate, and sometimes stateless societies of sub-Saharan Africa with which they came into contact, there clearly did not exist even the most basic elements of shared outlook that are presupposed in membership of a common international society.

What did exist during the centuries prior to the emergence of a universal international society, and was often invoked in Europe to show that there were rules governing the relationships between Europeans and other peoples, was the idea of natural law. This idea, or complex of related ideas, inherited from the Greek and Roman Stoics and elevated to a central position in the political theory of Latin Christendom, proclaimed that rights and duties attaching to human beings as such and apparent to the light of reason existed by nature throughout the world as a whole, whatever convention decreed at particular times and in particular places. The doctrine of natural law, of course, played an important role in early modern times in the relations among Christian or European peoples themselves: thinkers such as Vitoria and Suarez in the sixteenth century, and Grotius and Pufendorf in the seventeenth, based their claim that Christian or European rulers and peoples formed an international society partly, even if not wholly, upon the moral bonds alleged to bind human beings together by nature. In the case of relations among Christian or European peoples, however, these alleged bonds of natural law were supplemented by bonds of volitional or human law, inherited from the past or arising out of present intercourse, as well as by a common understanding of divine law; in the case of relations between Europeans and Amerindians, Asians and Africans, where these other bonds were initially weaker or did not exist at all, the idea of natural law assumed a more central position.

The doctrine of a natural law community of mankind that knew no geographical limitations provided a weapon with which to combat conceptions of obligation that treated non-Christian or non-European peoples as devoid of rights. Just as in ancient Greek times the Stoics proclaimed the unity of all mankind as moral beings, up against those who, like Aristotle, divided men into Greeks and barbarians and held the latter to be slaves by nature, and just as in late medieval times Paulus Vladimiri and other followers of Aquinas upheld the rights of pagan Lithuanians to independent political existence, as against those who followed the doctrine of Hostiensis that non-Christian communities had been deprived of their rights of political existence with the coming of Christ, so in the period of modern European expansion the doctrine of natural law was proclaimed to defend the rights of Amerindians against Spanish conquerors, of Africans forced into trans-Atlantic slavery, and of aboriginal peoples in many parts of the world against dispossession and demoralization by European settlers.

But the universal international society of mankind contained in the doctrine of natural law was a merely conceptual or theoretical one. It had no foundation in the will or consent of political communities throughout the world. In modern times it has been asserted only in the European countries, even if there are parallels to it in some non-European traditions. Its influence on European or Western practice was limited. Moreover, asserted unilaterally by the expanding Europeans the natural law doctrine of a universal international society existing by right provided a rationale for forcing non-European peoples into commercial and diplomatic intercourse against their will – the *ius commercialis* which in the sixteenth century Vitoria held to have justified Spain's wars in the Indies, and which in the nineteenth century was held to justify British wars to open the China trade, and United States coercion of Japan. Like the assumption of a right to spread the Christian message and so realize the community of all men in Christ, or the later assumption of a right to spread civilization and so bring into being a secular universal community of the civilized, the assumption of universal rights to trade and diplomacy conferred by nature was menacing to those whose consent to such rights had not been given.

An actual international society worldwide in its dimensions, as opposed to the merely theoretical one of the natural lawyers, emerged only as European states and the various independent political communities with which they were involved in a common international system came to perceive common interests in a structure of coexistence and co-operation, and tacitly or explicitly to consent to common rules and institutions. One of the elements in this process was the exchange of diplomatic representatives on a permanent basis, beginning with *ad hoc* envoys and leading to the establishment of resident missions and the adoption of common protocol and procedure. Another was the adoption of common forms of international law, at first indicated in practice in the making and observance of treaties according to common procedures, and later recognized by international legal publicists who spoke of the expansion of 'the family of nations'. A further element was the representation of states at those periodic multilateral conferences that have marked the evolution of modern international society from the time of the Peace of Westphalia. One way of charting the evolution of a universal international society is to trace the widening representation of non-European states at these conferences.

Developments such as these could not have taken place except as the consequence of processes of cultural change within the countries concerned, in which attitudes hostile to international norms based upon equality and reciprocity were replaced by attitudes more favourable to them. The Ottoman Empire could not enter into relations of a peaceful and permanent nature with infidel states without some attempt to abandon or at least to qualify the theory that the relations between the community of the faithful and unbelievers consisted only of unrelenting war. An exchange of diplomatic missions on the basis of reciprocal interest and in accordance with rules providing for equal treatment implied and presupposed a repudiation of the theory that the relation of Imperial China to outside powers was one of a suzerain to its vassals. The protest of Asian and African states against unequal treatment received at the hands of European powers increasingly able, as the nineteenth century progressed, to mete out such treatment with impunity, could not take place until Wheaton's *Elements* and other such Western works of international law had been first translated, and their message of the equal sovereign rights of states digested, even if only for tactical reasons.

More basically still, perhaps, the coming together of numerous and extremely diverse political entities to form a single international society presupposed that these entities had come to resemble one another at least to the extent that they were all, in some comparable sense, states. By the early twentieth century international legal doctrine came to insist that political entities were entitled to recognition as sovereign states only if they met certain formal criteria of statehood, e.g. that there must be a government, a territory, a population, and a capacity to enter into international relations or fulfil international obligations. It is true that recognition was often extended in practice during the process of expansion of the European international system without regard to such formal criteria. Moreover, the doctrine that states do not have sovereignty apart from recognition of it by others (the doctrine of so-called 'constitutive recognition'), which European states came in the late nineteenth and early twentieth centuries to apply to Asian and African states, is one which is widely viewed today as having been simply an instrument of European dominance. Nevertheless, it could hardly have been expected that European states could have extended the full benefits of membership of the society of states to political entities that were in no position to enter into relationships on a basis of reciprocity, and the process by which Asian and African political communities did come to enter into such reciprocal relations and to enjoy full rights as members of international society was inseparable from domestic processes of political and social reform which narrowed the differences between them and the political communities of the West, and contributed to a process of convergence.

The widening of an originally European society of states beyond the geographical confines of Europe began a century before Europe had entered the culminating phase of its colonial expansion, with the independence of the United States towards the end of the eighteenth century, followed by that of the Spanish colonies in the Americas in the early decades of the nineteenth. This initial expansion, to embrace peoples Christian in religion and European in race and culture, did not strain the criteria of membership and in itself did little to advance the prospects that non-Christian and non-European peoples could gain admission. Indeed, the independence of settler colonies implied the ultimate extinction of the remaining political rights of indigenous American peoples, and the rights of man and of peoples proclaimed in the American revolutions were not extended in practice to persons and peoples other than those of European race, just as the rights proclaimed in the French Revolution, and extended in theory to the black and mulatto peoples of Haiti (then called St. Domingue), were asserted in practice only by the bloody struggles of the latter against French and British attempts to suppress them. But the revolutions in America, and the entry of the 'new states' created by them into the international society evolved in Europe, extended its geographical scope. These revolutions also led to a doctrine and rhetoric of anti-colonialism, of non-alignment with regard to great power conflicts, of 'continentalism' or regional solidarity and separateness, of fresh starts and repudiation of past experiences in international relations, that was inherited by later generations of 'new states'.

Later in the nineteenth century, despite the tightening of Europe's grip on the rest of the world and the tendency to define admission into international society in stricter and more exclusive terms, a small number of powers neither Christian in religion nor European in race or culture entered into the originally European circle of states dealing with one another on a reciprocal basis in diplomacy and international law, and represented at multilateral conferences. At the Congress of Vienna in 1815 only European states were present, but at the Paris Peace Conference of 1856 the Ottoman Empire was represented; at the Hague Conference of 1899, together with the United States and Mexico, the Ottoman Empire was joined by China, Japan, Persia, and Siam; and at the Hague Conference of 1907 there were also a total of sixteen Latin American republics, whose considerable impact was a premonition of the influence of the Third World on the United Nations General Assembly. By the First World War, then, a universal international society of states clearly existed which covered the whole world and included representatives of the Americas, Asia, and Africa as well as of Europe.

The standard European view of this emergence of a universal international society was that non-European states entered an originally European club of states as and when they measured up to criteria of admission laid down by the founder members. Today, it is common to question this standard account. European statesmen before the nineteenth century do not appear always to have thought of international society as exclusively European. Natural law theorists from the sixteenth to the eighteenth centuries described an international society that was global in extent, even if they also recognized an inner circle of Christian and European states, among whom relations were more intimate. The practice of European states in the East Indies in the seventeenth and eighteenth centuries reflected a willingness to enter into commercial, military, and diplomatic relations with local powers on a basis of mutual acceptance. The standard view, moreover, neglects the influence of Asian international practices on the evolution of European ones: the international society to which non-European powers came to adhere was not one made in a Europe isolated from the rest of the world, but grew up concurrently with the expansion of Europe into other continents over four centuries, and was marked by this experience. There is, moreover, an element of absurdity in the claim that states such as China, Egypt, or Persia, which existed thousands of years before states came into being in Europe, achieved rights to full independence only when they came to pass a test devised by nineteenth-century Europeans.

Yet it cannot be denied that the role of the Europeans in shaping an international society of worldwide dimension has been a special one. It was in fact the European powers and not the powers of Asia, Africa, or the Americas that came to occupy a dominant position in the world as a whole. It was in fact their conception of an international society of juridically equally sovereign states that came to be accepted by independent political communities everywhere as the basis of their relationships. The non-European or non-Western majority of states in the world today, which played little role in shaping the foundations of the international society to which they now belong, have sought naturally and properly to modify it so that it will reflect their own special interests. It should not be overlooked, however, that by seeking a place in this society they have given their consent to its basic rules and institutions. While non-European communities in some cases were incorporated in the international system against their will, they have taken their places in international society because they themselves have sought the rights of membership of it, and the protection of its rules, both *vis-à-vis* the dominant European powers and in relation to one another.

If absurdities arise from the idea that non-European political communities were admitted into a club originally for Europeans only, there are also difficulties about the idea of a universal society of states that existed before the era of European colonial domination. While some Asian and African states today are historically continuous with states of pre-colonial times, the majority are genuinely 'new states' that are not the heirs of ancient policies but creations of the colonial system. 'Old states' which like China survived the colonial period, or like Vietnam disappeared but re-emerged, did have rights to independence in the pre-colonial period, at least by the standards that we apply today in retrospect, and so did the vast array of Asian and African political communities whose independence disappeared permanently. Moreover, these rights to independence in many cases enjoyed some form of recognition at the time, both by Europeans and by others; at the beginning of the process of expansion Vitoria and other observers considered that Amerindian political communities had the same rights of independence that European states had, and many of the Amerindian, Asian, African, and Oceanian communities that were subsequently absorbed in colonial empires had previously been given some form of recognition by treaty. But except in the case of late victims of colonialism like Ethiopia (which when it was annexed by Italy was widely recognized as a sovereign state and was a member of the League of Nations), these rights to independence could not be said to have been endorsed by a universal system of positive international law and did not reflect a universal international society that actually existed.

In assessing what I have called the standard view of the emergence of a universal international society we also have to bear in mind that the European international society of the nineteenth century which (in retrospect so arrogantly) presumed to lay down criteria for admission to its ranks was not a mere continuation of what had gone before in the eighteenth century but was in a state of progressive development: the century following the Congress of Vienna witnessed the experiment in management of the international system by a concert of great powers, the regulation of diplomatic precedent and protocol, the steady professionalization of international law, dramatic advances in communications and transport, the deeper involvement of many societies in an expanding international economy, the rise of technical international organizations, the first stirrings of internationally organized action about human rights in relation to the slave trade, and new ideas about disarmament and the peaceful settlement of international disputes. It was the Europeans (and Americans) who were at the forefront of all these developments, and the capacity of Asian and African powers to enter into relationships on a reciprocal basis with European states of the same nature that the latter had with one another was less than in earlier times. There is no reason to doubt that the European powers which insisted on criteria of admission to membership of international society did so in part because of assumptions they made about the superiority of their religion and civilization which to us appear unfounded. Nor should it be doubted that they sometimes used these criteria to deny others their rights and to acquire special privileges for themselves, or that they required others to meet standards of behaviour they failed to observe themselves. We should also recognize, however, that in the course of the nineteenth century participation in the life of international society was taking on a different meaning from what it had had before. Societies did in fact differ radically in their capacity to conduct the new forms of international relations, and the tests devised by the Europeans recognized that this was so.

But while by the time of the First World War European society had ceased to be exclusively European and had become universal in its membership, the European powers along with the United States held a dominant position. The greater part of Asia, Africa, and Oceania comprised colonial dependencies: the universal international society was one of states, but not everywhere of peoples or nations. With the important partial exception of Japan, those racially and culturally non-European states that enjoyed formal independence laboured under the stigma of inferior status: unequal treaties, extraterritorial jurisdiction, denial of racial equality. In the gradations of independence recognized by the European powers in the extra-European world, the spectrum of positions intermediate between full sovereignty and the status of a colony (spheres of influence, protected states, protectorates, subjection to imperial paramountcy), there could be seen the survival, alongside the concept of a society of equally sovereign states, of the older and historically much more ubiquitous concept of international relations as the relations between suzerains and vassals.

Nor did this situation change basically in the years between the First World War and the Second. In this period there occurred the rejection of the racial equality clause by the Paris Peace Conference of 1919, the further expansion of the British and French Empires through the device of the Mandates System, the completion of the partition of Africa by Italy's absorption of Ethiopia, the Jewish colonization of Palestine, the achievement of effective self-government by white settler minorities in South Africa and Rhodesia. The leading powers in the League of Nations, Britain and France, were also the leading colonial powers; their chief challengers in the 1930s, the revisionist states, did not seek to challenge the colonial system: Italy sought only a redistribution of colonies in its own favour, Germany sought a different kind of colony among the Slav peoples of eastern Europe, and Japan sought to undermine empire in the east only in order to replace it with an empire of its own, conceived in the image of those of the Europeans.

The movements that were to shake this structure of European dominance were already to be seen at work in the Japanese campaign against extraterritorial jurisdiction in the 1880s and 1890s, the success of mass nationalist movements in China and India in the 1920s, the impact of the Bolshevik Revolution in the East, the anti-imperialist congresses of the 1930s. But it was not until after 1945 that these movements came to fruition and the attempt was made to transform a universal society of states into one of peoples.

9

NEW STATES IN THE AMERICAS

Adam Watson

The long process of transition from a European to a global international society began at least a century before the expansion of European power over the rest of the world had reached its fullest extent. This transition took two principal forms. The first is the series of modifications introduced into the European system as it expanded, in order to manage more effectively the relations of the European powers with Asian (and to a trivial extent non-Asian) states. The second is the adjustments to the achievement of independence by European colonies of overseas settlement. The second is the more significant of the two.

The first period of this development runs from the revolts of the 1770s in certain British colonies on the American mainland, through the successful independence movements led by Washington, Bolivar, and San Martin, to the Spanish and Portuguese recognition of the independence of their mainland colonies in the 1820s. Three familiar aspects of this process are especially relevant to our inquiry, and to the subsequent course followed by the transition. First, it resulted from secessions by European settlers. Second, it was confined to the Americas. And, third, it effectively subtracted the new American states from the European balance of power.

I

Let us look first at the process of secession. In the eighteenth century many European settlers in the Americas became increasingly tired of interference by the metropolitan government in Europe in their affairs, and of the unresponsiveness of royal governments and officials to the views of colonial assemblies and councils of notables, especially in economic issues. An increasing number of these settlers adopted democratic and revolutionary ideas imported from Europe. The complaints of British American colonists symbolized by the slogan 'no taxation without representation' were much the same as those in the Spanish colonies against the ignorance, exploitation, and arbitrariness of Madrid. An anti-colonial tradition and rhetoric were developed. Many political leaders in Britain (a majority of the House of Commons) and later in Spain (both in the Napoleonic and Anglo-Bourbon camps) sympathized with the rebel settlers. American-Indian leaders generally favoured the Crown. The British and Spanish governments made half-hearted efforts to reassert their authority by force of arms against the rebels, who received some help from the European enemies of those governments – in the British case France and in the Spanish case Britain.

In the movement of secession it was the British rebels who gave the lead. This was for familiar reasons, including the greater degree of self-government already existing in British America and the more developed traditions of political liberty in England. Their unilateral declaration of independence was made in 1776 and accepted by the defeated British Crown in 1783. The Spanish rebels only became effective when Napoleon's invasion of Spain in 1807 led to revolutionary proclamations and the paralysis of the Spanish government. In medieval Spanish law a king's domains had the right to govern themselves in an interregnum pending the restoration of a lawful king. When Napoleon made Ferdinand VII abdicate and set up Joseph Bonaparte, the Spanish settlers in the Americas claimed this Spanish right, in the same way as the British settlers claimed the English right to be taxed only by parliaments in which they were represented. The liberalized Spanish government recognized the secessions, which between them covered the whole of the mainland empire, only in the course of the 1820s.

Unilateral declarations of independence and successful armed defiance of the forces of the imperial power were the classical method of establishing new states on the European model in the new world outside Europe, and certainly the more mythopoeic one. But there was another more evolutionary course, that of gradual independence by negotiation and mutual consent, with the maintenance of some symbolic constitutional link after the end of all imperial authority. This alternative low road to independence also began to take shape in the first years of the nineteenth century, and was, like the high road of unilateral independence, to play a major part in the transition to a global international order. Indeed the second and third powers of the American continent, Canada and Brazil, took this route.

The case of the Portuguese territories in America is instructive for our purpose as well as impressive in itself. While the Spanish Viceroyalties in the New World were established largely on the foundations of previous Indian empires, the Portuguese colonies were, like their British counterparts, maritime settlements strung out along the Atlantic seaboard. By the eighteenth century the settlers were acquiring some experience of self-government in municipal councils which enjoyed greater powers than in European Portugal. These councils maintained lobbies at the court of Lisbon, had the right to summon the royal Governor, and at times of crisis called in military, judicial, and church leaders and additional 'spokesmen for the people'. There were also local militias captained by large landowners, rather like the Virginian militia of George Washington. Enlightened despotism in Lisbon discouraged race prejudice, and Pombal decreed that any Portuguese in Brazil who married an Indian would improve his chance of preferment under the Crown. The most serious issue between the settlers and Lisbon was trade, which the Crown wanted to monopolize for Portugal whereas the settlers wanted to trade with other countries, especially Britain.

Self-government came to Brazil early in the nineteenth century without the need to resort to arms. When Napoleon overran Portugal in 1807 the Regent John and his government moved to Brazil under British protection, leaving only the bridgehead of Lisbon in Europe. Rio de Janeiro became the provisional capital of the Portuguese world. Settler influence soon made itself felt. Within a year the government yielded to settler demands and British advice, and declared the ports of Brazil open to all non-enemy flags. The government did not return to European Portugal when it was liberated from French occupation. John VI was crowned King of Portugal in Rio in 1816, and only returned to Lisbon in 1821, leaving his son Peter as his regent in the New World. By this time Portuguese America had consolidated itself into the Empire of Brazil, and was no longer disposed to take orders from Europe again, even on matters of general policy. When in the following year the Lisbon government summoned Prince Peter back to Europe 'to complete his education' the Brazilians refused to let him go and proclaimed him an independent Emperor Peter I. Because he was the crown prince of the Braganza house and had been installed by his father, his authority was accepted in Brazil as legitimate; and the problem of the legitimacy of power seized by force, so difficult to resolve in Spanish America, did not beset Brazil. After three years of dispute the issue was settled amicably through long negotiations in London, with Britain and Austria acting as mediators, by the father's inevitable recognition of his son's independence. President Monroe jumped in with his recognition of the Brazilian Empire just ahead of Portugal and the other European powers. The new Brazilian constitution of that year (1824) was a model of liberalism and balanced powers, based on British and American as well as Brazilian practice. Metternich's role is worthy of note in our study of the transition process. Emperor Peter's wife was the Habsburg princess Leopoldina, who maintained close contact with her father and Metternich: Austria therefore opposed the usual Holy Alliance policy of maintaining the rights of crowned heads, and Metternich skilfully dissuaded Russia and Prussia from assisting the Portuguese to reassert their dominion over Brazil. He thus ensured that the Empire of Brazil established its independence by the general consent of the Concert of Europe, instead of by a unilateral British fiat backed by unchallengeable seapower.

But this did not end Brazilian involvement in the Old World. When a few months later King John died, Peter actively supported the claims of his own daughter Mary and the liberal Constitutionalists against his brother Michael, whom the Absolutists and the Holy Alliance preferred. Michael prevailed, and in 1834 Brazil formed a Quadruple Alliance with the constitutional monarchies of Britain and France and the constitutionalist Queen Isabella of Spain directed against Michael, Russia, Prussia, and in this case Austria too. A Brazilian army led by Peter with smaller British and French forces placed Mary on the throne (where she stayed till her death nineteen years later). Peter's use of Brazilian blood and treasure for intervention in Europe was resented by most settlers. But the dynastic connection between the two halves of the Portuguese world continued until the abdication of Peter II in 1889 and the proclamation of the Brazilian Republic. A network of special agreements and close informal ties continues, and Brazil today is appreciably more Portuguese than Canada is British.

The parallel course of Canada's low road to independence is more familiar, and I need only indicate some relevant features. The British Crown's timely concessions to the French Canadians and their hostility to the British settlers ensured their neutrality in the American War of Independence. But after the successful United States secession strikingly large numbers of loyalist British settlers moved to Canada, which aggravated the feud between the two communities. Pitt's Canada Act of 1791 separated them, giving each an elected parliament but a nominated executive. The French Revolution, which kindled much interest in the settlers of the Spanish colonies, alienated the conservatives and the Catholic French Canadians who saw the British Crown as a lesser evil than the United States or the Jacobins, and noted Napoleon's disinterest in North America. But in spite of their feud the French and British settlers were both soon objecting to taking orders from London for all the usual settler reasons. In the 1830s disaffection grew into open rebellion in both provinces and secession seemed a real possibility. Unrest on a lesser scale also disturbed the four other British colonies in North America, Nova Scotia, New Brunswick, Prince Edward Island, and Newfoundland. The Whig government in London, which had just enacted Grey's Reform Act, sent out his son-in-law 'Radical Jack' Durham to be Governor-General of all six colonies. He suppressed the rebellions by force; but in his famous report of 1839 declared that the Crown's North American subjects had the same rights as those in Britain. 'The Crown must consent to carry on the government by means of those in whom the representative members have confidence.' But Durham had no such Whig solution for the enmity between the British and French settlers. 'I expected to find a contest between a government and a people: I found two nations warring in the bosom of a single state.' (At least Radical Jack did not deceive himself into thinking that this intractable ethnic problem was really a political and economic one in disguise, as has so often happened since.) The enactment of Durham's proposals in 1840 brought Canada back to the low road of independence by consent. Self-government was achieved by stages, and not without some bitterness. The great debate of the 1860s on how to bring about a union with the maritime and western settlements was due to local initiative for the most part. Those who wanted a wider federation were firmly monarchist, seeing in the Crown the common focus of all the otherwise particularist loyalties of the settlers. The Canadian request to call the new state the Kingdom of Canada was rejected by the Imperial Government in London so as not to offend the United States. The debate took place under the shadow of the American Civil War, which many Canadians attributed to the individual states having too much power; so a 'tight' federation was established by the Confederation Act of 1867, giving the provinces less autonomy than the states of the United States or Brazil, let alone the Spanish American solution of over a dozen independent states. The vital emotional link with the Crown and with Britain held Canada for the rest of the century as a willing reinforcement of Britain's position in the European balance of power in the world, and she entered both World Wars of the twentieth century alongside the 'mother country'. Only in this century have Canadian governments operated externally as fully independent members of international society.

The low road to independence avoided the destruction, bitterness, and rupture caused by the armed secessions (which were especially damaging to Venezuela). But the Brazilians and Canadians were only able to travel it because most of them were visibly ready to take the high road if the imperial power would not yield to persuasion.

The effective pressures towards independence from metropolitan control came from the European settlers. In all the American colonies, prominent settlers were involved in local government to a greater or lesser degree: on the one hand through elected assemblies in the British territories or nominated councils in the Spanish and Portuguese, and on the other hand by appointments under the Crown (e.g. Washington, San Martín). Only they had the necessary political consciousness; only they had the awareness and the experience of how a 'civilized' government should operate, in order to make self-government plausible and acceptable to a large section of European opinion. Most important of all, only they understood the techniques of European warfare well enough to push out the imperial authority where it did not progressively hand over power with good grace.

During their struggles for independence, often involving prolonged and risky military operations, the embattled colonials were normally quite unworried about revolts by African slaves or quasi-forced Amerindian labour. Nor were they unduly put out by the more serious nuisance of 'guerillas' by independent Indians encouraged and equipped by the Crown. This had been an accepted feature of the conflicts between European powers in the Americas all through the eighteenth century. Its main effect was to harden the determination of the settlers to eliminate future danger from that quarter in the territories they came to control.

How far were Mexico and Haiti exceptions to this general picture? They may seem at first glance to be so. Mexico at the turn of the nineteenth century had a history of mestizo and Indian unrest. The Napoleonic invasion of Spain in 1807 also brought to a head the opposition between those who wanted to maintain the Spanish connection and the criollos (white settlers) who wanted independence. But when in 1810 the criollo priest Father Hidalgo proclaimed a revolution to extend all rights and privileges to the mestizos and Indians, most of the white population was driven to make common cause against him and his successors in what became increasingly a racial war. The aims of the priestly leaders of the revolution were a mixture of the traditional demand of the Spanish Catholic Church for better treatment of the Indians and the new ideas of equality and fraternity. The revolution was finally suppressed by General Itúrbide, a conservative criollo soldier comparable to Washington and San Martín. In 1820 the Spanish Government introduced a liberal constitution in Madrid; and Itúrbide, hitherto a loyalist, now opted for independence with a more conservative constitution to be headed by a Spanish prince. When none could be found, he agreed to become Emperor on Napoleonic lines, with full rights for all criollos. Support for this solution was at first so general that the new Spanish Viceory sailed back to Spain within a few days of arrival. Yet within two years, republican opinion among the criollos became so strong that a military coup against Itúrbide established a republic. Thus the break with Spain, initiated by Hidalgo to better the lot of the Indians, became appropriated by the criollos, whom the threat from below made more conservative on internal issues. Hidalgo and his successors thought in terms of an egalitarian Catholic polity; they had no thought at all of resurrecting an Aztec or other Indian state. Neither then nor in the confused decades of the early Republic did Indians provide any significant leadership. Only when Napoleon III tried to re-establish the Empire under a Habsburg prince did Indian and mestizo leaders take over the fight for independence.

Haiti offers a more striking portent of events in our own time; and the danger of anachronism is therefore greater. Haiti was ceded to France in 1697, and in the century that followed there were a number of grisly slave risings. The French Revolution led to an uprising of the mulattos, which came under the leadership of Toussaint l'Ouverture, the able negro who became dictator of the whole island of Hispaniola, including the Spanish half, and defeated Napoleon's brother-in-law Leclerc whom the Emperor sent to suppress the rebellion. A formal unilateral declaration of independence was made in 1804, and the whites were expelled. Several brief empires followed under various negro leaders, and the kingdom set up by Christophe. These were all caricatures of Napoleon's empire, and not only very bloody but also grotesque. A republic was finally established in 1858. France recognized Haitian independence in 1825, followed by Britain. The United States only recognized the Haitian state in 1864, and it then gradually took a somewhat nominal part in international society. There can be no doubt that Haiti's international position suffered from prejudice against her by the majority of European and settler states: prejudice in the first half of the nineteenth century against sanguinary revolution, and in the second half against negro 'incompetence'. Moreover the rulers of Haiti were not very interested in formal participation in the comity of states. International society in the Americas was dominated by white settlers, and in general by Europeans: the very people whom the Haitians had driven out. What they wanted was sovereignty without outside interference, and facilities for carrying on trade and contracting debts. In practice the position of Haiti did not materially differ from that of other small central American states. Race was not considered a barrier to formal statehood in the first half of the nineteenth century.

There is, therefore, little reason to regard Mexico or Haiti as very significant exceptions to the general pattern of the first phase of the transition from a European to a global international order. In Mexico the men who established independence were white settlers, though a few had some Indian blood. They differed strongly among themselves about the position of Indians in the new society (but no more than United States settlers). Their attitudes towards Europe and towards the position of Mexico in the international community were like those of their fellow settlers in other countries. Haiti deviated more from the general pattern in that the revolution was consciously racialist and anti-settler. The Haitian case has certain symbolic value, and is a foretaste of things to come. Even so there was no thought in the period under discussion of any language but French: the regimes copied or parodied the Napoleonic empire; their attitude to the outside world was in its essentials a *reductio ad minimum* of general settler attitudes; and Haiti was regarded by the international community as too insignificant and too barbarous to require any notable modification of the rules of the game.

II

The fact that the new states which came into existence between 1776 and 1830 were (with one exception) established by European settlers is one of the keys to the second aspect under consideration, that the process of secession and negotiated independence was confined to the Americas. Indeed save for the two Hispaniolan states it was confined to the mainland: the islands were too small, and the settlers in them too few, to rebel successfully. In fact there were very few European settlers anywhere else at the beginning of the nineteenth century. There were Dutch and Huguenot settlements round the Cape of Good Hope; and a string of Russian posts through Siberia which were territorial extensions of European Russia and dependent on it for protection. Nor were there yet in Asia or Africa many of the other sort of colony, where a handful of 'home-based' officials administer sizeable non-European populations. In Asia there was nothing nearer than India, which had to be reached by the long haul round the Cape. The Dutch were the most enterprising: they administered parts of Java, and Ceylon until 1796, through native rulers. The British East India Company administered Bengal and some smaller territories in India more directly; and the French and Portuguese had toeholds on the sub-continent. In the Pacific the Spaniards were Hispanicizing the Philippines, also without settling them. Further afield the British Government accepted the strategic argument for settlements in Australia, which had to be effected at first by compulsory deportation. The European presence was still essentially maritime: and it manifested itself in coastal trading posts and strategic forts. Nor was there anything more in tropical Africa: the continent seemed unsuitable for white settlement, and unlike Asia remained very largely unexplored and unvisited by Europeans. A few of the islands in the Atlantic and Indian oceans were settled, like Mauritius; but they were even less suitable candidates for independent statehood than the West Indies.

III

Thirdly, the subtraction of the newly independent American ex-colonial states from the European balance of power is of particular interest to us in studying the transition from a European order. It was a major and decisive break. And it was made not by Asians or other conquered peoples, but by the European settlers across the Atlantic.

The major reason why the West European powers established overseas bases and colonies was to strengthen themselves economically and strategically against the other powers in the European system of states. The eighteenth-century European order was based on a 'Newtonian' concept of a multilateral balance of power, according to which each state was affected to a greater or lesser degree by all the other members of the system; and it was accepted that when a state grew stronger in relation to its neighbours, equilibrium was preserved by the rest moving away from it and closer to each other, regardless of religious, dynastic, or ethnic ties. But the colonies of a European state overseas did not move in this way: they were an extension of that state, and represented a permanent part of the weight which it brought to bear in the states system. The colonists in the Americas understood this very well. They saw that so long as a colony in the New World remained loyal to the mother country, it was an extension of that country's mercantile system in times of peace, and in wartime it had to supply the Crown with the resources of war and was subject to attack and harassment by other European powers.

When certain colonists began to perceive their interests as distinct from those of the mother country – which will have been quite an intellectual jump to make in most cases – the colonial connection seemed to them an *entanglement*, diverting them from their natural course of development. Once a colony or group of colonies took the plunge and proclaimed itself a separate state by armed rebellion, it had to counterbalance the military power of the former mother country by accepting the readily proffered aid of that country's European enemies of the moment. At that stage it became a new member of the European power system. It was natural for the European states, who had found the struggle for power and the need for watchfulness inescapable, to assume that these new recruits to their system would continue to behave in the same way as they themselves felt constrained to do; that for some time at any rate the weight of the new state would be brought to bear, in self-defence, against the former imperial power and thus in favour of its enemies. Lafayette and de Grasse saw their part in the American War of Independence in much the same light as the commanders of the French regular forces on the Stuart side in the '45 rebellion. Canning's familiar statement in the House of Commons on 12 December 1826, when the French intervened militarily in Spain to prop up absolute monarchy on behalf of the Holy Alliance, shows that he thought in the same way, as did his audience.

'Is the balance of power a fixed and unalterable standard? Or is it not a standard perpetually varying, as civilization advances and as new nations spring up and take their place among established political communities? . . . Contemplating Spain such as our ancestors had known her, I resolved that if France had Spain it should not be Spain with the Indies. I called the New World into existence to redress the balance of the Old.'

But in so doing the Europeans were reckoning without the colonists. Their aim was to disentangle themselves from the quarrels and exigencies of Europe altogether, to trade with whatever markets suited them, and to concentrate on the problems which faced them in the New World. Whether Washington's famous valedictory advice to his countrymen to avoid entangling alliances meant that he considered all alliances entangling, or was merely opposed to long-term commitments, and especially a semi-permanent alliance with France which could involve the United States in coming to France's aid in a quarrel which did not concern America, is disputable. But the general sense of his words was endorsed by majority opinion in all the new states. In spite of Canning, neither Bolivar nor San Martín saw their role as redressing the balance of Europe; on the contrary, this is what they wanted to stop doing. Like Washington, they wanted to disengage strategically not merely from their imperial member of the system but from the system itself.

They were after all a long way away. It is easy to forget how remote the Americas were in those days. In the days of sailing ships, and before the Panama Canal, Peru was as much subject to *The Tyranny of Distance* as Geoffrey Blainey (in his book of that title published in Melbourne in 1966) has shown was the case with Australia. This distance was not only a tyranny, it was an opportunity. In anti-colonial eyes the home govenment prejudiced the strategic interests of the settlers in two ways: it afforded them too little protection against hostile neighbours, and involved them too much in the interminable power struggle in Europe. This sentiment was echoed by the friends of the settlers at home. Burke in one of his deliberately memorable metaphors asked the House of Commons where England would be 'if our Colonies had not with truly filial piety put the full breast of their youthful exuberance into the mouth of their exhausted parent.' To many American colonists it seemed less filial, perhaps, but certainly more natural to use their youthful exuberance to raise new countries of their own begetting. And if the secessionists among the settlers in the Americas begrudged their milk to Britain or to Spain, how much less were they inclined to offer it to France or Russia or some other power in the gyrating European mobile?

The persistence of this attitude is well illustrated by the Monroe Doctrine. The germ of the doctrine can be found in statements by Washington and Jefferson. The Old and New Worlds were two separate spheres of political activity, they argued, and the New World should have as little to do politically as possible with the Old. By 1823, when the independence of Spanish America was fairly established, the Monroe Administration had two concerns. The first arose out of Russian activities in Alaska. The American continent, proclaimed Monroe, 'is henceforth not to be considered as a subject for colonization by any European power'. In return the United States would not interfere in European affairs. The second concern Monroe shared with the British Government of the day: the danger that the Holy Alliance would intervene in the Americas to restore the Spanish Crown. Canning proposed to Monroe a joint declaration on this subject; but Monroe and his advisers felt that association with imperial Britain would gravely compromise the principle of the American stand, and replied that the United States wished to make a unilateral announcement. The Secretary of State John Quincy Adams declared in impeccable anti-colonial language that the United States would not be 'towed like a cockboat in the wake of the British man-of-war'. The Doctrine was reaffirmed and strengthened in 1845 when President Polk felt the need to contradict Guizot's publicly announced thesis that the balance of power also applied to the New World, in the context of the United States annexation of Texas from Mexico, after a brief interlude of independence. The American Civil War effectively prevented further enunciations of the Doctrine in the 1860s, the period of Napoleon III's invasion of Mexico. But in the 1870s Grant more than once stated the principle that the remaining European colonies in the Hemisphere could not be transferred from one European power to another. In effect, only American powers might make changes in the Americas. In 1881 the Concert of Europe was even more specfically excluded: 'Any extension to our shores (i.e. the Americas) of the political system by which the great powers have controlled and determined events in Europe would be attended with danger to the peace and welfare of this nation.' The climax came with the imperious warning to Britain in the (still unresolved) territorial dispute between Venezuela and British Guiana: the United States could not countenance any British jurisdiction 'over any territory which after investigation we have determined of right belongs to Venezuela'.

The rule laid down separately but simultaneously by the United States and British governments in the 1820s, that the newly independent states in the Americas were excluded from the European balance of power, from European military intervention, and from European alliances, was generally accepted in Europe. The remaining European possessions in the Americas (except for Britain and Russia, only a few small territories in the Caribbean) were not affected by the rule; but there was an informal taboo on ceding these possessions to another European state. It is generally held that the observance of the Doctrine was made possible by the determination of the United States, the unchallengeable British naval control of the Atlantic, and the desire of the Latin Americans to contract out of the European system. Even so, it remains something to be wondered at, in the century of confident and irresistible European imperialism and expansion all over the Eastern hemisphere.

The new nations of the New World wanted to opt out of the Old World's balance of power. They wanted to be politically and strategically non-aligned. But they did not at all want to opt out of European society. On the contrary, they wanted to maintain the closest cultural ties with Europe: especially with the mother country whose blood, language, traditions, and tastes they shared, but also additionally with other centres of what they considered civilization. We see them consciously and often anxiously measuring their achievements against the standards of England or Spain, and also those of France and Italy. Every ship brought, alongside more mundane merchandise, its precious cargo of new books and fashions and returned travellers. The new states also wanted and expected to play their rightful part in international relations. In matters like international law and diplomatic practice they accepted the European rules and patterns without question. They also adhered to the postal and other conventions and negotiated a full range of multilateral and bilateral accords on non-political subjects – the whole network of agreements which formulate civil international order. In matters like neutrality, the rules governing interference with shipping, European intervention in the Americas, and other issues which touched them directly, they wanted to wear their rue with a certain difference. But they wanted these modifications to be accepted by all members of international society, to be incorporated in international law or at least in the society's codes of conduct. They evolved special diplomatic procedures within the Americas, such as the right of asylum in Embassies of American states but not others; and they expected these procedures to be respected as peculiarities by the international community as a whole. In short, they saw themselves as members of what had previously been European society, but excluded from the European balance of power and the strategic aspects of the system, and the system excluded from them. And the European powers, by and large, accepted this arrangement.

IV

The broad picture is of a whole hemisphere of new states developing from European colonization and on European lines which by the end of the eighteenth century were ready for independent statehood and capable of asserting it. In some cases virtually the whole population was of European stock; in others the Europeans were an educated managerial élite. Independence was conceived and established from the top, by the ablest and most educated of the settlers. They and the states they formed were accepted members of European society – rather boorish and provincial members, perhaps, but that was no great matter. In seventeenth-century common parlance an American, in London or Madrid, had meant a red man: in the nineteenth century it meant a white. Since the new states grew out of European settlements, none of them was in any sense a restoration of a previous form of government, or considered itself in any way a legal successor of a formerly independent state. To men steeped in the classics all this was right and proper. The Greek city-states had founded colonies by planned emigration with an eye to commerce and strategy. It was how the Corinthians founded Syracuse and the Megarans Byzantium. It was how Aeneas and his wandering Trojans founded Rome. And for the more pious, it was how the Book of Exodus described the Children of Israel taking possession of the land of Canaan. The inspiration of these great examples encouraged the pride of the settlers in their origins and their achievements. It did not encourage too much concern with the views and fate of the Sicels, the Sabines, or the Canaanites.

The first phase of the transition to a world order was the extension of the European society of states to the newly independent European settler states in the Western hemisphere under special conditions. Subsequent extensions and changes bear a family likeness to it. This is not only because decolonization is much the same now as it was then. The initial expansion also created precedents and a pattern to copy.

First we may note the establishment of an anti-colonial tradition and rhetoric. Overseas territories ought to become independent. A sense of moral obligation as well as self-interest impels leaders in dependent territories to hasten forward the day. The new states ought then to be admitted on terms of equality to the club. They ought to have a say – some would claim an equal say – in how the world is run. But the new states have a right, perhaps even a duty, to disentangle themselves from the conflicts of the great powers. The present heir of Washington and Bolivar in this respect is the non-aligned movement. Since what matters emotionally and in practice is disengagement from the former imperial power, the natural ally of the non-aligned, as Castro argues, is that state in the great power balance which is most opposed to the former imperial masters, even though it is just as imperialist and undesirable in the longer run, and the ultimate attitude of the non-aligned is Mercutio's plague on both your houses.

Secondly, the settler goal of full self-government, via the Canadian-Brazilian low road of independence by negotiation and a symbolic link through a shared royal family, came to be accepted by Britain, the foremost imperial power. At first this concept was only seen to apply to white settlers, capable of constituting a state that could take its place in international society, which was still European society writ large. Then gradually, in areas with few or no settlers, the concept was extended to include self-government by Western-trained non-Europeans. The two major Latin colonial powers evolved the counter-premiss of romanization, the gradual granting of full rights of citizenship to the assimilated non-European population of worldwide France or Portugal. These are two answers to the same question. What do you do when there is no European settler élite? You train a Europeanized local élite who correspond to the settlers, and who see their interests and responsibilities in the same way. In the last quarter-century we have seen romanization collapse in favour of multiple independence for states governed by small Europeanized élites (I include Marxist and American training in the term European). Today, unlike the position in 1830, the great majority of members of the United Nations which were formerly under European government have travelled the low road to independence by negotiation between the local élite and the imperial power.

There are two kinds of non-European élite: those from the ancient civilizations of Asia who seek in varying degrees to restore states and traditions that existed before the European conquests of the last century; and those from pre-literate societies in Africa and elsewhere who have in practice only European models to look to. Those from Asian and Islamic societies usually have a much greater cultural affinity with the peoples whom they govern than do the Europeanized élites of pre-literate societies in Africa and elsewhere, whose aim is much more like that of the settlers, to step into the shoes of the imperial authorities. The restored Asian and Islamic states may have a greater and more distinctive contribution to make to the refashioning of international society. But all, in their concepts of independence and of the role which newly independent states should play on the international stage, owe a great deal to the settlers in the Americas who worked out a new pattern for themselves between 1770 and 1830, and succeeded in getting it accepted by the Europeans at the very heyday of European expansion in Asia and Africa.

10

THE OTTOMAN EMPIRE AND THE EUROPEAN STATES SYSTEM

Thomas Naff

To a historian of Ottoman-European relations, the Ottoman Empire poses a large paradox: for half a millenium, from the fourteenth century until the nineteenth, the Ottoman Empire occupied, controlled, and administered one-quarter to one-third of the European continent. Through its wars, its political and economic policies, and its Islamic mission as the successor to the great Muslim caliphates of the past, the Empire became significantly involved in the continent's international politics. At first, the Empire played the role of dominant actor; by the eighteenth century it was a weak actor, with the sultan's shrinking domain a pivotal object in the power struggles among Europe's kings and emperors. The logical conclusion ought to be that the Ottoman Empire was, empirically, a European state. The paradox is that it was not. Even though a significant portion of the Empire was based *in* Europe, it cannot be said to have been *of* Europe.

Two equally formidable bulwarks of religious ideology and culture – one Christian, the other Muslim, both reinforced by ignorance, prejudice, and hostility – separated the European and Ottoman worlds. Profound differences in concepts of state, law, and government inhibited the mixing of systems and mentalities. Only in the eighteenth and nineteenth centuries, when European secularism and power overwhelmed the Ottoman Muslim barrier, was political integration possible. In 1840 and again in 1856, the *Sublime Porte* was formally inducted by treaty into Europe's state system. That simple formality codified a century and a half of precedent, embedded in an even longer process and complicated by variant rationales for the organization of human society.

The post-medieval European idea of the state – a territorially defined entity apart from ruler or dynasty, organized in accordance with man-made rules – was alien to Muslim political theory. Ottoman theories of state and government derived from the Muslim concept that God is the source of all authority and law, that government exists to enable the community of true believers (Muslims) to fulfil its obligations to God. The community, not the state, constitutes the basic Muslim polity, transcending all boundaries.

Since God, through the Prophet Muhammed, gave his community its law, that law was holy, perfect, unchangeable, and provided for all exigencies. Any Muslim community/state is, theoretically, morally superior to all other societies. Until God's intention of a universal true-believing community under a single law and ruler was achieved, the world would be divided into two spheres: *Dar ul-Islam* – the abode of Islam where Islamic law obtained; and *Dar ul-Harb* – the abode of war where infidels lived outside the law of God and against whom holy war, *jihad*, must be waged until the universal idea became reality.

Such a world-view was bound to have significant impact on Ottoman relations with Europe. The difference in the theoretical political construct of Europe and the Ottoman Empire was reflected in their international systems: Europe's was mainly secular and state-centred, while the Ottoman was imperial and Islamic. The Ottoman system did not admit the principles of equality of sovereignty and diplomatic reciprocity or the notion of a law of nations as the basis for regulating relations among states. These latter elements formed the political matrix of the secular international society created by Europe in modern times, from which the Ottoman Empire excluded itself. Instead, successive Ottoman governments, infused with a deep sense of Muslim tradition, remained faithful to their Islamic political order with its inherent belief that whatever was western was potentially corrupting and must be shunned or struggled against. Despite its enduring presence in Europe, and despite the efforts of a few reforming sultans, the Ottoman Empire remained at the outset of the nineteenth century essentially a medieval Islamic state in objectives, organization, and mentality.

However, the barriers dividing the Ottoman *Dar ul-Islam* from the European *Dar ul-Harb* were not altogether impenetrable. Inspired before the eighteenth century by the confidence of supreme power, later driven by need generated of weakness, the *Sublime Porte* participated gradually in Europe's alliance system. This process compelled the sultans to align Ottoman diplomacy with Europe's system of international relations. The determinants of that system were, by the nineteenth century, shaped by Europe's colonial rivalries across the globe. The men of the *Sublime Porte* had to expand their vision and knowledge accordingly. In the new world created by the West, survival of *Dar ul-Islam* required fundamental changes in self-perceptions, attitudes, and ideas. A process of cultural synthesis (albeit imperfect) between the Empire and Europe – made inexorable by Europe's dominance in every material sphere of life – became integral to the unification of systems.[1]

Each stage of the long journey to that condition is instructive. For practical purposes, the journey can be said to begin in the latter part of the fifteenth century, the days of expanding Ottoman power when sultans considered themselves protectors of the entire Muslim world. Significant Ottoman involvement in Europe's affairs began when the warring city-states of Italy sought Ottoman aid against their enemies. Sultan Bayezit II, already hostile towards Venice for its rivalry in the eastern basin of the Mediterranean and in Albania and the Morea, sided with Milan and Naples against a Franco-Venetian alliance. In the ensuing sporadic war (1495–1502) the Empire attained the status of a major naval power with newly aroused interest in the western Mediterranean.

Bayezit's fierce successor, Selim I (1512–20), consolidated Ottoman authority in Anatolia and achieved significant conquests in the Arab heartland, adding Syria (with the holy city of Jerusalem), the Hejaz (with the holy cities of Mecca and Medina), and Egypt to the Ottoman domain. With these accomplishments Selim I completed the transformation of the Ottoman Empire from the last vestiges of a *Gazi* frontier state to a Muslim empire in the tradition of the Islamic caliphate.

Sultans Mehmet II, his son Bayezit II, and Selim I, by their conquests and by their legal, administrative, and military reforms, made possible the emergence of the Ottoman Empire as a world power which, under Suleyman I the Magnificent (1520–66), overarched and determined the course of events in Europe and the Mediterranean throughout the sixteenth century. Not only did the Empire decisively influence issues of international politics; it also played a role in two profoundly significant movements of the age, the Protestant Reformation and the Catholic Counter-Reformation, which together with the Renaissance transformed European society and led ultimately to the creation of an international society in Europe's image.

Suleyman conducted Ottoman foreign relations by a simple technique: supported by an invincible military machine, the sultan pronounced his will and got his way, or went to war and, with few exceptions, emerged victorious. Europe's view of the Ottomans as expressed by a contemporary was – not surprisingly: ' . . . the present terror of the world'.

The First Ottoman – European Agreement

Suleyman took advantage of Europe's strifes to enhance the territory and power of the Empire. The most conspicuous of these occasions, which led to what is usually considered the first Ottoman alliance with a

European power, was the struggle for the Holy Roman Emperorship between Charles I of Spain and Francis I of France.

Suleyman's desire to carry on the task of creating a world Muslim empire oriented his ambition westward against the European frontier. Dynastic rivalries, power struggles, and religious dissidence centring on the competing claims of Charles I of Spain and Francis I of France for the title of Holy Roman Emperor gave ample scope to the sultan's cause. The election of Charles as Holy Roman Emperor (Charles V) in March 1521 led to war with Francis. Suleyman forthwith marched against the gateway to central Europe; Belgrade fell to the janissaries in August 1521, and the Knights of St. John were expelled from Rhodes in the following year. In 1529 Suleyman made Hungary a vassal and beseiged the walls of Vienna. From 1531, the French worked to persuade the sultan to attack Italy and conclude an alliance with France, but Habsburg machinations in Hungary and Safavid aggressions in Kurdistan and Iraq diverted Suleyman. A campaign in Hungary in 1532 produced in June 1533 a settlement whereby Ferdinand I of Austria gave up temporarily his claims to Hungary and an Ottoman vassal was installed. The next two years were absorbed by naval exertions in the Mediterranean and an expedition against the Safavids. Following the capture of Francis I at Pavia in 1525, the French had approached Suleyman for assistance against the Holy Roman Emperor. The sultan encouraged the French and other enemies of Charles V, but without entering into an agreement. French envoys continued their efforts, going so far in 1534–5 as to join harem intrigues against the great grand vizir, Ibrahim Pasha. The French ambassador wanted a vizir who would incline the sultan's policies more against the Habsburgs, away from the Asian frontier, and towards an alliance with France. The execution of Ibrahim was not only the first step towards rule from the harem following Suleyman's reign, but also inaugurated the involvement of European ambassadors in Ottoman court intrigue. The contemporary naval struggle, which made adversaries of Hazruddin Barbarossa and Andrea Dorea, two of the most able naval commanders of the age, was significant because it finally convinced Suleyman to enter into an agreement with the French.

The French ambassador, Jean de la Forêt, concluded an agreement on 19 February 1536. The written document, called capitulations because it was organized by chapters, was a trade agreement modelled on concessions granted in the previous century to Venice and Genoa. France was granted commercial privileges and, interestingly, extraterritoriality. The military and political terms were secret and oral only. The idea was to attack Charles V in Italy: France from the north and the Ottomans from the south and east.

The military articles came to nothing, because Francis yielded to papal pressure and made peace the next year with Charles. Nevertheless, friendship and co-operation continued to characterize Ottoman-French relations. Henry II, who succeeded Francis I, maintained his predecessor's Ottoman policy. On Suleyman's part, France was the key to undermining the power of the Habsburgs. He encouraged the Lutherans and Calvinists with a view to promoting European disunity, which would weaken the Holy Roman Empire and papacy, and put an end to crusades against the Ottoman Empire. Suleyman's support of the Protestants was an important factor in preventing the Holy Roman Emperor from taking sterner action against the German Lutheran princes and Calvinists. The sultan's pressure forced the Habsburgs to make concessions to the Protestants and was a factor in granting official recognition to Protestantism.

The French-Ottoman treaty of 1536 bears closer scrutiny for the precedents it set, and for its impact on Ottoman-European relations:

(1) The agreement crystallized Ottoman objectives in Europe into a general policy of using political and military co-operation to create disunity and weakness. At the same time, it established the precedent for granting capitulations to gain political allies.
(2) The treaty set the direction of France's Near Eastern policies for the next three centuries and made the Empire one of the bases of French commercial prosperity.
(3) The treaty established an enlarged framework within which Europe's system of alliances operated.
(4) The principle of extraterritoriality established the future legal terms of reference for the resident European community in Istanbul and allowed the introduction of western principles of international law.
(5) The treaty served as the model for all subsequent capitulations. From the eighteenth century onwards, the capitulations became an important instrument for regulating Ottoman-European relations – increasingly in Europe's favour – and a primary means by which European political and economic influences were injected into the Empire.

The treaty illustrates basic conceptual differences between the Ottomans and Europeans. While France and the rest of Europe regarded the agreement of 1536 as a treaty of alliance, to the Ottomans it was no more than an *ahdname* (contract) granted unilaterally by the sultan. These *ahdnames* (or capitulations in European parlance) were freely given concessions in which the sultan retained the unilateral right to decide when the pledge of friendship was broken and the *ahdname* was void. Moreover, a capitulation given by one sultan became invalid at his death unless reconfirmed by his successor. The unilateral character of the agreement reflected the Muslim-Ottoman view of the inferiority of Christian Europe; it did not accord European rulers equality of sovereignty with the sultan.

For Suleyman the 1536 *ahdname* was not a formal alliance but rather a convenient instrument of policy, fashioned unilaterally, against the Habsburgs. It would have been contrary to Islamic law to have made a formal military alliance with an infidel. Suleyman did not in fact confirm the written *ahdname*, an indication that he did not give great weight to its commercial terms. Consequently, there are, technically, no capitulations of 1536. The first capitulations granted to France were those confirmed by Selim II in 1569.[2]

The Wave Crests

When the seventeenth century opened, the Ottoman Empire had reached the limits of its expansion. Its military prowess had abated, and its hegemony was challenged on the Asian frontier, in the Balkans and western Mediterranean, and in the north by the rising power of Muscovite Russia that was to become its most implacable foe. The ruling circle of the Empire had turned in on itself, yielding to conservative religious influences often shading into fanaticism. Corruption and self-serving factions destroyed the system that had produced the great leaders of the past, while the Ottoman sense of moral superiority stifled curiosity about Europe, its societies, governments, and religions.

Throughout most of the seventeenth century the Ottoman Empire was perceived, with waning justification, as a formidable power. Alliances, coalitions, and marriage pacts aimed at the Ottomans continued as features of European international relations. For its part, the *Sublime Porte* was willing, on a diminishing scale and with less effectiveness, to use agreements with European powers – e.g. the British capitulations granted at the end of the sixteenth century and those granted to the Dutch in the seventeenth – to further its political ends.

Early in the seventeenth century came the harbinger of the shift in the balance of power in favour of Europe. In 1595 yet another anti-Ottoman alliance was organized by the Habsburgs. This alliance overleapt the Empire to include Shah Abbas of Iran, forcing the Ottomans to fight a two-front war. The Treaty of Zsitva in 1606 marked the first time an Ottoman sultan did not dictate terms to a European adversary but instead accepted the demands of the Habsburg monarch.

European progress during the seventeenth century in technological and military spheres produced significant strategic advantages over the Ottomans. On the seas, Europe outstripped the Empire, which stuck with galleys while Europe switched to tall ships. On land, partly owing to the Thirty Years War, the Europeans developed more effective weaponry, tactics, and military organizations. The Ottomans relied on increasingly undisciplined and rebellious janissaries and feudal cavalry, who resisted even the mildest innovation. The Empire's strength was sapped by revolts in the provinces, corruption in the ruling circle, and unrelenting pressures from the Habsburgs.

The tradition-minded reforms of Murad IV (1609–40) and of Mehmet IV's (1642–93) grand vizir, Mehmet Koprulu, temporarily gave the *Sublime Porte* enough sting to take Crete (1669), to lay seige to Vienna (1683), and to seize control of the Black Sea littoral (1699). Although France joined the anti-Ottoman coalition that gave up Crete, the sultan renewed France's capitulations to maintain France's good-will against the Habsburgs. Louis XIV took advantage of the Ottoman attack on Vienna to march on the Spanish Netherlands.

Despite a few successes, the Empire had lost its military superiority by the end of the seventeenth century. Military decline was accompanied by loss of trade in the commerce of silk, spice, and woven cloth, especially after the establishment of the British East India Company. European ships sailed farther and faster while Dutch, French, and Portuguese competition worsened the situation. The Empire possessed few industries beyond the craftsman level. From the late seventeenth century to the nineteenth century, the Ottomans increasingly exported raw materials to Europe and imported manufactured products; this trade was mainly in the hands of Levantines.

From the last quarter of the sixteenth century onwards, because of the flow of specie from the New World, Ottoman currency was repeatedly debased. Inflation impoverished the classes that depended on fixed feudal incomes. Wars and rebellions in the seventeenth and eighteenth centuries forced the *Porte* to raise more revenues, while chronic inflation reduced their value by half; corruption, profiteering, and usury siphoned off much of what remained. The Empire never wholly recovered from this economic crisis, but its leaders remained as closed-minded to economic reform as they were to political and military innovation.

In this mentality the *Sublime Porte* entered the last decade of the seventeenth century once more engaged in hostilities with a European coalition. The culminating disaster was inflicted on the Ottoman armies at Zenta in 1697 by Prince Eugene of Savoy. Only the desire of

Leopold, the Habsburg ruler, to free himself to face an impending conflict with Louis XIV of France enabled the Ottomans to survive. The Treaty of Karlowitz (26 January 1699) established Europe's permanent superiority and signalled the Empire's retreat from Europe. After Karlowitz, the *Porte* was unable again to alter events significantly on the Continent.[3]

The Induction is Prepared

The most consequential phase of the process by which the Ottoman Empire entered the European state system began with Karlowitz and ran through the events that culminated in the Tri-Partite Treaty of 1799. In those ten decades, reforms were introduced and precedents were set which permanently altered Ottoman-European relations, particularly as regards the conduct of Ottoman diplomacy.

For the first decade of the eighteenth century, successive grand vizirs, but principally Chorlulu Ali Pasha and Koprulu Numan Pasha, turned their attention to domestic problems and laid down a strict policy of peace in foreign affairs. The small improvements achieved by their reforms made possible the Ottoman victory over the Russians at Pruth in 1711. Inspired by this success, the *Porte* attacked Venice and recaptured the province of Morea which had been lost in 1699. The Habsburgs intervened and Prince Eugene inflicted another stunning defeat on the Ottoman army. At Passarowitz in July 1718, although the Ottomans retained the Morea, the Austrians dictated terms entirely to their own advantage and extracted profitable capitulations which served as a model for such treaties later in the century.

Subsequently, the *Sublime Porte's* foreign policy in Europe became more and more reactive – a sign of the Empire's waning power – and the advantage of military, political, and economic initiative gradually but steadily passed to the European powers. The Ottomans did not fight another war in Europe until provoked by Russia in 1736. The Ottoman-Persian hostilities of the 1730s diminished still further the sultan's military prowess, leading to the revolt which dethroned Ahmed III (1703–30).

The long periods of relative peace – 1718 to 1736; 1739 to 1768; 1774 to 1787; 1792 to 1798 – which characterized Ottoman-European relations in the eighteenth century held various consequences for the Empire. The janissaries were weakened as an effective fighting force and bureaucrats slowly filled the higher departments of government. The *kuttab* (scribes, bureaucrats) dominated the offices of the grand vizir and *reis ul-kuttab*, or *reis efendi* (from the eighteenth century, foreign minister); the office of *reis efendi* became a common route to the grand vizirate. Under the influence of the *kuttab*, the state was transformed from a military to a bureaucratic empire, an empire which nevertheless remained feudal. The men of the pen, while only a little less traditionally minded than their peers, tended to be more pragmatic, more open to new ideas, and thus more inclined towards reform. Indeed, the feature that distinguished the *kuttab* from their peers, especially among the *ulema*, lay in their attitude towards the state: they embraced the idea of the primacy of the state and were willing to act for the recovery of the central authority of the sultan.

Such bureaucratic vizirs as Nevshehirli Damad Ibrahim Pasha (1718–30), Ragib Pasha (1757–63), and Halil Hamid Pasha (1782–5) undertook not very successful attempts at reform of Ottoman military, diplomatic, and economic institutions. The reform movement reached a sweeping climax in the last decade of the century under Selim III. Because Europe served as the model for change, the Empire gradually became more European-minded at the top of its ruling hierarchy. This fact had significant long-range impact on Ottoman-European relations. At the same time, 'Westernizing' policies produced intense, often violent, opposition from the *ulema*, the janissaries, and all whose vested interests were threatened by reform. As Europe's military pre-eminence was repeatedly confirmed – by the Austrians at Passarowitz in 1718, by the Russians at Kuchuk Kaynarca in 1774 and in the Crimea in 1783, and by the French in Egypt in 1798 – the new breed of bureaucratic leadership recognized that the Empire could no longer be defended without European allies. They increasingly counselled their sultans to rely on effective management of foreign affairs to protect their domains. The apparatus and conduct of diplomacy consequently received a full share of reform in the last decade of the eighteenth century.

But formidable obstacles inherited from the past made rapid change difficult. The Ottoman's concept of their state as an Asian-based land empire that grew by warfare against infidels remained entrenched, however myopic. On the other hand, in the preceding two centuries several European nations had acquired overseas dominions through exploration, colonization, and commercial expansion; had developed a secular, rational outlook which promoted scientific discovery; and had produced technological, industrial, and agricultural revolutions, together with a new, more flexible economic system – and all of these achievements were linked with the rise of strong centralized monarchies. These accomplishments were the bases of Europe's supremacy and the genesis of a modern international system of politics and economics. In the eighteenth century the Ottoman Empire, with its survival at stake, stood outside that network of colonies and alliances.

The second deterrent to change was also embedded in traditional Muslim political thought. Prior to the eighteenth century, Ottoman relations with Europe had been conducted under the guiding principle of the inadmissibility of equality between *Dar ul-Islam* and *Dar ul-Harb*. Because *jihad* was the only legal basis for relations with infidels, treaties with European powers, in theory, could be neither religiously nor judicially valid. The only other sanctioned state of relations was a provisional truce, not to last longer than ten years. Some Muslim jurists recognized an intermediate condition, that of non-Islamic tributary states with whom relations were conducted on a contractual basis which applied to a broad range of dealings.

When military impotence forced the sultans to replace *jihad* with diplomacy and commerce as the basis of relations with Europe, jurists reinterpreted the concept of *jihad* to permit a *de facto* (even legal) state of peace – i.e., a truce could be renewed as often as interests required. Other concepts such as *maslaha* – acts for the good of the Muslim community – were also invoked. But these techniques of change were applied with difficulty and not always successfully.

Because the Ottomans failed in the eighteenth century to adapt their Muslim rationale of foreign relations to the political and economic realities of the age, they sacrificed a large measure of control over the forces which were to shape their destiny. Given Europe's ascendancy, particularly that of Russia, and the Empire's infirmity (the last major campaign the Ottomans were to win in Europe without an ally was against the Austrians in 1738–9), the Ottomans became dependent for survival on Europe's system of international relations. In the eighteenth century the determinants of the European balance of power were located increasingly beyond the confines of Europe, in the Western Hemisphere and Indian sub-continent, where the rivalry between England and France unleashed political and economic forces well beyond the ken or control of the *Sublime Porte*.

Survival on these terms demanded changes in eighteenth-century Ottoman diplomacy. There were more frequent special Ottoman diplomatic missions to European capitals and a large increase in the number of European resident envoys and consular representatives in Istanbul and other areas of the Empire. The number of European travellers and merchants in Ottoman territories increased as a result of capitulations which gave them greater freedom of action and movement.

The Empire's economic relations with Europe also underwent a profound change in the eighteenth century. The treaties of capitulation were no longer an indulgence granted by a sultan as an expression of his will. From 1718 onward, the European powers dictated the terms of capitulation and often outrageously abused the concessions. The Empire became an important object of commercial exploitation to the European powers, much of it centred on French-Russian rivalry in the Black Sea. These factors not only defined the *Porte's* relations with these two powers but, by way of the web of alliances, with other European powers as well.

Stages of Integration

Although the Empire's statesmen might still harbour feelings of Muslim supremacy, they were compelled by circumstances to steer a course towards integration with Europe's state system and foreign relations. The stages of this movement were highlighted by the acceptance of such European principles as equality of sovereignty and reciprocity of relations, the adoption of European diplomatic usages and communications, and the recognition of points of western international law such as extraterritoriality and the Law of Nations. All of these 'concessions' paved the way for the ultimate acceptance of alliances with Christian powers of the West.

These developments occurred sometimes as deliberate initiatives of policy, sometimes as the result of coercion by a European power, and sometimes as the result of the exigencies of the moment without awareness of the precedents being set. But above all, these changes in the conduct of Ottoman diplomacy came about without accompanying modifications in the relevant institutions of government. The organization of the bureaucratic infrastructure, the systems of recruitment and training so vital to the implementation of foreign policy, hardly altered in the eighteenth century, not even in response to Selim III's reforming efforts, which were feeble and ineffectual in this sphere.

The route by which the Ottomans entered the European alliance system is clearly marked out in the eighteenth century. After mid-century, the *Sublime Porte* reluctantly engaged in a series of disastrous hostilities with Russia, Austria, and France which accelerated the process.

Alarmed by the aggressive expansionist policies of Catherine the Great and urged on by the French, Sultan Mustafa III (1757–74) went to war in October 1768 to secure the Russian evacuation of Poland and the relief of Catherine's pressure on the Crimea. The war, an unmitigated calamity for the Ottomans, ended in an equally ruinous treaty signed at Kuchuk Kaynarca on 21 July 1774. The sultan gained nothing; he had to pay a 7.5 million *akcha* indemnity out of a destitute treasury, release the Crimea from its vassalship to the Empire thus losing a buffer against Russia, and give up territory that enabled St. Petersburg to dominate the Black Sea and penetrate the Balkans. He had to allow the Russians to build an Orthodox church in Istanbul, which was later interpreted by the czars as the right to intervene to protect Orthodox Christians in the Empire. The strategic advantage which Kuchuk Kaynarca gave Russia frightened the Austrians, French, British, and Prussians. In subsequent political manoeuvring to counter Russia's gains (ironically, Prussia and Austria compensated themselves with Polish territory), the Ottoman Empire was a pivotal factor. The British and the French particularly wanted to shore up the tottering Muslim empire as a bulwark against further Russian expansion. Thus, unwittingly, the Ottoman Empire became more enmeshed in Europe's power politics.

Catherine's next *démarche* came in April 1783. Taking advantage of English-French hostilities during the American War of Independence, Catherine annexed the Crimea. Sultan Abdulhamid I (1725–82), lacking a powerful European ally and faced with a janissary revolt, had to acquiesce. This success only stimulated Catherine's ambitions in Europe. In a secret agreement with the Austrian empire – which rewarded other powers for their co-operation – Catherine spelled out her design for the revival of a Byzantine Empire to include Istanbul, northern and western Greece, and Bulgaria, to be ruled by her grandson Constantine. Even France, the Ottoman Empire's chief advocate on the Continent, was tempted by the reward of Syria and Egypt, which would give French merchants an armlock on the Levant trade.

Excluded, England and Prussia exhorted the sultan to resist Russian expansion. These urgings elicited a responsive chord from the war party of the *Sublime Porte*. Already alarmed by the Crimean annexation and Russia's growing strength on the Black Sea, the war party, led by Grand Vizir Koca Yusuf Pasha, used Catherine's grandiose scheme to lever the sultan into a declaration of war on 14 August 1787.

Although the Ottoman forces made a better showing in this war, they were routed once more by the imperial armies of Russia and Austria: Istanbul stood exposed. However, events in Europe during 1789 and 1790 stayed the sultan's enemies. Swedish and Prussian moves in Finland and Poland diverted Catherine, uprisings in Hungary and the Netherlands pulled off Joseph II, and the French Revolution shook all the major powers. The new sultan, Selim III (1789–1807), tried to gain the assistance of Prussia and Sweden but to no avail; he was obliged to negotiate the Treaty of Jassy, signed on 8 January 1792.

Selim had to acknowledge the annexation of the Crimea and acquiesce in Russia's domination of the Principalities (Moldavia and

Wallachia) and the Black Sea; but he did win survival for the Empire and vital time for military and diplomatic reform. Selim's reforms were pursued until the wars of the French Revolution spilled over into his Empire with the invasion of Egypt in 1798. The French expedition led to the Tri-Partite Treaty of 1799 – the culmination of a century-long journey into the European network of alliances.[4]

The Forces of Change

Although established Islamic values were challenged, the traditional Muslim rationale of state continued to inspire loyalty, and its proponents were able to organize vigorous opposition to westernizing reforms. Nevertheless, the forces of change were by no means negligible. During the eighteenth century, the bonds of tradition were permanently loosened, the old institutions were shaken to their foundations, and the idea of reform itself acquired an inexorable momentum within Ottoman governing circles. One of the most significant changes was a more favourable attitude towards European civilization by a few influential Ottomans. This new outlook, which did not concede superiority to western values, was manifest in the sultan's court from the time of Ahmed III's reign (1703–30), the so-called Tulip Era. As European travellers in the Empire became more common, as the European communities burgeoned, and as, at the same time, the number of special Ottoman missions to the capitals of Europe increased, westward-looking Ottoman officials – small in number but influential – led the Empire, often unwittingly, into Europe's international system.

Since the Ottoman Empire had no permanent diplomatic representation in Europe, Europe brought its system to the *Sublime Porte*. Resident European envoys in Istanbul, most of whom were conversant with the intricacies of western diplomacy and the continental alignments of power, insisted on instructing the *Porte* in the niceties of European protocol. The abler among them succeeded in making the Ottomans the instrument of their sovereign's foreign policy in eastern Europe.

By the eighteenth century, the Ottoman authorities could no longer act unilaterally. With increasing frequency throughout the eighteenth century the European representatives in Istanbul were consulted by the *Porte*, and as a consequence came to play a role in the formulation of Ottoman foreign policy. The *Porte*, prevented by Ottoman tradition from developing adequate diplomatic communications with western capitals, had to turn to the European diplomats in Istanbul to find out what was happening. It was a rare occasion when the information supplied was not tailored to the interests of the nation whose envoy was consulted. Without a regular courier service of its own, the *Porte* made use of the couriers of European powers – with obvious consequences.

The principle of the inadmissibility of equality between *Dar ul-Islam* and *Dar ul-Harb* lost its validity the first time the sultan was forced to negotiate rather than dictate a treaty with a European power (at Zsitva in 1606). But Ottoman power remained such in the seventeenth century that the experience had little impact. Only in the eighteenth century, under the guns of the Habsburgs and Romanovs, was the *Sublime Porte* made to behave in accordance with the European principle of the equality of sovereignty.

One of the ways whereby the *Porte* demonstrated abandonment of its notion of the inferiority of Europe was in the use of diplomatic mediation. In the course of the eighteenth century, there were few treaties arranged between the Ottoman Empire and its enemies that were not either negotiated through the mediation of other powers or accompanied by offers of mediation. English and Dutch services were welcomed at Passarowitz, and France mediated at Karlowitz and later, more significantly, at Belgrade. In 1745, the *Porte* caused a mild sensation among European diplomats by offering to mediate the War of the Austrian Succession.

By deliberately seeking mediation and by attempting itself to assume the role of mediator, the *Porte* not only forsook a traditional religious principle, it allowed the Empire to be drawn further into the orbit of European diplomacy. As mediator, Louis XV had pledged to guarantee whatever treaty the Ottomans negotiated at Belgrade – so long as the terms worked in favour of France's interests, to be sure. By this surety, the Ottoman Empire came formally under the protection of a Christian power.

The Capitulations

No area of Ottoman-European relations is more significant or more instructive of the steps by which the *Sublime Porte* entered the European alliance system than the treaties of capitulation. These agreements, particularly those made in the eighteenth century, involved far more than commercial exchange. They changed the conduct of Ottoman diplomacy; they regulated political relations between the Empire and Europe and gave direction to rivalries among the European powers; and they influenced the economic and social structure of the Ottoman Empire. It can even be argued that the capitulations laid the foundation for Ottoman-European relations down to the First World War.

In the eighteenth century the primary Ottoman motives were the need to acquire political allies in Europe, the need to obtain scarce goods (such as cloth, tin, steel, etc.), and the need to increase the customs revenues which were the main source of hard currency. Although until the last decade of the eighteenth century the Ottomans practised non-reciprocal, unilateral diplomacy in political relations with Europe, they did invoke the principle of reciprocity in the capitulations. Reciprocal advantages were expected by the sultan in return for the concessions; until the eighteenth century, if these benefits failed to materialize the sultan, could abrogate the treaty.

The principle of reciprocity extended to the high seas. Indeed, it is among capitulatory articles pertaining to relations at sea that reciprocity is most apparent. The Ottomans regarded the Aegean, the Black Sea, the Dardanelles, the Red Sea, and the Strait of Otranto as being part of *Dar ul-Islam*. Any mutual protection granted under the capitulations was extended to those waters, and citizens of capitulatory powers could invoke *aman* (security) when threatened by a Muslim ship. Earlier, when the Barbary corsairs came under Ottoman suzerainty, articles were added to the capitulations extending guarantees to the western Mediterranean.

In the course of the eighteenth century, the European capitulatory powers controlled the degree and application of reciprocity. One of the causes cited by the *Porte* for the renewal of hostilities with Russia in 1787 was that power's failure to carry out the reciprocal clauses of the Capitulation of 1783. Reciprocity became more important to the Ottomans in their weakness than it was in their time of greatness. Given the Empire's subordination to Europe and the linkage of political with economic factors in the capitulations, it was a short inevitable step to the *Porte's* adoption of full diplomatic reciprocity by the end of the eighteenth century.

Extraterritoriality, based on European personal law, also came to the Ottomans by way of the capitulations. At first, Ottoman authorities treated resident ambassadors at the *Porte* as little more than consuls and regarded them as representatives of their *millet*s (a legally recognized religious community, usually non-Muslim). The parent governments and merchant companies of the envoys directed the internal organization of the resident foreign colonies through the issuance of detailed regulations administered by ambassadors and consuls. During the seventeenth and eighteenth centuries the European governments imposed on the *Porte* European formulas regarding the status of consuls, with nearly the same range of diplomatic privileges and immunities for consular officials as for ambassadors. All ambassadors and consuls were issued *berats* (patents) which empowered them to administer the commercial, personal, and legal affairs of their *millets*. In litigation involving foreign residents, the laws and customs of the parent state were applied. Envoys could invoke the assistance of Ottoman authorities in the execution of their responsibilities; hence the need for the issuance of a *berat*.

During the seventeenth and eighteenth centuries, by extension of the principle of extraterritoriality, the European powers extracted for their merchants many privileges pertaining to such matters as slavery, search and seizure, fugitives, and inheritance; such additional concessions were codified as specific articles in the capitulations. These concessions, together with the endless abuses which by threat of force were embodied in new articles, caused the capitulations by the end of the eighteenth century to work almost entirely in favour of the Europeans. Furthermore, the fierce competition among the European powers for the Levant trade in the seventeenth and eighteenth centuries not only led to a significant increase in the number of capitulatory states – at least six in the eighteenth century alone – but as well to the appearance of the 'most favoured nation' clause in all the treaties.

Towards the end of the seventeenth century, the capitulations entered a new political phase which had a marked effect on Ottoman-European relations in the eighteenth century. From 1683 onward, capitulatory privileges were granted with the undisguised aim of gaining political assistance in reciprocation. For this reason the capitulations serve as a barometer for the political and economic standing of a particular state at the *Sublime Porte*.

If in the eighteenth century the capitulations were pivotal in the Empire's relations with Europe, they were also important in producing a new era of Ottoman diplomacy. The imposition of European diplomatic concepts and practices, the multiplying links with the West's system of international politics, the constant necessity of having to negotiate the Empire's survival – all factors involved in the capitulation treaties – moved the *Sublime Porte* inexorably away from traditional Islamic unilateralism toward the adoption of a European-style reciprocity. Moreover, the continued success of the capitulatory states in extracting and exploiting the new commercial and political privileges resulted in transforming the Ottoman Empire into a virtual open and free market for Europe. This occurred at the time when the European industrial revolution was requiring new outlets for its manufactures. A few decades into the nineteenth century, the Empire's economic subjugation to Europe was well-nigh complete.

Other Imperatives

Other forces simultaneously at work impelled the *Sublime Porte* towards reciprocity in foreign relations and entry into Europe's alliance system. The overriding factors were the Empire's military incapacity, the growth of Russian power, and the struggle among European powers for supremacy on the Continent, of which the colonial wars were a crucial dimension. All these external issues, which became critical after 1740, had a vital bearing on the position of the Ottoman Empire as a European power and constituted a threat to its existence. From 1740 to 1763 the salient political questions in Europe were whether Austria or Prussia would dominate in Germany; whether Russia would prevail in the Black Sea region, in Poland, and in the Balkans at the expense of both the Ottomans and the Habsburgs; and whether France or England would rule in North America and India. This latter conflict affected the Ottomans because, if France triumphed, she would be in a stronger position to check Russian expansion in the Near East by diplomacy and by the maintenance of the Ottoman Empire.

Furthermore, French trade with the Empire was the most extensive in Europe. England, though considered a friendly nation, looked on events in the Near East as of lesser importance. Until Bonaparte's thrust into Egypt in 1798, the British pursued an ambiguous Mediterranean policy and tended to side with Russia for reasons of trade and rivalry with France. Complicating the picture for the Ottomans was the 'Diplomatic Revolution' of 1756 which joined France in alliance with Austria, and England with Prussia. Since the Russian-Austrian alliance of 1726 was operative, though barely, France was brought technically into co-operation with Russia. This shuffle of alignments, together with England's decisive victory over France in 1763 and her subsequent involvement in the American War of Independence, laid the basis for the *Porte's* isolation at the time of Kuchuk Kaynarca and the annexation of the Crimea.

Another tentative step during Selim III's reign drew the Ottoman government a little closer to the European bilateral system of diplomacy. Increasing reference was made by the Ottomans to international law in their dealings with the Europeans. For example, in 1799 the grand vizir informed Selim III that a squadron of Russian warships had entered the Straits unannounced. The Sultan commented:

> My vizir, the *reis efendi* ought to take this opportunity to remind the Russian interpreter in an amicable way of the international rules of conduct and of the reasons for the clauses in the treaty [with Russia] governing this matter. It is

contrary to the canons of international law that a war fleet should enter a foreign port without prior notification and without specifying the number of vessels. This act of the Russians causes agitation among ill-intentioned persons. They look on such acts as insults to our state.

These early references to international law, although used only to suit Ottoman convenience, are an important indication that the Islamic rationale of Ottoman diplomacy was being breached by western thought.

Another new element entered the workings of Ottoman diplomacy in Selim's reign – the element of public opinion. The idea of deferring to public opinion was, for Ottomans of the period, decidedly a modern one. True, public opinion was still rudimentary, uninformed, and confined mainly to the capital and a few of the larger provincial cities. But it warrants brief attention because Ottoman ministers were beginning to make use of popular feeling in devising their policies. In 1804, when the *Porte* came to fear that France might declare war over the sultan's refusal to recognize Bonaparte's emperorship, the *reis efendi* tried to persuade the Russian ambassador to withdraw his objections to recognition, arguing,

Why should the recognition of Bonaparte's title dissolve the treaty [of 1799]? The only circumstances in which the Ottoman government can go to war would be if the security and the territorial integrity of the Empire are threatened. How can it be explained to the public that the government has gone to war for the sake of a treaty? How can the people be told they will have to fight a war for the sake of one simple word [emperor]?

While the *reis*'s statement that the *Porte* could not fight to preserve a treaty agreement is an interesting example of how rapidly the Ottomans were becoming sophisticated in the workings of the European alliance system, the real point is that the only opinions that formerly counted were those of the sultan, the janissaries, and the *ulema*. That public opinion was even referred to was an indication of changes that were taking place, and of changes that were on the way.[5]

To Change or to Perish

Throughout the eighteenth century many a caveat had been sounded at the *Porte* by concerned Ottoman statesmen who saw that the Empire had to alter its policies or perish. Shortly after Kuchuk Kaynarca, this view was cogently argued by Ahmed Resmi who, as *sedaret kethudasi* (deputy of the grand vizir) was one of the negotiators of the treaty. He criticized the traditionalist belief that Islam was destined to overcome

Christianity irrespective of the decrepitude of Ottoman armies and armaments. He emphasized that Ottoman power was gone, that the traditional posture was ill-suited to meet the threat of Russian ascendancy. He urged the *Porte* to pursue a policy of peace towards the Europeans and seek out allies among them, an exercise in which Ottoman authorities now had some experience.

The real breakthrough came after the annexation of the Crimea and the accession of Selim III. The seizure of the Crimea, the first piece of Islamic territory taken by a Christian power, enraged the Muslim sentiments of many Ottomans. But, without an ally, the *Porte* simply was in no position to engage the Russians without risking total destruction. This experience starkly revealed to Ottoman authorities the need for European allies. Selim came to the sultanate in 1789 determined to seek alliances. While still heir apparent he had corresponded with Louis XV expressing his desire for a formal connection with France. At his succession, the Empire was at war with Russia and Austria. When Gustavus III of Sweden, who had attacked Russia in 1789, proposed a pact, Selim reacted quickly by signing an alliance and subsidy treaty in July 1789. But in July 1790, the Swedes, contrary to their treaty with the *Porte*, made a unilateral peace with Russia on the basis of the *status quo ante* in the Baltic, without reference to the Ottomans. Selim, unschooled in the *real-politik* of European affairs, complained to his vizir, 'This is a harmful situation. . . . Infidels are so unreliable.'

Undaunted, in January 1791 Selim embarked on his second venture into the European alliance system by accepting a defensive agreement initiated by Prussia. Prussia agreed to join hostilities as an ally against Russia and Austria in the spring of 1791 and to restore the Crimea and all other territories lost in the war by the Ottomans. Prussia then commenced a series of complex political manoeuvres, designed primarily to advance her own interests, by which in conjunction with the British and the Dutch she mediated peace treaties between the Ottomans and the Austrians at Sistovo in August 1791, and the Ottomans and the Russians at Jassy in January 1792. In both instances, the situation was restored to the *status quo ante*. While the Prussian initiative, combined with pressures from events in France, did bring peace, the Ottomans were disappointed, since Prussia did not restore the Crimea.

The *Sublime Porte* benefited little from these sallies into the European alliance system. On the contrary, the experience seemed to bear out the criticisms and warnings of Selim's conservative foes. The failure of the Swedish and Prussian alliances caused the *Porte* to be highly sceptical of inducements offered by European powers who subsequently tried to persuade the Ottomans to join one of their warring camps. After 1792, disillusion and absorption in domestic affairs caused the Ottoman government to revert to the old policy of non-involvement in Europe. Selim had in the meantime launched his reform campaign, the most significant feature concerning diplomacy being the establishment of permanent Ottoman embassies in Paris, London, Vienna, and Berlin.

De Facto Induction

When ultimately the *Porte* was driven by the French invasion of Egypt into the defensive Tri-Partite Alliance with Britain and Russia in January 1799, it was a significant departure from precedent. The most conspicuous attribute of Ottoman-Russian relations over the previous 300 years had been deep-seated mutual hostility. Conversely, France was the Empire's oldest European friend. In allying the sultan and the tsar against France, the treaty constituted a second eighteenth-century 'Diplomatic Revolution'.

Another unprecedented feature was the extent to which the contracting parties pledged mutual assistance. Both the Russians and the British warranted more to the Ottoman Empire than ever before, though less than in previous Continental alignments. However, the alliance was for the Ottoman Empire without parallel. The *Sublime Porte* not only broke sharply with past policies but also contravened Islamic rules of international relations laid down by the *sharia* (religious law). The sultan promised to contribute the Empire's resources to meet all the demands of his partners. He consented to the free passage of Russian warships through the Straits (on a 'this time only' basis, to be sure, but nevertheless a precedent not lost on the Russians). He agreed, if necessary, to the stationing of large numbers of Russian troops on Ottoman soil – a prospect which struck most members of the government with horror.

These aspects set the pact apart from earlier alliances, which had complied with the *sharia* by being far more circumspect in their terms and by adhering to the rule that such pacts endure only for the period of hostilities. This treaty was to last for eight years and the Ottomans honoured their agreement, albeit reluctantly, until two months prior to the date of expiration. By committing itself to a treaty of such long duration, well beyond the anticipated requirements of the campaign in Egypt, the *Porte* effectively joined the Continental alliance against France. It thereby became a *de facto* member – the first and only non-Western member – of the European network of alliances against Napoleon.

Towards Formal Induction

With this act, the *Porte* set Ottoman diplomacy on course towards the years 1840 and 1856 when, by treaty, the Empire was formally inducted into the West's state system. The instrument which charted the way was the Alliance of 1799.

After the Tri-Partite Treaty, the *Sublime Porte* was never again so bereft of allies or so isolated politically as at the time of the Crimean annexation. Nor, until its demise in 1923, was the Empire without a formal political connection on the Continent. Throughout the nineteenth century, alliance within one or another of Europe's camps was integral to the *Porte's* strategies for survival; the capitulations were a constant binding factor in alliance formulas.

The wars of the eighteenth century revealed to all but the most blinkered Ottoman authorities and notables that the Empire was incapable of defending itself without substantial foreign assistance. The paraphernalia of Ottoman diplomacy had few strong features to redeem its inherent weakness, and the military was too corrupt and weak to be effectual. Hence the only source of effective support was Europe. But the sultans learned painfully that to prevent such alliances from becoming liabilities, they and their ministers had to be thoroughly schooled in European politics.

Survival demanded comprehensive reforms with profound changes in the traditional bases of Ottoman statecraft. The Ottoman reform movement generated by Selim III did not lose political momentum until Abdulhamid II abrogated the first Ottoman constitution in 1877. Throughout the process, European ideas, institutions, and systems served as the model for change. In a brief span of time the upper social and political levels of the Empire were Europeanized. Even after Abdulhamid II ended political reforms, modernization continued in education, technology, and communications. When, around the middle of the nineteenth century, bureaucracy and education became Europeanized in language, ideas, and methods, the last obstacles to the Empire's entry into Europe's state system fell.

However, the journey began inauspiciously. The French had successfully invaded Egypt and Syria as far as Acre. Selim's European and Asian provinces were wracked by insurrection, sedition, and separatist movements. The Serbs mounted a serious revolt (1803–5). There were times when the sultan's effective authority hardly extended ten miles beyond his capital. The overriding necessity was to expel the French from Egypt and Syria, but Ottoman ministers were split into pro-British and pro-French factions. The former argued for fulfilment of the war aims laid down in the 1799 treaty, the latter wanted an immediate negotiated end to hostilities, restoration of amity with France, and termination of the alliance with Russia.

Selim himself wanted to slip Russia's embrace and adopt a posture of neutrality in Europe's wars. The tsar gave him ample cause for mistrust. Russia exercised the terms of the alliance to bolster its fleet in the eastern Mediterranean and tighten its protectorate over the Ionian Islands. At the same time, the tsar's agents fanned the flames of the Serbian revolt and gave material assistance to the rebels. Because the Empire would be vulnerable to both the French and the Russians without the protection of the British, Selim could not risk losing British support by rupturing relations with St. Petersburg. At England's insistence, he abided by the terms of the Tri-Partite Treaty and strove to steer a delicate course of balance among friends and foes alike.

The exigencies of war and diplomacy on the Continent once more rescued the sultan. Hostilities ended, and the French evacuation of Egypt and Syria was gained by the Peace of Amiens in June 1802. The British and Russian envoys negotiated terms on behalf of the *Sublime Porte*. Tallyrand won by diplomacy much of what Bonaparte had hoped to give France by war – particularly access for French merchants to the Black Sea. Not only was friendship between France and the Empire restored, but mutual assistance in the event of war was pledged.

This was another complicated step into Europe's alliance network. Since it was apparent (but not to the French party in the *divan*) that Amiens by no means ended the hostility between France and the British-led Continental coalition, and since the British and Russian envoys at the *Porte* insisted that the sultan reaffirm his Tri-Partite Treaty commitments, Selim could hardly avoid entanglement. Neutrality was beyond his reach.

A precipitating issue was not long in coming. Bonaparte strenuously invoked the friendship clauses of Amiens and, promising military support against Russia, demanded that Selim formally recognize his title as emperor. This controversy dominated Ottoman-European relations in 1804–5. In December 1805, when Napoleon broke off relations with the *Sublime Porte*, Selim was no longer able to resist the pressures of the British, Russians, and Austrians; he reaffirmed the Russian alliance and agreed to cooperate with the Coalition in its renewed war with France. However, Bonaparte's victories over the Austrians and Russians at the end of 1805 shifted Selim back into the French camp; he recognized Napoleon as emperor in February 1806.

These events set the Empire in the crossfire of Europe's wars and severed yet another bond with traditional Muslim practice. By October

1806 Russia had declared war on the Ottomans. England weighed in on the side of the tsar and sent a fleet to blockade Istanbul in early 1807. Selim now took the initiative in soliciting a formal military alliance with France for the defence of the Ottoman Empire.

This was an unprecedented act beyond the strictures of traditional Islamic international relations, but a precedent was set that became normal practice in the course of the nineteenth century. The sultan proposed placing the survival of the Empire under the protection of a European power in a bilateral treaty drawn up in accordance with the system of European international law and diplomacy. Unilateral diplomacy, inequality of sovereignty, and *jihad* as the basis for Ottoman-European relations had lost all practical validity. This act of realism by a sultan, who was himself a devout Muslim and a man of his era, was the logical extension of the treaty of 1799.

Selim III's reforms and tradition-shattering policies ultimately cost him his throne, his programme, and his life. Selim, buoyed by French help (but not the treaty he requested), drove the British fleet from the Straits and prepared to turn on the Russians. At this juncture (May 1807) his enemies overthrew him, girded Mustafa IV with the sword of Osman, and routed the reform party from the *Sublime Porte*. The British sailed from Istanbul to Egypt where they tried to re-establish Mamluk power but were foiled by Muhammed Ali in September 1807. Meanwhile, Bonaparte and Tsar Alexander reached an agreement at Tilsit in July 1807 whereby Napoleon would pressure the sultan to settle with Russia in return for the tsar's mediation of peace between Britain and France. If the new sultan refused, France would join forces with Russia against the Ottoman Empire. The sultan readily agreed, but the tsar, hoping to make his grip on the Principalities permanent, delayed signing a peace treaty until 1812. Then Bonaparte's preparations for invading Russia stimulated an eight-month negotiation with the new sultan Mahmud II, mediated by young Stratford Canning, the British chargé d'affaires in Istanbul. The Treaty of Bucharest, May 1812, essentially restored the *status quo ante bellum*, but left Serbia autonomous and Bessarabia as the only territorial acquisition for Russia. For the Ottomans, the most important gain was respite. Mahmud II, having resided with the deposed Selim for a year in the palace quarters known as the 'Cage', had been tutored by the latter in ideas of reform. He used the respite to consolidate his power and lay the basis for an era of change which transformed the Empire, in its organization and apparatus of government, into a secular European-style state.[6]

The Final Stage

The final phase of what had been part uncharted drift, part navigated transit, led the Empire inexorably into the vortex of Europe's international political and social systems. Certain landfalls mark the way: Muhammad Ali's challenge (1823–33) and the Treaty of Hunkyar Iskelesi; the Hatti Sherif Gulhane (1839); and the Convention of 1840 and the Treaty of Paris of 1856.

Roused by the ferment of nationalist ideas produced by the French Revolution and spurred on by Russian agents, a new generation of Greeks, led by a group that called itself the Society of Friends, precipitated a revolt in March 1821 to create an independent Greece. The movement escaped complete suppression for three years. Restiveness among the public and janissaries motivated Mahmud II to call on the assistance of Muhammad Ali, whose popularity in Istanbul was high owing to his success against the Wahhabis in Upper Egypt and Arabia. In return for a promise of the governorates of the Morea and Crete, Muhammad Ali sent a force commanded by his son Ibrahim Pasha which, in swift, devastating campaigns in 1825–6, seemed to have overwhelmed the revolt.

At about the same time, in June 1826, Sultan Mahmud responded to yet another janissary rebellion by destroying the corps and the power of its *ulema* allies. Within a month the janissary corps ceased to exist. With the janissaries disappeared a major barrier to reform. The sultans of the nineteenth century gathered into their hands more personal power and centralized authority than even the greatest of their predecessors – but too late to save the Empire.

Tsar Nicholas, fearing the presence of Muhammad Ali in the Morea more than the sultan, issued an ultimatum to Mahmud in March 1826. So interwoven had the Empire become with the post-Napoleonic European balance of power that this act precipitated a series of hostilities and political manoeuvres which severely tested the Concert of Europe, brought the Ottoman Empire to the brink of extinction, and then, in 1840, caused the European Concert Powers unwittingly to induct the Ottoman Empire formally into the European state system. In the course of the next four years, an allied fleet of British, French, and Russian warships blew the combined Ottoman/Egyptian navies out of the water at Navarino (20 October 1827); Muhammad Ali was forced out of Greece and Crete (October 1828); Russia gained the right of protection over Serbia, Greece, and the Principalities, and received the same capitulatory rights as the other European nations (1827); Greece won full independence (1830); and France conquered Algeria (1830).

Reeling from these events, Mahmud II was confronted in 1831 by a demand from Muhammad Ali that he be given Syria in compensation for his losses in Greece. Muhammad Ali's dynastic ambitions had already aroused the ire of the sultan, who ordered the governor of Syria to mount a campaign against Egypt. Ibrahim Pasha quickly dispatched the sultan's forces, completing the conquest of Syria by June 1832. When Mahmud organized another assault on the Egyptian forces, Ibrahim moved into Konya and inflicted a defeat on the imperial army which made possible the conquest of Anatolia and deposition of the sultan. By February 1833 Ibrahim was preparing to make winter camp in Bursa, only fifty miles from Istanbul.

Mahmud's pleas for help from the British and French produced nothing but advice intended to serve their interests and keep Mahmud from turning to the tsar – which is exactly what Mahmud did. Mahmud allowed the Russians to station a fleet before Istanbul and to post troops across from the capital in Anatolia at Hunkyar Iskelesi. To the outrage of the *ulema* and citizenry, other Russian troops were encamped just outside Istanbul itself. Moreover, following Selim III's precedent, Mahmud requested a defensive alliance with Russia against Muhammad Ali.

Having to depend on Russia for survival without the counterweight of British and French support, Mahmud was forced to pay a high price to ransom the Empire. In March 1833 he confirmed Muhammad Ali in the governorship of Crete as well as Egypt. To Ibrahim Pasha he accorded the governorship of Syria and Jeddah in Arabia, after which Ibrahim evacuated Anatolia.

In July 1833 it was the turn of the tsar. Mahmud agreed to the Treaty of Defensive Alliance of Hunkyar Iskelesi by which, if the territories of either signatory were attacked during the next eight years, each would go to the aid of the other. He confirmed the Treaty of Edirne (14 September 1829) which gave Russia rights of protection in Serbia, Greece, and the Principalities. In a secret article, the *Sublime Porte* was exempted from military stipulations if the sultan would close the Straits to all foreign naval vessels in time of war. The French and British, realizing the tsar's purpose was to exempt Russian ships from restrictions and prevent naval attacks against his Black Sea installations by any European international enemies, strenuously objected (August 1833).

Until the end of the decade the British and French expended considerable diplomatic energy on reversing Hunkyar Iskelesi and reducing the influence of Russia in the Ottoman Empire. Matters came to a head in 1839–40. Mahmud II and Muhammad Ali were once more at war and a significant shift occurred in the Continent's alliance system. France, convinced that the Empire's demise was at hand, abandoned its traditional support of the *Sublime Porte* and backed Muhammad Ali, precipitating counter-moves by Britain. Lord Palmerston, the British Foreign Minister, perceived that a debilitated Ottoman Empire dependent on Britain was preferable to an independent-minded powerful Muhammad Ali, attached to France and in control of a vital link in the route to India. He sought to preserve the Ottoman Empire by internationalizing responsibility for maintaining its territorial integrity. In a clever two-step manoeuvre, Palmerston concluded an agreement in December 1839 with Tsar Nicholas I, who gave up the Treaty of Hunkyar Iskelesi in return for joint action by the powers to end Ottoman-Egyptian hostilities. For the tsar, *rapprochement* with Britain prevented France from gaining in the Levant, split the British-French alliance, and curtailed the threat to long-range Russian interests from Muhammad Ali. For Palmerston, in addition to dissolving Hunkyar Iskelesi and thwarting French ambitions, the agreement kept Russia and France from making common cause against the British and assured the survival of the Ottoman Empire.

This arrangement was followed by a formal convention signed by Britain, Russia, Austria, and Prussia on 15 July 1840, which assured the sultan the protection of the signatory powers against his viceroy in Egypt. The new sultan, Abdulmecid I, agreed to close the Straits to the warships of belligerent nations with which the Empire was not itself at war. Muhammad Ali was given hereditary possession of Egypt and control of southern Syria for his lifetime provided he recognize the suzerainty of the sultan and apply the laws of the Ottoman Empire in his domain. After a revolt forced Muhammad Ali out of Syria, he accepted hereditary rule in Egypt and an end to hostilities in November 1840.

The last decisive step in the Empire's formal induction into Europe's international political system was taken on 17 September 1840. To the Convention of 1840 was added a Self-Denying Protocol which stated:

> . . . That in the execution of the engagements resulting to the Contracting Powers from the above-mentioned Convention, those Powers will seek no augmentation of territory, no exclusive influence, no commercial advantage for their subjects, which those of every other nation may not equally obtain.
>
> The Plenipotentiaries of the Courts above-mentioned have resolved to record this Declaration in the present Protocol.
>
> The Plenipotentiary of the Ottoman Porte, in paying a just tribute to the good faith and disinterested policy of the allied Courts, has taken cognizance of the Declaration contained in the present Protocol, and has undertaken to transmit it to his Court.[7]

At the moment the *Sublime Porte* became a full party to this agreement, that large historical paradox with which the Empire began its long journey towards integration with Europe was dissolved. J. C. Hurewitz has accurately observed that those instruments – the Convention and Self-Denying Protocol of 1840 – to which the sultan affixed his signature alongside those of the monarchs of England, Russia, Austria, and Prussia,

> . . . explained the purposes and laid down the rules of the collective European intervention into internal Ottoman affairs. Although it was not recognized by statesmen of the time, or by scholars later on, the convention of 1840 signaled the start of the Ottoman Empire's unqualified participation in the European state system.[8]

The synthesizing of political systems extended to the process of change within the Empire. Reform became an element of policy in Ottoman relations with Europe. Significant measures of reform called for by the European powers were introduced at critical junctures in European Concert diplomacy: the Hati Sherif Gulhane, the reform edict which ushered in the Tanzimat era, was issued on 3 November 1839, the eve of the Convention of 1840; the reform edict of 18 February 1856, which reaffirmed the privileges and immunities of the non-Muslim Ottoman communities, appeared only a month before the Treaty of Paris which terminated the Crimean War; and the first Ottoman constitution was promulgated on 23 December 1876, just as a conference of European powers met in Istanbul to settle another Balkan crisis that threatened to involve the Ottomans yet again in war with Russia.

By the time the Ottoman Empire completed its entry into Europe's state system, most Islamic societies outside the Empire had already been engulfed by Europe's colonial expansion. By this means, almost all of the Islamic world had already been incorporated at some level into the European international system. The Ottoman Empire was the last and most important in the process. The Treaty of Paris of 1856 codified what had been for some time a reality.

It would be wrong however, to suppose that the synthesis of European and Muslim societies was total; it was not. What occurred was an integration of *systems* and the material and technological accoutrements of modern societies. Values, outlooks on life, behaviour patterns, and beliefs remained culturally disparate, and despite the revolution in education and communications of the modern era, imperfectly matched.

11

CHINA'S ENTRY INTO INTERNATIONAL SOCIETY

Gerrit W. Gong

The process by which non-European countries such as China entered the international society is just beginning to be studied by those whose primary interest is in international relations. Viewed from the European centre, it is the story of the expansion of the European international society into a global society; from the non-European periphery, it is the story of the changes, adjustments, and adaptations, some voluntary and some not, made by non-European countries as they became members of the expanding international system and, later, of the international society. While the features which distinguish an international system from an international society are necessarily fluid and dynamic, the case of China serves to illustrate the difference between initially having 'sufficient contact' with the European states 'to act – at least in some measure – as parts of a whole', and eventually adhering to the common interests and values, binding rules, and institutions of the nineteenth-century international society which self-consciously characterized itself as 'civilized'.[1]

As formal and sustained intercourse with the extra-European world burgeoned during the course of the nineteenth century, the European powers faced the challenge and difficulty of drawing the non-European countries into their system of international relations in an orderly and humane way, as much as possible within the international legal guide-lines which were themselves evolving to cope with the expanding domain of international law. Indeed, as Alexandrowicz notes: 'It seemed logical that in the confrontation of different civilizations and political traditions a way should be found to enable the newcomer to the Family of Nations to take sooner or later his rightful place in the framework of the latter.'[2]

Despite European efforts to find logical and humane ways to draw the non-European newcomers into their international system, the expanding European international system posed a threat to China which was already part of an established, albeit, non-European, international order. Indeed, as the Middle Kingdom in a Confucian Family of Nations, China vigorously resisted the European challenge to its historic civilization and traditional system of tributary relations. In the ensuing confrontation, the European system expanded to supersede the Confucian order in East Asia.

The European confrontation with East Asia proved to be more than merely political, economic, or military. It was also cultural and involved the clash of fundamentally irreconcilable standards of 'civilization'. Generally speaking, a standard of 'civilization' embodies the assumptions, tacit and explicit, used to distinguish those that belong to a particular society (by definition the 'civilized'). It expresses the way a society, domestic or international, self-consciously characterizes its members; stipulates the rules, norms, and precepts of their mutual interaction; and differentiates them from those excluded as outsiders. As societies are dynamic (again, both domestic and international), so are their standards of 'civilization': the Sino-European interaction changed both the Chinese and the European standards of 'civilization'. In the course of the late nineteenth and early twentieth centuries, China's standard of 'civilization', especially regarding international trade, diplomacy, and legal relations, came to reflect the dominant European standard of 'civilization'. At the same time, the European standard of 'civilization' – which was codified in treaties with non-European countries and later articulated in the writings of the European publicists as part of customary law – emerged in increasingly explicit terms to delineate the requirements necessary for non-European countries like China to enter international society.

Sustained trade, diplomatic, and legal relations according to the European standard of 'civilization' were first regulated by the treaties China was forced to sign following the Opium War of 1839. Although they served as the basis for the treaty port system, which introduced China to the rules, norms, and practices of the European international system, these early treaties earned the opprobrium 'unequal treaties' both in China and the West, for at least three reasons. First, they were imposed by European military force; second, they dictated unequal obligations which compromised China's sovereignty; and third, they came to symbolize China's evolving perceptions of humiliation and injustice. Initially, China suffered profound cultural trauma when its historic standard of 'civilization' was forcibly assailed by foreign powers with 'barbaric' standards of 'civilization'; later, as China sought to 'civilize' itself according to European standards and to judge its international situation according to Western liberal, Communist, and pan-Asian doctrines, the cultural humiliation of its 'unequal treaties' took on added dimensions of international legal injustice and ideological inequality.

This essay traces China's entry into international society in three parts. First, prior to the Opium War, China stubbornly maintained its own standard of cultural superiority and thereby refused to enter into equal relations or treaties with the West. Second, beginning with the 1842 Treaty of Nanking, 'unequal treaties' became the basis for the treaty port system which served as a vehicle of Western impact in China and which acted as a catalyst for and during China's transition from universal empire to sovereign state. The third part of this essay sketches the processes by which China attempted to conform to the European standard of 'civilization' by establishing accepted diplomatic practices, adopting international law, and gradually becoming a 'civilized' member of the international society.

Sino-Western Relations and the Traditional Chinese World Order

From the earliest days when the Marco Polo explorers and adventurers first visited China, the Chinese asserted that they would deal with Europeans according to the same patterns and principles they had used to rule the Empire for thousands of years. Though the Chinese Empire had expanded and contracted with the fortunes of successive dynasties; though ruling houses had waxed and waned; and though emperors had risen and fallen for millennia, these cycles of dynastic change reinforced the Chinese sense of historical continuity and confirmed the traditional wisdom that the early Confucian sages knew best; that older and more experienced civilizations were wiser and more virtuous ones; that, indeed, China alone offered the blessings of civilization to man.

Traditional China's standard of 'civilization' was enshrined in Confucian doctrine. As the Son of Heaven, the Chinese emperor possessed the mandate of heaven to rule the Middle Kingdom, which in principle encompassed the entire world, both 'civilized' (Chinese in culture) and not yet 'civilized' ('barbarian' or foreign in culture). Within this world order, everything from the most mundane daily events to the most significant affairs under the distant reaches of the heavens were intimately related in a hierarchy of order maintained and symbolized by the faithful performance of prescribed ritual kowtows. Children kowtowed to parents; parents to grandparents and ancestors; ministers to the emperor; and the emperor to heaven itself. The Confucian classic, *The Great Learning*, described the universality and indivisibility of order throughout the Chinese cosmos in this way:

'Rectify yourself; put your house in order; regulate the kingdom; and there will be peace under all the heavens.' Peace under all the heavens began with the kowtow at home.

The same Confucian principles and traditions which ordered China's domestic affairs also determined its relations with its non-Chinese neighbours. As the father or elder brother, China rewarded the respect and tribute of its surrounding tributary states by offering due Confucian benevolence and fair if patriarchal relations. Even though couched in the language of cultural superiority, the Chinese world order, buttressed at crucial times by Chinese military strength, was regarded not only by nomadic groups outside the Great Wall, but also by Korea, Annam, Siam, Burma, and for a time Japan,[3] as universal, historically proven, and thereby acceptably prescriptive in its demands for ritual respect and periodic tribute.

Indeed, Europeans arriving in China soon discovered that they could not violate the prescribed ceremonial kowtows without confronting China's standard of 'civilization' and the culture and world view which it undergirded. Thus the kowtow became a potent symbol in such Sino-Western confrontations as the 1645 Rites Controversy (where an issue was whether or not Chinese Christians could kowtow as part of the Confucian ancestral rites); the 1689 Treaty of Nerchinsk (where agreement between the Muscovite and Chinese courts to reciprocate ritual observances finally permitted the signing on 27 August of China's first treaty with a Western country); and the troubles associated with the British efforts to open China for trade in the middle of the nineteenth century.

It was, of course, Lord Macartney's adamant refusal in 1793 to kowtow to the self-proclaimed superiority of the Chinese standard of 'civilization' which proved to be a harbinger of disaster for the traditional Chinese world order. Tradition dictated that China deal with the Europeans not in accordance with the developing European philosophy that states represented by respected plenipotentiaries interact as sovereign equals, but rather in accordance with the Confucian patterns and principles which demanded that all from near and far acknowledge China's standard of 'civilization'. Though the Chinese finally permitted Macartney to bow on one knee in lieu of the kowtow, the concessions he had hoped to obtain were not achieved until they were imposed by the Treaty of Nanking. Still, it was not totally Macartney's blustering which limited the success of his mission; in the trough of the dynastic cycle, the weak Ching government perceived trade with the West not only as unnecessary, but also as a potential threat to an already moribund dynasty. Trade according to western practices may have seemed life-blood for the European countries, but it sounded the death-knell for old China.

The Impact of the West

Of undisputed importance are the Opium War and the Treaty of Nanking, as turning points in Sino-Western relations. According to Hsin-Pao Chang, 'Whether Chinese or Western, radical or conservative, scholars have invariably taken it [the Opium War] as a starting point in the study of modern China.'[4] The Opium War and the signing of the Nanking treaty marked the beginning of the use of Western military force in China, the initiation of sustained if forced Sino-Western contact, the imposition of the European standard of 'civilization' in China, and the start of what is generally referred to as a hundred years of unequal relations due to 'unequal treaties'.[5]

At least three main issues, each arising at least in part from conflicting standards of 'civilization', contributed to the outbreak of the Opium War.

First, Western merchants and diplomats accustomed to European practices of direct representation on the basis of equality complained that the hierarchical Chinese system denied them the right of direct representation in Peking and required them instead to deal through monopolistic Cohong trading firms which were inefficient intermediaries even after the necessary and sometimes exorbitant bribes had been paid. These merchants and diplomats complained too that the crippling restrictions on travel could not be rescinded without Peking's permission. The Europeans repeatedly protested that they were being treated not only as unequals but as inferiors by Chinese contemptuous of 'barbarians'.

Second, Chinese insistence on traditional codes of justice caused Europeans to feel that they were being subjected to an 'uncivilized' standard of justice. The Chinese concept of group responsibility seemed as benighted and unjust as Chinese forms of torture and execution, e.g., strangling, seemed barbaric.

Third and most immediate, after decades of frustrated efforts to penetrate China's essentially self-sufficient economy, British merchants discovered that opium, easily imported from India, commanded a high price and such a ready market that by the mid-1820s, the silver flow between Britain and China had finally reversed.[6] Tension mounted as Commissioner Lin Tse-hsu took firm measures to control the opium trade which threatened to undermine both China's economy and the health of her people. Thus, although Commissioner Lin's detention of the foreign community at Canton and the destruction of 20,000 chests of opium provided Britain with a *casus belli*, underlying the opium issue were British demands for equality of diplomatic representation, judgement by their own legal concepts and courts, and freedom of trade, conditions assumed granted by all 'civilized' countries.

The battle of Chuenpi, the first of the Opium War, occurred on 2 November 1839 when two rather small British warships decimated an inexperienced and ill-trained collection of Chinese war junks and fire-ships. The overwhelmingly superior firepower of the British forces quickly became evident; the threat to bombard Nanking hastened the signing of the thirteen-article Treaty of Nanking on 29 August 1842. Following the Nanking Treaty, the Western powers signed the Treaty of the Bogue (1843), the Treaty of Wanghia (1844), and the Treaty of Whampoa (1844) in rapid succession. These four treaties became the basis of a unified Western approach to relations with China and formed the 'foundation on which has been erected the superstructure of the diplomatic and commercial relations between China and upwards of a score of foreign nations which have entered into common treaty relations.'[7] For this reason, H. B. Morse describes the first treaty settlement as 'four treaties one settlement'.[8]

After twelve years, when the Nanking treaties came due for revision, the European countries insisted on broader treaty privileges. What they demanded in essence was 'the opening of China as a market for Western manufactures and commerce on the basis of China's incorporation, by force or otherwise, into the modern state system'.[9] More specifically, the West demanded permanent residence in Peking for diplomatic representatives and the opening of the China market through increased numbers of treaty ports, freedom of navigation on inland rivers, travel into the interior, and abolition of the kowtow. Under the threat of renewed Western military force, China signed the Tientsin treaties in 1858.

When China temporized in implementing the Tientsin treaties, British and French troops marched on Peking where they burned the Summer Palace and where, on 24 October 1860, Lord Elgin dictated to Prince Kung the Convention of Peking. The Convention finally established the Western right to permanent diplomatic residence in the Chinese capital, increased China's indemnity, and opened Tientsin itself to foreign trade and residence. Britain acquired the lease of an extension in Hong Kong at Kowloon, while France secured the right for Catholic missionaries to acquire property in China's interior.

By 1860, the West was in a position to dictate the conditions of its relations with China. Beginning with the Nanking and Tientsin treaties, the imposition of what gradually became formalized as a standard of 'civilization' forced China to open its ports, to trade on Western terms, and to conduct its relations with the West according to international law and Western diplomatic practices. While at least initially the Europeans may have only intended the treaties to create an international system of diplomatic representation, trading rights, and judicial process, equal to those granted by and to all 'civilized' states, the Chinese saw the treaties as imposing a foreign standard of 'civilization' and as forming the spearhead for increasing Western penetration. In time, however, China's early treaties with the West gradually replaced the traditional Chinese tributary system by forming the foundation for a Western treaty port system.[10]

The treaty port system was so named because the treaty ports, demanded in increasing numbers after the Treaty of Nanking, became a symbol of the West in China. The first five treaty ports were on the coasts at Amoy, Canton, Foochow, Ningpo, and Shanghai. The Tientsin treaties opened ten new ports, and Tientsin itself was added after the Western march on Peking. By 1920 there were 69 treaty ports dotted about China, on the coasts and in the interior.

The treaty ports became the permanent residences of increasing numbers of Westerners, the centres for trade and commerce, the home stations of the Western gunboats, and the sites of consulates and military barracks, all protected as semi-autonomous units with their own tax and legal-judicial systems and thereby exempt from Chinese jurisdiction. Concessions granted in the Nanking and Tientsin treaties were added to and built into a treaty port system through further agreements, arrangements, conventions, and supplementary conventions, ranging over Rules of Trade, Customs, Commerce, Official Intercourse, etc. In this way, the treaty port system became a complex and far-reaching arrangement of interrelated rights, interests, and privileges acquired or claimed over the course of almost a century.[11] Within their enclaves, foreign nationals enjoyed the rights, privileges, and protection they associated with 'civilization'.

A major exception to the gradual and relatively peaceful growth by accretion enjoyed by the treaty port system occurred in 1900 when the Boxers, later with support from xenophobic officials and gentry, erupted in a campaign to exterminate the foreign presence 'root and branch'. An international concert of 'civilized' powers mobilized to enforce their collective standard of 'civilization' against the Boxer rebellion. After the Boxers surrendered, the treaty powers demanded more stringent guarantees of foreign life, liberty, and property and increased protection for diplomatic and legal communication channels.

It is ironic that the Boxer excesses which sought to eliminate the foreign standard of 'civilization' in China increased the severity with which that standard was ultimately enforced.

The treaty port system reached the peak of its influence in the 1920s and 1930s. In addition to the original and basic treaty concession of consular jurisdiction, these privileges evolved to include:[12]

(1) national courts of the major extraterritorial powers at Shanghai, and the 'mixed courts' which extended Western judicial functions far beyond those originally granted in the 1840s and which gave foreign assessors a degree of jurisdiction even in cases involving Chinese as defendants when a foreign plaintiff was involved;
(2) foreign-administered bureaucratic services such as the Chinese Maritime Customs Service, the Postal Service, the Salt Gabelle (tax agency);
(3) treaty provisions which bound China to a fixed and low *ad valorem* tariff and granted the Western powers immunity from direct taxation by China;
(4) foreign-controlled settlements and concessions at the principal treaty ports which, protected by the gunboats at the coastal ports and on the Yangtze River, were the main manifestations of the Western presence. In Peking, the treaty powers maintained the Legation Quarters with legation guards. Western troops were also stationed at Tientsin and at strategic points along the railways from Peking to the sea. The rights to coastal and inland navigation were included in the right to travel. Missionaries were not only permitted to travel freely but to settle, acquire real property, and proselytize throughout the country.

Despite the gradual but pervasive extension of the treaty port system, the Western economic impact, excepting special areas such as Shanghai, remained relatively circumscribed. However, the widespread social and political impacts introduced by the system remain incalculable. Eyewitnesses of the now-infamous 'No Dogs or Chinese' signs outside some Shanghai parks remember their sense of humiliation and outrage as twofold: first, because Chinese people and dogs could be compared and treated in the same manner; second, because the unwanted foreign presence which was undermining traditional Chinese society could not be expelled from what should have been Chinese territory.

However, the European order prevailed and China gradually made the transition from universal empire to 'civilized' state as it was forcibly drawn into the international society.

THE STANDARD OF 'CIVILIZATION'

An expression of the universalist aspirations of the late nineteenth- and early twentieth-century international society which evolved self-consciously to characterize itself as 'civilized', the standard of 'civilization' had become part of customary international law in a two-stepped process. First codified in the early treaties signed with non-European countries from the mid-nineteenth century, e.g. the Treaty of Nanking, the requirements of the standard were made increasingly explicit as they were articulated in the writings of Wheaton and subsequent international publicists. By the turn of the century, the standard had emerged sufficiently to define the legal requirements necessary for a non-European country like China to gain full and 'civilized' status in 'civilized' international society. Included in these requirements were the ability of the country to guarantee the life, liberty, and property of foreign nationals; to demonstrate a suitable governmental organization; to adhere to the accepted diplomatic practices; and to abide by the principles of international law.

China's acceptance of the elements and institutions required by the standard of 'civilization' was due both to Western pressure to 'civilize' and to increasing domestic demands for reform. Sustained European influence and the example of nearby Japan (which as described in the following chapter, had methodically 'civilized' itself with dramatic results) gradually caused China to object to the 'unequal treaties' on grounds of previously foreign notions such as the inviolability of sovereignty and the equality of 'civilized' states in international law. By 1880, China had begun to employ European principles of diplomacy and international law and, increasingly, to accept a role in the international system. By January 1912, when the Republic of China was founded as China's first attempt to conduct its affairs as a sovereign state after the pattern of the European states system, a constitutional government was established in part, as Jerome Ch'en writes, 'to replace the Confucian orthodoxy which had hitherto been the fundamental principle of the state with a new concept, legitimacy'.[13] A fountainhead for both these domestic and international changes had been the establishment of permanent diplomatic relations.

THE ESTABLISHMENT OF PERMANENT DIPLOMATIC RELATIONS

It was only after the 1858 *Arrow* war and the subsequent Tientsin treaties that Western diplomats were finally permitted to take up residence in Peking for the first time in Chinese history. By 1862, Sir Frederick Bruce, Alphonse de Bourboulon, Colonel Balliuzek, and

Anson Burlingame had begun residence as the ministers from Britain, France, Russia, and the United States, respectively.

Early in 1861, China established a *Tsungli Yamen* or official 'Office for General Administration' as its first formal and permanent central organ for the handling of foreign affairs. The establishment of the *Yamen* marked 'a turning point in China's foreign relations'[14] because it represented an institutional change in China's conduct of foreign affairs and the end of the traditional tributary relations conducted among unequals. A College of Foreign Languages or *T'ung-wen kuan* was established in Peking in 1862 as an adjunct office to the *Yamen* with the commission to teach foreign languages to the Chinese officials selected on a competitive basis.

The European powers saw the *Yamen* as a potential key to treaty enforcement. As Bruce argued in a dispatch of 8 September 1862:

> Our true policy is to give weight and authority to the Foreign Board [*Tsungli Yamen*], by compelling it to deal with foreign questions and to punish, if necessary, officials who violate Treaties, and thus to teach the latter to tremble when a consul threatens to bring a matter under the notice of the Minister at Peking.[15]

Britain, France, Russia, and the United States joined in a 'Co-operative Policy' during the 1860s in a joint attempt to secure treaty enforcement through diplomatic pressure exerted upon the Peking government. Consuls in the treaty ports were discouraged from using gunboats to enforce the treaties, and every effort was made to support and encourage Prince Kung and the progressives working towards China's modernization.

China also sought to protect its interests through diplomatic channels. In the decade following the ratification of the Tientsin treaties, the Ching government, as Mary Wright states, 'accepted and mastered the principles and practices of Western diplomacy and succeeded in using them as the main bulwark of Chinese sovereignty'.[16] China's diplomats repeatedly insisted that its strict observance of the treaty provisions not only removed potential Western excuses for punitive action but also limited Western activities in China to those already specified in the treaties.

The Introduction of International Law

After the founding of the *Tsungli Yamen*, China became increasingly aware that some knowledge of international law was necessary to deal with the West. An American missionary, W. A. P. Martin, translated Wheaton's *Elements of International Law* and began distributing it under the title *Wan-kuo kung-fa* (Public Law of All States) in 1864. Even after translations of Woolsey, G. F. de Martens, and other publicists started to appear, Martin's translation of Wheaton remained the standard international legal treatise for the *Yamen*. By the turn of the century, Martin had been appointed Professor of the Law of Nations at the Imperial College of Tung-wen; students were also being sent to Europe and America to study international law.

Though it acquired a sense of the importance of international law, China continued to apply it in only a limited fashion. It came to accept the treaty port system and its undergirding system of international law more as a defensive means to enforce the treaties which kept the West from further encroaching on Chinese sovereignty, than as a positive means to secure favourable treaty revisions. Further, China only gradually accepted international law as a means for dealing with former tributary states such as Korea.

Still, even before the birth of the Republic of China, representatives from China had attended the Hague Peace Conferences of 1899 and 1907; adhered to many multilateral conventions dealing with the laws of war, the pacific settlement of disputes, and other matters; joined the Universal Postal Union (UPU) and the International Institute of Agriculture (IIA).[17] Beginning with the sixth meeting in 1878, China sent delegates to the Association for the Reform and Codification of the Law of Nations; Kuo Sung-t'ao, also China's first minister to England, was even elected honorary vice-president of the Association.

ENDING EXTRATERRITORIALITY

China's efforts to conform to the principles and practices of the prevalent international society made evident its transition from Middle Kingdom to probationary member of that society ('probationary' as defined by that society). Though this transition was nominally completed with the establishment of the Republic of China on 1 January 1912, many saw the national revolution, which had begun only eighty-three days before with the uprising against the Ching dynasty, as yet incomplete. Though China had proclaimed itself a new state, it was not yet a 'civilized' member of the international society. On the day the Republic of China was formally inaugurated, Provisional President Sun Yat-sen announced that 'with the establishment of the Provisional government we will try our best to carry out the duties of a civilized nation so as to obtain the rights of a civilized nation'.[18] Even at Sun's death a decade later, however, 'unequal treaties' were still an issue. Sun's Will, dated 11 March 1925, disappointedly admitted that 'the work of the Revolution is not yet done', and urged that 'the abolition of unequal treaties should be carried into effect with the least possible delay'.[19]

In its efforts to revise the 'unequal treaties' and to abolish extraterritoriality, China purposefully entered the First World War on the side of the Allies, thereby voiding its treaties with Germany and Austria-Hungary and securing a place at the victory table; it made the issue of extraterritoriality a focus of international controversy at the 1921 Washington Conference, which responded to China's Ten Points by delegating an international Commission on Extraterritoriality to investigate the situation; and, after the League of Nations court system was established, China became the first country to appeal to its machinery for the revision of the 'unequal treaties' on the basis of equality and reciprocity.[20]

China's efforts to revise the 'unequal treaties' and to abrogate extraterritoriality were made more complex by at least two additional factors. One was the internal weakness and dissent which encouraged factionalism and power rivalries in China and which, even after Kuomintang leader Chiang Kai-shek loosely united the country in 1928 after the unsuccessful Northern campaign, still left China divided and unstable. A second was that the goal to restore China's territorial integrity and national sovereignty was shared by Chinese leaders of all political persuasions including Sun Yat-sen, Chiang Kai-shek, and Mao Tse-tung. Further, in their own times and ways, the Western liberals, the Communists, and the Japanese all espoused China's quest for treaty revision as their own. This kind of burgeoning support guaranteed the eventual abolition of extraterritoriality in China, though it also left it unclear who could claim the victory when the 'unequal treaties' were finally revised.

As early as the 1902 MacKay Treaty, the Western powers had expressed their willingness to abrogate extraterritoriality, contingent on China's ability to bring its own judicial system into line with 'civilized' standards. But, even into the 1920s, China's inability to guarantee foreign life, liberty, and property, or to maintain effective political control made the treaty powers reluctant to surrender their extraterritorial privileges. The negotiations to revise the 'unequal treaties' which had dragged on through the 1920s were suspended in draft form after the Japanese invasion of Manchuria; they were concluded in short order after the Japanese attack on Pearl Harbour. The Western decision to end extraterritoriality in China was announced on China's 'Double Ten' Independence Day and formalized on 11 January 1942.

CONCLUSIONS

First imposed by the Western powers on a proud and isolationist China in 1842 and not ended until the abrogation of extraterritoriality in 1943, 'unequal treaties' symbolize the first century of formal relations between China and the West. In their initial and deepest emotional sense, the 'unequal treaties' represented a cultural humiliation for the Middle Kingdom, the shattering of China's tradition of cultural superiority by Western 'barbarian' powers which were not only China's military superior, but which tacitly and explicitly asserted the superiority of their standard of 'civilization' over China's as well. In practice, the 'unequal treaties' became the means by which China was gradually if forcibly drawn into what it perceived as a European international society. As the treaty port system irrevocably drew China into greater and more sustained contact with members of that society, China perceived that it had no viable alternative but to adopt the institutions and practices required for 'civilized' countries, including those relating to the protection of foreign life and property, to governmental organization, to diplomatic representation, and to international law.

Official Chinese protests against 'unequal treaties' also evolved to reflect China's growing acceptance of a role in the international society. China ceased to demand the preservation of its historic standard of 'civilization' and its traditional status as the 'Middle Kingdom', arguing instead for revision of 'unequal treaties' and extraterritoriality on the grounds of formal legal inequalities. That modern China discussed 'unequal treaties' in international legal terms, e.g. as treaties signed under duress or as encroachments on sovereignty, underscored the extent to which it had accepted the principles and practices of the European international society.

Thus, in this case study of China's entry into international society, 'unequal treaties' as a manifestation of different standards of 'civilization' were seen to be both a constant and a changing theme. They were a constant theme because they were a consistent element in China's formal relations with the West from 1842 to 1943; they were a changing theme because China's perceptions of 'unequal treaties' evolved as China gradually became a sovereign and 'civilized' member of international society. By 1943 this transition was at least nominally complete; it was not foreseen that the civil war would bring yet another government to power in China, and with its rise, an ideology that raised new questions about China's relation to international society.

12

JAPAN'S ENTRY INTO INTERNATIONAL SOCIETY

Hidemi Suganami

Commodore Perry's arrival in Japan in 1853 may be commonly remembered as the starting-point of Japan's relations with the Western Powers, but her first encounter with the West began with the 'discovery' of Japan by Portuguese castaways in the mid-sixteenth century. From then on Japan's foreign relations went through three stages.

In the first stage, lasting to the early decades of the seventeenth century, there was a great deal of interaction between the Japanese and foreigners inhabiting the Far East. In the second stage, up to the mid-nineteenth century, Japan under the House of Tokugawa adopted the policy of seclusion. During the third stage, from the mid-nineteenth century onwards, Japan reluctantly abandoned the seclusion policy and later strove for equality and Great Power status in international society. Here we shall concentrate on Japan's relations with the outside world during the seclusion and post-seclusion periods up to the end of the First World War.

The Period of Seclusion

The years from 1603 to 1868 are known in Japanese history as the Edo Period. Edo, renamed Tokyo in 1868, was where the House of Tokugawa, a warrior clan, having terminated a long period of war among feudal lords, established the central administration of Japan, called the 'Bakufu'. The Bakufu was headed by a 'Shogun', which in the ancient time was the title of the Emperor's *ad hoc* military deputy, but which had come to mean the supreme feudal lord formally authorized by the Emperor to rule Japan. The office of Shogun was hereditary in the House of Tokugawa throughout the Edo Period. The Imperial Family and Court Nobles survived in the ancient capital of Kyoto, but were politically impotent until the very last phase of the Edo Period.

A part of Japan was under direct Tokugawa rule, and the rest was divided up into feudal domains governed by the 'Daimyos', or feudal lords. There were three classes of Daimyos: those of Tokugawa blood;

those descended from the vassals of Ieyasu, the founder of the Tokugawa Bakufu, during his rise to power; and those who submitted to Tokugawa control after the battle of Sekigahara in 1600 which won Ieyasu the title of Shogun. The Tokugawas treated the third category of Daimyos with suspicion. It was chiefly to prevent them from allying with foreign powers against the Tokugawa hegemony, and gaining power through foreign trade, that in the early part of the seventeenth century the Bakufu introduced the policy of seclusion.

According to the official doctrine of the seclusion period, foreigners were divided into three categories. The Dutch and the Chinese were classified as 'Tsusho-no-kuni', or 'nations-for-trading'. Korea and Ryukyu came under the category of 'Tsushin-no-kuni', or countries whose official envoys were invited as state guests to Edo on important ceremonial occasions for the exchange of goodwill. The rest of the world was to be repelled.[1] Despite their classification as 'Tsusho-no-kuni', however, the Dutch and the Chinese were not treated in the same way by the Japanese; nor were the positions of Korea and Ryukyu the same *vis-à-vis* Japan despite their title 'Tsushin-no-kuni'.

At the beginning of the seventeenth century, there were four European nations which had relations with Japan: the Portuguese, Spanish, English, and Dutch. The first two were expelled by the Tokugawa seclusion edicts, while the third temporarily withdrew on account of the lack of profit. When in 1673 the English attempted to resume trade, the Bakufu's seclusion policy had become too rigid to allow for their return despite the Charter of Privileges accorded them earlier by the first two Tokugawa Shoguns. This left the Dutch as the sole Europeans to be accepted in Japan.

The Dutch were confined to Dejima, an artificial island in the port of Nagasaki, and subjected to all manner of restrictions. They did, however, share one burden with the Daimyos, which by that very fact was a sign of privilege. This was the Shogun's audience. The Daimyos, with certain exceptions, had an obligation to alternate their residence between Edo and their fiefs, leaving their families as hostages in Edo. On their arrival, the Daimyos were to be conducted to the Shogun's presence in Edo Castle to pay their respects. Similarly, the Dutch Factory had to send envoys regularly to Edo with presents to pay their respects to the Shogun. The head of the Factory was brought into the Shogun's presence in a manner similar to that in which the Daimyos were introduced, and although he had to perform obeisance to the Shogun, which might have seemed undignified from the European viewpoint, he was at least on a par with any of the great Daimyos in this respect.

The Chinese were in a different position. There were no formal relations of 'Tsushin' (communication of goodwill through official envoys) between China and Japan during the Edo Period; by the mid-sixteenth century this form of intercourse, which Japan had maintained with the Ming in the early part of the fifteenth century in order to facilitate trade, had fallen into desuetude. The Bakufu's desire to re-establish 'Tsushin' with China through Korean mediation was not fulfilled. Nevertheless Chinese merchants continued to visit Japanese ports for private trading. In 1636 Nagasaki was declared the only port open to them, but no envoys were sent to Edo from the Chinese community, which thrived in Nagasaki. In the relationship with the Chinese, therefore, we find a purer example of 'Tsusho' (trade).

In the case of relations between Korea and Japan in the Edo Period there were three principal actors: the Korean Court, the Bakufu, and Tsushima, an island midway between Korea and Japan. The Bakufu invited envoys from Korea, while Tsushima traded with her, maintained a small settlement in Pusan, and acted as an intermediary for Japanese-Korean relations. The relationship between Japan and Korea was not a product of the seclusion period. There had been similar relations between them since the fifteenth century. It is of interest that the Bakufu's relations with Korea were conducted on the basis of formal diplomatic equality, and that the protocol was worked out in detail by the Bakufu's official Confucian scholars.[2]

There were twelve missions from Korea throughout the Edo Period, each of which contained a large number of delegates. The first mission, for instance, that of 1607, consisted of 467 members, including circus riders and musicians.[3] The nearest contemporary equivalent of the Korean missions may be found in the practice of sending special envoys to attend important occasions, such as state funerals, or in the exchange of cultural missions for the promotion of goodwill. It is important to note, however, that the main aim of the Bakufu in inviting missions from Korea was political. The Bakufu attempted to enhance its prestige, and reinforce its legitimacy, by means of international recognition, which was to be obtained from the Korean envoys' occasional visits to the Shogun's capital.

In contast to the case of Korea, Japan's relations with the Ryukyu Islands were not based on equality, as the King of Ryukyu had been subjugated by Satsuma, Japan's southernmost domain, in 1609. Ryukyu maintained a tributary relationship with China, which facilitated trade, but Satsuma, far from objecting to the islands' formal subservience to another country, positively encouraged it, because Satsuma's chief aim in subjugating the islands had been to establish an indirect trading link with China. Satsuma even directed the Ryukyu authorities to conceal their relationships with Japan from the Chinese lest the disclosure of the Ryukyu King's double loyalty should displease the Chinese and result in the loss of trade.[4] The King of Ryukyu began to send congratulatory missions to Edo in 1644, which heightened the prestige both of the Bakufu and of Satsuma.[5] Japan under the Meiji Government was to declare full sovereignty over the islands in 1871, originally incorporating them in the Kagoshima Prefecture, a former Satsuma domain, and shortly afterwards according them the status of the Okinawa Prefecture. However, unlike the Meiji Government, equipped with the modern notion of absolute territorial jurisdiction by the state, the feudalist Tokugawas tolerated a less exclusive relationship with what was, after all, their vassal's vassal in a distant place.

In addition to contacts with these four peoples, there was also some trade between Matusmae, Japan's northernmost domain, and the Ainu, who traded between themselves and brought animal pelts from the northern Kuril Islands and Kamchatka.[6] All these, however, were exceptions to the rule. Under the strict policy of seclusion, all other nations were to be refused any contact with the Japanese. Naturally, the effectiveness of this policy depended not only on the power of the Bakufu to enforce its laws but also upon the willingness of the foreign countries to acquiesce. Unfortunately for the Bakufu's seclusion policy, ships began to approach the coast of Japan from Russia, Britain, and the United States in increasing numbers from the early part of the eighteenth century. The official treatment of unwanted foreigners arriving on the ships reflected to a large extent the laws that the Bakufu enacted to implement its policy of seclusion.[7]

The first such law was the edict of 1791, which consolidated customary rules that had begun to develop in the treatment of foreign vessels approaching Japan. Given the general principle that foreigners were not allowed to visit Japan, the tone of the 1791 edict was relatively moderate, although it severely restricted the freedom of those who arrived.

The Bakufu was impressed by the willingness to comply with the laws of Japan shown by two Russian envoys (Laxman in 1792 and Rezanov in 1804). This led to the revision of the Bakufu attitude in 1806 in favour of the Russians. The new edict recommended a particularly gentle treatment of the Russians, although all it amounted to was an instruction that the Japanese officials should try to be as gentle as possible in telling them to depart and never to return.

However, the Bakufu's special favour to the Russians was soon abandoned in response to the Khvostov/Davidov affair of 1806–7, when two naval officers seconded to the Russian American Company, of which Rezanov was a leading figure, attacked Japanese settlements in Sakhalin and the southern Kuril Islands. They had acted under the personal instruction of Rezanov, who had been outraged by the fact that his painstaking effort to open trade with Japan had completely failed. The Bakufu now decreed that all Russian ships must be repelled, and failing this, their crews detained, or executed in case of resistance.

Another unfortunate event occurred in 1824 when some English whalers attacked Satsuma officials, attempting to steal some bullocks for food. Insignificant though it might appear as a political event, this in fact caused the Bakufu to promulgate in 1825 the most uncompromising repulsion edict of all. All foreign vessels approaching the Japanese coast were to be repelled unconditionally. The Bakufu, however, did hardly anything to strengthen coastal defence and the edict's efficacy was precarious.

Meanwhile, European naval and military capabilities were developing rapidly. Already in 1840 the news of the Opium War had reached Japan through the Dutch Factory and shaken the Bakufu's confidence in China's status as a Great Power, and *a fortiori*, its confidence in its own power to maintain the 1825 edict. Moreover, the idea of an unconditional repulsion was thought by the Bakufu's official Confucian scholar to be unreasonable and contrary to moral obligation towards foreign countries. A report, which had reached Japan through the Dutch Factory, that the *Morrison*, which had been repelled in 1837 in accordance with the 1825 edict, in fact intended among other things to return some Japanese castaways raised a strong sense of shame among some Bakufu officials. The result was the abolition in 1842 of the unconditional repulsion edict and reversion to the decree of 1806. Aid to ships in distress was assured, although landings were firmly refused.

The Bakufu legislations generally proscribed unnecessary violence. However, some degree of violence was necessary for the very implementation of the seclusion policy. This, and some inaccurate reporting by the castaways who had been imprisoned (or quarantined) in Japan, as well as unfortunate incidents during the unconditional repulsion period, caused the Western nations, particularly the Americans, who were the most frequent victims, to regard the Japanese as barbaric in their treatment of foreigners. This explains much of Commodore Perry's uncompromising attitude towards Japan and his conviction that civilization must be forced upon the Japanese. Perry determinedly refused to comply with the usual restrictions that the Bakufu had imposed upon foreigners approaching Japan, and resisted all attempts by the Bakufu officials to employ their customary techniques of hindrance and procrastination. Perry's approach worked because the Bakufu, intimidated by his show of superior force, concluded that there was little it could do to avoid accepting some of his demands, at least temporarily. The Bakufu did not attempt to resist Perry by force because it thought that it would be even more undignified to accept the American terms after having been seen to have lost a battle.

Entry into International Society

As we saw, during the seclusion period, Japan operated what might be called an ethnocentric system with herself at the centre surrounded by Korea, Ryukyu, the Chinese, and the Dutch. In addition, there were sporadic contacts with Russia, Britain, and America. These relationships did not constitute an 'international society' of the kind which existed in the West. However, Japan by the end of the century had transformed her uncertain relationship with the West into a full 'societal' one, while her traditional ethnocentric system lost its practical relevance. The question arises as to when this transformation took place.

It is to be noted that between 1853 and 1858, during the Bakumatsu (End-of-the-Bakufu) Period, treaties were negotiated and concluded between Japan and the Western Powers, and consuls were sent to Japan. Thus during this period Japan can be said to have begun to participate in the operation of some of the basic rules and practices of international society. However, her knowledge of these rules and practices, or institutions, was very limited. She did not appreciate the value of preserving these institutions, or indeed of becoming a member of an international society with such institutions. The strong anti-foreign factions in Japan still maintained that the Bakufu should pursue the policy of seclusion, that any concessions offered by the Bakufu to the Western Powers through the treaties of 1854–8 were temporary measures, and that, when Japan had rebuilt her strength to match the West, she should revert to the ancient laws of seclusion. The Western Powers, on their part, as is clear from the terms of these treaties, did not regard the Japanese state as an equal member of their international society. Thus, despite her gradual abandonment of the policy of seclusion, it is doubtful whether Japan can be said to have become a member of international society in any proper sense during the Bakumatsu Period.

Meanwhile, the Tokugawas continued to exhibit their inability to revert to the seclusion policy. The anti-Tokugawa forces in Japan used this weakness of the Bakufu to their best advantage. The Tokugawas were now being shown to be unfit to govern Japan, for they could not abide by their own ancestral laws, and failed to protect Japan from the encroachment of the 'barbarians'. The Tokugawas fell, and the power of government was restored to the Emperor in 1868, because they were outbalanced by the coalition of anti-Tokugawa factions who rallied round the slogan, 'Revere the Emperor; Expel the Barbarians.' It was argued that only through unification under the leadership of the Emperor could Japan rebuild her strength to repel the Western Powers. Although the leading factions of the anti-Tokugawa forces had come to realize by 1864 the futility of attempting to repel the Western Powers, they clung to the latter half of the slogan because it effectively disclosed the Bakufu's weaknesses.

The policy of seclusion, however, was not a realistic alternative for the new-born Government of Emperor Meiji. Contrary to Japanese expectation, that the new government would adopt a seclusionist policy, it announced that the goal of the whole nation should be to restore the glory of Japan in the eyes of all nations, that the iniquitous aspects of the treaties the Bakufu had concluded with the West would be revised, but that foreign relations should be conducted in accordance with the law of nations.[8]

Japan can be said to have entered international society somewhere between this time and the turn of the century, when she finally managed to persuade the West that the 'unequal' treaties imposed upon Tokugawa Japan should be revised. In 1868 Japan declared her intention to become a member of international society by formally abandoning the policy of seclusion and undertaking to comply with Western rules and the practices of foreign intercourse. Some thirty years later the Western Powers upgraded Japan from an inferior status by agreeing to revise the 'unequal' treaties.

The Advancement of Japan in International Society

The development of Japan's foreign relations from the arrival of Perry to the early decades of the twentieth century can be divided into three stages.

In the first, between Perry's initial visit (1853) and the Iwakura Mission to the West (1871–3), Japan was still learning to understand Western conceptions and the methods of foreign relations.[9] At the beginning of this stage, Japan's attitude was that of an unwilling pupil, but practical necessity soon turned her into a keen student of Western diplomacy. After the Meiji Restoration of 1868 the process was irreversible. By the end of this stage Japan was engaged in an earnest endeavour to adopt the behaviour appropriate to the Western-dominated international society in order to be accepted as one of its full members.

The quest for equality, which has its roots in the formal abandonment of the seclusion policy by the Meiji Government, is the predominant theme of the second stage in Japan's foreign relations after Perry. It stretches from the time of the Iwakura Mission (1871–3) to 1911, when Japan, having abolished consular jurisdiction in 1899 (an agreement to terminate it had been reached in 1894), finally succeeded in removing the restrictions on her tariff autonomy.

Japan's transition during these two stages necessitated change in her relations with Korea and China. No formal relations existed between Japan and China, and 'Tsushin' with Korea had ended in the early part of the nineteenth century. One of the first diplomatic acts of the Meiji Government was to attempt to establish full relations on the European model with the governments of these countries.

It is to be noted that Meiji Japan's intercourse with these countries closely resembled that between the Western Powers and the Tokugawa authorities in both form and substance: in form, it was based on treaty obligations; in substance, it was an exercise in power politics. Just as Japan was at the receiving end of 'unequal' treaties with the West, so she herself imposed an 'unequal' treaty upon Korea in 1876, thereby ending the seclusion of that country and, in 1896, gained most-favoured-nation status in relation to China. Thus this second stage of Japan's foreign relations is one in which she began to apply what she had learnt from the West in her external affairs. Clearly, Japan's success in putting into practice what she had learnt was the major source of her advancement in international society.

The most significant events during this stage, from the viewpoint of Japan's status in international society, included war with China (1894–5), participation alongside the European powers and the United States in the Boxer Intervention (1900–1), the Anglo-Japanese Alliance (1902), war with Russia (1904–5), and the annexation of Korea (1910). Japan's meticulous observance of international law during the Sino-Japanese War, the Boxer Intervention, and the Russo-Japanese War was also an important factor in helping her win a reputation among the Western Powers as a civilized nation, while the formation of the Anglo-Japanese Alliance gave her not only international prestige but also a pretext under which she was later to participate in the First World War against Germany. Clearly, by the end of the second stage, Japan had begun to behave like a Great Power, and to be accepted by the Western

Great Powers as a member of the ruling directorate of international society.

In the third stage of Japan's foreign relations after Perry, which is from about the second decade of the twentieth century, she tried to consolidate her position in international society as a Great Power of Asia equal in importance to those of the West. Japan secured a formal expression of such a status by becoming a permanent member of the Council of the League of Nations after the First World War, while her Twenty-One Demands to China during the War were a clear indication of the imperialist path Japan had set out to follow in the decades to come.

Westernization in Japan's Foreign Relations

We must now examine how the Japanese came to accept Western practices of foreign relations which were entirely alien to them during the period of seclusion. When the Westerners approached the Japanese in the Bakumatsu Period there was a gap between the foreign visitors and the Japanese governing class as regards the purpose of foreign intercourse: the Japanese saw very little, for the tradition of seclusion had been accompanied by the cultivation not only of an inarticulate anti-foreign sentiment, but, combined with it, a belief in autarky. It came to be held, except by a negligible minority, that what foreigners brought were unnecessary luxuries, that they took away what Japan could hardly spare, and that therefore foreign trade was harmful to the Japanese economy and society. This belief was reinforced by the warrior ethos, which emphasized austerity and disdained commerce.

Thus the reluctant abandonment of the seclusion policy in the Bakumatsu Period, and the radical departure from it in the Meiji Period, involved Japanese acceptance of the Western conception of the purpose of foreign intercourse, which reflected the current Western international economic theory and practice.[10] In this sense the abandonment of the policy of seclusion can itself be said to have involved Westernization.

Westernization in Japan's purposes in engaging in foreign intercourse was accompanied by the Western Powers' imposition of their formal methods, or institutions, of foreign relations. This had already begun with the arrival of Perry, who successfully ignored the traditional Japanese methods of dealing with unwanted foreigners. Among these new methods, or institutions, introduced by the West, the most fundamental were the diplomatic/consular system and international law.

The idea of sending letters and envoys abroad had existed among the Japanese prior to seclusion, and the practice of receiving missions from overseas continued in the Edo Period. But the distinctively European idea of a permanently resident diplomatic mission or consul was entirely alien to the Japanese. Perry's proposal to set up a US Consulate in Japan was strongly resisted because the Bakufu assumed a consul to be just an alien civil administrator incompatible with Japan's sovereignty.

However, Perry was also insistent. A solution was found in what appears to be a deliberate mistranslation: the English text of the 1854 US–Japanese treaty secured to the US government the right to send 'consuls or agents to reside in Shimoda' automatically after the expiration of eighteen months from the date of signature, whereas the Japanese text made this conditional on an agreement between the two governments after the eighteen months' period.

There was no provision in the treaty indicating which of the four versions was the original text: the Dutch, English, Chinese, or Japanese. Through such an arrangement, Perry obtained what he wanted, while the Japanese negotiators appear to have tried to cover up their weaknesses.[11]

In accordance with the English provision, Harris arrived in Shimoda in 1856 as a US consul-general. The Bakufu officials strongly protested against his arrival, and severely restricted his freedom, but in the end acquiesced in his presence. By 1858 commercial treaties had been concluded with the West, and the Western Powers secured the right to keep resident diplomatic and consular agents in Japan and obtained extraterritorial rights for their nationals. These developments owe much to Harris's negotiating skills, while the growth of the anti-seclusion party in the Bakufu was also decisive. Japan herself, however, did not send resident missions abroad till the Meiji Period when the policy of seclusion was finally discarded without reservation.

Given its initial insistence that a resident diplomatic or consular agent was incompatible with Japan's sovereignty, it is curious that the Bakufu should have given away extraterritorial rights to foreign nationals on a non-reciprocal basis. Three reasons may be noted here. First, the Japanese negotiators did not have sufficient power to avoid such an arrangement. Second, they negotiated within the seclusionist frame of mind, which meant that, with the one notable exception of the 1855 Russo-Japanese Friendship Treaty, all the treaties envisaged the existence of foreigners in Japan, but not that of the Japanese abroad. This one-sidedness in the balance of interest seems to have reinforced that of the balance of power. Third, the Japanese negotiators were so ignorant of the workings of international relations that they could not foresee the inconvenience and injustices that could result from the arrangement. It should be noted in this connection that Japanese ignorance also explains in part why they unquestioningly gave away the most-favoured-nation clause to Perry, and accepted fixed tariff rates in the negotiations with Harris.[12]

Compared with the case of the resident diplomatic/consular system, the Japanese acceptance of international law went more smoothly, despite the fact that the existence of international law was totally unknown to them. This was because some understanding of international law was essential to the Bakufu in order to cope with the new concepts and rules employed by the West since the arrival of Perry. Moreover, when the Meiji Government was established, it was popularly expected to carry out the expulsion of foreigners, because the anti-Tokugawa forces had used chauvinistic slogans as a means of pressure upon the Bakufu. The new government, however, had neither the power nor the intention to revert to the policy of seclusion, and thus felt the need to justify its foreign policy as soon as it came to power. In this respect, the concept of the law of nations was most appropriate, because the Government could try to pacify the people with the idea that the Western Powers complied with the law of nations and should not be regarded as lawless barbarians. The fact that most textbooks of international law imported to Japan had Natural Law overtones suited the Government well, because the Western Natural Law vocabulary was translated into Japanese through the basic language of Confucianism, which added grandiosity to the new body of rules.[13]

It should also be noted that the Meiji Government used international law both to defend Japan against Western interference in her domestic affairs and as a means of breaking up China's suzerainty over Korea. The Japanese were to achieve this through the use of force, but they also tried to make use of the basic conceptual tools of the Western theory of international relations embodied in international law, such as sovereign equality, independence, and non-intervention, to which the Chinese idea of suzerainty was opposed. At the same time, Japan tried to impress the Western Powers by meticulous observance of international law. Two eminent Japanese jurists were attached to the Army and the Navy respectively during the Sino-Japanese War as the legal adviser of each headquarters. In the Russo-Japanese War many more advisers were involved, some of whom worked at the front.[14] There was a tendency among the Japanese élite to respect international law as part of their West-worship.

Factors Favourable to Japan

Several factors favoured Japan in her struggle in the Western-dominated international society. A comparison with China is particularly instructive.

First, we may compare the two nations' self-images. The Chinese divided the world into the civilized centre, where the Emperor's rule was effective, and the barbaric periphery, where, they thought, Chinese influence had not brought up the standard of morality and living. It is important to note that this division was cultural rather than territorial or ethnic.[15]

The Japanese also had a sense of national superiority. In particular, the scholars of the Japanese classics who were self-consciously opposed to Chinese culture became influential in the nineteenth century. They argued for Japan's uniqueness and superiority on the grounds of Shinto beliefs: that the Japanese Emperor was descended from the Sun-Goddess, that the Japanese Islands and people were also of divine origin, and that therefore Japan was superior to the rest of the world. The Japanese sense of superiority, by contrast with that of the Chinese, was thus closely bound up with the unity of the race and the integrity of the territory in which they had developed their peculiar blend of culture.

This difference between the two nations favoured Japan over China as the Japanese authorities, being more conscious of territory and race than their Chinese counterparts, could perceive the threat from outside more vividly. The 'Black Ships' created an acute sense of crisis among the Japanese leaders, while the Chinese appear to have seen them rather as just another source of nuisance.

A second factor which favoured Japan over China was the difference in the nature of the leadership. Japan was governed by the warrior class. Although 200 years of domestic peace had made Samurais redundant in their original functions as fighters, and turned them virtually into civil administrators, they maintained their traditional mode of thinking as military experts. This helped the Japanese leaders rule out strategically irrational options in responding to the Western threat, and encouraged them to import superior Western technology. By contrast, the Chinese civilian mandarinate had almost no interest in military and technological matters, and even disdained them.

Compared with the Bakufu leaders, anti-foreign factions of the powerful Satsuma and Choshu domains were more deeply misguided by their chauvinism; but through the events of 1863 and 1864, in which they exchanged fire with Western naval forces, they too had to come to realize their impotence in the face of new Western technology, and therefore speeded up their efforts to modernize their forces through foreign aids. In this connection it may also be noted that, unlike their counterparts in China, peasant uprisings in Japan did not develop into a large-scale anti-foreign movement, which would not only have cost Japan military intervention by the Western Powers but also have led to further curtailment of her political independence.

A third factor is the Japanese readiness to learn from abroad, which the Japanese sense of national superiority was not so overwhelming as to rule out. In fact, even during the seclusion period, strong West-worship developed among the so-called Dutch scholars, especially after the middle of the eighteenth century. Although few in number, they nevertheless illustrate the Japanese readiness to seek any new form of knowledge regardless of its cultural or ethnic origins. One tangible result of the scholars' efforts was the production of modern cannon in one of the domains in 1853, the year of Perry's arrival. Westernization in technology and military science, however, was negligible during the Edo Period. The Meiji Period saw a systematic effort by the government and people to import from the West all necessary artefacts and paraphernalia to qualify as a civilized, modern, nation.

A fourth factor was a peculiar structure of dual authority in Japan: the presence of the Emperor in addition to the Shogun. As we saw, the opening up of Japan went side by side with the decline in the power and authority of the Bakufu, but, fortunately for Japan, the Emperor provided a rallying-point for the anti-Tokugawa factions and enabled Japan to avoid a long period of national division. Moreover, a timely change in the government provided Japan with an opportunity to reform its political institutions along Western lines. In China, by contrast, there was no similar second authority to make such a transition possible. The view that the revitalization of China in the face of the Western encroachment required the modernization of her political institutions as well as the importation of Western technology was defeated by the conservative intellectual outlook of the ruling class and the inertia of the old institutions.[16]

Westernization in both technology and institutions distinguishes the experience of Japan in the nineteenth century from that of China. This institutional Westernization helped Japan to attain the position of equality with the Western Powers because the revision of 'unequal' treaties had been made conditional upon her internal law reforms on the Western model. Moreover, the abolition of the feudal system and introduction of a centralized form of land-taxation by the Meiji Government gave Japan a national basis for state-led industrialization.

How real this institutional Westernization has been in Japan since the latter part of the nineteenth century is a question that cannot be dealt with in this chapter. It should be noted, however, that at the level of ethics, traditional Confucian values were stressed through state-controlled education, and at the deeper level of social psychology, the Japanese conceptions of personal relationships appear to have remained largely unchanged despite the West-worship of the Meiji Period.

Fifthly, geographical factors and their implications should be noted. Japan was far smaller than China and, viewed from Europe, lay beyond the Chinese subcontinent. This had made China the more compelling centre of attraction for European capitalism and its first victim in the Far East. The resultant time-lag was valuable for Japan. It enabled some enlightened Japanese leaders of the Bakumatsu Period, who learnt about the developments in the neighbouring country through the Dutch Factory, to try their utmost to avoid repeating China's mistakes.

Moreover, Japan managed to maintain the policy of seclusion precariously in a distant corner of the world until the leading European Powers' expansion began to slow down. Britain and France had enough on their hands in China, as witnessed by their involvement in the Taiping Rebellion and the Arrow War. In addition, Britain, France, and Russia became engaged in the Crimean War. This momentary deceleration in European expansionism left America to take the initiative in the opening up of Japan. Fortunately for Japan, the change in the United States Presidency from Fillmore, a Republican, to Pierce, a Democrat, reduced the militancy of American policy towards the Far East. What the Americans saw in Japan was chiefly port facilities, vital for their trade with China, and for their whaling industry in the Northern Pacific, but not a territory to colonize.[17]

In addition, the small size of Japan made it relatively easy, when the new government came to power, for it to extend its rule effectively to the whole territory and to maintain a centralized system – something that was much more difficult for China partly because of her sheer bulk.

A number of other factors can be added to the above list, for example, the level of Japanese economic development, and that of literacy in the Bakumatsu and early Meiji Periods. The above analysis tends to show, however, that Japan's advancement in international society is due partly to a fortunate set of circumstances and partly also to Japan's conscious effort to strengthen herself and respond rationally to the pressure from outside. Her eagerness to satisfy Western standards of civilization in external affairs was also vital. The proofs that she had achieved these standards included not only her acceptance of international law and the diplomatic system but also the winning of wars against China and Russia. As Martin Wight remarks, 'as the head-hunters of Borneo entered into manhood by taking their first head, so a power becomes a great power by successful war against another great power'.[18] The case of Japan was no exception.

13

THE ERA OF THE MANDATES SYSTEM AND THE NON-EUROPEAN WORLD

Wm. Roger Louis

At the time of the invention of the condominium of the Sudan in 1899, Lord Salisbury, according to Lord Cromer, 'joyfully agreed to the creation of a hybrid State of a nature eminently calculated to shock the suceptibilities of international jurists'.[1] In 1919 at the Paris Peace Conference a sense of humour from time to time also relieved the ponderous deliberations of the founders of a similar fabrication in international history, the mandates system of the League of Nations. At one stage in the discussions, Clemenceau said to Lloyd George that it was time to hear from the 'cannibals' of Australia and New Zealand. The 'cannibals' were the Prime Ministers of the two antipodean Dominions. The latter proceeded successfully to argue that the 'head-hunters' of New Guinea and the 'primitive' peoples of Samoa and South West Africa did not fall into the same category as the more 'advanced' peoples of the Middle East and differed even from those of tropical Africa.[2]

The colonial settlement of 1919 in effect defined three classifications of mankind: the 'A' peoples of the Middle East, who in a relatively short period of time would be able 'to stand alone'; the tribal 'B' peoples of tropical Africa, who would require an indefinite number of years or decades of economic and political advancement under European tutelage; and the 'C' 'primitive' peoples of the Pacific and the 'Hottentots' of South West Africa, who probably would remain European subjects at least for a period of centuries, if not forever. Though it was not the purpose of the founders of the mandates system to generalize, the American respresentative, at least, could well have extended the categories of 'A', 'B', and 'C' to apply to such countries as (a) India, Indochina, and Indonesia; (b) all of tropical Africa and the Caribbean; and (c) peoples of the island groups and other remote territories who still existed in the 'stone age'. Those paternalistic distinctions held good for the leaders of the anti-colonial movements as well as for supporters of empire. For those who made the actual decision to establish the mandates system, the Sudan condominium provided an example of how to deal with the problem of expanding empires without blatantly adopting a policy of annexation pure and simple. The representatives of the colonial powers no doubt believed in their civilizing mission. They also found it politically expedient to pay homage to international convention and the tradition of trusteeship.

The principles set forth in Article 22 of the League's Covenant (the 'Charter' of the mandates system) were only implicitly universal, and the imperial powers agreed to be held accountable to the League only for the specific ex-territories of the Ottoman and German Empires. The heart of the mandates system was accountability. In the interwar period the administering authorities submitted annual reports to the Permanent Mandates Commission to prove that they were fulfilling the obligation of holding the mandates (in the words of Article 22) as 'a sacred trust of civilization', in other words, for the welfare of the 'natives' and not for purposes of exploitation. The territorial settlement agreed upon in Paris was:

'A' mandates	Iraq	Great Britain
	Palestine	,, ,,
	Syria	France
'B' mandates	Togo	Divided between Britain and France
	Cameroons	,, (nine-tenths to France)
	Tanganyika	Britain
	Ruanda-Urundi	Belgium
'C' mandates	South West Africa	South Africa
	New Guinea	Australia
	Samoa	New Zealand
	Marshall, Carolines, and Marianas	Japan

Despite considerable discussion in the 1930s about the possible return to Germany of her former colonies, the administration of the mandates remained constant during the interwar period.

For the purposes of this volume, the mandates system will represent a prism that disperses light on the 'colonial question' of the interwar period. To comprehend the mentality of those who presided over the colonial regimes during that era, it is helpful to examine both the antecedents and the legacies of the mandates as well as the racial assumptions of the European protagonists. The immediate antecedent of the mandates was the Berlin Act of 1885 and the principal legacy was the trusteeship of the United Nations. The overriding racial preconceptions, implicit in the 'A', 'B', and 'C' categories, may be described in the words of the grandson of Lord Salisbury of the 'Scramble', the 5th Marquess of Salisbury, who at the San Francisco Conference of 1945 spoke of a 'colonial ladder' which the colonial peoples would climb at their own time and pace. The general outlook in 1945 was remarkably similar to that in 1919. It altered substantially only after the close of the Second World War when the pace towards independence accelerated dramatically. Political groups in England such as the Fabian Colonial Bureau demanded reform and political progress, as did individuals such as President Wilson and President Roosevelt; but even the reformers foresaw colonial development as an evolutionary process that would take place over many decades and, in the case of New Guinea, over many centuries. 'Gradualism' is the best word to summarize the tenets of 'enlightened imperialism' in 1919 and 1945.

In the realm of the history of ideas the origins of the mandates may be directly traced to the era of the partition of Africa. At an early stage of the 'Scramble' the European powers in 1884–5 attempted to regulate the opening up of Africa by establishing freedom of trade in the basins of the Congo and Niger. Agreement on this basic point could be reached because none of the European powers wished to be afflicted by trade barriers of another. King Leopold's Congo consequently was established as a buffer between commercial and territorial rivalries of the great powers in central Africa. The Congo Free State subsequently became notorious for violating, among other things, the free trade provisions of the Berlin Act. King Leopold's regime caricatured the spirit of 'free trade' to an extent that the creators of the mandates system in 1919 looked back on this grotesque failure of 'international law' with a determination to make the 'A' and 'B' mandates genuine free trade zones (in which they largely succeeded). Another basic provision of the Berlin Act was the protection of the 'natives'. King Leopold's Congo also made a mockery of the phrase 'native welfare', and again the inventors of the mandates system resolved to make improvements on the Berlin Act (and it is arguable that the progress in education, health, and agriculture in the mandated territories at least matched the development in neighbouring colonies because administrators knew that the mandates stood as showcases exposed to the glare of international publicity).

The Berlin Act of course was not the only precedent for the establishment of the mandates system. In the Middle East the history of the British occupation of Egypt seemed especially pertinent to the British

Colonial Secretary in 1919, Lord Milner. He believed that Britain had amply fulfilled a sacred trust:

Lord Milner pointed out that the mandatory principle was not altogether an innovation. Our administration of Egypt for thirty-five years was carried on on that principle, and subject to innumerable obligations which we consistently fulfilled, at one time to the extent of giving a decided preference to other nations over ourselves.[3]

Since the occupation of Egypt, even when justified on grounds of trusteeship, did not appeal to the French or the Americans, the British in 1919 decided to emphasize the relevance of the Berlin Act. In Lloyd George's words, there was 'no large difference between the mandatory principle and the principles laid down by the Berlin Conference'.[4] To put it more directly, the mandates were regarded, in the phrase current at the time, as 'colonies in all but name'. Winston Churchill said publicly and candidly in his capacity of Colonial Secretary in 1921 in regard to Palestine and Iraq: 'we are . . . in possession of those territories.'[5]

It would be a mistake entirely to dismiss the traditional idealistic version of the history of the mandates system. To some extent it was a triumph of internationalism over nationalism, free trade over monopoly, humanitarianism over slavery, and self-determination over imperialism. These idealistic elements of the mandates had deep and different sources: international control emanated from the concerted action of the great powers as 'trustees' of peace and order; free trade was connected with the open door policy of equal commercial opportunity; 'native welfare' flowed from the anti-slavery tradition; and self-determination appeared to be derived from European nationalism.

'Self-determination' – the principle championed by the leaders of the Russian Revolution and by Woodrow Wilson alike – is indelibly associated with the mandates system and the colonial controversy between Churchill and Roosevelt during the Second World War. It is the catchphrase that the British and French accepted only with great circumspection. At the close of the First World War no one could predict for certain that a referendum in Syria, Palestine, or Iraq would be satisfactory to the British or the French, or for that matter whether the result might be in favour of the Americans because of local antipathy towards the British or French. It could also not be assumed the plebiscites would inevitably lead eventually to independence or irrevocably to incorporation in the existing British or French Empires. President Wilson for example thought that the best solution to the problem of South West Africa would be absorption into South Africa. South Africa would merely have formally to prove worthy of the 'sacred trust'.

By contrast General Smuts was especially aware that the principle of self-determination might backfire against South Africa because of the principle's ambiguity. He after all was one of the principal inventors of the mandates system, which he had mainly envisaged as a solution to the problems of central Europe and the Middle East. When the future of the Ottoman territories became linked with the disposal of the German colonies, Smuts became hoist on his own mandatory petard. Since South West Africa was a German colony, and since *all* German colonies logically would become mandates, Smuts had no choice. He could only lament that he felt like the girl who wanted to keep her illegitimate child – South West Africa was only a very small baby.[6]

After considerable soul-searching, the British War Cabinet decided to endorse the principle of self-determination, for reasons well stated by Lord Curzon in December 1918:

> I am inclined to value the argument of self-determination because I believe that most of the people would determine in our favour . . . if we cannot get out of our difficulties in any other way we ought to play self-determination for all it is worth wherever we are involved in difficulties with the French, the Arabs, or anybody else, and leave the case to be settled by that final argument knowing in the bottom of our hearts that we are more likely to benefit from it than anybody else.[7]

Little over two decades later such confidence had given way to suspicion that the Americans might use the principle of self-determination to subvert the British Empire.

By the time of the Second World War the principle of self-determination had been identified in England, in Tory circles at least, as one of the most dangerous spirits escaping from the Pandora's box of the First World War settlement. Churchill was eager to apply the principle to conquered territories 'under the Nazi yoke' in Europe, but he resolutely refused to extend it to the colonial world. There lay the issue at stake in the famous colonial controversy between Churchill and Roosevelt over the interpretation of the Atlantic Charter. Article three of the Charter endorsed the right of all peoples 'to choose the form of government under which they will live'. Roosevelt maintained that the principles of the Atlantic Charter were global in scope. So also did an influential segment of the British political Left. According to the headlines of the *Daily Herald*, after an interview with Clement Attlee: '*The Atlantic Charter: IT MEANS DARK RACES AS WELL'*.[8] In this controversy the stalwarts of the British Empire such as Leo Amery argued that self-determination of 'the form of government under which they will live' could merely mean self-government. But even this seemingly innocuous interpretation alarmed the Colonial Secretary in 1941, Lord Moyne:

Some Colonies are so small, or strategically so important, that complete self-government seems out of the question; and I cannot, for instance, imagine any conditions under which we would give Dominion status to Aden, Gibraltar, the Gambia or British Honduras.[9]

The more that Colonial Office officials studied the problem, the more they became alarmed at the far-reaching consequences of self-government:

Gibraltar, Aden, Mauritius, Seychelles, Fiji, the Western Pacific islands, the Falklands, British Honduras, Bermuda, the Gambia, Hong Kong. All these Colonies, and probably others (Cyprus, Malta, the dependencies in Borneo, and even Malaya) are too small or too important strategically ever to become independent self-governing units.[10]

The Colonial Office's fears were realized. After the Second World War the affirmation of the principle of self-determination by countries of the 'Third World' contributed substantially to the multiplication of national sovereignties and in particular to the 'balkanization' of the African continent. The present-day politically-fragmented map of the world represents the opposite of the Colonial Office's vision of large regional configurations that would have been, it was hoped, economically viable and politically stable.

As the European powers consolidated their administrations in the interwar period, publicists and supporters of empire provided an ideological basis of colonialism. Sir Frederick (later Lord) Lugard's *Dual Mandate* is a paramount example of the argument that the European powers had an obligation to develop colonies for the benefit of the local inhabitants and for the world at large. Lugard served from 1923 to 1936 on the Permanent Mandates Commission. He made himself thoroughly unpopular in the Colonial Office because of his meticulous criticism of the annual reports. But there was no disagreement between Lugard and the Colonial Office about the purpose of colonial rule which he saw as gradual economic and social development , and, in due course, political progress through representative institutions. Roland Oliver has written of the civil servants who created this colonial consensus:

After 1919 colonialism has so far seemed in comparison distinctly gentler and more law-abiding – its moral outlook conditioned by the mandates system, its new concern for the welfare of its African subjects expressed in a score of major reports and policy statements. The colonialism of the 1920's and 1930's has been seen as smug and paternalistic, and certainly as very unrealistic about the time at its disposal; but the people operating it have so far emerged as a decent and forward-looking lot, very different from the swashbucklers and scallywags of the Scramble.[11]

In the interwar years and especially during the Second World War, critics of the colonial system increasingly identified racial tension as a major problem in the colonies. They demanded elimination of the 'colour-bar' and here, in theory at least, the mandated territories and the European colonies generally stood in advance of such multi-racial countries as the United States.

The question of race is essential in a broad understanding of attitudes of the mandates area. Officials of that generation not only tended to classify groups of 'backward races' into 'A', 'B', and 'C' categories of 'civilization' but also identified national races. The British for example held firm ideas about the 'British race' and more often than not regarded it as superior to any other. They saw the difference between their race and the Latin or Teutonic races as distinctly as they saw the difference between the Chinese and Japanese or Arab and Jewish races. There was often a question of 'colour' and 'kinship' involved in the distinction. British statesmen at the beginning of the era referred to the 'yellow men' of Japan as their brave but dangerous allies during the First World War and to the Americans as their 'kith and kin', at least those Americans of old stock, meaning of course those of English descent. In the latter part of the era the racial policies of Nazi Germany exacerbated the relations between the Jewish and Arab 'races' by driving an increasing number of Jews to Palestine. The following sections attempt to take the racial as well as the ethical and strategic aspects of the 'sacred trust' into account.

The 'A' Mandates

Of all the mandated territories, and indeed in all the 'colonial world', Palestine stands out as a unique case. Its complicated history for purposes of this chapter may be summarized in relation to the Balfour Declaration of 1917, which Zionists regarded as a solemn promise to establish a Jewish 'national home' (and sometimes a national 'state') in Palestine – a commitment that must be studied in relation to the labyrinth of contradictory assurances given to Arab nationalists.[12] From 1917 until the late 1930s the British followed a wavering course of reconciliation between Jews and Arabs while at the same time they attempted to anchor the security of the British Empire in the eastern Mediterranean. It is possible in the space here only to hint at the complexity of the problem, but the themes of racial conflict, ethical commitment, and strategic security can be made clear.

In 1921, when Winston Churchill was Colonial Secretary, the British government attempted to make a final clarification of the Balfour Declaration by reaffirming the Jewish 'national home' and by creating Transjordan as a separate territory that would remain Arab. The final form of government in Palestine, whether unitary or federal, remained open. Churchill expressed the crux of the issue in relation to other mandated territories when he said in 1921: 'The difficulty about this promise of a National Home for the Jews in Palestine is that it conflicts with our regular policy of consulting the wishes of the people in the Mandated territories and of giving them representative institutions as soon as they are fit for them.'[13] Churchill exaggerated the reality of a 'regular policy', but as one did evolve in Palestine it amounted to the hope that the problem of self-determination could be resolved by Arabs and Jews reaching a consensus about the future form of government.

Until the late 1930s British policy in Palestine was based on the premiss that the two races would be able to sink their differences and live harmoniously in a single state. Leo Amery, who had been involved in the Palestine question since the time of the Balfour Declaration, stated in 1939: 'Palestine, like Canada or South Africa, must always be a State in which two different elements had to recognize each other's equal rights.'[14] The famous White Paper of 1939 was interpreted by the Zionists and many others as an abnegation of the Balfour Declaration. It limited Jewish immigration, thereby seeming to ensure an Arab majority and a Jewish minority of about 33⅓ per cent. The British, facing the global crises of the late 1930s and an actual Arab rebellion in Palestine itself, attempted to placate Arab nationalism. The significance of this episode in relation to the question of the Palestine mandate as a 'sacred trust' is that robust champions of the British Empire such as Churchill and Amery regarded the White Paper of 1939 as a violation of mandatory accountability and an ethical breach of faith with the Jews. In any case the developments of the late 1930s and the 1940s belied the conviction of A. J. Balfour that the principle of self-determination in a small territory with an insignificant population would never be a matter of great moment for the British Empire.

The question of self-determination was closely linked with Britain's future as a strategic power in the eastern Mediterranean. In this regard the views of Colonel Richard Meinertzhagen are illuminating because he served as military adviser on Middle Eastern questions at the Paris Peace Conference. Unlike most of his colleagues in the War Office and the Colonial Office, he took a strong pro-Zionist line. His ideas help to put the general pro-Arab attitudes of the Foreign Office in relief. He argued that the British could never be on good terms with both Jews and Arabs. He therefore thought it would be best to cement the friendship with the Jews on the basis of the Balfour Declaration because, among other reasons, they would eventually hold the supreme strategic position in the Middle East. He wrote in March 1919:

This Peace Conference has laid two eggs – Jewish Nationalism and Arab Nationalism: these are going to grow up into troublesome chickens. . . . In fifty years time both Jew and Arab will be obsessed with nationalism, the natural outcome of the President's [i.e. Wilson's] self-determination. . . .

The British position in the Middle East is paramount; the force of nationalism will challenge our position. We cannot befriend both Jew and Arab. My proposal is based on befriending the people who are more likely to be loyal friends – the Jews. . . .[15]

In contrast with the Arabophile strategists of the Chiefs of Staff and the Foreign Office, who wished to forge a line of defence through Arab alliances, Meinertzhagen believed in the opposite solution, an alliance with the Jews. 'Palestine is the corner-stone of the Middle East', he wrote. 'Bounded on two sides by the desert and on one side by the sea', it possessed 'the best natural harbour in the East Mediterranean'. In sum an alliance with a Jewish state would provide the best strategic defence of the British Empire in the Middle East.[16]

The long and the short of the history of imperial strategy in the eastern Mediterranean in the interwar years is that Meinertzhagen's analysis proved to be right in at least one negative aspect. The British in 1939 attempted to appease the Arabs and remain friends with the Jews. They succeeded in neither. Nevertheless the British White Paper of 1939 pacified the Arabs to the extent that, in Elizabeth Monroe's words, 'it helped to secure enough Arab compliance to tide Great Britain over the war years.'[17]

Strategic assessments of all the other 'A' mandates – Syria (and Lebanon), Iraq, and Transjordan – were made against the background of a possible single, united Hashemite state stretching across the fertile crescent. The alternative was separate mandatory regimes. One of the reasons behind British determination to hold on to Palestine following the First World War was to counterbalance French influence in Syria. Syria, like the other 'A' mandates, seemed to possess distinctive strategic characteristics. Syria was the heartland of Arab nationalism, geographically forming the northern frontier of the Arabian penisula and strategically providing a major overland route to Iraq and the Persian gulf. Iraq in turn also was a vital link in the British-Palestine-Transjordan-Iraq-Bahrein 'connection'. Transjordan, the only Middle Eastern country where the British achieved their defence goals in the 1940s, similarly occupied, in the words of the British Chiefs of Staff, 'a central position in relation to the Middle East area as a whole and in the fact that direct communications between the oil producing areas of Iraq and Persia and our main base and supply areas in Palestine and Egypt traverse the country'.[18]

The pan-Hashemite scheme to unite those territories is associated with Hussein I, King of the Hejaz and Sharif of Mecca. His idea of a single state failed in part because of the French acquisition of Syria as a mandate and other international developments, but his two sons, Abdullah and Feisal, eventually became Kings of Transjordan and Iraq respectively, and their countries remained within the orbit of Britain's 'informal empire' until the mid-1950s. For purposes of this chapter the most important event of the interwar years was the treaty concluded between Britain and Iraq in 1930. It granted Iraq independence and paved the way for her admission to the League of Nations in 1932. Britain's relinquishment of the mandate and Iraq's unanimous acceptance into the comity of nations was watched enviously by Syrian nationalists and was widely publicized at the time as Britain's fulfilment of the 'sacred trust'.

The recently divulged secrets of the British archives re-enforce contemporary suspicions that the British intended to grant only nominal independence to Iraq. The treaty of 1930 heralded British attempts to transform mandates and protectorates into 'independent' states bound economically and militarily to the 'informal' British Empire. A remark made by Stafford Cripps in the House of Commons in 1939 in regard to Palestine summarizes the general goal of British Middle Eastern policy in the 1930s and 1940s: Palestine, like Britain's other mandates, was 'to continue as an annex of the British Empire, though it will be annexed by treaty and not by conquest.'[19]

THE 'B' MANDATES

The 'B' mandates of tropical Africa were the heart of the mandates system. The 'A' and 'C' mandates in comparison were makeshift solutions, the former to be converted into semi-independent states as soon as possible, the latter to be transformed into permanent acquisitions as soon as international circumstances permitted. Tropical Africa was the part of the world where most of the members of the Permanent Mandates Commission had acquired their expertise, either as administrators, diplomats, or scholars. Lord Lugard again is the paramount example of a tropical African explorer, administrator, pro-consul, publicist, and philosopher. His name is virtually synonymous with the theory of 'indirect rule'. Like most of his colleagues he displayed considerable caution about stirring up new problems in the cauldron of Middle Eastern troubles, and he thought that colonial rule in the Pacific should adhere to the general precedents established in tropical Africa. The major debates of the Permanent Mandates Commission concerned such African questions as land tenure, commercial monopolies, taxation, justice, and education. The decisions of the Permanent Mandates Commission on those issues set standards for the entire colonial world as well as for the specific mandated territories. The mandates system acted as a negative check against economic exploitation and religious discrimination, and the Permanent Mandates Commission insisted on minimum standards of colonial administration. In a more positive vein, the mandates sytem encouraged economic and political progress in order to enable the 'child-like' races of tropical Africa eventually to climb the colonial ladder and become fully developed children of the parent state.

The 'B' mandates were significant militarily and strategically. Militarily the mandates for the Cameroons and Togo specifically gave France, in contrast to the other 'B' mandatory regimes, the right to raise African troops 'in the event of a general war'. Lloyd George referred to this provision as the French 'nigger army' clause. It caused British Colonial Office officials to speculate that the French might eventually attack British territories with African troops. Leo Amery, Under-Secretary at the Colonial Office after the First World War, held the view that the French 'want nigger conscripts not against us but to hold down Arabs & Germans'.[20] The War Office argued that 'the French are aware of the comparative immunity and peace of the territories in which they will be raised, and of the great assistance they can render in more disturbed areas elsewhere'.[21] The War Office also held the view that the First World War had weakened the British military position in India and therefore the British, like the French, should look to Africa for conscripts. The British did not in fact request permission from the League to raise troops in East Africa, but the extensive discussions on this point indicate how carefully British officials weighed each humanitarian, legal clause of the mandates in relation to military strength and security throughout the world.

Tanganyika provided the richest ground for strategic speculation. According to General Smuts in August 1918:

> The British Empire was the great African Power right along the eastern half of the continent, and securing East Africa would give us through communication along the whole length of the continent – a matter of the greatest importance from the point of view of both land and of air communications . . .[22]

The revival of the idea of the 'Cape to Cairo Route', one by air if not by rail, titillated armchair strategists of the interwar period, and during the Second World War some British officials penned lines identical with those of Smuts two decades earlier. In the more hard-headed view of the Chiefs of Staff, Tanganyika at least had a denial value. By retaining Tanganyika as a mandated or trust territory, Germany would be denied the opportunity to build a base for submarines, which, with greatly increased cruising range and torpedo power, might paralyse British movements in the Indian Ocean. Such speculation almost rivalled Smuts's idea at the close of the Second World War that it would be desirable to establish a British atomic arsenal in Cyrenaica in order to hold the strategic balance between the United States and the Soviet Union.[23] The colonial world continued to provide fertile ground for imaginative minds intent on strategic security.

The 'C' Mandates

All of the 'C' mandates, with the partial exception of Samoa, were regarded as strategically indispensable to each of the mandatory powers. The South Africans regarded South West Africa as an 'integral part' of South Africa. They thought that its absorption into the Union would be indispensable in guarding against the danger of resurgent German militarism in South Africa as well as in the former colony. The Australians viewed New Guinea and the Bismarck archipelago as an outer defence perimeter shielding Australia from Japan. The Japanese believed that the mandated islands would provide an effective defence barrier against the United States in the event of a Pacific war. The New Zealanders regarded the possible re-entry of the Germans into Samoa as only a remote danger and were the only ones to consider the return of the colony (provided Samoa was not converted into a naval base). The general significance of New Zealand's trusteeship lies in the response to the nationalist movement, the Mau, rather than in the strategic dimension of trusteeship. All of the 'C' mandates were administered as integral parts of the madatory power. The colonial powers possessed complete control over immigration, commercial, and defence policies. Apart from the requirements to submit annual reports to the League of Nations, the 'C' mandatory powers held their mandated territories as colonies in all but name.

The 'C' classification in relation to the themes of this chapter is especially relevant because Japan was a 'C' mandatory power, the only non-white maritime colonial power in the League of Nations and the only nation in Asia with ambitions of territorial aggrandizement. There were two ways in which Japan's expansionist aims directly jeopardized the British Empire, and, less substantially though no less important, the United States. The first was the attempt to reduce China to the status of a Japanese satellite. The second was the ambition to create a 'co-prosperity sphere' that would have eliminated Western colonialism in South East Asia. And there was a third important dimension of Japanese imperialism. Japanese hegemony in Asia would undermine the moral pretence of the Western powers ruling the non-Western world. It would subvert the tacit assumption that the white man's rule was innately superior. It would destroy such crude classifications as 'A', 'B', and 'C' peoples at different levels of 'civilization'.

As an ally without whom Britain could not have won the First World War, Japan at the Paris Peace Conference expected to be admitted to the League of Nations on an equal footing. Instead the Japanese failed to obtain a 'racial equality' clause in the League's Covenant. The smouldering resentment of the Japanese consequently became a mainspring of the Pacific war.[24] A Japanese diplomat explained to an Australian military officer in 1920:

> Mr. Hanihara begs leave to remind Major Piesse that the utterances of Japanese delegates and steps taken by them at the Conference, demonstrated that Japan's object was not 'the removal of restrictions on immigration', but the elimination of racial discrimination – a discrimination which, for no reason but of the colour of skin, deprives men of equal opportunity in life, and often subjects them to an unbearable humiliation.[25]

One of the Far Eastern experts of the British Foreign Office wrote in the aftermath of the Peace Conference: 'If we probe this problem to its depths it cannot be disguised that in the last analysis it is primarily and fundamentally racial in character, and that the political and economic aspects, important as they are, are in reality only secondary compared with the underlying racial problem.'[26] In the 1930s the Japanese came to believe that a pan-Asian movement under Japanese leadership would liberate Asia from Western imperialism and end the implicit assumption of racial inferiority. The racial irritation suffered by the Japanese through the League of Nations and its component, the mandates system, contributed only in a minor way to the origins of the Pacific war of 1941–5, even if the war is viewed pre-eminently as a racial struggle. Yet in the resurrection of the mandates system at the San Francisco Conference of 1945 can be found a reflection of the racial conflict. The trusteeship system of the United Nations was not based on the implicit racism of 'A', 'B', and 'C' peoples but on the premiss of racial equality.

Part III

The Challenge to Western Dominance

14

THE REVOLT AGAINST THE WEST

Hedley Bull

By the time of the First World War, as we saw in Part II, there existed not only a worldwide international system but also an international society that was universal in the sense that it covered all the world and included states from Asia, Africa, and the Americas as well as Europe. In this universal international society, however, a position of dominance was still occupied by the European powers, or more broadly (since Europe's offshoots in north and south America, southern Africa, and Australasia partook of this dominance) by the Western powers, which continued to occupy this position until the Second World War. After the Second World War a revolt against Western dominance – a revolt which had been growing in strength earlier in the century, and whose roots lay late in the last century – became powerful enough to shake the system.

The dominance of the European or Western powers at the turn of the century was expressed not only in their superior economic and military power and in their commanding intellectual and cultural authority but also in the rules and institutions of international society. This society was still seen as an association of mainly European and Christian states, to which outside political communities could be admitted only if and when they met the criteria for membership laid down by the founding members – as Japan by 1900 was widely deemed to have done and China not yet to have done. The rules of international law which then prevailed had been made, for the most part, by these European or Western states, which had consented to them through custom or treaties concluded among themselves; the governments and peoples of Asia, Africa, and Oceania, who were subject to these rules, had not given their consent to them. The international legal rules, moreover, were not only made by the European or Western powers, they were also in substantial measure made *for* them: part, at least, of the content of the then existing international law (e.g. treaty law, which upheld the validity of treaties concluded under duress; the law of state sovereignty, which took no account of the self-determination of peoples; the law governing the use of force, which made resort to force a prerogative right of states) served to facilitate the maintenance of European or Western ascendancy.

At the turn of the century the chief pillars of this system of dominance were the European colonial powers, especially Britain and France, and to a lesser extent the latecomers, Germany and Italy; and even as late as the early years of the Second World War, this still appeared to be the case. But the United States, the white dominions of the British Empire, the Latin American republics, and indeed the Russian Empire were also supporters and beneficiaries of Western dominance, even if in some cases ambiguously; and as the revolt unfolded against it, later in the century, they too became its targets.

The United States, it is true, saw itself as an anti-colonial power, sympathized with anti-colonial rhetoric, which was the rhetoric of its own war of independence, and resented the exclusiveness of European imperial structures, in which its trade was sometimes put at a disadvantage. But the American colonies which gained their independence from Britain were themselves a product of the process of European expansion; the United States carried this process further by extending its dominion across the north American continent to consolidate its territory, subjugating aboriginal peoples as it did so; it expanded in the Caribbean and the Pacific to become a colonial power in its own right; its denial of equal rights to black Americans aligned it with European policies of racial exclusiveness; and the economic position it acquired for itself in Asia and Africa was such that, when European colonial rule eventually disappeared and neo-colonialism became the principal target of Third World protest, the United States came to be viewed as the main antagonist.

Russia, it is true, has always been perceived in Europe as semi-Asiatic in character, a perception confirmed by the ambivalence in Russia's own mind as to whether it belongs to the West or not; it was, until recently, a relatively backward and under-developed country, vulnerable to the Western great powers as Asian countries have been; the efforts of Russian reformers, from Peter the Great onwards, to learn from the West so as to be able to compete with it provide a model which Asians and Africans have followed; and since 1917 the Soviet state has rendered powerful assistance to the forces struggling against Western dominance as their ally and champion. But like the United States, the imperial Russia of the turn of the century was the product of European expansion; like the maritime expansion of the Western European states, the expansion of Russia by land proceeded by the subjugation of indigenous communities and immigration and settlement by metropolitan peoples. Its frontiers, determined in places by 'unequal treaties', and its non-European peoples, originally subject to Russian dominance, still partly define the character of the Soviet Union today, rendering it also a potential target of Third World hostility.

The Latin American republics, like the United States, have an anti-colonial and national liberationist tradition. In the late nineteenth and early twentieth centuries, moreover, at a time when the United States saw itself as a newly arrived great power, the Latin American states saw themselves as victims of great power dominance and intervention; their attempts to impose legal limitations on the use of force in international relations and to strengthen the principle of non-intervention were an anticipation of the later policies of the Third World. In the post-colonial world their posture in world affairs has been that of poor, under-developed states, allied with Asians and Africans in the Group of 77 and the Non-Aligned Movement. But they, too, are the products of the process of European expansion; they are founded upon the subjugation of aboriginal peoples, whom some of them continue to oppress; they are chiefly Western in language, religion, and other aspects of culture, and if anything distinguishes their position from that of the United States in the context of the revolt against Western dominance, it is only their conspicuous failure to match it in economic or political development.

European or Western dominance of the universal international society may be said to have reached its apogee about the year 1900. It is true that at that time the Western impact on the world was in many respects less far-reaching than it has since become. European colonial expansion did not reach to its fullest extent until the period between the two world wars. African and Asian societies, even under colonial rule, were not then as entangled in the world economy as they were to become in the post-colonial period. The technological distances between the most advanced Western societies and most Asian and African societies, although this is difficult to measure, may be judged to be in some respects greater now than it was then. The intellectual and cultural penetration of Asian and African societies by the West was less profound then than it was to become later.

But at the turn of the century the dominance of the European or Western powers expressed a sense of self-assurance, both about the durability of their position in international society and about its moral purpose, that did not survive the First World War. In non-Western societies also the ascendancy of the West was still widely regarded as a fact of nature rather than as something which could or should be changed. The spiritual or psychological supremacy of the West was at its highest point, even if its material or technological supremacy was not. In their attitudes to other peoples, moreover, the Western powers displayed a measure of unity, of which a striking expression in 1900 was their intervention in China to suppress the Boxer Rising. The leading states of the old, European-dominated international order sank their differences and sent an international army that inflicted humiliation upon the greatest of non-Western societies. The presence in this international army of a Japanese contingent, however, showed that the system was already changing. The Japanese did not respond to the Dowager Empress's request to the Mikado for Asian unity against the West, but joined in the defence of the international society of states, to membership of which they had graduated.

The revolt against Western dominance, which had already begun at this time, comprised five phases or themes. First, there was what we may call the struggle for equal sovereignty. This was the struggle of those states which retained their formal independence, but enjoyed only a subordinate or inferior status, to achieve equal rights as sovereign states. The marks of their inferiority included so-called 'unequal treaties' – treaties concluded under duress, conferring conspicuously unequal benefits on the parties to them, and impairing the sovereignty of the non-Western states concerned – and especially those conferring rights of extraterritorial jurisdiction on the citizens of Western states within the territories of non-Western states. The lead in this struggle was taken by Japan, which freed itself of extraterritorial jurisdiction in the course of the 1890s, and went on to achieve the status not merely of a sovereign state equal in rights to the Western powers, but of a great power able to impose "unequal treaties" of its own on Korea and China. Turkey achieved the elimination of extraterritorial jurisdiction through the Treaty of Lausanne in 1923 (the system had been unilaterally repudiated by the Ottoman Empire on entering the war in 1914, but re-imposed by the victorious Allies through the Treaty of Sèvres in 1920); Egypt through the Anglo-Egyptian Treaty of 1936; China through agreement with the United States and Britain in 1943. In the Persian Gulf, where the old international order survived for a period after it had disappeared elsewhere, as the Empire of Trebizond survived the fall of Byzantium, extraterritorial jurisdiction continued until the British withdrawal in 1971.

Secondly, there was the anti-colonial revolution, by which we normally mean the struggle of Asian, African, Caribbean, and Pacific peoples for formal political independence of European and American colonial rule, although it is worth noting that Korea between 1912 and 1945 was a colony not of any European power but of Japan, that the Sudan between 1899 and 1956 was a quasi-colony of Egypt in conjunction with Britain, and that the European peoples of Cyprus and Malta still had the status of colonial dependencies after the Second World War. Although the colonial system was disturbed by the prominence given to the principle of national self-determination in the Bolshevik Revolution, the 1919 Peace Settlement, and the evolution of the British Commonwealth in the interwar period, the revolution that overthrew it in the non-Western world belongs chiefly to the post-1945 era: the Asian colonial dependencies became independent for the most part in the late 1940s and 1950s, the African territories in the 1960s and 1970s. With the collapse of the Portuguese empire in 1974–5 the era of classic, European colonialism came to an end, even though the anti-colonial movement had further targets in white minority rule in southern Africa and Jewish rule in Palestine.

Thirdly, there has been the struggle for racial equality, or more accurately the struggle of non-white states and peoples against white supremacism. The old Western-dominated international order was associated with the privileged position of the white race: the international society of states was at first exclusively, and even in its last days principally, one of white states; non-white peoples everywhere, whether as minority communities within these white states, as majority communities ruled by minorities of whites, or as independent peoples dominated by white powers, suffered the stigma of inferior status. The struggle to change this state of affairs spans many centuries and touches the internal history of states as well as their relations with one another. It encompasses the eighteenth-century doctrine of the rights of man, at first applied effectively only to persons of European race, the movements for abolition of slavery and the slave trade in Europe and America, the emergence of Haiti as a black state, the Japanese victories over Russia in 1904–5 and the Western powers in 1941–2, the pan-African movement in the first half of the century. But it has been in the post-1945 period that the decisive changes have come: the Afro-Asian movement launched at Bandung in 1955; the achievement of independence by so many non-white states that the white have become a minority; the victories of the civil rights movement in the United States in the 1950s and 1960s, profound in its repercussions on other Western countries; the virtual expulsion of South Africa from the Commonwealth, and its reduction to the status of a pariah in the United Nations; the development of human rights instrumentalities under the aegis of the UN, and especially the Convention on Elimination of Racial Discrimination of 1966. The solidarity of non-whites against whites has been one of the principal elements making for the cohesion of the loose coalition of states and movements to which we refer as the Third World.

Fourthly, there has been the struggle for economic justice. Although anti-colonial movements from the beginning maintained that imperialism was bound up with economic exploitation, and included goals of economic development or betterment in their programmes, and although the assertion by Third World states of sovereignty over their natural resources may be traced back through the nationalization of the Anglo-Iranian oil company in 1951, the Mexican expropriations of foreign oil companies of the 1930s, the experience of the Bolshevik Revolution, and the Calvo and Drago doctrines asserted by Latin American states late in the last century against foreign intervention in their economic affairs, it was not until the 1960s that economic objectives attained pride of place in the agenda of the coalition of Asian, African, and Latin American states, which by then had become known as the Third World. By the time of the formation of the Group of 77 at the first meeting in 1964 of the UN Conference on Trade, Aid, and Development, concern about colonialism was giving place to concern about economic domination by the Western powers of the post-colonial world; the gap between the living standards of most Western and most Third World states was growing as a consequence not only of the economic boom in Western countries but also of their new policies of state promotion of minimum standards of welfare; and consciousness of the gap was growing as a result of the revolution in communications. In the 1960s the debate between Western and Third World countries over what was called international development assistance took the form of a discussion of the terms of a partnership between rich and poor countries that had common interests in development – the rich having a stake in the development of the poor, and the poor in the further development of the rich. In the 1970s by contrast, under the impact of the 1973–4 oil crisis, the world recession, the radicalization of Third World opinion and the reaction against this in the West, the terms of the debate changed: the idea of a partnership between rich and poor gave place to that of a struggle for the world product, non-zero sum conceptions of the relationship to zero-sum, development assistance to redistribution of wealth – a change reflected in 1974 in the Declaration of a New International Economic Order and the Charter of the Economic Rights and Duties of States endorsed by Third World majorities in the UN.

Fifthly, there has been the struggle for what is called cultural liberation: the struggle of non-Western peoples to throw off the intellectual or cultural ascendancy of the Western world so as to assert their own identity and autonomy in matters of the spirit. The revolt against Western dominance in relation to the four earlier themes that have been mentioned has been conducted, as least ostensibly, in the name of ideas or values that are themselves Western, even if it is not clear in all cases that these ideas are exclusively or uniquely Western: the rights of states to sovereign equality, the rights of nations to self-determination, the rights of human beings to equal treatment irrespective of race, their rights to minimum standards of economic and social welfare. Perhaps the right to cultural autonomy may also be regarded as a Western value, or at all events as a value which Western countries (for example, as signatories of the Covenant on Economic, Social and Cultural Rights of 1966) now support. But the re-assertion by Asian, African, and other non-Western peoples of their traditional and indigenous cultures, as exemplified in Islamic fundamentalism, Hindu and Sikh traditionalism in India, manifestations of ethnic consciousness in Africa, has raised the question whether what has been widely interpreted as a revolt against Western dominance carried out in the name of Western values, is not a revolt against Western values as such.

We need to bear in mind, in speaking of the repudiation of 'Western values' in Third World countries, that the former are neither monolithic nor unchanging. Different Western countries, and different regimes within those countries, stand and have stood for values of very different kinds: in the post-1945 period the West for some Third World peoples has been represented by the resurgent imperialism of the French Fourth Republic and the post-war Netherlands, by the Spanish and Portuguese dictatorships, and by a South African government committed to strengthening rather than removing barriers between races. In the period during which the revolt against Western dominance has been unfolding, there have been vast changes in the values prevailing in all Western societies; public attitudes towards the equal rights of non-Western states, national liberation from colonial rule, equal rights of non-white races, the rights of poor peoples to economic justice and cultural autonomy have been transformed in recent decades. Moreover, in noting the gap between Third World behaviour and what Western persons like to think of as 'Western values', we should not fall into the error of assuming that Western peoples are themselves always faithful to them; they are at most a statement of Western ideals, not a description of Western practices.

Yet as Asian, African, and other non-Western peoples have assumed a more prominent place in international society it has become clear that in matters of values the distance between them and Western societies is greater than, in the early years of national liberation or decolonization, it was assumed to be. In making their demands for equal rights on behalf of oppressed states, nations, races, or cultures, the leaders of the Third World spoke as suppliants, in a world in which the Western powers were still in a dominant position. The demands that they made had necessarily to be put forward in terms of charters of rights (the Declaration of the Rights of Man and the Citizen, the American Declaration of Independence, the League Covenant, the Atlantic Charter, the UN Charter) of which Western powers were the principal authors. The moral appeal had to be cast in the terms that would have most resonance within Western societies. But as Asian, African, and other non-Western peoples have become stronger relative to the Western powers, they have become freer to adopt a different rhetoric that sets Western values aside, or at all events places different interpretations upon them.

The collapse of the old, Western-dominated international order has been brought about by perhaps five factors on which we may briefly touch. First, there has been the psychological or spiritual awakening of Asian and African, Caribbean and Pacific peoples, beginning among small groups of the Western-educated, later affecting masses of people, that led them to perceive the old order no longer as a fact of nature, but as something that could be changed, to recognize that by mobilizing themselves to this end they could indeed change it, to abandon a passive for a politically active role in world affairs. The great instrument these peoples have used to advance their purposes has been the state: they began by capturing control of states and then used them – domestically to build nationhood, to establish control of their economies, to combat local vestiges of external dominance; internationally to establish relations with outside states, to combine with their friends, drive wedges among their enemies, and expound their views in the councils of the world.

A second factor has been a weakening of the will on the part of the Western powers to maintain their position of dominance, or at least to accept the costs necessary to do so. The First World War destroyed the self-assurance of the European powers which had been so cardinal a feature of the old order, while also leading them to embrace a principle of national self-determination contradictory of the legitimacy of colonial rule. The Second World War left the European imperial powers too weak to maintain old kinds of dominance, even though it left the United States with a commanding position in world affairs. As Third World peoples mobilized themselves politically in defence of their interests, the use of force to maintain Western positions of dominance became more costly. At the same time it came to be questioned whether colonial dependencies were a source of material gain: the old liberal thesis, that the true interests of the metropolitan peoples lay in non-interventionism and avoidance of empire, was revived, and appeared to be confirmed by the economic triumphs of Germany and Japan, achieved without military pre-eminence or colonies. Nor were the peoples of the metropolitan countries always insensitive to the aspirations of non-Western peoples: both in Europe and in America there were many for whom the emancipation of the former dependencies represented the fulfilment of their own ideals.

It would be wrong, however, to countenance the idea that the Western powers offered little or no resistance to the dismantling of the old order, or that this dismantling came about essentially in response to their own policies. That the process of decolonization was an act of policy of the colonial powers themselves is the thesis both of apologists for the policies of the colonial powers (as in the argument of writers about the British Commonwealth that the purpose of empire was preparation for self-government), and of those who see the transition from colonialism to neo-colonialism, from direct to indirect domination, as the result of a conspiracy by the colonial powers themselves to bring about a form of domination that they had come to prefer. There were indeed cases in the latter stages of the process of national liberation, especially in Africa and the Pacific, in which the independence of former colonies came about through co-operation between the metropolitan power and local representatives. But such instances were made possible only by the fact that the will of the colonial powers had already been broken. The reverses that were inflicted upon the Western powers in Indonesia, Indo-China, Algeria, Suez, Cyprus, Vietnam, and elsewhere had first to be suffered before the lessons from them could be drawn.

A third factor making for the demise of the old order was the impact of the Bolshevik revolution and the rise of the Soviet Union as a major power. The influence of the Soviet Union, it is true, has not always been perceived as a positive one from the point of view of the Afro-Asian or Third World nationalist struggles. Classical Marxism was basically unsympathetic to nationalism, and although Leninism has aligned the communist movement with it, the heritage of the ideas of Marx and Engels has sometimes proved a handicap in this respect. Stalin's Russia during the Second World War was aligned with European imperialists against Germany, and thus withdrew its support for anti-imperialist movements. Even after the War, Soviet support for communist revolution in the Third World stood in the way of an understanding with Third World nationalism until after the death of Stalin. The Soviet Union has never been able to compete with the United States and the Western European countries in providing economic and technological assistance to Third World countries. The Soviet Union's frontiers, as we noted above, result from European expansion and subjugation of non-European peoples, which means that some Third World sentiment may be mobilized against it, as China has sought to do. The Soviet Union's capacity for direct military intervention in Third World countries, demonstrated in Afghanistan since 1979, has attracted some of the Third World antagonism against external domination previously directed chiefly at the Western powers.

Nevertheless, the rise of Soviet power, especially since the Second World War, including its attainment of crude strategic parity with the United States by the early 1970s and development of global interventionary capacity, has been basically helpful to the struggle of Third World peoples against the dominance of the Western powers. It is not merely, or perhaps even chiefly, that the Soviet state has provided a model of socialist planning and control of economic, social, and political life that has exerted an immense attraction over Third World countries and movements. It is rather that, since the collapse of Germany and Japan, the Soviet Union has been the chief centre of power in world affairs outside Western Europe and North America. Since it is the established ascendancy of Western Europe and North America in Asia, Africa, and Latin America that the Third World has been struggling to overthrow, the alliance of the Third World and the Soviet Union against the West, at least on a limited range of issues, that has been a basic feature of world affairs for many decades, has been natural and perhaps inevitable.

A fourth factor assisting the efforts of non-Western states and peoples to transform the system has been the existence of a more general equilibrium of power, to which the rise of the Soviet Union contributed, but of which it was only part, that has operated to the benefit of those challenging the old order. It is not a new circumstance that 'divisions among the imperialists' should operate in favour of the independence of weak peoples. But from the very beginning of the process of Western expansion, when the Papacy sought to contain the rivalry between Spain and Portugal, there were attempts, often successful, to preserve a common front *vis-à-vis* the non-Christian or extra-European world, or at least a common framework for competition within it. We have noted how, in the nineteenth century, such a framework was provided by the Concert of Europe.

In the post-1945 world also some elements of this common framework still survive: it is not wholly fanciful, for example, to see in the tacit understandings through which the North Atlantic powers and the Soviet Union have excluded war from their own area of the world, while exporting their military conflicts to the periphery, an echo of the arrangements reached between France and Spain at the Peace of Cateau-Cambrésis in 1559, whereby armed conflicts in the New World were allowed to continue on the understanding that they would not disturb the peace of Europe. It is clear, however, that the divisions among the advanced powers are today much deeper than they were at the time when the West could agree to send an international force with a German commander to keep a dissident China in order; and that this new circumstance has operated to assist the weaker members of the system. Deeply divided as they are, the North Atlantic states and the Soviet Union serve to check one another's interventions in the Third World. At the same time, the existence of several major centres of power – in Western Europe, Japan, and China, as well as in the United States and the Soviet Union – provides Third World countries with a range of diplomatic options for combining with one major power against another.

Finally, the dismantling of the old order has been assisted by a transformation of the legal and moral climate of international relations which the Third World states themselves, grouped with one another in the Afro-Asian movement, the Non-Aligned Movement, and the Group of 77, have played the principal role in bringing about. Commanding majorities of votes as they do in the political organs of the UN, and able to call upon the prestige of numbers, not merely of states but of persons, accruing to the states claiming to represent a majority of the world's population, they have overturned the old structure of international law and organization that once served to sanctify their subject status. The equal rights of non-Western states to sovereignty, the rights of non-Western peoples to self-determination, the rights of non-white races to equal treatment, non-Western peoples to economic justice, and non-Western cultures to dignity and autonomy – these rights are today clearly spelt out in conventions having the force of law, even though in many cases they are not enjoyed in practice and no consensus exists about their meaning and interpretation.

The Western powers have fought a rearguard action against this rewriting of international law and quasi-law, which may be studied in the debates that led up to the passing of such historic resolutions of UN organs as the 1960 Declaration on the Granting of Independence to Colonial Peoples, the 1965 resolution recognizing the right to use force in a war of national liberation, or the 1974 Declaration of a New International Economic Order. As a result of the challenge delivered by the Third World to the old legal order there is today deep division between the Western powers and Third World states about a wide range of normative issues. As the political organs of the UN were made to subserve the political purposes of the Third World coalition, the Western powers, once able to make the UN the instrument of purposes of their own, became disillusioned about it. It is possible to argue that as a consequence of these disagreements and attempts to paper them over by resort to concepts of 'soft law', the integrity of interntional law has been debased and the role actually played by international law in international relations, as opposed to what John Austin once called positive international morality, has gone into decline. It is not possible, however, to doubt that the changes wrought by Third World majorities have affected the legal and moral climate of world politics profoundly, and in such a way as to assist the challenge to Western dominance.

Theorists of international 'dependence' tell us that the position of the Western countries in the international system is still one of dominance. It is indeed true that the present distribution of wealth and power in the world falls far short of the aspirations of Third World peoples and their well-wishers elsewhere for justice and equality. But if we compare the position occupied by non-Western states and peoples in the universal international society of today with the position in which they found themselves at the turn of the century, it is difficult not to feel that the revolt against Western dominance has had a measure of success.

15

THE EMERGENCE OF THE THIRD WORLD

Peter Lyon

The term 'the Third World'[1] was first coined in France in the early 1950s at a time of apparently increasing polarization of the international system, as the two principal poles, the United States and the Soviet Union, sought to sustain and extend their leadership and discipline over their respective alliance systems. Undoubtedly the use of the phrase 'le Tiers Monde' by a number of French writers (most notably by Claude Bourdet, Alfred Sauvy, and Georges Balandier[2]) conveyed a conscious echo of the older concept of 'le Tiers État', and perhaps of Abbé Sieyès's famous rhetorical question in his pamphlet 'What is the Third Estate?'

But the notion that a third estate or 'world' was developing in the international system at large gained rapidly in currency and credibility from the congealing of an Arab- (later widening to become an African-) Asian group meeting both within the UN system and outside it, in the latter respect most notably at the Bandung conference in Indonesia in April 1955.

The Bandung conference resulted from initiatives taken during 1953 and 1954 by the so-called Colombo powers – Ceylon, India, Pakistan, and Indonesia. It was in part a protest at more than four years of deadlock over new United Nations memberships (Indonesia had been the last to secure membership, in January 1950) and about the failure to achieve much decolonization since 1947–8. It was also emphatically an expression of objection to the way the UN arena was dominated by Cold War rivalries and was not in practice giving effect to the principle of universality of membership. In part at least it was also implicitly an occasion to proclaim the political renaissance of Asia and Africa and to protest at the continuance of white man's hegemonies. It was not, though many subsequent writers have wrongly supposed it was, a non-aligned conference: Turkey, Pakistan, China, Japan, Thailand, and the Philippines, each in its distinctive way then aligned, were present at Bandung. Indeed, although non-alignment was to become a strong and perhaps the central ingredient in subsequent pan-Third

World dealings, more significant than the Group of 77 (hereafter G77), in the mid-1950s it was still novel, *ad hoc*, and inchoate, and the phrase 'Non-Aligned *Movement*' (hereafter NAM) does not really become appropriate, nor is it used, until the early 1970s.[3]

I

Non-Alignment, in an *ad hoc* and individualistically self-ascribed sense, preceded the Non-Aligned Movement. As is by now well known[4] the Yugoslavs, Egyptians, and Indians – and especially Tito, Nasser, and Nehru – played pioneer initiating roles, in defining their own country's foreign policies as non-alignment and in terms which other leaders were soon to regard as exemplary and worthy of emulation in some respects. The nature of Non-Alignment in the 1960s was revealed most clearly at its first two general Summit Conferences.[5] Indeed, before 1970 these two meetings provided the only really emphatic evidence that Non-Alignment amounted to more than the declaratory foreign policies of an assorted company of Third World countries.

The first general Summit of the Non-Aligned was held in Belgrade (appropriately enough, as it stemmed principally from Yugoslav initiatives) in September 1961 and was attended by twenty-five full members – eleven from Africa, eleven from Asia, two (Yugoslavia and Cyprus) from Europe, and one – Cuba – from Latin America. Its final Declaration devoted most space and attention to what was characterized as the threat posed to world peace by the further decline in East-West relations and the urgent need to establish an international system on the basis of 'peaceful co-existence'. Disarmament also featured prominently in the Declaration, with the Non-Aligned demanding their own participation in all future international debates and negotiations on the subject. Predictably, a number of currently highly topical issues – Cuba and the Bay of Pigs affair, nuclear testing, the French naval base at Bizerta, Berlin – were mentioned, as were colonialism, apartheid, and the Middle East.

During the conference deliberations there was a marked difference between those who were characterized in the western press as 'moderates', notably Nehru of India, who wanted principal stress to be put on issues of world peace and how to ease relations between the major powers, and those 'militants', such as Sukarno of Indonesia and Nkrumah of Ghana, who emphasized anti-colonial issues and the need for the Non-Aligned to practise a confrontational style of diplomacy. In the event, at this conference the moderates affected the temper and tone of the final Declaration rather more than the militants, though contributions from both wings may be detected in what was inevitably a somewhat catch-all document.

The second Non-Aligned Summit held in Cairo in October 1964 with forty-six delegations in attendance (the increased numbers since Belgrade mostly coming from Africa) was once again primarily the result of an active partnership between Tito and Nasser. They were joined more positively than in 1961, though at a late stage, by Nehru again, who favoured a second Non-Aligned Summit not least as a preferable alternative to a second Bandung Afro-Asian conference to which China and Pakistan would have been able to come. India was still smarting from its war with China in 1962, and, although not many of the self-declared Non-Aligned had supported India then, Egypt and Yugoslavia had done so. The expanded ranks of the Non-Aligned in 1964 as compared with 1961, as many newly independent African States now joined, and greater permissiveness being practised in defining which countries were non-aligned, were certainly seen by India as a way to dilute the impact of the militants. The ambiguous notion of the 'democratization' of international relations could be and was thus invoked here. Indeed, diplomacy by 'consensus', meaning assumed general tacit agreements, came to be cultivated deliberately, precisely because the Sino-Soviet dispute, the Vietnam war, and intra-Third World quarrels (e.g. the Indo-Pakistan war of 1965, the Arab-Israeli war of 1967) made active positive agreement among the increasingly heterogeneous company of the Third World more and more difficult.

Thus throughout the 1960s, rather as in the second half of the 1950s, non-alignment took on whatever formal characteristics it had primarily from opposition – individual and to some extent concerted – to participation in either of the two Cold War blocs. As the dominantly bi-polar international system loosened, however, this negatively conferred identity lost its earlier sharpness and there was mounting evidence that anti-colonialism was the core concern of the Non-Aligned. Although at the second Non-Aligned Summit at Cairo in 1964 stress was still laid – as at Belgrade three years earlier – on the need for peaceful co-existence and the responsibilities of the great powers for global peace, considerable and heavily accented attention was also given in many of the delegates' speeches, and in the Final Declaration, to the threats posed by 'imperialism, colonialism and neo-colonialism'. These emphases no doubt in part reflected the presence of many more newly independent states in the company of the Non-Aligned, and also the sense that the tides of decolonization were running strongly.

President Nasser, in his opening address to the conference, anticipated a future major motif for the NAM when he called for the eradication of the 'fateful disparity' in the living standards amongst the world's peoples. A specific section in the final Declaration of the Conference was subsequently devoted to 'Economic Co-operation', and underscoring the heightened emphasis given to economic development issues the Non-Aligned jointly enjoined themselves to 'pledge their co--operation to the strengthening of the Group of 77' – which had recently been formed at the first United Nations Conference on Trade and Development (UNCTAD-1) held in Geneva in 1964.

The Cairo conference was none the less an *ad hoc* occasion and there was no firm commitment to hold future conferences, still less for Non-Alignment to assume any continuing organizational forms. Indeed, in the world of the second half of the 1960s it was far from clear that Non-Alignment had any collective or organized future at all. It was to take almost six years – and much strenuous lobbying by Tito during 1968 and 1969 – before a third Summit could be convened. Indeed, in these years it seemed as if the more modest arrangements of the G77,[6] inside international organizations, or even at specially convened meetings such as the G77's Ministerial meeting in Algiers in 1967, preoccupied as they were with economic matters, might be the only way the Third World could agree to convene in plenary sessions.

II

From the late 1970s the Non-Aligned Movement emerged as an international grouping, recognizably influenced by the experiences and procedures current in the United Nations and in some other contemporary fora, but none the less distinctive in its own right, with its own membership and modalities.

Although only slightly more delegations attended the third Non-Aligned Summit (53 as compared with 46 at Cairo six years earlier), both in its proceedings and outcomes the Lusaka Summit marked a new departure for collectivized Non-Alignment. The very fact that the Summit met in southern Africa symbolized the numerically large component of African Non-Aligned countries and inevitably gave greater prominence to anti-colonialism and opposition to apartheid. Kenneth Kaunda's active, eloquent, and skilful chairmanship helped to give credence and credibility to the idea that collectivised Non-Alignment should be regularized and maintain some continuing momentum. Accordingly, it was from Lusaka that three important innovations for the Non-Aligned were launched and soon became generally acceptable: that a Summit Conference of the Non-Aligned should be held regularly at intervals of about three years; that the host country of the last Summit Conference should act as the principal spokesman for the Non-Aligned in the intervals between Summit meetings; and that the host country, acting in effect as Chairman for the Non-Aligned, should assume responsibility for convening such other meetings as may be deemed desirable or necessary, as well as assuming responsibility for some servicing arrangements at and between conferences. In this last point we can see an implicit acceptance of the idea that more collective activities were desirable and also the embryo of the idea of a secretariat, or at least of a co-ordinating bureau – such as actually developed in the 1970s.

The years 1971–4 marked a real watershed in the international economic system: with the floating (in effect the devaluation) of the US dollar in August 1971 formally signalling the end of an international monetary system mostly operating in terms of fixed exchange rates relative to the dollar; with the quickening boom in many world commodity prices (in fact this was the last feverish upswing of what in retrospect can be seen as the tail end of about twenty years of expansion in world trade), and then the unprecedented demonstration of OPEC solidarity in fixing much higher world trading prices for oil in the wake of the Yom Kippur or Ramadan war. Undoubtedly the early 1970s saw a heightening sense of optimism among spokesmen and leaders of Third World countries who sensed that they were increasingly capable of taking matters into their own hands, of ensuring that issues were discussed increasingly in North/South rather than East/West terms, and that matters of economic justice were accorded greater priority.

The Georgetown Conference of Foreign Ministers, held in Guyana in July 1972, had continued the process of institutionalization within the NAM and a greater concentration on economic matters, when it was agreed that henceforth Ministers of Non-Aligned countries should meet every two years to consider economic issues of mutual concern and that four member countries selected on a regional basis should be made responsible for co-ordinating co-operation among Non-Aligned and other developing countries on a variety of economic issues. The discussion of economic matters at the Lusaka Summit in 1970 had been addressed mainly to the question of how to promote self-reliance among the Non-Aligned States through co-operation at a functional level, e.g. in planning and in trade, in industrial, mineral, and agricultural production. The Georgetown Meeting of Foreign Ministers two years later added, mainly at Algeria's instigation, a sharpened and expanded dimension to the Movement's approach to economic issues: with consideration of private foreign investment aid, announcements of the intention to control 'vital' economic activities, including the exploitation of resources involved, and censure of the activities of trans-national corporations. Latin American experience and expertise (the ideas, for example, of Raul Prebisch and the experience of William Demass of the Caribbean Development Bank) were significant here too.

There can be no doubt, however, that it was the fourth Non-Aligned Summit which met in Algiers in August 1973, and Algeria's active chairmanship then and for three years thereafter, which imparted a strong sense of dynamism, purposefulness, and forward-looking momentum to what was now – and increasingly widely spoken of as – the Non-Aligned Movement. These middle years of the 1970s mark a major landmark in the world's economic system, from the American 'modifications' of the Bretton Woods system in 1971–2 to the OPEC price increases on 1973–4, and the launching of the campaign for a New International Economic Order (NIEO) at Algiers in 1973 and at the Special UN Session on Development in mid-1974. These same years are also important for the rapid evolution of Non-Alignment away from an *ad hoc* approach and towards more frequent and more specialized consultations and co-operative measures: in fact, then, towards greater organization and institutionalization.

Rhetoric alone, it was increasingly appreciated, was not enough. More programmatic concerns and specific practical proposals begin to obtrude more prominently in the Summit conferences and to be taken up subsequently in the more specialized follow-up meetings which increasingly were seen to be the necessary and well-nigh natural sequel of the more intensive and certainly more complex conference that the Algerians had organized in 1973. Furthermore, it was now undeniable that the NAM was gaining considerably increasing membership, principally fuelled by the dynamics of decolonization. In numerical terms the African states were the largest group, followed by the Arab states, but Caribbean and South-East Asian voices, views, and interests were made manifest from time to time as well. By the mid-1970s almost every ex-colony sought with independence to join the UN, the G77, and the NAM, and increasingly Third World spokesmen were inclined to stress, with some plausibility, that the latter two associations were complementary, not competitive associations for the prosecution of their causes.

Undoubtedly, the Algiers Summit of the NAM in 1973 marked a much increased assertiveness and self-reliance of the NAM and with it the consolidation of a general strategy which has since then formed the main basis of the collective posture of the Non-Aligned and developing countries towards the richer developed world. Some commentators have suggested that Algiers produced a reorientation of Non-Alignment, away from East/West and towards North/South preoccupations. Certainly at Algiers the earlier, more tentative tendencies of the Non-Aligned to ascribe the major blame for their underdevelopment to the developed world was made explicit and emphatic. Both the Lusaka and the Georgetown meetings had touched on the Leninist theme that 'capitalism, colonialism and imperialism' were responsible for the inequalities in the international system. The Algiers Summit asserted this with a new vehemence, claiming that the economic imbalance between developed and developing countries was a function of 'selfish colonialism, neo-colonialism and imperialism'. The developed countries were censured for lack of 'political will' and insufficient 'co-operation'. In addition to such general indictments, the Economic Declaration from Algiers in 1973 recommended 'the establishment of effective solidarity organisations for the defence of the interests of producers of raw materials'. The Summit stopped short, however, of endorsing the concept advocated by Algeria of using raw materials not only as instruments of development but as economic weapons against the developed world. The use in the Algiers Declaration of the terms 'non-aligned', 'developing countries', and 'the Third World', without apparent distinction, seemes to testify to a new solidarity: the Non-Aligned identified their interests as those of all developing countries and vice versa. In fact, however, the short but sharp commodity price boom which peaked for some hard-metal (tin, lead, copper, zinc) and a few other commodity exports (coffee, cocoa, but not tea) in 1973–4, and came at the end of nearly twenty-five years of expansion of world trade, actually showed again the diversity and differentiations of real interests within the Third World just below the surface canopies of rhetorical agreement. The onset of a combination of rampant inflation and little or no real growth in the world economy swiftly reduced and probably undermined any real chance there was of achieving an NIEO by agreement – conditions which have prevailed, and still prevail today.

None the less, the pre-eminently economic emphasis established at Algiers and the tone of criticism directed towards western industrialized countries and their arrangements (symbolized in the swift currency achieved from about this time by the metaphor North/South) had supplied the NAM with a central motif which continues to be at work today. In that sense the Algiers Summit was seminal and everything that has occurred since then in the NAM seems like embellishments or footnotes to the Algiers meeting.

While the close student of the NAM needs to study carefully the proceedings of the Colombo Summit of 1976,[7] of Havana in 1979,[8] and of New Delhi in March 1983, and can learn much about topical preoccupations from these major conventions of the Non-Aligned, the main lineaments were laid bare in Algiers in 1973.

III

In the early 1980s, even more emphatically than in the early 1960s, the large number of states, certainly a very heterogeneous company, which attended summit meetings of the Non-Aligned Movement and/or participated in its activities did not together contribute any marked unity in political institutions, values, and diplomatic attitudes. The various nuances of non-alignment, of Third World-ism, are determined by multiple causes, much more political than economic, of which the character of an incumbent ruling élite at a particular time is in many cases the most important single determinant, but the general international context and what are currently the most topically controversial crises are undoubtedly crucial 'defining' factors as well.

In the 1980s both the NAM and the G77, as compared with even ten years previously, confronted a more complex, disillusioned, even pessimistic world and were wracked by intra-mural and external tensions. Afghanistan, Kampuchea, the Falkland Islands, Palestine, the Lebanon, the Polisario Front – each name spelt a whirlpool of problems. More generally, the Sino-Soviet Cold War continued despite faint signs of some possible abatement. Pressures for nuclear proliferation intensified, progress on general disarmament was nugatory. The United States under the Reagan administration was stolidly hostile or indifferent or stonewalling on a number of issues of considerable moment to the NAM – from the NIEO proposals, to North/South dialogue, to an agreement within UNCLOS, for example. Indeed, nothing substantial was gained towards achieving the NIEO as first spelled out by the NAM in 1974, though already a rather different actual international economic order was functioning in the 1980s than that of ten years previously.

Within the large and heterogeneous world of the NAM today its two largest internal groupings – those of the African and of the Arab states – are patently in disarray, unable to agree in practical terms on common policies, despite verbal concurrence in identifying such common enemies as the Republic of South Africa and Israel.

To date, the NAM has avoided establishing its own machinery for conflict resolution among its members – though a case for having such machinery has been urged, notably by the Yugoslavs, from time to time.

The NAM has in effect sought generally to practise a diplomacy of conflict limitation and conflict dampening through mediation, good offices, etc. – inevitably with mixed and, on the whole, undramatic results. Such approaches seek to avoid aggravating and aggregating existing divisions within the Movement. It is also clear from the record that the members of NAM on the whole tend to avoid submitting their disputes to the United Nations for settlement (but self-righteous proclamations there as to the justice of one's own cause are, of course, commonplace), no doubt because it is feared that this will expose them to the uncertainties and escalatory potential of the big powers.

Pressure for further institutionalization of the Third World (whether generally or specifically) is likely to remain, fuelled in part by the evident gap between deeds and words, between high-sounding declamation and relatively small actual achievements. In some cases where machinery has been set up, dissatisfaction is rather with the low degree of actual implementation achieved than with the absence of instruments.

If the Third World is seen as an aspect of contemporary international organization with broad agendas of economic and political concerns, and an ever-ramifying range of regular or *ad hoc* activities, then it seems more reasonable to expect it to persist rather than to break up in the immediate future. International organizations are not immortal, but the demise or supersession of international organization is likely to occur only as a by-product of general war or because of acute and protracted general crisis in the international system.

16

RACIAL EQUALITY

R. J. Vincent

One of the marks of the transition from a European to a global international order has been the passing, at least in terms of the number of white states compared to non-white, of white predominance in international society. The society of sovereign states, once composed almost exclusively of states with white populations, is now made up mainly of members with predominantly non-white populations, and there is no thought any longer that colour is a bar to their belonging. So while it is far from being the case that racial discrimination (and not only by white men) is a thing of the past, international society has now branded as illegitimate all doctrines to justify it. This is a dramatic change from the attitudes that typified the age of European ascendancy, when notions of a biological hierarchy among different human types that justified and even required the subjection of one to another were considered respectable. Indeed, in some accounts of the need for European ascendancy, it was above all race, not religion, or civilization, or mere Europeanness that imposed the duty of empire. According to a few extremist writers like Lothrop Stoddard, the basic factor in human affairs was 'not politics, but race'.[2] Civilization of itself meant nothing. It was merely an effect whose cause was the 'creative urge of superior germ-plasm. Civilization is the body; the race is the soul.'[3] A racial account of international relations followed. The *Pax Romana* of antiquity, the *Civitas Dei* of the medieval Christian Commonwealth, and the European Concert of nineteenth-century diplomacy were declared by Stoddard to be expressions of the instinctive comity of the white race which was 'one of the great constants of history'.[4]

This placing of race and civilization in the positions of cause and effect, providing a biological account of the difference between advanced and backward peoples, was never the official doctrine or justification of any European empire. The Portuguese especially, and more recently the French, saw it as their imperial mission to Christianize and civilize – to romanize, some of their spokesmen said – the non-European populations over which they ruled. Civilization was regarded as something that could be imparted to others, as it had been to the ancestors of the Portuguese and the French. Prominent in the British justification of empire was the idea of trusteeship over backward races,[5] who could and should be civilized and educated. In this enterprise, narrow British interest joined with a contribution to world civilization. Lord Rosebery thought that it was 'part of our responsibility and heritage to take care that the world so far as it can be moulded shall receive the Anglo-Saxon, and not another character'.[6] France, the official formula ran in the hey-day of the French empire, is a nation of a hundred million, all with the same rights to liberty, equality, and fraternity.

None the less, in the popular mind the notion of racial superiority was woven into the pattern of European empire, and affected relations both between European settlers and non-European 'natives' and between imperial states and their non-European dependencies. Some political leaders went, as they saw it, one better than Lord Rosebery, seeking to bestow not merely Anglo-Saxon, or French, character on the less fortunate, but also to stiffen them with European blood. Even as late as the Second World War, Leo Amery thought that the infusion of Nordic blood would make India more capable of holding its own in the future, and Franklin Roosevelt wondered whether the interbreeding of European and Asian races would not produce a less 'delinquent' Asian stock.[7] And when the problem was seen not as one of ordering the lesser breeds, but of coping with 'the rising tide of colour' that threatened to engulf the white world demographically and economically, then it was necessary to construct a white redoubt to preserve the higher civilization.[8]

If racial attitudes played some part in the age of European ascendancy, they accompanied also its passing, in two ways. In the first place, the seriousness with which many Europeans took their supposedly superior genetic endowment, especially at the height of imperial enthusiasm in the late nineteenth century, meant that the shock of the demonstration of their mere mortality, when it came, was felt the more severely. The victory of the Japanese over the Russians in 1905 was widely interpreted not as a local triumph of one nation over another, but as a victory, with global implications, of the Mongolian people over the European. And if this event shattered the myth of white invincibility from without, the Europeans were interpreted as doing this for themselves in the great 'European Civil War' between 1914 and 1919.[9] Not only were the whites laying to rest the notion of their instinctive comity by butchering each other in such unprecedented numbers, but they were also showing their neglect of race in favour of nation in using non-white troops to advance the slaughter. Just as the Peloponnesian War had brought the great age of Greek civilization to an end in destroying the sentiment of

Greek race-unity, so the First World War, after the Periclean Age of the nineteenth century, spelled the end of white dominance, and of the idea that civilization was essentially European.[10]

The second way in which the factor of race featured in the passing of European ascendancy was in giving a racial flavour to the new emerging forces, the after-taste of which is still with us. This theme of Europe racializing the world, and suffering now from the effects of a colour-consciousness that it itself implanted, is a prominent one in the account that follows of race in the transition from a European to a global international order.

I

Both the idea that there is such a thing as racial inequality, and the notion that such inequality justified the superior in subjecting the inferior, tend now to be called racist or racialist and to bear the opprobrium attached to these labels.[11] In nineteenth-century Europe, such racialism was thought by some to have a scientific basis; it was possible on physiological grounds alone, said the French racial theorist Gobineau, to distinguish three great and clearly marked types, the black, the yellow, and the white, and to arrange them in a hierarchy with the lowest, the negro, being hardly more than a mere brute, the yellow race committing none of the strange excesses so common among negroes but tending to mediocrity in everything, and at the top the white race gifted with energetic intelligence, perseverance, an instinct for order, and a love of liberty.[12]

Less repellent to the modern reader, and more sophisticated, were the later nineteenth-century ideas of social evolution influenced by Herbert Spencer's analogy between societies and organisms, and Darwin's account of the survival of the fittest in the animal world. Benjamin Kidd wrote that the road along which man had come was strewn with the wreckage of nations, races, and civilizations. Social systems, like individuals, were organic growths apparently possessing laws of health and development. Societies flourished until they gave way before other associations of men of higher efficiency. The weaker races disappeared before the stronger through the effects of mere contact. But this was not to assert any great intellectual difference between the higher and lower races. Even the Australian native who had been 'the zero from which anthropologists . . . have long reckoned our intellectual progress upwards' could learn quite as easily and quickly as Europeans. It was the qualities contributing to social efficiency that mattered in making any claim to superiority, and they consisted not in brilliance, but in the more plodding virtues of strength, energy of character, humanity, probity, integrity, devotion to duty.[13]

'The gradual extinction of inferior races', wrote Sir Charles Dilke, 'is not only a law of nature, but a blessing to mankind.'[14] Social Darwinist ideas had given a civilization that might now be interpreted as having a temporary lead in some areas of human endeavour, notions of its manifest destiny to rule the world. Biology in the twentieth century has not followed Dilke's law of nature, and has eschewed the idea not merely of a hierarchy among the races, but also of race itself. It has dealt instead with statistics about populations. 'There are no races,' we are told, 'but only clines – gradients of change in measurable genetic characteristics.'[15] The conventional wisdom as now distilled by UNESCO has as much diversity within so-called races as between them; no coincidence between races and blood-groups; factors grouped together and said to be transmitted *en bloc* in fact passed on independently and in varying degrees of association; and cultural advance as a more profound factor in human evolution than genetic inheritance.[16]

The difficulty with this dismissal of race as a scientific concept is that it allows no treatment of certain obvious, if superficial, differences between peoples which have some political significance. For the purposes of this paper, we might think of race as at the same time a biological and a sociological notion. Races are not pure types but populations differing from each other in the relative commonness of certain hereditary traits,[17] and thinking of themselves as socially distinct. Our question is now what part has the idea of equality or inequality played in relations between such groups during the expansion of international society.

II

Viewed in terms or race, the first phase of the transition from a European to a global international order might be said to be the establishment of independent states that took as their *raison d'être* the extension of the liberal ideas of the French Revolution to include non-Europeans as well as Europeans. In this movement, there was, in Adam Watson's terms, a high road to independence taken by Haiti, and a low road taken by Liberia and Sierra Leone, which, in the latter case, led back to dependence. The high road involved non-Europeans in taking up arms and winning a famous victory against Europeans. The low road was the result of white conviction, enterprise, and interest in regard to the welfare of non-whites.

The high road was taken by Toussaint L'Ouverture. In joining the insurrection of the slaves in St. Domingue and then leading it, it is said that his first objective was nothing so grand as to cause the French unswervingly to follow the logic of their own revolutionary ideas, but merely to secure an additional day each week during which the slaves might cultivate their own allotments of land.[18] But his objectives became more ambitious with the success of the uprising. The emancipation of the slaves was ratified by the French Convention in 1794, and by 1801 Toussaint was strong enough to issue a constitution tantamount to a declaration of independence.[19] Independence proper was not to come until Dessalines' proclamation of it in 1804, after the betrayal of Toussaint to the French and his death in prison. But it was Toussaint who had seen and taken the high road.

The low road derived mainly from European and American abolitionism. Agitation for an end to the slave trade, and to the institution of slavery itself, made much of slavery as a 'colour problem'.[20] The idealized black man, the noble savage, was prominent in European literature of the eighteenth century. One group of French abolitionists called themselves *Les Amis des Noirs*. Pitt affectionately called two of the leading abolitionists, Ramsay and Clarkson, 'Wilberforce's white negroes'.[21] The idea of a connection between being oppressed and being non-white, much aired as we shall see in contemporary international politics, goes back at least to this time. And it was the abolitionists' resolve to make amends for this, not merely by ending the slave trade, but also by making a constructive contribution to African civilization. From this resolve came the foundation of Sierra Leone and Liberia as settlements for freed slaves. Unlike Sierra Leone, Liberia moved early to something like an independent statehood and from the beginning saw its purpose as one of upholding black liberty generally, her constitution announcing that the state was formed 'to provide a home for the dispersed children of Africa'.[22]

For both sides in this phase of the transition – the non-Europeans who seized or were given their independence, and the Europeans who wanted to free the slaves – the idea of the moral and juridical equality of all men was an important one. The abolitionists relied on the argument that the slaves were our fellow-creatures. In St. Domingue, the doctrine of equality cut through the elaborate distinctions between *grands* and *petits blancs*, shades of *gens de couleur*, and the black slaves. In the case of Haiti, and of Liberia, the idea of equality extended to the equal sovereignty of black states with the European states that had been pronounced equal in the international legal doctrine of the previous century. The implications of these developments were profound, both for the emancipation of the slaves, and for the independence of states. Toussaint is supposed to have said:

> It is not a fortuitous concession of liberty, made to us alone, that we want, but a recognition of the principle that whether a man be red, black or white, he cannot be the property of any other man . . . the First Consul maintains slavery in Martinique, which means that he will make us slaves when he feels he is strong enough to do so.[23]

This is the familiar doctrine that the revolution is not safe anywhere until it is safe everywhere. Europeans were not slow to draw their conclusions. Napoleon was not alone in thinking that unless Toussaint were overthrown, 'the sceptre of the New World would sooner or later pass into the hands of the Blacks'.[24]

It may be that classing Haiti, Sierra Leone, and Liberia as the first phase of the transition is dignifying them with a title that they are not noble enough to bear. Toussaint's campaigns were regarded by some as squalid rather than inspiring, and Haiti has been more often the object of the scorn of the European powers than the subject of their esteem. The people of Sierra Leone calling themselves Englishmen and boasting of Lord Nelson and Waterloo were treated as faintly absurd by a Victorian writer.[25] And in the twentieth century, the insistence of President Tubman of Liberia on frock coats and top hats made it hard for western observers to take him seriously. But disdainful interpretations of this kind miss the dramatic confrontation, achieved by Toussaint above all, of Europeans with the practical effect of their own universal political theory. The rights of men and nations were the rights of all men and all nations. French revolutionary ideas about national self-determination were given a racial aspect that was to become a battlecry of new African states at the United Nations a century and a half later. It turned out that Toussaint's revolution remained for a long time within one country, and the conservative fear of contagion was exaggerated. But a breach had been made in the wall of European ascendancy.

III

A common western view of the Japanese in the nineteenth century was that they shared with other orientals a capacity for lying and a lack of moral scruple which arose, in the Japanese case, from an apparent ability to do without religion.[26] They were regarded as at best semi-civilized. Japanese awareness of this classification led to their determination to improve their position, to show the Europeans who had brought them into international society that they had reached their standards, that they were, in all except colour, Europeans.[27] This demonstration took place most spectacularly in the military field: the victories against China in 1895 and more importantly, from the point of view of her appenticeship as a power that would be civilized, against Russia in 1905; the vigorous participation with the great powers in the putting down of the Boxer Rebellion in 1900; the alliance with Great Britain of 1902 and involvement in the Great War including the dispatch of a Japanese fleet to the Mediterranean. The alliances with Britain, and later with the Western powers in the First World War, were contracted not against other Asian powers but against European powers: Japan was an honorary white power in this respect long before the South African Department of Immigration allowed the Japanese this status. Moreover, when Japanese troops landed with a British contingent in China in the opening year of the First World War it was an operation under Japanese and not British command. This was a far cry from the exclamation of a British naval officer in nineteenth-century China that 'the notion of a gentleman acting *under* an Asiatic barbarian is preposterous.'[28]

When it came to the peace settlement after the Great War, Japan's achievements as a military power did not bear diplomatic fruit. Japan proposed that the clause in the League of Nations Covenant providing for religious equality should be broadened to embrace racial equality. The principle of the equality of all men might have been taken to mean all men, yellow and even black, as well as white, but the consequences of such a doctrine for the domestic policies of the powers – the treatment of the negroes in the United States, the 'White Australian policy' – militated against its acceptance. Billy Hughes of Australia pronounced the theory of racial equality nonsense, and President Wilson deemed that the motion failed from want of securing unanimous approval.[29]

Nor did Japanese military success persuade the powers that Japan was no less a force to be reckoned with than European rivals. Churchill was not alone in continuing to think of the Asian races as inferior, and Christopher Thorne has assembled a number of instances illustrating complacency and scorn for the Japanese among those maintaining the position of the West in the Far East up to and during the Second World War.[30] The story of the Hong Kong garrison, lulled by the Western tradition of Japanese ineptitude, finding it hard to believe that the accurate fire being trained on them from Japanese planes was the work of Japanese, and not imported German pilots, has uncomfortable associations with the assumed incompetence of the 'gooks' in Vietnam and the 'gyppos' in the Arab-Israeli conflict: in these instances, it was the Russians who were held to be providing the stiffening.[31]

Thorne goes on to argue that 'in one of its vital aspects, the Pacific War of 1941 to 1945 was a racial war.'[32] It brought to a head long existing tensions on both sides: the Western powers worried by the implications of the threat to white predominance and seeking to avert the banding together of Asian powers after the war; the Asian powers in revolt against a world order that was white. Thorne says that one of the senses in which the United States and Great Britain were *Allies of a Kind* during the Second World War was in their concern to defend the prestige of the white race.[33]

The Western powers were also allies of such a kind in their relations with China. The policy of preserving a united European front against Asians was more successfully executed in China than it was in the case of Japan. The idea that this was a front maintained by a superior race against an inferior one was perhaps most luridly presented in Western dealings with China after 1840. Europeans had previously regarded Chinese civilization as strange but impressive. The Chinese failing that hostile Western observers noted most frequently was their dishonesty, and one writer speculated about the connection between this attribute and the shortcomings of the Chinese language – making no provision for fine distinctions and predisposing to a disregard for accuracy.[34] The general image of China in the period in which we are interested, says Jerome Ch'en, was one of a 'depraved race governed by a despotic and corrupt ruling class'.[35] There were three options for the West: to wipe the race from the face of the earth (the view of the Shanghai merchants); to treat it with contempt (the attitude of the diplomats); or to reform it (the task of the missionaries).[36] This idea of the Chinese as a race that had to have something done to it was not fundamentally to change until Western radical opinion, expressed, for example, in Edgar Snow's *Red Star Over China*, presented a possible alternative. But this might be said to have come from the same decline in Western self-confidence that led to the celebration of the Soviet Union by the European Left in the 1930s.

The 'yellow peril' lumped the Asiatic races together but was applied more to the Chinese than the Japanese. It had a military and an economic and social aspect. Militarily, there was the fear, from Kaiser Wilhelm II through to the allied leaders during the Second World War and beyond, that the next great conflagration was to take place as a result of the menace to the white from the yellow races. This fear was and still is strongest in Russia. The new Mongol hordes were a threat to a superior civilization from an inferior one in the tradition of Goths, Vandals, and Tartars.[37]

While some in the Western world frightened themselves with this prospect, action was taken against the other aspect of the yellow peril manifested in the coolie-trade or the pig-trade. The need for cheap labour on colonial plantations after emancipation had started this trade, and the gold rushes in California, Victoria, and the Transvaal brought Chinese immigrants to the United States, Australia, and South Africa. The one area in which the Chinese were superior to the Anglo-Saxon race was in their industry. They could outwork white men and there was the fear that the 'cheaper would starve out the dearer race'.[38] Concern on this economic ground, together with suspicion of the alien and apparently exclusive culture of the Chinese workers, combined into a hatred of their race. 'In America, as in Australia,' wrote Dilke, 'there is a violent prejudice against John Chinaman. He pilfers, we are told; he lies, he is dirty, he smokes opium, is full of bestial vices – a pagan, and – what is more important – yellow!'[39]

The result in the United States was the series of Exclusion Acts beginning in 1882 and not finally repealed until 1943, and after the wave of Japanese immigration at the turn of the century the Gentleman's Agreements of 1907–8 by which the Japanese government agreed to issue no more passports to coolies going directly to the United States. In Australia, the result was the Commonwealth Immigration Restriction of 1901, which followed legislation by separate Australian colonies in seeking to keep Australia white.

Preserving the purity of the race was not the sole justification of these policies, though a defence of the White Australia Policy has been that it was a particular expression of the general myth of white superiority extant in the Western, and especially the English-speaking, world, at that time.[40] There were also economic arguments about preserving the ratio of labour to capital.[41] But these arguments too tended to be poured back into a racial mould: restriction of one class of immigrants in particular; the idea that to preserve economic opportunities for one's own people was 'only the claim of a creator to possess and enjoy that which he has created' – for centuries it had been open to the Asiatics to develop Western America or Australia;[42] the observation that Europeans brought in capital and raised the standard of living of the country at large, while the coolies sent savings home draining the country.[43]

IV

The phase during which the expansion of international society has been most rapid is that one which is still with us, but is now very nearly at an end: the formation of new states from the old European empires after the Second World War. The doctrine of racial equality has had a substantial part in this story, not least, as we shall see in the following discussion of India and Africa, because of the attitudes of the imperialists themselves.

The frankness of its racialism has been regarded by an Indian writer as the most prominent characteristic of British rule in the East in the nineteenth century.[44] For the British, the burden of a God-given mandate to govern in India meant that there were standards to be kept up, rituals to be enacted for the benefit of the natives, and the social hierarchy intricately constructed and maintained. The orthodox attitude was to despise the natives, and those who failed to do so were regarded as eccentric, or worse.[45] The threat to the racial identity of Anglo-Saxons from contact with an alien culture, especially to children who had not yet learned the rules and might mix too freely with the natives, was constantly in mind. Kipling's Strickland of the police was sent home when he was 7 'and they flicked it out of me with a wet towel at Harrow'.[46]

For many Indians, the pattern of British rule meant no advancement beyond a certain level either in the military, or socially. The British treated India, said Nehru, as an enormous country house.[47] The British, the gentry, owned the house and occupied the comfortable parts aloft, while the Indians regimented below stairs remembered their position beneath an impassable social and political barrier. What was surprising about this, Nehru continued, was not the attitude of the British but that of the Indians in accepting the hierarchy and wishing merely to prosper so well as they could within it. This psychological achievement of getting the slave to think as a slave is what, for Nehru, was the triumph of the British in India.

And yet the impression gained from Nehru's account of the struggle for Indian independence is not of a quest for racial dignity, but rather for nationalist goals of a classical European kind: India as the Italy of Asia. 'All my predilections (apart from the political plane) are in favour of England and the English people, and if I have become what is called an uncompromising opponent of British rule in India, it is almost in spite of myself.'[48]

The argument for European rule in India applied the more strongly to Africa. According to a widespread mid-nineteenth-century notion, as we have seen, it was the negro who stood most in need of civilization, for he was the lowest of human types. European intervention would liberate the African from the cruel and irrational system which bound him.[49] And in the later evolutionist view, the problem of the tropical lands that were unfit for colonization by Europeans, but whose riches might not be exploitable by the inefficient indigenous populations, was how to develop them in the interest of civilization as a whole. The idea of administration from Europe as a trust for all mankind was a gloss on Burke's doctrine that 'all political power which is set over men . . . in derogation from the natural equality of mankind at large, ought to be some way or other exercised for their benefit.'[50] And it was an idea that was deployed in defence of empire elsewhere: the Dual Mandate put most crisply by Balfour, 'We are in Egypt not merely for the sake of the Egyptians, though we are there for their sake; we are there also for the sake of Europe at large.'[51]

The presumption of superiority which shored up the notion of benefit involved in this splendid piece of imperial selflessness came under fire from the critics of empire in a way that cleared much of the ground for the argument for racial equality. Mary Kingsley started this by separating civilization from Westernization.[52] The black peoples should not be viewed as underdeveloped whites, but as races with a course of their own to chart. Our duty as imperialists was to allow them to follow it, not us. This did not demolish the presumption of superiority, even for Mary Kingsley who argued that the black races were inferior in kind not degree, but it let in a relativism whose implications were equalizing. J. A. Hobson used the Cobdenite argument that the appeal to a higher standard of civilization in defence of empire assumed a uniform scale of civilized values which was a European conceit bearing no relation to reality.[53] Where there was no such scale, it came to be argued, there were no grounds for discrimination.

A longer-standing argument against discrimination, having no need for this anthropological sophistication, was that of the rights of man. The liberal policy towards the natives of the Cape, advocated especially by the missionaries, and opposed to the segregationism of the Boers, drew on Christian doctrine regarding the worth of individual human souls, and on the conscious extension to individuals from uncivilised races of the liberties of European free persons.[54] During the debate in Britain before the establishment of the Union of South Africa, the humanitarians argued for a comprehensive declaration of equality between Europeans and non-Europeans.[55] And the idea that this equality ought eventually to be achieved, and the regret that it could not now be endorsed owing to Boer intransigence, was common ground among most participants in the debate.[56] But common ground too was the notion that equality could not be established there and then. Europeans and non-Europeans were in different stages of civilization, and nothing was to be gained by equating the more-advanced with the less-advanced, the superior with the inferior. Even Keir Hardie said in the House of

Commons that 'none of us here are pressing that natives should get the franchise',[57] and Morley thought that parliamentary government was inappropriate for non-European peoples.[58]

But the genie of equality was out of the bottle. 'Indian leaders quoted Locke, Durham and J. S. Mill just as French Canadians and Afrikaaners had learnt to do'.[59] And West Indians and Africans followed. The idea of racial equality, in particular, may be said to have played its part in decolonization in three ways. In the first place, it encouraged non-Europeans to believe, and then to show that they were the equal of Europeans. Making the argument for independence in the Gold Coast Legislative Assembly, Kwame Nkrumah said the civilizations of the Ghana Empire were in existence long before the modern age of imperialism.

In the second place, the idea of racial equality, and the memory of inequality, may be said to have encouraged not imitation but the anxiety to be different. The insistence of Europeans in Asia on their European-ness has been said to have led Asians to develop in response a common feeling of Asian-ness, so that a racial as distinct from national division became an important factor in world politics.[60] Similarly, in Africa there has been the celebration of negritude and the search for an African personality. 'We are as good as you' becomes 'we are different from you, and we do not necessarily have the same values as you.'

Then, in the third place, this relativism is defended, in however muddled a way, by reference to the European principle of self-determination. By this principle, nations, and in an African interpretation, races, have the right to decide for themselves who is to belong to the separate units and the institutions that will rule them. Racial equality, in this interpretation, means the preservation of the integrity of a race, a doctrine that was so alarming in the hands of a soi-disant master-race, but is less so when deployed as now in the defence of the underdog.

V

Against the lurid racialism of some nineteenth-century imperialists can be placed the relative lack of colour-consciousness among Europeans in earlier ages of expansion, and also the doubts about doctrines of race supremacy expressed in the Victorian age itself.[51] Benjamin Kidd's arguments about social evolution, which were cited earlier, can be taken as examples of the fanaticism of a lunatic fringe which 'equated the strongest with the fittest, might with right, and the Elect with the big Battalions'.[62]

If we might, accordingly, hesitate to take racial differences, and the postulate of a racial hierarchy, to be a reason for empire, we may notice their part in its rationalization. From an anthropological point of view, it might be said that the function of racialist doctrine was to legitimize European dominance, and to buttress the idea of cultural superiority. Not merely was there a God-given mandate to rule, but the Europeans were to appear God-like themselves in the eyes of the natives;[63] and if not quite God-like, then at least in the relationship of masters to servants, or, a common theme, parents to children. This last metaphor might seem very unracial because it calls up a family similarity and not ethnic difference, and children grow to become adults themselves. But adults who are placed in the relationship of children by a governing class of different racial stock might see it differently. In any event, by reference to both cultural and racial superiority, parents and children were confirmed in their roles: Europeans sustained the will to govern; non-Europeans remained deferential.

The popularity of these rationalizations of empire gave, as we have seen, the emergence from it a racial flavour. The colour-consciousness of Asians or Africans stemmed in part from the dominance of Europeans who were conscious of their whiteness: 'The Negro, never so much a Negro since he has been dominated by the whites, when he decides to prove that he has a culture and to behave like a cultured person, comes to realize that history points out a well-defined path to him: he must demonstrate that a negro culture exists.'[64] It may be that the practical effect of this on international politics was small. The self-consciousness about ethnicity involved in the shedding of colonial nomenclature in Mali, or Bangladesh, or Sri Lanka, or Zimbabwe might be a one-shot affair, celebrated in independence before the assumption of routine diplomacy.

There is also the question of the connection between the idea of racial equality and the achievement of independence. Certainly, it has been argued, native awareness of the disjunction between what was preached and what was practised by white colonizers, and observation by the colonized of the colonizer when given an opportunity to visit the metropolis, both led to doubt about the universal superiority of the white race.[65] But we may doubt in turn whether it was the sudden unmasking of the impostor that led to the granting of independence on the grounds of the absence of any hierarchy among the races. The idea of racial equality got short shrift, as we have seen, in the preparation of the Covenant of the League of Nations, and Article 16 made reference to 'peoples not yet ready to stand by themselves under the strenuous conditions of the modern world'. In the Charter of the United Nations, however, these peoples had become, in Article 73, those who 'have not yet obtained a full-measure of self-government', and respect for and observance of human rights and fundamental freedoms without distinction as to race, sex, language, or religion had become a principle of international society. In contrast to the Covenant, the Charter was a declaration for racial equality and self-government.

What stood behind this change was not a recognition on the part of the white world that they had been racialist long enough in their relations with the non-white world, but the abhorrence felt at the working-out of a noxious doctrine of racial superiority within the Western world. The non-white world benefited, according to this view, from a Western lesson learnt, but it was the Nazis and not the non-white world that taught it. Benefit too was to be had from the new dominance of two strongly anti-colonial great powers, the United States and the Soviet Union, though their anti-colonialism did not necessarily derive from a belief in racial equality. But whatever the immediate cause of their acceptance, the principles of racial equality and of anti-colonialism were now part of the official doctrine of international society. What had been a protest against orthodoxy, in the debate on the Union of South Africa and elsewhere, was now itself the orthodoxy.

Its pronouncement as orthodoxy has led neither to the uniform acceptance of the idea of racial equality throughout international society, nor universally to its practical fulfilment. This unevenness is perhaps no surprise. The racialism of the imperialists had varied with time and place. French ideas about integration, for example, differed in their consequences for the colonized from what came to be the British model of indirect rule. And the emergence from empire varied in its racial component: Nehru saw the Indian struggle as a national rather than a racial one, while racial rhetoric played a more prominent part in the African independence movements – the search for an African personality reflecting the quest for dignity of a race that had always been at the bottom of the European list.

It is in relation to African affairs that the question of race relations features most prominently in contemporary international politics. It is on this continent, where one country still insists on patterns of racial segregation that go back to the beginnings of Dutch settlement in the seventeenth century, and where several others seem determined to expel their racial minorities, that the transition to racial equality seems the furthest from completion. At the United Nations, the guardian of the orthodoxy of racial equality, agitation against the colonial remnant in South Africa, led by the black African states, marks the anomaly. Out of this agitation has come the doctrine of racial sovereignty or pigmentational self-determination: a right to independence based on the racialist notion that rulers and ruled should be of similar stock.[66] This is majority rule, but the rule of an ethnic majority rather than a majority democratically returned in the Western liberal sense. And while this principle provides a new gateway into international society (or at least turns Toussaint's practice into doctrine), it is a gateway intended for only one newcomer.

There is also a more profound sense in which the transition is said to be incomplete. Here the argument is that the battle against racialism might have been won domestically in the victory against colonialism, but not in world society which has been rendered as a global caste-system.[67] Not merely, on this view, does it happen to be the case that the rich world is predominantly white, and the poor world predominantly coloured, but since the gap is widening between them it has been argued that this is evidence for the existence of a caste-system characterized by separation, division of labour, and hierarchy. Separation is not hermetic, but universally immigration laws preserve the characteristics of established populations. Where contact does take place, this argument alleges, white Brahmins oversee the Third World, black Harijans fulfil menial functions in the First World. The division of labour is the familiar one between white manufacturers and coloured primary workers. And hierarchy exists in virtue of the inequality of reward in this division, surplus value accruing to the manufacturers who then reinforce their position of superiority.

If there is anything in this, the phase of the transition to racial equality in world society has hardly begun. In relation to the liberal consensus, the conventional wisdom of which was referred to at the outset, it would assert a practice far distant from the principles written into the Charter of the United Nations. If this is no surprise, it would, by its insistence on the palpability of the racial factor in international politics, undermine the liberal wish to talk about something else – clines, or class, or culture. But it is much exaggerated. The notion of a global caste-system overlooks the cosmopolitanism of, say, the international diplomatic élite. Further, non-white countries that in the nineteenth and early twentieth centuries suffered the indignity of capitulation and the imposition of extraterritorial courts, are now not merely equal members of international society with their former exploiters, but powers of close to the first rank. And the several East Asian countries that have enjoyed such economic success since the Second World War can hardly be said still to be straining under a racial yoke. In view of this the argument that it is no accident that the 'less-developed countries' and the 'most affected nations' are non-white, that they are the Harijans in a global caste-system, is false. But the extent to which it has some propagandistic value reflects the extent to which it is still true to say that the affluent and the hungry worlds stand on either side of a colour line.

17

CHINA AND THE INTERNATIONAL ORDER

Coral Bell

As swiftly, suddenly, and mysteriously as a transformation-scene in pantomime, the image of China in the West changed in a few years from that (around 1967, at the height of the Cultural Revolution) of the most determined and implacable revolutionary enemy of the existing international order, to that (by about 1972) of a co-belligerent of the status quo powers, a strategically useful friend to NATO, and a prospective customer for American arms. As an example of diplomatic reversal over a period of barely five years, it will take some matching in the history books. From the point of view of the study of international politics, the chief interest of the change of stance and image is probably as an illustration of the dominance of power-calculations over ideology in foreign policy, even for a revolutionary élite. But paradoxically, the episode may also be presented as a case-study of continuity rather than change, provided one uses a somewhat longer time-span. For the things Mr Deng Xiaoping was saying about Soviet 'social imperialism' during his visit to America in 1978, and the mixture of hope and doubt with which he was contemplating the decision-makers in Mr Carter's Washington, seemed almost identical with the things Chiang Kai-Shek had been saying about Soviet imperialism in the 1940s, and the mixture of hope and doubt with which he then was looking to the decision-makers in Mr Truman's Washington. So over thirty years the wheel seemed to have turned precisely full circle. From a geopolitical determinist point of view, one might from this argue that China's interests as a sovereign entity in the society of states had in effect re-asserted themselves: the natural enemy was (as earlier) the predatory neighbour, Russia (in its Soviet incarnation as previously in its Czarist incarnation), and therefore the obvious potential ally became that enemy's chief enemy, the United States. All in all, the traditionalist might hold the story to be a particularly cogent illustration of that very old maxim of international politics, 'Neighbourhood maketh enmity.'

But actually it has been rather more complex that that, because China's attitude to the world order has been conditioned, since 1949, by its policy-makers' membership of the distinctly fratricidal brotherhood of Communist movements, as well as those same policy-makers' vested interest in the power and well-being of the society they command. It has been the interaction of those two influences on the sovereign personality of contemporary China which seems to account for the changes over the thirty-plus years in question.

To examine the process in more detail, we must return to 1949. Between the proclamation of the Communist regime in Peking in October of that year, and the mid-1980s, six phases of Chinese foreign policy may be distinguished. I will call them the 'United Bloc' period (1949–54), the 'Independent Hand' transition (1954–7), the 'Covert Strategic Divergence' period (1958–62), the 'Open and Polemical Divergence' period (1963–9), the 'Reinsurance Diplomacy' transition (1969–74), and the 'Anti-hegemony Drive' from 1975 to the time of writing. Arguments will be addressed later to the point that each of these phases induced some modifications either in the Chinese definition of the existing international order, or in assumptions about the desirable international order, or both.

The first or 'United Bloc' period was characterized by a theoretical proletarian internationalism: its basic assertion was the natural and complete solidarity of interests of China with other Communist powers, especially the Soviet Union, against the non-Communist world as a whole, especially the United States. The chief document of this phase of Chinese policy is Mao Tse-tung's essay 'On the People's Democratic Dictatorship', in which he enunciated the well-known 'lean to one side' principle, which many Westerners then assumed would prove the permanent centre-piece of Chinese foreign policy. The policy of the new China, Mao said, would be 'to ally with the Soviet Union, to ally with the new democratic countries of [Eastern] Europe, and to ally with the proletariat and masses of the peoples of all countries'. This might bring the accusation of 'leaning to one side', but the forty years experience of Sun Yat-Sen, and the twenty-eight years of experience of the Communist party had convinced them that to win victory and consolidate victory, they must lean to one side. 'One either leans to the side of imperialism or the side of socialism. *Neutrality is a camouflage and a third road does not exist.*'[1]

The Sino-Soviet Treaty of February 1950 in effect provided a formal expression of this initial identification of China's interests with those of the Soviet-led Communist world of the time. But even in 1949, Chinese experience of Soviet fraternal advice and help had already been quite ambivalent. And Mao's own memories of his treatment by Stalin must have been bitter enough.[2] So that the bland phrases of the communiqué, and the proclaimed official expectation of thirty years of common diplomatic purposes, barely disguised the possibility that the treaty would prove to be a fragile papering-over of some large gaps between perceived national interests, once the diplomatic honeymoon was over.

In the light of later polemics, it appears that the experience of the Korean War (in which the Soviet Union sat on the sidelines and later presented a bill for $700 million in weaponry[3]) apparently sharpened the consciousness among Chinese policy-makers like Chou En-lai and Mao himself of the necessity for the new regime beginning to 'play for its own hand' in world diplomacy. Certainly that impression emerged strongly from Chou's visible independence of operation from the Russians at the Geneva Conference on Indo-China and Korea in 1954, and still more so from the Bandung Conference of 1955, at which his skill in making Third World contacts for the new China was strikingly deployed.

This period of the mid-fifties marks the beginning of serious ideological and diplomatic competition between the Soviet Union and China, since (whether the decision-makers of either country wanted it or not) the two regimes were inevitably seen by ambitious young radicals, plotting their own respective revolutions in the Third World, as alternative possible 'models'. The advantages of China in this competition initially seemed considerable, because China was still essentially a very poor peasant-subsistence economy, like most of the Third World countries concerned, and thus easier for them to identify with in situation and experience. The Soviet Union, to the contrary, was an industrialized superpower, relatively rich by Third World standards, and the Russians who made the decisions in Moscow were Europeans with a long imperial history, still openly determined to hold on to tzarist acquisitions. Besides, the Chinese Revolution was newer, and Mao a more charismatic figure than either Stalin or Khrushchev. The possibility that Third World leaders might see the Chinese model and 'Mao Tse-tung thought' as more relevant and useful than the Soviet model, and what the Russians presented as Marxist-Leninist orthodoxy, must have been vividly obvious to policy-makers in Moscow by 1955.

That same year also saw the beginning of a more traditional kind of diplomatic clash of interests between China and the Soviet Union, over attitudes to India. Bulganin and Khrushchev (then apparently joint decision-makers for the Soviet Union) visited India in 1955, had a noticeable popular success, and promised the Indian government advanced weapon-systems, including late-model MIG aircraft. That was the beginning of an arms-supply relationship which has been sustained ever since, and has undoubtedly been seen as a diplomatic asset in the Soviet Union. But China was already, by 1955, in a situation of potential or growing friction with India over the Aksai Chin road and the border areas. (Those frictions eventuated in a brief war in 1962.) So the sight of the Soviet Union providing military supplies to India (including aircraft more advanced than those China itself had been given) was not calculated to re-establish Chinese faith in the already somewhat dubious and battered concept of the brotherhood of Communist powers. This phase to my mind should be regarded as a three-year transition to the sharper conflicts after 1958.

The third phase, which I have called that of covert strategic divergence, was marked by acrimonious but still behind-scenes arguments between Chinese and Russian leaders over the handling of various diplomatic crises, beginning with the Iraq-Jordan-Lebanon crisis of mid-1958, and the Quemoy-Matsu crisis of late 1958. On the basis of the polemics released later, one would say that the gravamen of the argument was the Russian insistence on rather cautious crisis-management strategies, despite the Chinese demand for bolder ones. One might also say that Russian caution was based on a realistic understanding of the true balance of forces at the time between the Soviet Union and the West, whereas the Chinese demand for boldness appears to indicate that Mao had hypnotized himself (though not necessarily all his colleagues) into believing his slogan of the time about 'the East Wind prevailing over the West Wind'.In domestic policy this was a period of a political line (the so-called 'Great Leap Forward') which was later (after Mao's death) revealed by his successors to have precipitated major disasters: great waste of resources and mass starvation. In foreign policy, at least *vis-à-vis* the US, the Russians could of course veto any corresponding strategic notion of a 'great leap forward' internationally, since they alone, then, controlled such nuclear weapons as the Communist camp possessed. But late in the fifties (about 1957) Soviet policy-makers made a decision which might be regarded as a surprising gesture of faith in the 'United Bloc' concept, or a desperate bid to reassert the natural brotherhood of Communist governments. They gave the Chinese aid which enabled China to start along the pathway to nuclear weapons.

Soviet help to China in the nuclear field only lasted about eighteen months: according to the Chinese, the Russians reneged on the agreement about the time of Mr Khrushchev's visit to Washington in 1959. They have referred to the Soviet change of mind as 'a gift to President Eisenhower'. But that brief period of co-operation, when added to the earlier training of Chinese physicists in American institutes like MIT and Caltech, in effect endowed China only a few years later with the ability to mount a devastating last-ditch threat to at least a few cities in the Russian Far East. (The Chinese tested their first atomic weapon in 1964.) The Cuba missile crisis at the end of 1962, or rather the Russian mishandling (as the Chinese saw it) of that crisis provided Peking with a useful occasion for bringing the conflict with the Soviet Union out from behind the scenes into full international view. Judging that move as part of the Chinese strategy in the competition with the Soviet decision-makers for influence over other Communist regimes and movements, it seems logical enough. That particular crisis certainly provided a highly dramatic occasion on which the Chinese could accuse the Russians, with considerable plausibility, of 'adventurism' in putting the missiles into Cuba, and with 'capitulationism' in taking them out again. Both of course are grievous sins among Leninists.

Up to and for a time after this crisis, the Chinese leadership appeared still to be adhering to a 'two camps' concept of the international order, even though with steadily increasing readiness to make visible and audible its distrust of Soviet strategy in the conflict with the West, and its readiness to challenge the Soviet Union for leadership of the 'camp of socialism and peace'. However, in the next phase, beginning about the mid-sixties, a new and violent radicalism became temporarily dominant in Chinese polemics. The new phase was inextricably involved with a vast Chinese domestic upheaval, the 'Great Proletarian Cultural Revolution'. From the retrospect of the early eighties, at a time when the Cultural Revolution is officially described by the successors to Mao as a catastrophe, the status of the set of intellectual concepts associated with it in Chinese foreign policy must necessarily appear dubious. They might be regarded as not more than a by-product of a sort of domestic frenzy. Such episodes as the burning-down of the British Embassy in Peking, the physical mistreatment of various foreign diplomats there, the summoning home of senior Chinese diplomats to be harangued and 're-educated' by teenage Red Guards, the ramming of 'Mao Tse-tung thought' down the throats of travellers, and so on, seem at this distance like a half-forgotten nightmare. The political leaders and officials who at the time had to co-operate in such behaviour (including to some extent Chou En-lai himself) presumably did so in fear of their lives.

The intellectual strategy associated with the Cultural Revolution in foreign and defence policy was attributed at the time to Lin Piao, then Mao's 'close comrade in arms', heir-apparent, and Defence Minister. Lin fell from grace in 1971, perhaps because of disagreement over Mao's turn by that time to the US, but the official Chinese charge against him is still that of attempting to assassinate Mao, mount a *coup d'état*, and flee to the Soviet Union when his plots failed. So doctrines associated with his name can hardly be accorded official status or rehabilitation even by the present leadership. Nevertheless an essay attributed to Lin, published in Peking in September 1965[4] provides the most coherent account from this period of the then-prescribed Chinese analysis of the world order, and the strategy proposed for transforming it. The essay remains an interesting piece of Chinese revolutionary utopianism, even if one regards the Cultural Revolution as a disastrous aberration on Mao's part and accepts the official view (since 1971) of Lin as a traitor.[5]

With the growth of anger against the Soviet Union in the late sixties (a period marked by border clashes between Soviet and Chinese troops in Sinkiang and the Amur-Ussuri area) the original 'two-camp' theory of the existing world order was transmuted into a 'three-camp' theory. The first camp comprised the two superpowers, the 'imperialists' and 'social imperialists' (Americans and Russians) initially presented as equally infamous and dangerous. Then there was the 'second intermediate zone': the industrialized powers of Europe, seen as temporarily allied to one or other of the superpowers but who might conceivably be recruited as tactical allies against them, since their interests were in reality in conflict with those of both superpowers. Finally, there was the Third World: China was seen as belonging to this grouping and as being its natural leader, especially since it would 'shun hegemonism' and 'never behave like a superpower', even though it had nuclear weapons.

The Third World was also referred to as the 'countryside of the world', whereas all the industrialized powers, east and west, were 'the cities of the world'. And, in an obvious approximation from the strategy by which Mao won the long civil war in China, the revolutionary 'countryside of the world' was somehow to surround the 'cities of the world', depriving them of the sustenance they draw from it, and so achieving final victory. The whole existing society of states was seen as a structure of injustice, fit only for the scrap-heap of history.

The image of China as a totally revolutionary society, intent to a reckless and irrational degree on the destruction forthwith of the whole existing international order, an image which was widespread during the years of peak frenzy in the Cultural Revolution (1966–7) derived mostly from a misinterpretation of the revolutionary utopianism of Lin's essay, plus the actual physical events of the period in China. Beneath the verbiage the essay was outlining basically a defensive strategy for meeting a Soviet attack, if one should come, 'drowning the invaders in a sea of people's war'.

To a few far-Left radicals in the West, the Cultural Revolution seemed like a sort of Second Coming: there was much enthusiasm in the predictable quarters, academic and otherwise. But to most Third World regimes, the whole spectacle was quite frightening: enough to give revolution a bad name. To orthodox Communists it seemed a proof that the Russians were right about the Chinese. Thus one can say that while no doubt Mao won his point through this technique (in that he restored himself to power, and managed to hang on to power until his death in 1976), that triumph of revolutionary machiavellianism was at staggering cost to China, as his successors have been saying in recent years. The domestic costs were obviously much the greater, but in international relations it cost China practically all that Chou En-lai had built up earlier in the way of influence and connections. By 1968, China seemed to have no friend in the world except Albania. If Chinese policy-makers had ever believed the notion put forward in Lin's essay, of the 'countryside of the world' rallying behind China and surrounding the 'cities of the world', such optimism could hardly have survived the experience of the years concerned.

Thus in a way the isolation which Mao brought upon China during the Cultural Revolution period made the next turn of Chinese foreign policy less rather than more surprising. That turn was, of course, towards Washington.

Dr Kissinger's account[6] makes it clear that signals hinting at the possibility of coming to terms were being sent from Peking for quite some time before they were identified as such by American 'China-watchers', even though Mr Nixon had decided on a China initiative before taking office. The chief factor behind the Chinese push for *rapprochement*, on the evidence, was a judgement by the decision-makers (Mao as well as Chou) that the Soviet Union had become, and was likely to remain, a far more dangerous enemy for China than the United States. And that therefore, in accordance with Maoist strategy, Washington must be regarded as a potential diplomatic or even military ally against Moscow.

Though that assessment may seem startlingly at odds with Leninist theory, and with the Chinese analysis of just twenty years earlier, the events of 1968 more or less imposed it upon Peking. On the one hand, the relative fragility of American will to intervene overseas was indicated by President Johnson's being unwilling or unable to make the effort for a second term, after five years experience of Vietnam. To a hardened old revolutionary like Mao, who had just turned his own country upside down in order to reassert his control over party and government, that must have seemed to rule out America as any kind of formidable antagonist. The signal as to Soviet political will, however, had been exactly the reverse: Brezhnev's using Soviet tanks to put down a fraternal communist party in Czechoslovakia (also in 1968) because it had drifted into heresy. The contrast could hardly have been more pointed. The Chinese may not have believed that the Russians would dare to try applying the Brezhnev doctrine in China, but clearly Soviet restraint had to be interpreted as evidence of lack of means, rather than lack of will.

Moreover, it has from time to time been reported (though never officially confirmed) that during the Sino-Soviet border clashes of early 1969 over the island variously called Chen Pao or Damansky according to one's point of view, the Russians attempted to cow Chinese decision-makers into withdrawal by sending a group of Soviet bombers on a 'dry run' over some Chinese cities, clearly intending to convey to Peking a signal that the bombers could readily come again, if necessary, perhaps with nuclear weapons. At the same time the Russians allegedly dropped heavy hints of a possible joint strike at Chinese nuclear installations to the Americans, who snubbed them – and adroitly let the Chinese know about it all.

If there is any substance in that story, it would explain the notable vigour and persistence with which the Chinese set about what I have called the 'reinsurance diplomacy' of this period. And if Lin argued that the better strategy would be to make some concessions to the Russians, in order to reinsure with them as the more dangerous of the two superpowers, it would explain both his fall from favour with Mao, and the nature of the accusations brought against him at the time, and sustained by the successor Chinese governments after Mao's death. Unlike Liu Shao-chi and many others, he has never been rehabilitated.

During the early years of *rapprochement* with the United States, the tone of Chinese comment on the two superpowers seemed to bracket the 'imperialists' and 'social imperialists' together in general infamy, and assume them equally responsible for the dangers to peace. For instance, Chou En-lai in 1973:

> The US-Soviet contention for hegemony is the cause of world intranquility. It has met with strong resistance from the Third World and has caused resentment on the part of Japan and the Western European countries.[7]

But four years later, with Chou and Mao both dead, the Russians are unambiguously the villains of the piece:

> Of the two imperialist superpowers, the Soviet Union is the more ferocious, the more reckless, the more treacherous and the most dangerous source of world war.[8]

A year further on, and what I have called the anti-hegemony drive is emerging clearly as a first priority of Chinese foreign policy:

The urgent task for people of various countries is to unite with all forces against hegemonism, foil the Soviet offensive, sabotage the Soviet strategic arrangements and strive to postpone the outbreak of a world war . . . The international united front against hegemonism is consolidating and expanding.[9]

That prescription has since continued to be the official one from Peking, with the implication that it provides a mode of avoiding war:

It is our view that if only all peace-loving countries and peoples unite and take firm steps to curb the hegemonists' aggression and expansion, it is possible to postpone or even prevent the outbreak of a great war.[10]

Though the 'three camps' concept of the world order is not specifically disavowed, the pressures of the anti-hegemonial drive have tended towards a presentation of the world as, for most practical purposes, reducing itself essentially to just two camps: the would-be hegemonial power with its captives and proxies (the Soviet Union, the other Warsaw Pact powers, Vietnam, Cuba, maybe Angola and Mozambique) on the one hand, and the rest of the world, the potential anti-hegemonial alliance, on the other.

Thus, ironically, China had moved in thirty years from a United Front *with* the Soviet Union against the capitalist world to a United Front *against* the Soviet Union, with the capitalist world and anyone else who could be persuaded to join. One could even re-apply, making only a slight variant, an earlier Maoist maxim. 'One either leans to the side of Soviet hegemonism, or one resists it. Neutrality is a camouflage and a third road does not exist.'

The reasons for that further turn of the foreign-policy wheel (like those for the turn towards Washington in 1969) clearly derived from the world of practical international experience, not that of theory. In 1975, the Americans accepted their defeat in Vietnam, unresisting, and appeared for several years to be altogether opting out of South-East Asia. In those same years the Russians consolidated their alliance with Vietnam, and the Vietnamese consolidated their hold on Kampuchea and Laos. Furthermore, the Soviet navy considerably stepped up its presence in the Sea of Japan, and Soviet naval and air power began to be deployed from Vietnamese bases at Cam Ranh Bay and Danang. So in effect, the decision-makers in Peking had to see China as prospectively encircled by the would-be hegemonial power, and its ally the 'regional hegemonist' (Vietnam). Further, the decay of American influence in the Persian Gulf, with the overthrow of the Shah (again, from Peking's point of view, with no effective American resistance), plus the Soviet move into Afghanistan (with consequent implied dangers to China's one South Asian ally, Pakistan), along with the growth of Soviet influence in Angola and Mozambique and Ethiopia and South Yemen provided extra plausibility to the notion of a Soviet 'great leap forward' in diplomatic influence and strategic capacity, a notion even more dismaying to Chinese than to Western policy-makers.

So President Carter, despite his normalization of relations with China, obviously was not seen in Peking as adequate to the role of chief decision-maker for the potential anti-hegemonial alliance. President Reagan, despite pre-election leanings towards Taiwan, and a tendency to re-assert them from time to time even after assuming office, was in most respects far more in line with Chinese thinking on the world conflict. His adminstration's demonstrative tough-mindedness towards the Soviet Union, its rejection of *détente*, its scepticism of arms-control, its obvious abandonment of any Kissinger-type concept of 'equidistance' between Moscow and Peking, and its willingness to sell armaments to China, all represented a much closer approximation to the proclaimed views of Deng Xiao-ping and his closest allies, and these attitudes clearly offset the black marks incurred by the Taiwan affiliations of right-wing Republicans, including the President.

Thus it was not surprising that the May 1981 meeting of the Politburo in Peking, at a time when the Chinese decision-makers had had a reasonable interval in which to digest the policies of the Reagan administration, decided to re-affirm the general line of co-belligerence (if not actual alliance) with the United States, Japan, and Western Europe. A faction of the party which reportedly wanted a more 'equidistant' stance between Moscow and Washington was defeated, and there appeared no interest in presenting China as a 'third force' in world affairs. There were by that date two large American-supplied surveillance installations on Chinese soil watching matters of strategic interest in the Soviet Union. (They apparently provided replacements for those previously operating in Iran.) Chinese faith in the revolutionary potential of the Third World appeared to have dwindled to a point where it had little impact on allocation of resources. Ambitious earlier efforts to build up influence with Third World governments through expensive schemes like the Tanzam railway found no successors. (Which was not necessarily regrettable because there was little indication that they had paid off either for the local peoples concerned or for China itself.) Chinese support for insurgent movements in areas like Thailand was also reported to be dwindling, though at least one earlier enterprise in that line, help given to Robert Mugabe in Zimbabwe, might be regarded as a considerable success.

All in all, the diplomatic stance of the government in Peking in the 1980s was uncommonly like what might have been expected if the political party which controlled it had still been the Kuomintang: on bad terms with the Soviet Union, and deeply suspicious of it; on wary good terms with Washington and Tokyo, though not entirely satisfied with the policies of either; temporarily tolerant of Hong Kong, and finding it a useful source of foreign exchange, though intending to reassert sovereignty as soon as it was convenient; determined to reclaim Taiwan, but willing to await a propitious moment; determined to maintain full control over Tibet, and willing to be on bad terms if necessary with India; on very bad terms with Vietnam and in a prolonged contest with Hanoi over the control of Cambodia; working with a Third World bloc at the United Nations, but discovering the industrialized Western powers and Japan to be more useful to Chinese purposes, both diplomatic and strategic. And in particular, wanting a peaceful world in which to pursue economic development (the 'four modernizations') with all speed possible.

That was a far cry from the wild revolutionary assertions of 1967, or even the more sober earlier ones of 1949. It would however be too much to say that demands for a revolutionary change in the world order have been abandoned. They persist at the level of declaratory policy, though operational policy appears to assume a continuance of the present international order for the foreseeable future, and China's most useful diplomatic connections are with the major status quo powers (the United States, Western Europe, and Japan) and their fellow-travellers, like Australia.

The notion of the world order comprises not only analysis of the-world-as-it-is, but concepts of the-world-as-it-should-be, and the connection (or perceived disconnection) between the two may be expected to generate some kind of strategic assumptions on how to get there from here. Present Chinese concepts of the world order as-it-should-be presumably continue to embody the vague Marxist notion of the eventual withering-away of the state, a development which (if it ever occurs) will obviously make the notion of a society of states obsolete. The world order, in that improbable case, will presumably be seen as a universalization of a benign domestic order, in which the government of men has been replaced by the administration of things.

However, as the almost seventy years experience of Communist governments is intellectually digested, that vague happy-ever-after stage of the human story must look increasingly less plausible, even to those actually operating within Communist systems, including China. They are not likely to hold their breaths waiting for it to happen. For actual experience has been that the state apparatus in Communist societies not only shows no sign of withering away, it flourishes like the green bay tree, and generates no less intransigent attitudes towards other states than towards its own citizens. The history of conflict between Communist regimes (the Soviet Union versus Yugoslavia and versus China, China versus Vietnam, Vietnam versus Cambodia), considering the brevity of the historical period involved, seems in itself enough, at least to non-believers, to indicate that a society universally of Marxist states would be no less conflict-ridden than a society universally of capitalist states once was.

Though Chinese policy-makers no doubt continue to attribute conflicts between governments claiming to be Marxist to the revisionism, bad faith, treachery, and hegemonism of the Soviet Union and its proxies, rather than to any essential flaw in the original theory of proletarian internationalism, there is in their own intellectual tradition an alternative concept of the desirable world order which might perhaps one day challenge the Maoist one, if the 'downplaying' of Maoism (which is at present apparent in many aspects of Chinese life) becomes still more thoroughgoing.

That alternative tradition is the classical Chinese concept, not so much of a world order as of a world state. The historic Chinese experience, up to the time of the Western impact in the mid-nineteenth century, had been of China as the central and light-bearing civilization of the world, surrounded by local barbarian peoples who might rise in due course to the level of benefiting by, or sharing in, the Chinese enlightenment, and more remote barbarians in whom they were not much interested. As a world-state, the Chinese Empire not only lasted vastly longer than the Roman Empire but was more absolute, in that the Roman decision-makers had to be conscious that other independent systems of an advanced kind had existed, like Alexander's empire, or the Greek city-states, or the ancient civilization of Egypt, whereas China was unique and unrivalled within its own world.

That immensely long historical experience had its own world view, derived from Confucian doctrine:

> The Confucian view of the foreigner depends partly on the stress given to the unique nature of the earthly authority delegated to the Son of Heaven. Such authority precludes the need for or the legality of other political units, and comprizes a temporal power over all members' of the civilized world. . . . Thus once a barbarian people has shown itself sufficiently well educated to appreciate the benefits of Chinese authority, it qualifies to become a full member of the Empire. Subject peoples can acknowledge his [Emperor's] authority by the payment of material tribute whose presence at court serves to enhance the

Emperor's majesty and to demonstrate the universal acceptance of his title to power.[11]

Remote though Maoism may seem from Confucianism, there were times during the Cultural Revolution when Mao was referred to by ideographs previously reserved for the Son of Heaven, and the insistence on 'Mao Tse-tung thought' as a treasury for all the peoples of the world came close to the old Chinese claim to provide tutelage to barbarians, near and far, in the ways of enlightenment. Until very recently it would have seemed absurd even to speculate on any other doctrine but Maoism making a distinctively Chinese input into the concept of a world order. Perhaps now, however, one might venture a tentative assumption that the classical vision may prove the more lasting one. On the face of it, that vision is totally incompatible with the usual Western assumption that an open and pluralistic society of states will and should persist as the world order of the foreseeable future. Yet the present Chinese strategy (of the anti-hegemonial alliance directed against the Soviet Union), and the present Western strategy (of a balance-of-power alliance directed against the Soviet Union) appear so usefully complementary that no one is likely to be disturbed by differences in underlying concepts. At least not for a long time yet.

18

INDIA AND THE INTERNATIONAL ORDER – RETREAT FROM IDEALISM

Gopal Krishna

I

At the end of the Second World War the world order built up by the European powers over the preceding two centuries stood dramatically transformed. The dominant power centres had shifted out of Europe to North America and the USSR, the world-wide empires of the European powers were on the verge of dissolution, and, though this was less evident at the time, a new force in world affairs in the form of the newly independent countries of Asia and Africa, later to be joined by the nations of Latin America, was taking shape. The emergence of India as a free nation in August 1947 was the first major event in the post-war process of the liberation of subject peoples in what is now known as the 'Third World'. Indians considered this an event of world-historical significance. It had a double import: it marked the beginning of the end of the era of European imperialism and domination of the world, and it heralded the emergence of new power centres which would inevitably bring about a reconstitution of the international system; above all, the hitherto disenfranchised multitudes of Asia and Africa would become citizens of the world and, it was felt, would play their proper part in fashioning a new and just world civilization.

The independence of India was soon followed by the victory of the Communist armies in China and the proclamation of the Chinese People's Republic on 1 October 1949. K. M. Panikkar, the Indian historian, diplomat, and administrator, had, among the Indians of his generation, the unique good fortune of witnessing the withdrawal of European power from India in 1947 and from China in 1949. Panikkar's remarkable book, *Asia and Western Dominance*,[1] was mostly written in 1949 in Nanking during the final phase of the Chinese civil war, and he saw the European warships evacuating their bases on the mainland of China and the departure of the diplomatic representatives of the European nations from Shanghai after the proclamation of the People's Republic in Peking.[2] For Indians of Panikkar's generation the end of the

European epoch of Asia's history was a moment of great excitement. For the best part of two centuries India, with much of Asia and Africa, had been subject to the ultimate form of inequality – political subjection – and its end promised a new life to the liberated peoples as well as the prospect of a more equitable world order.

When Indians visualized free India's position in the international system and the role India would play in world affairs, they thought of it primarily in terms of India's intrinsic claims. In the realm of power India might not count for a great deal – at least not until it had overcome its economic and technological backwardness – but it was a major constituent of world civilization and as such entitled to an honourable place in the international order. India's potential for sustaining a major role was felt to be much greater than its current condition suggested, and to many Indians it seemed certain that with its large, talented population, natural resources, and potential for the application of modern science India was bound to emerge as one of the great powers. But the drive for power as such was never a strong element in Indian domestic or foreign policy. The leaders of the Indian national movement who gave shape and solidity to the Indian state, in particular Jawaharlal Nehru, had a dispositional aversion to the application of power in domestic or international affairs. Itself a victim of superior power in the past and barely capable of resisting its encroachment in the present, India under Nehru's leadership exerted itself to reduce the role of power in the contemporary world order and to ground this order instead in rules of general application.

The post-war world was characterized by three basic features: it was still anarchic,[3] although the United Nations Organization was intended to put limits to the anarchy of sovereign states; there was (and still is) extreme inequality of power and resources between nations; and the peace of the world was (and still is) under threat from the conflict between the Atlantic and Soviet power blocs. Free India's foreign policy was conceived in this context. It was in the main the work of Jawaharlal Nehru, who brought to bear on his task a mixture of pragmatic idealism and regard for India's national interests. The principal constituents of Nehru's foreign policy were: friendship with all countries, support for independence movements in order to bring about rapid decolonization, regional co-operation in Asia (later extended to Africa and yet later to the 'Third World'), partnership in a reformed Commonwealth, support for the United Nations, non-alignment and the preservation of peace. India's own rather limited capabilities did not seem to him an insuperable handicap in the pursuit of a policy he considered good for India and good for the world. The particular constellation of forces in the international arena at the time made it appear feasible for an economically and technologically underdeveloped country, which yet entertained a high degree of self-esteem and aspirations to future greatness, to adopt such an ambitious policy.[4]

II

It was a strong, and rather distinctive characteristic of Indian nationalism that its attitude towards the world order, freed of imperialism, was wholly positive. Nehru had as long ago as 1929 expressed the view that free India 'will welcome all attempts at world cooperation and federation, and will even agree to give up part of her own independence to a larger group of which she is an equal member'.[5] A decade later, in 1939, he reiterated that India's independence had to be thought of 'in terms of the world and world cooperation'.[6] As early as 1933 he had drawn attention to the inequality of wealth between the nations of the north and the south.[7] He believed that 'imperialism and the anarchy of sovereign states are inevitable developments of the present phase of capitalism',[8] and therefore if, as many thoughtful people everywhere desired, the 'anarchy of sovereign states, with their hatreds, fears and conflicts' had to be ended, the world order had to be reconstructed on the basis of a socialist ideal.[9] When India became independent this broad, international orientation informed the Indian attitude towards the world.

The key premiss of Indian foreign policy was that the most active force in the post-war world was 'Third World' nationalism, and that this, unlike the pre-war nationalism in Europe, would be the basis for a reconstruction of the hitherto Western-dominated international order in which the priorities relevant to the greater part of mankind, the removal of poverty and backwardness, would take due precedence and the power conflicts of the major nations, which, given nuclear weapons, threatened the whole of civilization, would be moderated or controlled. The conflict between the Atlantic and Soviet power blocs, while presented in ideological terms, was perceived as essentially a power conflict, but one in which nuclear parity had removed the possibility of the use of war as an instrument of policy by either side; however the peace so maintained was precarious and, if only because of the nuclear danger, the great powers needed as never before to cultivate a temper of peace and mutual accommodation. In this context the cause of peace, allowing the application of world resources to the problem of backwardness, was best served by as many nations as possible keeping out of this conflict; the new nations should apply themselves foremost to preserving and strengthening their own political and economic independence.

It was above all to ensure the free development of the new nations that Nehru emphasized the need for constraints on the use of force in international relations. The only circumstances in which he held the use of force justified were self-defence, to repel aggression, and exceptionally, after the exhaustion of peaceful means, to eliminate colonial rule, itself a form of prolonged aggression against the colonized people.

The primary objective of Indian foreign policy was to preserve and further India's autonomy in a world dominated by the Atlantic and Soviet power blocs. This quest for autonomy was pursued through the policy of non-alignment. Though conceived in the context of the Cold War, non-alignment was not a policy only for the Cold War condition. It was neither a moral posture designed to achieve greater influence than India's capacity to exert power justified, as suggested by Henry Kissinger,[10] nor simply a formula for keeping India out of other peoples' conflicts in which she had little substantive interest, nor yet a clever device to get the best terms possible for herself from both sides to the global conflict, as in the vulgar view of it presented in much American Cold War literature on the subject. In its stronger version pursued by Nehru non-alignment was an ambitious proposition. By declaring that India would be non-aligned as between the two power blocs and would judge international issues on their merits, Nehru asserted India's independence and claimed for it a right to play a major role in world affairs. Unlike neutrality, non-alignment was an activist policy designed to influence the outcome of the major and minor conflicts in the world and to promote the transformation of the international order.

The ideological and power conflict of the post-war world was, in Nehru's view, derived 'from the background of Europe', and 'the background of Europe is not completely the background of India or the world';[11] consequently there was no reason why India should choose one or the other ideology or power bloc. Nehru considered both communist and bourgeois ideologies to be out of date and rejected the ideological mode of thinking as irrelevant and dangerous. It was neither desirable nor feasible to impose conformity of ideology on the diverse nations of the world and such an attempt by powerful nations would result in the oppression of weak nations, distract them from their pressing tasks of development, generate domestic divisions, and undermine their capacity for autonomy. Military alliance between the powerful and the weak was of advantage to neither; the former had no need of it, while the latter incurred the hostility of the rival great power, which could threaten its security and stability. The inevitable dependency relationship with the powerful ally Nehru considered abhorrent for a country attaining independence after prolonged subjection.

India's non-alignment was rooted in her non-aggressive but robust nationalism. Nehru believed that an international order allowing countries to work out their destinies in freedom and co-operation necessarily imposed constraints on all countries by ruling out foreign interference in most circumstances. He told the French author Tibor Mende, 'I may not like something for myself . . . But anyhow, *my* objecting to what they do, necessarily would lead to *their* objecting to what I do. Now, I do not want their intereference and I do not wish to interfere with them, or with any other country for that matter.'[12] Nehru regarded interference by outside powers as the principal source of instability in newly independent countries and as a practice contributing to tension between the great powers.

The adherents of non-alignment claimed to be a third, and somewhat saner, constituent of international society with the right to be heard with respect by the rest of the world on matters of war and peace, decolonization, and the distribution of the world's resources. It was also a claim of the non-aligned, though never quite specifically stated, that their very powerlessness made them natural defenders of world peace.

Nehru believed that India was particularly well placed to pursue the policy of non-alignment in that it had no security problem of its own, other than that with Pakistan which it was capable of containing with its own resouces without a high level of military expenditure; for the rest it posed no threat to anyone and no one threatened it. He considered that in the international context of the time, India's non-alignment would be a positive factor in preserving peace by preventing polarization of the world into two antagonistic power blocs. It would also serve the national interest by strengthening India's independence and providing security; both blocs would have an interest in protecting India's non-alignment as it became an indispensable element in the balance of power, and this would enable India to limit its defence expenditure, leaving resources free for economic development. Nor was Nehru insensitive to the domestic considerations favouring non-alignment. He told the Indian Council of World Affairs on 22 March 1949, 'Any attempt on our part . . . to go too far in one direction would create difficulties in our own country. It would be resented and we would produce conflicts in our own country which would not be helpful to us or to any other country.'[13] National interest thus seemed to dictate that India should not involve itself in the Cold War but should work for the reduction of international tensions.

The principal constituents of Indian foreign policy found their comprehensive expression in the ill-fated agreement between India and China – Agreement on Trade and Intercourse between the Tibet region of China and India – signed in Peking on 29 April 1954.[14] For Nehru it represented a major achievement for his policy of peace and mutual understanding between nations committed to different ideologies and having different political systems. The Agreement included the famous five-point formula – mutual respect for each other's territorial integrity and sovereignty; mutual non-aggression; mutual non-interference in each other's internal affairs; equality and mutual benefit; and peaceful coexistence – which Nehru commended to Parliament as '. . . a statement of wholesome principles, and I imagine if these principles were adopted in the relations of various countries with one another, a great deal of trouble of the present day world would probably disappear.'[15] The five principles were Nehru's rules for the conduct of international relations in the post-war world.

III

The international associations that India endeavoured to strengthen were the Commonwealth (at first the British Commonwealth, and later the Commonwealth of Nations), the Non-Aligned Movement, and the United Nations. They were the most appropriate agencies for promoting the Indian objectives of autonomy, co-operation and world peace. The Commonwealth and the United Nations were also the two international organizations that the newly independent, relatively weak nations could aspire to turn to their benefit by virtue of their numerical preponderance.

(a) *The Commonwealth*

Nehru's pragmatic idealism found its most creative expression in free India's link with the Commonwealth. The tranformation of the British Empire into a multiracial association of free nations, drawn from all the continents and culture zones, owed much to Nehru's statesmanship, reciprocated by the British leadership at the time. The Indian decision to seek membership of the Commonwealth on pragmatic considerations of national interest, and the willingness of the older members to accept the Republic of India to full membership represented a triumph of rational accommodation on both sides. It also transformed the nature of the Commonwealth.

The idea of a formal association with the British Commonwealth, then consisting of Britain and the white Dominions (some with pronounced racist orientation), was not popular in India at the time of independence. Indian radical critics of the Commonwealth held that membership of it would limit India's freedom and make her an adjunct to the Atlantic bloc. But Nehru saw in it an expanding relationship between erstwhile opponents and a prospect for building a mutually beneficial association between Britain, other white Dominions save South Africa, and the new Asian, African, and Caribbean members of the organization. He told the Constituent Assembly that the Commonwealth was not, and was not intended to become, a supra-national body and was not going to concern itself with disputes between member nations. There were no military commitments of any sort, the association rested entirely on mutual goodwill and tangible benefits, and for India there were practical considerations, resulting from long-established ties, which favoured membership.[16] This reasoning was accepted by the Constituent Assembly and by public opinion.

In the first eight years of India's independence the Commonwealth proved to be a useful institution for exerting a moderating influence on US policy in times of crisis, as in Korea in 1951, and in bringing about a settlement in Indo-China in 1954. The Indian appraisal of China influenced the British decision to accord recognition to the People's Republic despite the opposition of the United States and some Commonwealth members. However the members of the Commonwealth, including those belonging to the Western alliance, shared a common concern in moderating international antagonisms and this for a time seemed to bring it closer to India's non-alignment posture. This was especially true of Canada and Britain. The Commonwealth connection without doubt assisted India in playing a major role in international affairs during the first half of the 1950s, both to its own advantage and probably to more general benefit. This fortunate conjuncture was short-lived.

The basic condition for the growth of the Commonwealth, following the admission of the new South Asian nations, was a genuine commitment on the part of its members to multiracialism, decolonization, respect for the independence of the new nations, co-operation in developmental efforts, and the preservation of world peace. These were the basic tenets of India's foreign policy. As long as the Commonwealth – but above all its leading member, Britain – subscribed to them it was an important resource for India. Britain's commitment to decolonization held firm and over two decades led to the liquidation of the Empire. Its position on racial discrimination was initially weak but became stronger with the emergence of the black nations of Africa, and led to the departure of the Union of South Africa from the Commonwealth in

1961. Though the Colombo Plan was a useful beginning the developmental effort of the Commonwealth as a whole has been modest and of declining significance to its poorer members. But the Commonwealth was above all a political association and what caused it the gravest injury was the Anglo-French invasion of Egypt over the nationalization of the Suez Canal in 1956. The invasion caused dismay in India. The Government of India had worked for an amicable settlement between Egypt and the Canal users, but after the invasion Nehru took up a firm position against Britain and France, fearing that this use of force threatened the freedom of the weaker countries of Asia and Africa.[17] The Eden Government reacted angrily against Nehru's criticism, adopting an anti-Indian posture in the UN Security Council over the Kashmir issue. The result was that the special relationship between India and Britain that had been developed over a period of nearly a decade withered away. The Suez affair marked the beginning of the political decline of the Commonwealth. In its aftermath Britain turned away from the Commonwealth, seeking a new role in the European Economic Community. Over the years the economic and political relations between Britain and India have steadily declined. The deteriorating race relations in Britain and the treatment accorded to persons of South Asian origin in immigration control procedures have given a quietus to the original idealism about the Commonwealth. Inevitably it has become a marginal element in Indian, as in British, foreign policy.[18]

(b) *Asianism and the Non-Aligned Movement*

The Nehru policy of non-alignment found its concrete form in the Non-Aligned Movement. This movement had its origins in the romantic belief once widely held in India that Asia, freed from Europe, was going to play a major, peaceful role in world affairs.[19] To Indians of Nehru's generation the historical relationship between Asia and Europe was a subject of considerable intellectual and political interest. That relationship was seen as unequal and violent. The independence of India and the consolidation of China seemed to promise the beginning of a new age in human affairs. This expectation was the product of a perspective on modern Europe which viewed it as a relatively young, aggressive civilization given to violence, while Asia was ancient, wise, and peaceful. Asians, freed from European domination, would co-operate with each other and with the rest of the world for their own good and for the benefit of mankind. Nehru often spoke in this vein, and between 1947 and 1955 he devoted considerable effort to realizing Asian unity in tangible form.

On the eve of India's independence, in March 1947, Nehru convened the first Asian Relations Conference in New Delhi to mobilize Asian opinion in favour of the independence of Asian countries and to promote co-operation between them. He told the participants that the mutual isolation of the peoples of Asia, imposed upon them by the colonial powers, must now end, and that 'All the countries of Asia have to meet together on an equal basis in a common task and endeavour.'[20]

As the first major Asian country to become independent after World War II, India under Nehru had almost automatically assumed the leadership of the newly independent nations, and the passion for Asia was not unrelated to that role. It is relevant to note that neither China nor Japan nor any of the Islamic countries of West Asia were in a position to contest India's claim at the time. On the basis of its historical cultural links India assumed a special concern for South-East Asia, but Nehru displayed prudence in continuing his support to the non-Communist nationalist movements in the region. With the emergence of Communist China in late 1949 the Asian scene dramatically changed and from early 1950 India began to take steps to protect its interests in the north-central and north-eastern regions. From then on a less strident Asianism becomes evident in Nehru's public statements.[21]

The Bandung Conference of Asian and African Nations, held in April 1955, was the last major Indian endeavour in the pursuit of political Asianism. By the time the Bandung Conference met the Asian scene had greatly altered. The outcome of the Korean war had strengthened the position of China, who had emerged as a competitor with India for influence among the Afro-Asian nations. Many countries of Asia, among them India, were deeply involved in local conflicts and it was at Bandung that Nehru confronted Asia in its full diversity and range of mutual incompatibilities. His concern with world peace and non-alignment encountered opposition from nations who saw their security interests better served by strategic alignment. His angry outburst –

> Has it come to this, that the leaders of thought who have given religions and all kinds of things to the world have to tag on to this kind of group or that and be hangers-on of this party or the other, carrying out their wishes and occasionally giving an idea? It is most degrading and humiliating to any self-respecting people or nation. It is an intolerable thought to me that the great countries of Asia and Africa should come out of bondage into freedom only to degrade themselves or humiliate themselves in this manner [22]

did not dispel the reality. The rhetoric of Asia disappears from his speeches after Bandung. In December 1955 Nehru told Tibor Mende that Asia is too large an area, 'and to talk about it as one entity is to confuse ourselves', and 'to talk of Europe and Asia and America as separate entities is also misleading, for the future at any rate'.[23] It is no accident that the Afro-Asian conference never met again.

Over the years Asia has dissolved into several mutually antagonistic parts. In so heterogeneous a continent this was inevitable. As the reality of Asia caught up with the romantic vision, the latter gave way to a perception of many Asias, with India confined to its own subcontinental home ground and even there confronting opposition from its most important neighbour, Pakistan.

The Asian-African movement pioneered by Nehru and his associates in Indonesia, Burma, Sri Lanka, Egypt, and Ghana was absorbed into the non-aligned movement jointly launched by Tito, Nasser, and Nehru at Belgrade in 1961. Over the past two decades this movement has grown and now enjoys the adherence of nearly all the countries of the Third World.[24] The primary condition of membership of the movement – a commitment to pursue an independent foreign policy based on peaceful co-existence and non-alignment – ensures that the newly independent countries at least aspire to genuine independence and restricts the area of the world subject to great power manipulation. But no claims to moral excellence are made on behalf of the Third World as they were once made on behalf of Asia.

During the Nehru era the Non-Aligned Movement was dominated by political concerns — the threat to world peace, decolonization, racial discrimination, foreign intervention. By the end of the 1960s the concerns of the movement shifted to economic issues. This can be accounted for in part by the liquidation of the European empires, the receding threat to world peace as a result of superpower *détente*, and the global consensus against racism, as well as by the changes in the composition and leadership of the non-aligned movement itself. The successive non-aligned conferences beginning with the Lusaka Summit of 1970 have focused attention on the structural imbalance between the developed and developing countries and have emphasized the need to mobilize resources for assisting the latter in accelerating economic growth. This concern India has shared, and Indian representatives have played an active role in formulating the Third World demand for a new international economic order.

The achievements of the Non-Aligned Movement may be assessed thus: it accelerated the pace of decolonization, expanded the international system to make it universal, considerably reduced great power domination of the international system, and, by preventing polarization of the world into two antagonistic blocs, reduced the danger of a catastrophic world war. It also brought to the forefront the problems of economic development and equitable distribution of the world's resources.

This change of emphasis has, however, not been without a price. The Third World now presents itself in its unadorned deformity and poverty. Its impoverished state has made the issue of global poverty a matter of active concern, but at the same time the political role of the newly independent countries in the functioning of the contemporary world has been abolished. Nehru would have found this disheartening and as denuding independence of its other major purpose after nation-building, to play a worthwhile role in reshaping the international order. Since he did not subscribe to the idea of the primacy of the economic over the political element either in national or in international affairs, he would have regarded the loss of a political role for Third World countries in world affairs as unfortunate.

(c) *The United Nations*

India was one of the original signatories to the Charter of the United Nations, and subsequent Indian behaviour in the UN has been marked by sustained support for the organization. India looked upon the UN as a forum for all nations, representing all points of view, and as a body promoting the interests of mankind as a whole. The UN as it was constituted fell far short of the Indian ideal but, given the anarchic nature of international society, it was seen as the best the world could have. The principle of equality of states had been acknowledged in the 'one state – one vote' rule in the General Assembly, while in the constitution and powers of the Security Council the existing hierarchy of power was legitimized, especially in the form of the veto power conferred on the permanent members. India recognized the inevitability of this compromise in the given international situation and held that it was in the general interest to preserve and strengthen the structure that actually existed, although eventually it should be made more egalitarian. 'The main purpose of the United Nations', Nehru believed, 'is to build up a world without war, a world based on cooperation of Nations and peoples.'[25]

Because India believed the UN to be a world body, among the first causes it espoused was that of universal membership. During the first decade of the UN's existence the question of the admission of new members, whose applications had to be approved by the Security Council and were often subjected to veto by the USA or the USSR, was particularly contentious. India firmly pressed for universal membership, arguing that politically motivated restriction of membership would destroy the organization. For the same reason India advocated the admission of Communist China to the organization and to its rightful place on the Security Council. The Indian argument was that it was unwise to exclude from the UN a major country like China, and this position was maintained even after the border conflict between India and China in 1962.

The membership issue was closely linked to the power balance within the UN. With the addition of new members from Asia and Africa it became increasingly difficult to manipulate the organization to the advantage of the Atlantic bloc, as the United States had done for several years with the help of the Latin American countries. The Afro-Asian countries with India in the lead were able to accelerate the pace of decolonization, effectively utilizing the machinery of the United Nations to that end, and in the process to modify the power structure of the UN itself. In 1960 Nehru had complained that the structure evolved at San Francisco 'was not very fair to Asia and Africa', and that 'under the present structure they did not have the opportunity to pull their weight . . .'.[26] The 1963 reforms went some way towards meeting this criticism. The expansion of the membership of the Security Council from eleven to fifteen and of the Economic and Social Council from eighteen to twenty-seven gave the Third World countries greatly increased representation on both bodies. With their increased membership in the General Assembly and the two Councils, the Third World countries have been able to put their problems, initially of freedom from colonial rule and later of economic development and fairer distribution of the world's resources, in the forefront of the UN's most active concerns.

If on the membership issue India was radical, it was extremely cautious over changes in the basic structure of the organization and opposed those changes in rules that might upset the power balance between the Atlantic and Soviet blocs. Thus despite the Indian dislike of the veto power conferred on the permanent members of the Security Council by the UN Charter, Nehru and Krishna Menon, the latter then leader of the Indian delegation at the UN, took the view that its removal would endanger the UN itself. The veto was a necessary instrument for protecting the interests of the great power not enjoying majority support in the General Assembly. For this reason India opposed the US move to overcome the obstacle of the Soviet veto in the Security Council by conferring executive power upon the General Assembly through the 'Uniting for Peace' resolution in 1950. The UN Charter envisaged great power unanimity on critical international issues, and although this was no longer to be expected in the Cold War context, the Indian view was that the smooth working of the UN and the preservation of world peace still required mutual accommodation between the two power blocs.

The prudent course in the circumstances was to adhere to the provisions of the Charter as closely as possible, respecting the claims of each bloc and exercising maximum restraint. India opposed any move to amend the Charter for fear that it would lead to attempts to secure advantage for one bloc, which controlled the majority in the General Assembly, at the expense of its rival, and that this would threaten the disruption of the organization. It was the Indian view that any change in the Charter had to be effected only through agreement between the various constituents of the United Nations.

The Indian attitude to the UN could best be described as a combination of idealism and pragmatic good sense. The UN was a necessary instrument of world peace and had to be preserved as such, but it could not be allowed to diminish the sovereignty of member states. Thus while India supported the UN peace-keeping activities and contributed troops to the UN Emergency Force in the Middle East after the 1956 Suez war and to the UN Force in the Congo in 1961, it opposed the establishment of a permanent United Nations force or the introduction of UN forces into any country without specific invitation from the Government of the country concerned. On the other hand India was anxious to preserve the effectiveness of the UN within the limits of the Charter and therefore opposed the Soviet proposal to establish a 'Troika' in place of a single Secretary-General.

The Indian view of the UN, as it evolved with experience of the working of the organization, shifted from an earlier vision of it as a supra-national authority or world government in the making to considering it as a world forum in which international concerns were debated and conflicts between nations resolved through negotiations. Even this view had to be modified. Over the years the UN became more of a forum for legitimizing (or de-legitimizing) the claims of members against each other, that is, it became an instrument of diplomacy, and since its decisions, although not binding on governments, carry considerable political weight, this role of the United Nations, which India was slow to appreciate, became all-important. India itself took two issues to the UN, one concerning the status of persons of Indian origin in South Africa, and the other relating to the dispute with Pakistan over Kashmir. The Indian experience with both matters led to disenchantment with the organization, and over Kashmir there were demands in the Indian Parliament that the reference to the UN be withdrawn. But Nehru told Parliament that 'in spite of its many faults, in spite of its having deviated from its aims somewhat', the UN is 'a basic and fundamental thing in the structure of the world today. Not to have it or to do away with it would be a tragedy for the world. Therefore I do not wish this country of ours to do anything which weakens the gradual development of some kind of a world structure. . . .'[27]

Although Nehru maintained this position, he became gradually more cautious about taking issues to the UN, and advised Nasser in 1956 not to go to the UN over the Suez Canal dispute except in the event of a threat to Egypt's independence.[28] India's Defence Minister, Krishna Menon, saw to it that the expulsion of the Portuguese power from Goa was accomplished in less than twenty-four hours so that the Security Council had no opportunity to interest itself in the matter. Menon told Michael Brecher:

> . . . if we hadn't finished the action [in Goa] in twenty-four hours it would have got bogged down in the Security Council. It would have been difficult for us to defy it. Had the Security Council intervened we would not have stopped the action. We had learned some lessons. What happened to the Kashmir business? We had person after person such as MacNaughton, Owen Dixon, and various others who were in effect always using the machinery of international affairs against us. The nation that behaves well is always in a bad position.[29]

This aversion to UN interference in India's or other nations' affairs has persisted in post-Nehru foreign policy. In none of the major crises affecting India during the post-Nehru era, and there have been several of them, have the Government of India allowed any role to the United Nations. They did not go to the UN over the Rann of Kutch boundary dispute with Pakistan in 1965, preferring it to be settled through arbitration by Britain, nor did they seek UN intervention in the war with Pakistan in the autumn of that year. In the Bangladesh crisis of 1971, when Pakistan's Western allies strenuously tried to mobilize the UN in a manner designed to assist Pakistan, the Indian Government refused to allow any role to the organization, and through the Simla Agreement with Pakistan in 1972[30] it effectively excluded the UN policing of the new cease-fire line in Kashmir. It is now a settled Indian policy to seek bilateral solutions to its disputes without interference from outside sources, whether it be the United Nations or any other power.

IV

The conduct of Indian foreign policy in the first decade of independence was marked by certain bold and constructive initiatives. Nehru combined regard for India's national interests with a concern for the resolution of some of the most intractable international issues of the time, as in Korea and Indo-China. The Indian initiatives in these areas demonstrated the practical merits of non-alignment. With the support of the Commonwealth, in particular of Britain, India promoted the cease-fire in Korea and the liquidation of the French Empire in Indo-China. There were beneficial consequences for India's own international position. Its diplomacy during the Korean war brought about greatly improved relations with China and the Soviet Union; its opposition to the UN forces crossing the 38th Parallel demonstrated its independence of the Western bloc, despite membership of the Commonwealth, while the formula for the resolution of the prisoners-of-war issue earned it Western tolerance after initial US opposition. This activity established its utility to both blocs as an honest broker and thereby enhanced its own autonomy. It seemed to validate Nehru's over-all policy; India could simultaneously maintain a low defence budget and pursue a major role in world affairs.

The pursuit of autonomy without power was premissed, first, on a balanced stalemate between the Atlantic and Soviet blocs, which created a useful role for a non-aligned India, and, secondly, on good relations between India and most other leading countries, in particular the United States, the Soviet Union, and the People's Republic of China. The first of these two requirements was present in the world situation; the second Nehru sought to construct on the principle of reciprocity, on the assumption that India had no substantive conflicts of interest with any of the leading countries. Ideological differences were not seen as an obstacle to good relations given that there was a commitment to peaceful co-existence.[31]

The emphasis on a policy of peace was reflected in India's relatively modest defence expenditure and firm intention not to acquire a nuclear weapons capability. Between 1950 and 1961, the year preceeding the border conflict with China, Indian defence expenditure was maintained at less than 2 per cent of the GNP.[32] When questioned in the Lok Sabha about India's military weakness as revealed in the border conflict with China, Nehru told Parliament that his Government had accepted in the past 'about one-tenth' of what the military establishment had asked for, and he went on to affirm yet again his hatred of war and preference for peace.[33]

V

Under Nehru's direction, Indian nuclear policy was designed to ensure India's autonomy in the development of this energy resource, but not to acquire a weapons capability. He had taken the view as early as 1948 that if India aspired to 'remain abreast in the world as a nation which keeps ahead of things', she must develop atomic energy 'for the purpose of using it for peaceful purposes'.[34] With this end in view the Government of India built up a comprehensive nuclear industry with a programme oriented towards the generation of power and the utilization of radio-isotopes in industry, medicine, agriculture, and other fields, and aimed at achieving self-reliance in the skills, materials, and technology needed to sustain the programme. Nehru's commitment to restricting atomic energy to peaceful purposes was complete, but he was equally committed to ensuring India's independence in this field. When Eisenhower proposed the establishment of an international agency for the control of nuclear energy, Nehru raised pertinent questions about the kinds of control proposed, who would be subject to them, and whether the agency would have the power to deny states the right to develop nuclear energy.

There should be international control and inspection, but it is not such an easy matter as it seems. . . . We are prepared in this, as in any other matter, even to limit, in common with other countries, our independence of action for the common good of the world . . . provided we are assured that it is for the common good of the world and not exercised in a partial way, and not dominated over by certain countries, however good their motives.[35]

India's refusal to sign the Nuclear Non-Proliferation Treaty of 1968 on the ground of its discriminatory character was in conformity with the Nehru policy.

The Indian opposition to the Nuclear Non-Proliferation Treaty in its existing form focuses on its discriminatory features. The Treaty did not merely reflect in an implict way the hierarchical character of contemporary international society, 'it was explicitly, and officially, an unequal treaty'.[36] It distinguished between two different classes of signatories who incurred different responsibilities: the states without nuclear weapons promised not to acquire them; the nuclear powers were forbidden to assist them in acquiring a weapons capability, but were not required to renounce their own. The non-nuclear weapon states were required to open their nuclear establishment to inspection by the International Atomic Energy Agency to ensure that no nuclear material was being diverted to make bombs, while the nuclear weapons states incurred no such obligations. The suppliers of nuclear materials and technology were given powers to impose restrictions on the use of the supplies which were capable of creating a dependency relationship of potentially wider application. A Treaty so derogatory of the principle of equality of nations was contrary to the primary thrust of India's foreign policy since independence. The Indian position remains one of opposition to proliferation and to nuclear weapons, but Indian governments have refused to submit to unequal treatment in the nuclear sphere. The Indian nuclear explosion of 1974 was not, and was not intended to be, a first step towards the acquisition of nuclear weapons. As Ashok Kapur, the leading specialist on India's nuclear policy, pointed out, '. . . a single test has utility as a political signal rather than as an expression of interest in the military use of atomic energy.'[37] In Kapur's view, a country like India may have good reasons for not acquiring nuclear weapons, related for example to their possibly declining military utility, their definite unusability, and their costs; the value of retaining the nuclear weapons option as part of a security strategy is a different matter.[38]

VI

The Indian drive for autonomy without power before long encountered the realities of power in the international system. For its success the strategy of non-alignment without power needed to be accepted by both power blocs and by India's two neighbours, China and Pakistan. This condition was not fulfilled. The conflicts resulting from that failure radically altered India's security environment and over time brought about important modifications in India's attitude to power, in its expectations for the evolution of the international order, and in the quality of non-alignment.

A serious conflict of interest developed between India and Pakistan over the disposition of the state of Jammu and Kashmir soon after independence, leading to three wars between the two countries and the entry of outside powers into the affairs of the subcontinent to the detriment of India's fundamental national interests. A moderate conflict of interest developed between India and China in 1950 over the Chinese occupation of Tibet. Although subsequently Nehru retrieved India's relations with China, the Tibet factor, along with the border dispute, eventually led to a rupture between the two countries. India's relations with the Soviet Union began on a note of antipathy, but were gradually transformed into cordiality and later friendship, while those with the United States began with ambiguity and developed into antipathy.

India's need for economic assistance compelled Nehru to keep his resentment against US policy in South Asia, as well as in the broader international arena, muted. Since his death, policy differences between India and the United States have become sharper, with the US supporting India's two adversaries, China and Pakistan, and this has resulted in a partial modification of non-alignment in favour of a closer security relationship with the Soviet Union. The Soviet Union has emerged as the principal supplier of arms to India, accounting for as much as 81.2 per cent of the monetary value of all arms purchased abroad by India over the 1967–77 period.[39] The relationship was consolidated by the twenty-year Friendship Treaty concluded in 1971 in the midst of the developing Bangladesh crisis. India found itself in need of the treaty to safeguard its security in the face of the Pakistan-US-China alliance and the prospect of a major war in the subcontinent later in the year. The treaty signified that the stronger version of non-alignment was no longer sustainable. India required the support of at least one superpower when faced with a combination of adversaries consisting of a superpower, a great power who was also a hostile neighbour, and another neighbour armed by the adversary superpower. After the resolution of the Bangladesh crisis India retured to a posture of non-alignment, but one qualitatively different from Nehru's original conception.

Nehru's legacy has proved burdensome for India. Strong in aspiration, the Nehru policy came to grief on account of its worthy but untenable assumptions. His successors had to acknowledge that the 'Five Principles' had not protected India from 'trouble, conflict and war'; the precept of reciprocal friendship was found to be empty of content when substantive national interests were at stake. India could not be immune from the application of power just because it had rejected the power principle as 'uncivilized'. Nehru's obsessive concern with world issues of war and peace now seems curious. His hatred of war, his view of it as an expression of the irrational and unworthy passions of collectivities and his devotion to peace had their source not in Gandhian influence but in the British tradition of radical rationalism. This tradition was not pacifist and its concern for peace was not grounded in religion as was Mahatma Gandhi's. It was deficient in its understanding of the interrelated nature of power and freedom, for while it is self-evident that the abolition of power will create conditions of freedom for all, it is equally self-evident that as long as power continues to be the critical factor in international relations, the possession of power will remain a necessary condition of freedom. This unwelcome truth received no recognition in Nehru's foreign policy. His brave attempt to act on his chosen precepts in defiance of the prevailing reality, to maintain a degree of consistency between precept and practice, and to protect India's national interests without the requisite power was difficult to sustain in the best of circumstances; in adversity it proved to be unviable.

Nehru misperceived the implications of the nuclear stalemate. The exclusion of war as an instrument of policy applied only to general war between the superpowers; it did not exclude either small wars or wars by proxy instigated and fuelled by the superpowers. Indeed, the exclusion of general war made it likely that competitive co-existence would lead to tension and armed conflicts, in particular in the Third World areas over which the competition between the power blocs was to be acted out. India and the Third World were not strong enough to exclude the superpowers, and the powerful had no moral or practical incentive to act on the 'Five Principles'. As long as India was not itself subject to any security threat, it could practise a weaker version of non-alignment – neutrality, or honest brokerage between the two power blocs, or equal alignment with both – but once such a threat emerged Indian policy had to be fundamentally reoriented. It was evident that India could not meet the requirement for practising Nehru's stronger version of non-alignment – an ability to ensure national security without outside assistance. The weaker version was unviable over the longer term, subject as it was to other people's designs. Consequently in the post-Nehru era the fundamental postulates underlying Nehru's foreign policy have been substantially modified. Mrs Gandhi explicitly recognized that it is not the principle of reciprocity but national interests that govern the foreign policy of nations,[40] and therefore while India must always seek the friendship of other countries, it must be prepared, should circumstances so conspire, to do without it. The thrust of her foreign policy has been towards creating conditions which would, as far as possible, preclude harm being done to India's interests. Under her leadership India has opted to create the capacity for effective autonomy and has modified non-alignment to the extent of developing a purposeful relationship with the Soviet Union. In the aftermath of the border conflict with China a systematic build-up of India's defence capability was undertaken, mainly with Soviet support. Military expenditure rose to 3.9 per cent of the GNP in 1963 and has been maintained at a little over 3 per cent since. This has given India a basic defensive capacity, and military self-reliance is being sought. The Nehru aspiration to autonomy remains central to India's foreign policy, but there has been a scaling down of India's global role. On the great political issues of contemporary international society her voice is muted, if not silent.

19

AFRICA ENTRAPPED: BETWEEN THE PROTESTANT ETHIC AND THE LEGACY OF WESTPHALIA

Ali Mazrui

The West's cruellest joke at the expense of Africa is the construction of two contradictory prison-houses – one incorrigibly and rigidly *national* and the other irresistibly *transnational*. One is the prison-house of the sovereign state, a fortress of political and military sovereignty. The other is the prison-house of capitalism, compulsively transnational and constantly mocking the very principle of national sovereignty.

How has Western civilization succeeded in creating these two incredibly resilient prison-houses for Africa – the fortress of the sovereign state and the all-embracing market-place of capitalism? The politico-military prison of the nation-state is now the basis of the global system as a whole – it is hard to believe it was almost purely European a little more than a century and a half ago.

Also globalized this century is capitalism. Even the most fanatically socialist of contemporary societies are ensnared by the tentacles of international trade; the profit motive haunts socialist commodities; and the hard currencies of international exchange are the currencies of leading capitalist powers. Third World countries have discovered that going socialist in their domestic arrangements is not necessarily an adequate exit visa out of the global capitalist system. Many Third World socialist regimes soon discover that they are as heavily dependent on international capitalism as ever – in spite of adopting socialist or neo-socialist policies in their own countries. The regimes continue to struggle to compete in the market-place with their coffee, cocoa, or copper – desperate for 'foreign exchange' defined in terms of dollars, sterling, Deutsche marks, or Japanese yen. The bars of the capitalist prison are omnipresent.

The territorial sovereign state was not a universal category in pre-colonial Africa. From a political point of view the continent of Africa was a miracle of diversity – ranging from empires to stateless societies, from elaborate thrones to hunting bands, from complex civilizations to rustic village communities. But in this paper we address ourselves especially to the emergence of the state in Africa. We shall relate that phenomenon to the triple political and cultural heritage of the African continent – the indigenous, the Islamic, and the Western.

Let us first explore some of the main attributes we have come to associate with the state. The first is the relative centralization of authority. When Louis XIV said 'L'état c'est moi', he was formulating this doctrine of centralism at its most extreme, when it actually focused on a single individual at the pinnacle of authority. In reality the centralism can be relative rather than absolute. After all, although the United States of America uses the term 'states' in the plural, the country as a whole is a sovereign state within the tradition of the Treaty of Westphalia of 1648. The Federal Government of the country becomes both the focus and the mechanism of centralized authority.

Related to such centralization is Max Weber's principle of 'the monopoloy of the legitimate use of physical force'. Weber regarded this principle as virtually the definition of the state. But from our point of view we may accept the twin principles of centralized authority and centralized power as the defining characteristics of the state. What should be borne in mind are additional accompanying characteristics usually associated with the state but not necessarily of definitional import.

One of these accompanying characteristics of the state concerns a fiscal system of some sort. This could be a case of collecting tribute from integral units of the state, an evolving system of taxation still in the making. A relatively centralized system of revenue collection has come to be associated with institutions of this kind. Also basic as an accompanying characteristic of the state in history has been a centrally supervised judicial system. The judicial system may in fact be internally pluralistic, accommodating different religious courts or customary courts, but the centralization is partly a case of over-all jurisdiction, with the state sometimes modifying customary law to conform with some central principle. The state would in any case keep an eye on the system which selects those who interpret religious or customary law and those who implement it.

In Africa's experience state formation has been linked to the broader triple heritage of Africa's history and culture – the heritage which encompasses indigenous, Islamic, and Western traditions. Some states in Africa were primarily products of purely indigenous forces; some were products of interactions between indigenous and Islamic elements; and others were outgrowths of a basic interaction between indigenous and Western ideas. There have been occasions when the triple heritage has indeed been a fusion of all three – indicating an historical meeting-point involving Africa, Islam, and the West. However, in this essay our approach will be particularly comparative, focusing more on at least two traditions at a time, rather than on pure models of the state. After all, Africa has indeed been a melting pot of political cultures, a laboratory of diverse experiments in political formations.

Africa's interaction with Islam antedates European colonization of Africa by at least a millenium. In the seventh century Islam conquered Egypt and started the process of penetrating North Africa. Islam then spread down the Nile Valley as well as into North West Africa. The politics of those societies responded to the impact of Islam, and some of them began to evolve institutions which reflected this basic interaction between Islam and indigenous responses.

Especially important in state-formation is the precise balance between trade and warfare, between economic aspects and military dimensions. The history of Islam itself from the days of Muhammad is partly an equation involving exchange of goods and balances of arms. The Prophet Muhammad was himself a trader in his earlier years before he became a warrior in the name of Allah. Islam has itself divided the world conceptually between *Dar el Harb*, the Abode of War, on one side, and *Dar el Islam*, the Abode of Islam, on the other. Within the world of Islam political co-operation and economic trade would be facilitated. Between the world of Islam and the world of war lines of difference and strategies of protection would be evolved.[1]

Islam's penetration of the African continent continued this dialectic between the economic and military. When Islam became an empire, Egypt for a while became the pivot of an international Muslim economic system. There was a time when the merchant class of Egypt became what has been described as a group so influential that it 'increasingly shaped the policies of the Muslim states, developed commercial law and custom, and gave the civilization of Islam its strong emphasis on the bourgeois virtues of saving and sobriety, avoidance of waste or ostentation, and respect for scholarship . . .'.[2]

Then the spread of Islam into West Africa betrayed another economic process. The Trans-Saharan trade produced missionaries in the market-places. The Muslim shopkeeper was at times the equivalent of the clergyman. Islam was spreading as an additional commodity accompanying the grand paradigm of trade. Out of this began to emerge special kingdoms and emirates in West Africa, instances of new state-formation. There is a Hobbesian concept in Islamic statecraft – encouraging obedience to those who exercise authority, provided they do no violence to the principles that Muhammad advocated and God willed. This side of Islam is concerned with submissive fatalism.

But Islam is also a product of defensive fanaticism. While submissive fatalism might encourage acceptance and peaceful conformity, defensive fanaticism could generate rebellion. Again it went all the way back to the life history of the Prophet Muhammad. Against the political establishment of Arabia in his own day, Muhammad decided that his duty was to resist or go into exile. Under pressure he decided to flee into exile. The Islamic calendar to the present day is a commemoration of exile – since it begins neither with the birth of Muhammad nor with his death, nor indeed with the moment when he felt that God had favoured him with the revelation. On the contrary, the Islamic calendar goes back to the Hijra, the moment when Muhammad decided to flee from persecution and seek refuge in another city, Medina.

When Islam came to West Africa it certainly betrayed the same dialectic between submissive fatalism and defensive resistance. Islam was mobilized to resist European imperialism. Indeed, a substantial portion of Western Africa's primary resistance to European colonization was Muslim-inspired:

Militant Islam presented the greatest challenge and mobilized the sternest resistance to the European occupation of Africa in the nineteenth century. Muslim polities, with their written languages, their heritage of state-making, and the cohesive force of a universal religion preaching the brotherhood of all believers, could generally organize resistance on a wider scale than political units whose extent was limited by the ties of common ancestry. Muslims also had a strong incentive to oppose the advance of Christian power.[3]

When European pressures were getting too strong for the leadership of the Sokoto Caliphate in nineteenth-century Nigeria, the leadership thought of the Hijra – 'obligatory flight from the infidels'. Sultan Attahiru Ahmadu led a Hijra after the conquest of Sokoto, going eastwards. As a historian has put it:

The British finally overtook him at Burmi and killed him. However, many of his followers continued to the Sudan where their descendants still live today under the chieftaincy of his grandson, Mohammadu Dan Mai Wurno.[4]

On the other side of Africa, Islam also betrayed its own versions of defensive fanaticism, opposing the encroachment of European power and statecraft. Muhammad Abdulla Hassan, 'the mad Mullah', revealed his credentials against the British in the 1890s. As a British historian later described him, Muhammad Abdulla Hassan was 'a little African Napoleon – equal to the great Corsican only in his hatred of the English'.

It was Muhammad Ahmed el-Mahdi who revealed his own potentialities in the realm of defensive fanaticism. He was the precursor of

Sudanese nationalism, rallying religion behind nationalistic causes, marrying piety to patriotism. But Islam also had its other face – the face of submissive fatalism, a readiness to accept the inevitable. The same Islam which had fought so hard against European colonization later seemed to be ready to accept the inevitable hegemony of the West. Again no one has put it better than the British Africanist Michael Crowder:

> Islam, whose hatred of subjection to the infidel would have provided, as it did for a short while between 1889 and 1893 in the Western Sudan, a unifying theme for resistance against the French and British, also held the seeds of a fatalist acceptance of the inevitable.[5]

The preservation of pre-colonial state institutions, especially in Northern Nigeria, made the consolidation of post-colonial national institutions more difficult. Clearly the British had become more respectful of African institutions through their policy of indirect rule than the French had been through their policy of assimilation. After all, the French policy of assimilation denied validity to indigenous structures and values, asserting a supremacy and uniqueness of French culture, and proclaiming a mission to Gallicize those over whom France exercised hegemony. The British policy of indirect rule, in contrast, allowed for cultural relativism among societies and was based on an assumption of cultural diversity in the universe. Hence British reluctance to tamper with local native institutions where they could be recognized by them, and British eagerness to use those institutions instead of inventing new ones. But there was a heavy political cost in places like Nigeria. Pre-colonial statehood militated against post-colonial statehood. The survival of the Emirates of Northern Nigeria and the Kabakaship in Buganda, legacies of pre-colonial statehood, came to militate against the construction of one Nigeria or one Uganda after independence.

The Sultanate of Zanzibar in East Africa presented distinctive problems of its own without altering the basic tension between the pre-colonial and post-colonial African state. From the days before European colonial rule Zanzibar had been a racially and ethnically plural society. By the end of the eighteenth century the ascendancy of the Arabs was already clear. It was consolidated by the rise of Seyyid Said bin Sultan. Sultan Barghash later provided the transitional rule from pre-European Arab ascendancy to the Arab oligarchy under European overlordship. Once again the British, having recognized monarchical institutions in Zanzibar reminiscent of their own in England, proceeded to give some kind of validity to those monarchical institutions and use them as a basis of indirect rule. In one sense the

Arabs of Zanzibar were the equivalent of the Hausa-Fulani of Northern Nigeria. In both cases the maintenance of their particular political institutions from pre-colonial days augured ill for the transition to post-colonial nationhood. In the case of Zanzibar, the tensions between the privileged ethnic group and the others could not be mitigated by a shared rivalry of all of them against still other groups elsewhere. After all, the tension between the Hausa-Fulani and others in Northern Nigeria was eased by the fact that all Northerners had a sense of defensiveness against Southerners. Zanzibar was too small a society to have those built-in safeguards of cross-cutting alignments. The result was the disastrous revolution of January 1964, barely a month after the British had departed. Those very Arab institutions of statehood which the British had so affectionately protected became the Achilles Heel of the new nation as it struggled to have modern statehood after independence.

But why were pre-colonial state formations so difficult to reconcile with the demands of post-colonial statehood? Why did indirect rule in Nigeria, by preserving greater recognition of traditional institutions of statecraft, make the business of building the modern Nigerian nation-state tougher? Why was respect for the Kabakaship in Buganda a disservice to the task of the state-formation in Uganda?

Here it is worth bearing in mind another triple heritage – the heritage of the city-state, the empire-state, and the nation-state. To some extent Zanzibar was a city-state, though it gradually established enough hegemony in parts of what is today Coastal Kenya and Coastal Tanzania to be on the verge of becoming a proper empire-state. In the case of Zanzibar the empire-in-the-making was a dynastic empire, with an Arab Sultanate at the top.

In African history it is difficult to disentangle the origins of the city as against the empire. Some of the Emirates in West Africa were at once city-states and part of a wider empire. Subsequently the names of some of the greatest African empires were used after independence as names of the new nation-states. The empire-states of Ghana and Mali had bequeathed their historical names to modern states. We know less about ancient Zimbabwe than we know about ancient Ghana or ancient Mali, but Zimbabwe too may be a case of a former empire-state bequeathing its name to a modern nation-state. There is the alternative theory that Zimbabwe was an ancient city-state – but it had still contributed a name to a modern nation-state. No modern African country has as yet adopted the name of Songhai, but that is yet another ancient empire-state in search of modern reincarnation.

The most durable of all Africa's empire-states turned out to be

Ethiopia. Its last emperor was Haile Selassie. Both he and Kabaka Mutesa II were incarnations of pre-colonial statehood about to confront sooner or later their moment of truth with post-colonial statehood. Mutesa had his confrontation with President Milton Obote in 1966, a struggle for power partly between an ancient institution and a modern state, a regional king and a national prime minister. Obote won, partly with the help of Amin's arms, and King Mutesa fled to England where he died in 1969.

The creeping revolution of Ethiopia began in February 1974. By that time it appeared that the dynastic empire-state would no longer be permitted to masquerade as a modern nation-state. The soldiers of Ethiopia, for a while cheered by the students and peasants of Ethiopia, solved the dilemmas by abolishing the ancient imperial statehood and replacing it with a modern ideology dedicated in the long run to the principle of the 'withering away of the state' itself.

We might therefore conclude that one of the difficulties in the transition from a pre-colonial to a post-colonial state is precisely the normative and moral gap between the two. The values have fundamentally changed, the responsibilities have been redefined, the perspective newly focused, the policies demand reformulation. An important disruptive factor was the evolution of the principle of equality. In Africa this principle was far better realized among the so-called stateless societies than among either city-states or empire-states. Many indigenous societies along the Nile Valley, or societies like the Tiv of Nigeria and the Masai of Kenya and Tanzania, have relatively loose structures of control and substantial egalitarianism. In contrast, societies like those of Buganda, Northern Nigeria, Ashanti, and other dynastic empires of West Africa were hierarchical and basically unequal.

The new nation-state provided a basic contradiction. On the one hand, it championed almost as much equality as the so-called 'primitive' and stateless societies which did not have kings or identifiable rulers. On the other hand, the new nation-state explicitly expected identifiable rulers, and asserted what Max Weber called the state's 'monopoly of legitimate use of physical force'. The new post-colonial state was supposed to be as egalitarian as the Masai and the Tiv, and as centralized as the Baganda, the Ashanti, and the Hausa-Fulani. The new nation-state was supposed to be morally as egalitarian as the stateless societies of Africa: but politically as structured as the nation-states of Europe. This basic tension between moral equality from acephalous societies in Africa and political hierarchy from monarchical societies in Africa has been one of the central divisive elements in the post-colonial experience. In places like Rwanda and Burundi this dialectic pitched hierarchical Tutsi against egalitarian Hutu; in Nigeria it pitched deferential Hausa against individualistic Ibo; in Uganda it pitched monarchical Baganda against neo-republican Nilotes.

Another area of tension between the pre-colonial African states and the post-colonial concerned attitude to territoriality. Most African societies have a high degree of land reverence. On the other hand, the principle of the modern nation-state includes a high sensitivity to territoriality. The mystique of land reverence in traditional Africa has had to seek a *modus vivendi* with the principle of territoriality of the modern state. The mystique of land reverence in Africa is partly a compact between the living, the dead, and the unborn. Where the ancestors are buried, there the soul of the clan resides, and there the prospects of the health of the next generation should be sought. Land was quite fundamental to both stateless African societies and to empires and city-states.

On the other hand, territory became increasingly important in Europe, and became almost sacrosanct in the legacy of the Treaty of Westphalia of 1648. Political communities under the new doctrine of the sovereign state became increasingly definable in terms of boundaries between one state and another. Sovereignty was subject to territoriality; power was land-bound.

The pre-colonial African state carried the legacy of land reverence:

> My Negritude is no tower and no cathedral
> It delves into the deep red flesh of the soil.[6]

But while the pre-colonial African state indulged in this land worship in relation to both agriculture and the burial of ancestors, the post-colonial state indulged in the worship of territory in relation to power and sovereignty rather than cultivation and ancestry. The dichotomy between the land worship of old, and territorial worship in post-colonial states has not yet been resolved. All we know is that the last legacy of the colonial order to be decolonized is likely to be the territorial boundary between one African country and another. That colonial boundary currently helps define one African political entity as against another. Each is jealous of its own inherited boundaries. Kenya defies Somalia; Ethiopia defies Somalia; Niger defines Nigeria; Morocco defies Mauritania; and most post-colonial African states defy any territorial changes. The ghosts of ancestors and land worship have been overshadowed by the imperative of sovereignty and territorial possessiveness.

The Second World War was an important divide in this aspect of Africa's history. There is widespread consensus that the war contributed towards Africa's *political* liberation. It helped Africa's quest for modern statehood. But what about *economically*? Did the war tighten the shackles of dependency or loosen them? Did it lay the foundations of economic self-reliance or prepare the way for greater external capitalist control of African economies?

The war facilitated Africa's political transition to modern statehood partly by undermining Europe's capacity to hold on to empires. Britain was exhausted and also impoverished by the time the war ended. France had been humiliated by Germany. Related to this exhaustion and impoverishment of Western Europe following its own fratricidal war was the destruction of the myth of European invincibility in the eyes of the colonized peoples. Suddenly somebody noticed in Bombay that the Emperor's clothes of modern technology were not clothes at all – the British Raj was naked! And when the Indians started pointing fingers and exposing the nakedness of their Emperor, other subject peoples elsewhere heard it too. That is one reason why the precedent set by India in challenging British rule became an important inspiration to many African nationalists.

At a more individual level the war also cut the white man down to size in African eyes. The colonial situation until then cried out loud for two processes of humanization. The colonized Africans had had their humanity reduced partly because they were regarded as part devils and part monkeys. They certainly had their adulthood reduced when they were often equated with children.

On the other hand, Europeans had been portrayed as superadult and virtually superhuman. The war in turn humanized white men in the eyes of their African colleagues as they fought together in the Horn of Africa, in North Africa, in places like Malaya and elsewhere. To witness a white man scared to death under fire was itself a revelation to many Africans, who had previously seen white men only in their arrogant commanding postures as a colonial élite. So, while the image of the African was humanized by being pulled up from equation with devils, monkeys, and children, the image of the white man was humanized by being pulled down from equation with supermen, angels, and the gods themselves.

The third effect of the war was to broaden the general social and political horizons not only of ex-servicemen who had served in the war, but of many Africans who had remained behind. The idea of listening to the radio for *overseas* news concerning the war gathered momentum during the war. For millions of Africans all over the continent the

Second World War was an important internationalizing experience. By the end of it many Africans were ready to agitate for freedom and independence.

The Second World War was also politically liberating for Africa because at the end of it the pinnacle of world power was no longer in Western Europe but had divided itself between Washington and Moscow. The two superpowers both had a tradition of anti-imperialism in at least some sense, though both superpowers are also guilty of other forms of imperialism. What is clear is that the rise of the Soviet Union and the pre-eminence of the United States after the Second World War created two pressures on European powers to make concessions to African nationalists struggling for independence. The West's fear of the Soviet Union sometimes retarded the process of liberation, but in the end facilitated that process, convincing Westerners that it was a good idea to give independence to moderate Africans while there was still time and avert the threat of radicalizing Africans still further and driving them into the hands of the Soviet Union.

But although the Second World War was indeed politically liberating in the sense we have mentioned for Africans, that same war was an important stage in the incorporation of Africa into the world capitalist system. Partly in pursuit of war needs, African agriculture was modified to produce urgently needed supplies of food for Europe at war. In some parts of Africa there was a major depression later when the war demand for African-produced goods declined, but the structure of African agriculture had by then already entered a new phase of export bias. The trend towards slanting African agriculture in this direction continued unabated. But on balance the principle of developing African agriculture to serve European needs was quite well entrenched. The war had helped to consolidate it.

Another way in which the war created the foundations of further economic dependency lay in the manner in which it helped to transform colonial policy from the morality of maintaining law and order in Africa (*Pax Britannica*) to a new imperial morality of increasing development in the colonies and pursuing the welfare of the colonized peoples. Britain established the Colonial Development and Welfare Fund as part of the machinery of this new imperial vision. It was not enough to stop Africans fighting each other. It was not enough to control cattle raids between different communities and tribes. It was not enough making an example of political agitators in order to maintain the mystique of *Pax Britannica*. It was not enough to use the slogan of law and order. Imperial power was a kind of trust, a mandate to serve the subject peoples.

The vision itself was of course much older than the Second World War. It was even explicit in Rudyard Kipling's notorious poem 'The White Man's Burden' first published in *The Times* on 4 February 1899.

> Take up the White Man's burden –
> Send forth the best ye breed –
> Go bind your sons to exile
> To serve your captive's need.
> To wait in heavy harness,
> On flattered folk and wild –
> Your new caught, sullen peoples,
> Half-devil and half-child.
> . . . .
> Take up the White Man's burden –
> The savage wars of peace –
> Fill full the mouth of Famine
> And bid the sickness cease;
> . . . .
> Take up the White Man's burden –
> No tawdry rule of kings,
> But toil of serf and sweeper –
> The tale of common things.
> The ports ye shall not enter,
> The roads ye shall not tread,
> Go make them with your living,
> And mark them with your dead.

The developmental imperative of service was certainly very explicit in this poem. But on balance it was not in fact until the Second World War that development as a major imperative of colonial policy became a genuine exertion. New projects for rural development were more systematically implemented, and new trends in educational policy were soon discernible. Virtually all the major universities in black Africa were established after the Second World War, many of them soon after the war in response to the new developmental imperative in colonial policy.

But these thrusts of development were themselves a further aggravation of Africa's incorporation into Western capitalism. The Colonial Development and Welfare Fund contributed in its own way towards deepening both Africa's economic dependency on the West and Africa's cultural imitation of the West. Important biases in the direction of development included, firstly, the export bias we have just mentioned. Cash crops for export were given priority as against food for local people. One-quarter to one-third of the total cultivated area in some of the more fertile colonies was devoted to the production of such export commodities as cocoa in Ghana, coffee in Uganda, groundnuts in Senegal and The Gambia, pyrethrum in Tanganyika, and tea in Kenya.

Another distortion which occurred in the development process was the urban bias. Much of the economic change internally subordinated the needs of the countryside to the needs of the towns. One consequence was the volume of migration from rural areas to urban centres. The crisis of habitability continued to beset the lot of country folk. Young men struggled for a while, then downed their tools and hit the high road towards the uncertain fortunes of the capital city.

A third bias within each country was the subregional distortion. Some parts of the country were just much more developed than others. This burden of uneven development had its own stresses and strains. By being more developed than its neighbours the Buganda subregion of Uganda, for example, acquired not only extra leverage, but also the passionate jealousies and distrust of other parts of the country. With less than one-fifth of the population of Uganda, Buganda held sway and exercised undue leverage over the political and economic destiny of the country as a whole. Uganda is now very difficult to govern with the help of the Buganda, and very difficult to govern without their help. The chronic instability of Uganda is partly the result of ethnic confrontations and partly the outcome of uneven development among the different subregions and groups in the country.

The fourth distortion in the history of development in Africa was the distortion which occurred in parts of the continent settled and, at least for a while, controlled by white settlers. In 1938, out of a total of £1,222 million capital invested in Africa no less than £555 million was invested in South Africa from outside. A further £102 million was invested in Rhodesia. These countries under white settler control acquired in addition considerable economic muscle in their own parts of the continent, with leverage over their neighbours. Rhodesia exercised economic influence over Zambia, Malawi, Botswana, and Mozambique.

Kenya, while it was still a colonial territory, exercised considerable economic influence on the neighbouring countries of Tanganyika, Uganda, and Zanzibar. South Africa itself is now basically a giant in the southern African subcontinent with considerable potential for buying friends or neutralizing enemies.

The fifth bias in Africa's development takes us back to capitalism. For in this case we are indeed dealing with the capitalist bias in Africa's recent economic history – absorption into international structures of trade and capital flows, belief in the efficacy of market forces, faith in the profit motive and private enterprise, distrust of state initiatives in the economy, and optimism about the developmental value of foreign investments.

It is partly the nature of these five biases in the history of economic changes in the continent that has condemned the continent to the paradox of retardation – a continent well endowed in mineral wealth and agricultural potential which is at the same time a continent of the countries which the United Nations has calculated to be the poorest in the world. Until the 1970s, the terms 'poor countries' and 'underdeveloped countries' were vitually interchangeable. Clearly countries like South Yemen or Tanzania were both poor and underdeveloped. But the emergence of oil power has shattered this easy equation. Virtually all Third World countries are still technically underdeveloped, but only some of them are now poor.

In the 1980s is has become difficult to think of Saudi Arabia as a poor country. On the contrary, this is one of the best-endowed countries in the world in oil-wealth and dollar reserves – while being at the same time one of the least developed. What is true of Saudi Arabia as a country is potentially true of Africa as a continent. In terms of resources, Africa is one of the best-endowed regions of the world, but it is still the least developed of the inhabited continents. This is the pathology of technical backwardness. A related paradox is that, per head of each group's population, the richest inhabitants of Africa are non-Africans. The poorest in per capita terms are indigenous Africans themselves. Of course, there are rich Blacks as well as rich Whites in the continent. But again, we find that there are more white millionaires per head of the white population of the continent than there are black millionaires in relation to numbers of Blacks. This is the pathology of maldistribution.

The third interrelated paradox is that while the continent as a whole is, as indicated, rich in resources, it is so fragmented that it includes the majority of the poorest nations of the world. The paradox here is of a rich continent which contains many poverty-stricken societies. This is the pathology of a fragmented economy.

Estimates of Africa's resources are on the whole tentative. Not enough prospecting for resources under the ground has taken place, but it is already fair to say that Africa has 96 per cent of the non-Communist world's diamonds, 60 per cent of its gold, 42 per cent of its cobalt, 34 per cent of its bauxite, and 28 per cent of its uranium. Africa's iron reserves are probably twice those of the United States, and its reserves of chrome are the most important by far outside the Soviet Union. In the 1970s the United States imported 98 per cent of its manganese from abroad, nearly half of which was from Africa.

The West's interest in Africa's oil has also significantly increased, partly in proportion to the political uncertainties surrounding the Middle Eastern suppliers. Had Nigeria joined the Arab oil embargo of the United States in 1973, the consequences for America would have been severe. In 1974 – the year following the embargo – the United States' balance of payments deficit with Nigeria was already $3 billion. It rose to $5 billion two years later. For the time being America's dependence on Nigerian oil continues to be critical.

Then there is Africa's agricultural potential. The Republic of Sudan, Africa's largest country in square miles, may indeed develop into a major bread-basket for parts of Africa and the Middle East before the end of the century. More effective irrigation would facilitate full exploitation of the impressive fertility of this part of the continent.

Then there are Africa's water resources, with some of the greatest rivers of the world. Potentialities for building dams and generating hydro-electric power have only just begun to be exploited. Solar energy for domestic and public purposes is still in its infancy. But it should be remembered that Africa is the most exposed of all continents to the sun. The Equator cuts Africa right in the middle. And Africa is the only continent which is cut by both the Tropic of Cancer and the Tropic of Capricorn. Tapping solar energy in Africa, once the technique becomes sophisticated, could be an additional impressive source of power and energy. With regard to uranium, Africa's resources may be significantly greater than at present estimated. One country that became a uranium-producing state fairly recently is Niger, formerly a French colony.

Against this background of mineral, agricultural, and other resources in Africa there is also the disconcerting fact that Africa has some of the least-developed countries in the world. The overwhelming majority of the countries that the United Nations regards as the 'poorest' in the world are in fact in Africa. They range from Upper Volta to Rwanda and Burundi, and from Somalia to Tanzania. The continent itself seems to be well endowed with resources, but a disproportionate number of people in the population of the continent are undernourished and underprivileged. A situation where a continent is well-endowed but the people are poor is a situation of anomalous underdevelopment. A substantial part of the explanation lies in the nature of Africa's economic interaction with the Western world across time. And a major stage in that interaction was the Second World War and its distortive consequences.

Has the attainment of formal African sovereign statehood changed any of this? Links between African countries and the former colonial powers, and links between African economies and international capitalism, have at times turned out to be severed abruptly. Those African countries that have attempted to do so precipitately have sometimes found themselves in the agonies of serious economic haemorrhage.

The links may sometimes be with a country other than the former colonial power as such. This is particularly true of Mozambique with its own historical connections with the Republic of South Africa. Mozambique still hires out thousands of workers to the Republic of South Africa in exhange for gold and related contributions to Mozambique's foreign exchange reserves. Other economic links between the Marxist regime in Maputo and the racist regime in Pretoria, which were temporarily severed on attainment of Mozambique's independence, may in fact be restored in the years ahead. The possibility of encouraging South African investment in Mozambique and certainly the probability of increasing trade with South Africa are all part of the picture of historical continuities in Mozambique's predicament.

Then there is the problem that African countries encounter when they assume that to go socialist domestically is a way of disengaging from the international capitalist system. Many soon discover that they are as heavily dependent on international capitalism as ever – in spite of adopting socialist or neo-socialist policies in their own countries.

One reason is simply the fact that global capitalism is much more obstinate and resilient that its critics assume. Even the largest of the Communist countries – the Soviet Union and the Peoples' Republic of China – are sensing a growing dependency on the world market, which in turn is dominated by capitalism and its methods. International trade is substantially born out of the rules of capitalist interaction. The major currencies of world exchange are currencies of capitalist powers. The major centres of the technology of production are disproportionately capitalist. The nerves of the world economy are at the same time nerves of world capitalism. Small countries in Africa that decide to go socialist domestically may find that they are still prisoners of the international monetary system, of the international market for copper and cocoa, of the international rules of credit, and the international fluctuations of supply and demand. Going socialist in Nkrumah's Ghana or Nyerere's Tanzania is not an exit visa from world capitalism. Because African economies are particularly fragile, this global background of capitalism makes even domestic socialism shaky. That is one major reason why there has not been a single really successful socialist experiment in Africa – not even the equivalent of the success story of either Kenya or the Ivory Coast as *capitalist* models.

A related difficulty which confronts socialism in Africa is the prior distinction between dependent capitalism and indigenous capitalism in Africa. This is a matter of degree rather than a sharp dichotomy.

Dependent capitalism is the kind in which, even locally within a society like the Ivory Coast, there is a disproportionate role for foreign capital, personnel, and expertise. Thus the French role in the Ivory Coast economically is much greater than seems necessary to most impartial observers. Therefore capitalism in the Ivory Coast is more dependent than capitalism in, say, Nigeria.

Kenya lies somewhere in between. Radical African analysts of the Kenyan economy in the past tended to draw no distinction between it and the model of the Ivory Coast. But there has been a growing realization that the local entrepreneurial class in Kenya is more assertive, aggressive, and autonomous than its equivalent in the Ivory Coast. From the point of view of prospects for socialism, the question has arisen as to which one is the surer road to radicalization.

A British political economist, Colin Leys, wrote an influential book about 'neo-colonialism' in Kenya some years ago.[7] The main thrust of the book at the time was that Kenyan capitalism was of the 'comprador' variety. But less than three or four years later Leys was busy re-examining his original thesis, and was coming to the conclusion that capitalism in Kenya was less dependent and more autonomous than he had at first assumed.

One classical debate among Africanist Marxists is whether endogenous capitalism of the Kenyan variety, or of the Nigerian model, is a more effective prelude to socialism than dependent capitalism of the Ivorian variety. Western history would seem to teach us that when capitalism reaches a certain level of maturity it becomes difficult to dislodge. Marxists have been expecting a socialist revolution in places like Great Britain since the nineteenth century – but Marxists are still waiting.

On the other hand, situations where capitalism has only just begun and is still very dependent have turned out historically to be precisely the appropriate breeding grounds for effective radicalism. The history of countries as diverse as the Soviet Union and North Korea, Cuba and South Yemen, would seem to imply that *dependent* capitalism is a surer way towards socialism than indigenized (and more deeply entrenched) capitalism.

But history is one thing and doctrine is another. Marxist theory in its classical formulation did assume that a bourgeois stage of development was a necessary and inevitable pre-condition for a socialist revolution. As Engels put it:

> A bourgeoisie is . . . as necessary a pre-condition of the socialist revolution as the proletariat itself. A person who says that this revolution can be carried out easier in a country which has no proletariat or bourgeoisie proves by his statement that he has still to learn the ABC of socialism.[8]

By this argument, Kenya must surely be closer to socialism than Tanzania is – since Kenya has more of a bourgeoisie and more of a proletariat than Tanzania has evolved so far. Similarly the Republic of South Africa is closer to a genuine socialist revolution than Mozambique is – since South Africa is at a higher stage of capitalist development and has evolved a much bigger African proletariat class proportionately as well as absolutely than Mozambique can claim to have done.

Although framed differently, such debates have been known to shake the political climate of such ideologically active campuses as the University of Dar es Salaam. Are there autonomous process of class-formation taking place in Africa or are these mere reflections of the wider forces of imperialism? What should be clear is that Africa is unable to break out of the frontiers of international capitalism – whether or not an African regime decides to go socialist.

The most elaborate traps that the West has set for Africa are the state-system with each state a fortress of political and military sovereignty, the heritage of Westphalia; and the bequest of the 'Protestant' ethic, a capitalism which is compulsively transnational and constantly mocks the principle of sovereignty. But statehood itself is older in Africa.

We have attempted to demonstrate in this chapter that there are two levels of a triple heritage of state-formation in the history of Africa from pre-colonial times to post-European independence. At one level the triple heritage consists of the indigenous heritage, the Afro-Islamic heritage, and the Western heritage of state-formation. The purely indigenous heritage is exemplified by Buganda before the European impact. The impressive diversity of Nigeria illustrates the interaction between an Afro-Islamic heritage on one side, and indigenous heritage on another side of the country, and the repercussions of the stimulation which European contact inaugurated. But the Afro-Christian component in the history of state-formation in Africa did not always include European stimulus. The striking exception to the intrusion of *European* Christianity is in fact Ethiopia, which has been Christian for a longer period than many parts of Europe, going back to the fourth century after Christ. The rise of the Ethiopian State was quite indistinguishable from the rise of Christianity in Ethiopia, just as the nature of statehood in Nigeria, especially in the North, was often indistinguishable from the nature of Islam in Nigeria. But there was the subsequent impact of the system of Westphalia of 1648, consummated after the Thirty Years War in Europe, and clearly an aftermath of the conclusion of religious wars in Europe and the emergence of the sovereign states in the global system.

We have also attempted to demonstrate another level of the triple heritage – the heritage involving the city-state, the empire-state, and the new modern nation-state. Places like Kano and Zanzibar were partly settings for the city-state. But Songhay, Ghana, Mali, the Hausa-Fulani empire, Ashanti, and possibly Zimbabwe were manifestations of the second tradition of empire-states. The third structure of statehood was the sovereign state, very much a product of European history and very much a legacy of the Treaty of Westphalia of 1648.

This chapter has attempted to point out a basic discontinuity between the pre-colonial African state and the post-colonial state. In the transition the British especially attempted to provide a *rite de passage*, a ceremony of transition from pre-colonial to post-colonial statehood. This ceremony of transition was the British policy of indirect rule, which attempted to use native institutions of government as instrumentalities for colonial control and as intermediate stages before full African incorporation into the global state system.

But in the ultimate analysis the transition from pre-colonial statehood to post-colonial statehood was bedevilled by two crises – the crisis of normative egalitarianism and the crisis of territoriality. The crisis of normative egalitarianism arose because African city- and empire-states were, on the one hand, less egalitarian than African stateless societies; and, on the other hand, less egalitarian also than the new, evolving European nation-states. The kingdom of Buganda was less egalitarian than England; the religious Marabouts of Senegal were less egalitarian than at least the legacy of France after 1789.

But it was not merely the normative and moral cleavage which distinguished pre-colonial statehood from post-colonial manifestations. It was also the nature of responsiveness to land. Post-colonial statehood had a kind of mystical deference to land, an obsession with the aesthetics and religiosity of the soil. The grand compact between ancestors, the living, and the unborn found an area of fulfilment in the religiosity of the land. The land was where crops were cultivated so that the living could continue to live, and the future infants could be sustained. But the land was also a graveyard, a place where the ancestors were indeed laid to rest, a place where the last incarnation found repose before a new incarnation received stimulus.

But the other major cleavage between the pre-colonial and the post-colonial is not land but morality. This is a conflict of values and principles, a tension between preferences. The pre-colonial state was basically inegalitarian, tracing its roots to hierarchy, privilege, and power. Indeed the pre-colonial state sometimes began as a city-state and then acquired enough expansionism to become an empire-state.

One of the great ironies of the European era in Africa is that the Europeans colonized the African imperial-state and, by so doing, disimperialized it. Thus Buganda under British rule was indeed colonized, and after a while Buganda's capacity to imperialize the rest of Eastern Africa was blunted. British colonization of African empires reduced the imperial capacities of those empires.

This was repeated elsewhere in the continent. British colonization of the Hausa-Fulani helped to disimperialize the capacities of those groups to exert hegemony over others. British colonization of Zanzibar helped to disimperialize Zanzibar's expanding hegemony over parts of Tanzania and Kenya.

After independence in any case some of the most acute tensions of African societies were tensions between legacies of egalitarianism and legacies of hierarchy. Legacies of egalitarianism had a dual ancestry – the ancestry of the values of African stateless societies and the ancestry of the values of European liberalism and European socialism. The legacies of African hierarchy could be traced on one side to the impact of the city-states and the empire-states in pre-colonial Africa, and on the other side, to the legacy of the inequalities of European imperialism and European capitalism.

Perhaps the state system, whatever its origins, ought to give way to a more humane and more equitable global system. But while the state system persists, it is important to bear in mind that its African manifestation is indeed tripartite in two fundamental senses. It covers the basic interaction between indigenous cultures, Islam, and Westernism. That basic interaction also includes the accompanying tripartite communication between the city-state, the empire-state, and the nation-state in the agonizing tensions of Africa's political experience.

But we have also tried to demonstrate in the essay the economic side of Africa's predicament – the consequences of capitalist penetration especially from the Second World War onwards. This has been Africa's economic prison-house. The state system of Westphalia is excessively national and 'sovereign'. Capitalism, on the other hand, is compulsively transnational and increasingly corporate. Africa has been entrapped between the territoriality of statehood and the supra-territoriality of capitalism.

Most African economies have already been deeply integrated into a world economy dominated by the West. African countries which go socialist domestically find that they are still integrated in the world capitalist system. The rules of that system are overwhelmingly derived from principles evolved in the history of capitalism. In international trade countries seek to maximize their returns and to acquire profit.

The rules of business and exchange at the international level, the banking system which underpins those exchanges, the actual currencies used in money markets and in meeting balance of payments, are all products of the capitalist experience. Countries like Vietnam, Angola, and even Cuba discover soon enough that their best economic salvation is to gain international legitimacy by Western standards. Vietnam and Cuba may fail in gaining that legitimacy, but it is part of their ambition to begin receiving Western benefaction and to have easy access to Western markets for their goods, and Western currency markets as well.

What all this once again means is that Third World countries can make their internal domestic arrangements socialist while remaining deeply integrated in the international capitalist system at the same time. It has also been argued that a country like Tanzania is today more dependent on the world capitalist system than it was before it inaugurated its neo-socialist experiment under the Arusha Declaration in 1967.

Independent Africa has already discovered that the last thing it is willing to decolonize are the colonial boundaries of its post-colonial statehood, but it has yet to discover that the last thing it can conceivably socialize are its obstinate links with world capitalism.

20

ISLAM IN THE INTERNATIONAL ORDER

James Piscatori

There is no doubt that Muslims almost everywhere are reaffirming the importance of Islam to their social and political lives. Some of them object that this relatively greater emphasis on Islam is not a 'revival', a 'renaissance', or a 'resurgence', for to them each term erroneously implies a return of the lapsed to faith. They prefer rather to speak of Islam as a constant tug on the Muslim's heart, but they do concede that it has only recently assumed a pronounced political significance. Why has Islam seemed so important in the past few years?

One Western writer gives principal credit to the oil boom of the mid-1970s. He argues that this new-found wealth gave rise to independent centres of power, chiefly Saudi Arabia and Libya; that it set in motion the process whereby a charismatic leader, Khomeiny, came to dominate the Islamic stage; and that it gave Muslims an opportune infusion of vitality.[1] There is some sense in this explanation, but it gives too much weight, I think, to what is essentially a secondary phenomenon. The possession of vast amounts of capital is doubtlessly related to the pace of activity, but the reasons for Islamic reassertion are deeper and have a longer perspective. There are perhaps four broad reasons.

First, the defeat of Egypt, Syria, and Jordan in the 1967 war with Israel shattered the morale not only of the Arabs but also of most Muslims. It accentuated the Arabs', and by extension, the Muslims' sense of inferiority which they had developed over recent centuries of militarily unsuccessful encounters with outsiders, particularly the technologically superior Westerners. The defeat also displayed the hollowness of Nasirism, the ideology that had seemed the panacea for all the Arabs' problems, and prompted many to search for an ideology and programme now both coherent and effective; it forced people to reconsider basic principles. Many Muslims concluded that they needed to be better Muslims if God was to spare them further calamity, or if they were ever to have a chance of recapturing the holy city of Jerusalem. The loss of Jerusalem particularly inflamed Islamic sentiment, and in the common outrage Muslims everywhere found a stronger identification with each other than had existed previously in the modern era.

Second, modernization is running a rough course in these developing countries and so has induced people to turn to ancient symbols and rites for comfort and part of their orientation. Islamic societies, like all developing ones, are contending with the effects of rural migration to the cities and the resulting over-urbanization; the development of new middle classes which are impatient with old ideologies and anxious to better their political lot; and Western counsel and example presuming to point the way to a more efficient and prosperous future.

The example of the Shah's Iran, of course, comes to mind. The process of rapid modernization which he set in motion naturally created disturbances in the social equilibrium and caused people to feel that their world had become topsy-turvy. In this confusion the only safe mooring seemed to be in attachment to Islamic values; they were familiar, whereas the Shah's talk of liberating women, redistributing land, relying on American expertise, and curbing the mullahs' power seemed strange and even threatening. It made little difference whether or not these initiatives actually benefited the people – some did; what mattered, however, is that these reforms upset the traditional way of life without replacing it with a obviously preferable alternative. The result was not preferable to the big landowners, because they were being displaced; to the technocrats, because they were not getting as much wealth and power as they thought they deserved; and to the many urban poor, because they had moved to the cities in hope of a brighter future, only to find there no opportunity to better their lot. The Islamic backlash, then, did not arise because modernization *per se* is unacceptable to Muslims but, rather, because the *effects* of the modernization programme were unacceptable.

Although this pattern was taken to an extreme in oil-rich Iran, it is present in varying degrees in other countries of the Islamic world. But there is nothing in the nature of Islam which precludes modernization occurring, despite what many believe in the West. The bad reputation which Muslims gained, and not entirely undeservedly, is due to the emphasis on imitation or *taqlid* which prevailed from the tenth century. According to this idea, Muslims were to follow rigorously the early guidelines of the faith and to avoid all kinds of innovation as deviations from God's word. This obviously circumscribed the right of Muslims to use their independent judgement (*ijtihad*) in order to think through the application of their faith to changing circumstances. But since the nineteenth century there has been a discernibly growing consensus among Muslims that it is permissible to exercise *ijtihad* and to question the relevance of precedent. This has meant that Islamic law is not the frozen edifice many assume it to be; although its basic principles cannot be altered, for it is revealed law, interpretations and adjustments can be made to allow the law to move with the times.

It is by virtue of such flexibility that many Muslim intellectuals are able to call for an Islamic strategy of development to counter what they see as an unduly Westernized model of development. Although few Muslims seem to agree on what such an Islamic strategy is and, in fact, on what 'Islam' itself means, almost everybody feels that economy and society should be 'nativized' or 'retraditionalized' – that is, that proper, Islamic, values should suffuse planning schemes. The search for general consensus is bound to fail, even as the general idea proves to be durably attractive. But as these societies confront what appear to them as the anomic consequences of development and as Muslims therefore look for their own approach, there is a remarkably widely shared opinion that Western models are substantially part of the problem and that Islam is substantially part of the solution.

Third, there has been an increased emphasis on Islam because Islamic societies have been caught up in the universal crisis of modernity. Most Muslims, like practically everybody else in the developed and developing world, are feeling ill at ease with a world which places less and less emphasis on loyalties to the family and which seems to find the church an increasingly irrelevant institution. In the past century there has been a discernible shift towards individualizing within cultures – i.e. towards lessening the individual's dependence on the extended family, weakening parental authority, liberating women, and questioning the authority of the clergy. But modernism has seemed more recently to have had its costs in the diminution of belief: 'After the dizzying history of the last fifty years, the world has grown strange, and people floated.'[2] Indeed, the notion that something is missing in one's life has now generated a time of 'secular discontents'[3] when many are seeking in religion the answer to, not 'am I a modern man?', but 'after all, what is it to be a modern man?'

It is a basic search for identity, with many accepting that knowing oneself comes through associating with the crowd rather than seeking to rise above it. As Daniel Bell has put it, 'What I think the deeper currents of meaning are calling for is some new rite of incorporation, simplifying membership in a community that has links with the past as well as the future.'[4] To turn to religion is thus natural because it provides moral links and common world-views to its followers. In this one respect, born-again Christians and veiled-again Muslims are perhaps responding to the same broad phenomenon. But Islam supplies a particularly potent rite of incorporation because of its fervent devotion to the *umma* (community of believers), its view of the early Prophetic and caliphal community as the paradigmatic 'open society',[5] and its graphic view of the transcendence of trial and time in the afterlife.

Fourth, the conditions of political development in these societies have tended to amplify the importance of Islam. Because most of these societies are poor in institutions and dominated by unelected rulers, it is natural for them to look for a way of legitimizing themselves easily. Islam represents an especially easy way to do this because it is vague in content, and hence can be manipulated, and because people respond to it readily as a symbol. As development schemes lose momentum or run into trouble, leaders may increasingly find Islam attractive. This is happening in Malaysia where the government is daily affirming its religious credentials.

But just as Islam can be used to legitimize, so it can be used to express opposition. And there are signs that this use of Islam is increasing too. This is partly because of the example of the Shah's overthrow, but it is also because in many countries without regular outlets of political expression Islam is being discovered as the convenient cover for taking a political position. Governments are hesitant to suppress groups speaking in the name of Islam because of their need to appear orthodox themselves or because they may receive aid from an Islamic 'patron' such as Saudi Arabia. For whatever the precise reason, many Islamic groups are able to criticize their governments, albeit in a circumspect way. This is happening in Algeria where Islamic groups act as a kind of pressure group trying to influence policies rather than to replace the regime.

Islam acquires a more contentious political centrality when there is a marked division between the haves and have nots, between the 'oppressors' (*mustakbarun*) and the 'disinherited' (*mustadʿafun*). The rural poor and new urban immigrants constitute the latter, whereas the large landowners and urban middle class professionals constitute the former. Politics becomes increasingly polarized and vicious as all are caught up in a double 'revolution' of expectations: peasants anticipate the good life in the dazzling metropolises, while professionals and intellectuals anticipate ever greater influence over that life. There is also a sort of revolution of falling expectations, for there are many, in the cities as well as the countryside, who find no solace and place no hope in the rapid, uneven changes of their society. For the rural poor, rallying about the traditional faith becomes a natural reaction to what seems a senseless abandonment of tried values; for the urban poor, emphasizing Islam becomes the natural antidote to the frustrations and indignities of living on the margin. For both there is a good chance that, as in Iran or perhaps Egypt, they will come to regard the professionals, bureaucrats, and technicians of the new middle class as new oppressors, who use Islam as a tactic to gain mass support but are attracted by alien living styles and foreign values. The dissatisfied might even look upon Islamic modernists, those who say they are trying to make Islam relevant to the conditions of the modern world, as having sold out to or at least compromised with the secularizing leadership. In this situation, modernist groups would lose the initiative to traditionalist ones, as the example of the Masyumi party losing ground to the Nahdatul Ulama in Indonesia might testify.[6]

It is hard to make further generalizations since the reasons for Islamic activity are as many and as specific as Islamic countries themselves. Yet the four broad stimuli I have outlined provide enough common ground to make us wonder if there might not be, after all, revolutionary changes occurring, changes that would, when piece is added to piece, pose an actual and conceptual threat to international order as we know it today.

Challenges to International Relations

It has become the standard fare of news commentary since the Iranian revolution to leave the impression that Islam is anti-Western. Not unnaturally, medieval stereotypes spring easily to mind when we hear almost daily from the Islamic world boisterous denunciations of the West's satanism and watch helplessly as international conventions are flouted. The images are all the more unflattering since today's 'Muhammadan' is all the more menacing: he trades in a commodity a great deal more important than myrrh and wields a weapon far mightier than the scimitar.

But the astute observer of international relations will note that there is no such thing as a monolithic Islam, let alone a monolithically anti-Western Islam. Islam has become nationalized, producing as many Islams as there are countries with Muslim majorities. In this situation in which various Islamic ideologies mix with specific national interests, it is unlikely that we will find Muslim statesmen whose overriding ambition is to push back the frontiers of the Christian West. Even Qadhdhafi's policy, which many suspect of being a particularly virulent form of Islamic militancy, is much, much less Islamic than it is militant.

Destabilization

If Islam can be said to pose a practical challenge to the contemporary international order, it may do so in the sense of destabilizing the political order of key states. One way of doing this is, as in Iran, displacing the *ancien régime* without being capable of organizing an effective, broadly based *nouvel ordre*. Egypt and the Sudan are two other potential examples. What makes these internal political upheavals worrisome is that they occur in countries that, by virtue of their locations, size, and resources, are of strategic import to both East and West. Since the three mentioned have been recently in the Western camp, it is understandable that Western policy-makers would be alarmed by the prospect of Islamic movements helping in any way to tilt the balance in favour of the Soviet Union.

Another way in which Islam might destabilize the political order of states is to help break up those that are multi-ethnic. Once again, Iran might be an example since the Kurds, long desirous of establishing their autonomy if not their independence, are predominantly Sunni and thus differ from the vast majority of Shiʿi Iranians. A more significant example might be the Soviet Union which has over 43 million Muslims and ex-Muslims in the Central Asian republics. There is no hard evidence that the multi-national Soviet empire is immediately to become undone, but many observers are beginning to wonder whether the impact of Khomeiny's revolution in neighbouring Iran might only accelerate a process of disintegration which is already under way. Indeed, one can point to several reasons why Islam could be playing a disintegrative role. For example, Soviet Muslims are increasingly aware of what is going on in the Islamic world, if for no other reason than that there are fairly regular contacts between *muftis* (of the official Islamic establishment, though) and Islamic associations abroad. But there are other contacts as well: Soviet Muslim soldiers in Afghanistan have had a sobering confrontation of their own with the phenomenon of Islamic freedom fighters (*mujahidun*). As another reason, there has been a drawing together of Sunnis and Shiʿa since the 1917 Revolution, thereby minimizing divisions within the Soviet Union's Islamic ranks and contrasting with the situation in so many other Islamic countries. Furthermore, Soviet Muslims generally lag behind Soviet Russians in economic and social position, whereas their population is increasing at a greater rate; presumably, therefore, they harbour basic discontents.

Most important, there is a vibrant 'parallel' Islam which consists mainly of Sufi *tariqas*, or brotherhoods, and which is gaining new followers at a remarkably rapid rate. As one indicator, there are reportedly in the Chechen-Ingush and Daghestan republics alone some 500,000 members, what one expert calls 'a fantastic number for an underground society banned by Soviet law'. As another indicator of Sufi growth, the same specialist notes that 'at present, adepts of Sufi orders are not merely mountain peasants or poor artisans as before the revolution: the proportion of industrial workers and of the intellectuals is increasing'.[7] The functions of these brotherhoods are also expanding, for they are now actively involved in the teaching of the Koran and Arabic, the maintenance of many alternative mosques to the few official ones, and the propagation of ideas to counter the propaganda of the religious establishment – the Council for Religious Affairs of the Council of Ministers and its four regional directorates.

Other observers, however, will point out with good reason that in both these cases of potential destabilizing there are other considerations at work. In the first case, one can argue that there is no certainty and some doubt that the Soviets would maximize their position in countries such as Iran whose political orders have been destabilized; these are rarely zero-sum games. And certainly there is no evidence to suggest that if an Islamic group emerges as the dominant political force it would be accommodating to the interests of a Communist state. In the second case, one can stress that we must not underestimate the power of the Soviet central government to repress dissent and to co-opt potential dissenters. Appeals to national unity, one can also argue, are likely to find some response, particularly as the national adversary, the Chinese, try to score propaganda points over the comparative treatment of minorities. The maddening reality, however, is that just about anything is possible. At least it is clear that Islam, in the form of ideologies and movements, retains strong potential for undermining political orders at key intersections in world politics.

Restructuring

We may still wonder whether the ferment among Muslims is heading towards the reordering of contemporary international relations. Particularly if we listen to the voices of some traditionalists, we would conclude that Muslims have launched a full-scale attack on the very basis of the present system, the nation-state. Attracted by the lodestar of unity, these Muslims hope for a regeneration of the fideistic community, the model of which was the closely knit band of the Prophet's followers in Medina and Mecca. They point to the Koranic references to the need for suppressing dissension among the believers and to the lack of guidance as to how separate Muslim communities should interact as evidence that God ordains one Islamic commonwealth.[8] This compact fellowship, according to them, made possible the wider union of the Umayyad, ʿAbbasid, and Ottoman periods, but it was rent by imperialist interventions and colonial designs. It was the West, then, which imposed disorder upon the Muslims and moulded them into wholly artificial political and national subdivisions. So entrenched have these divisions become, so manipulable were earlier generations, that even today's Muslim political scientists are imprisoned by their deference to the national paradigm.[9] These particular traditionalists see in the Iranian revolution the opening gun of a new era when the believers will have no higher loyalty than Islam and no other identity than Muslim. Most of them, however, are vague about what precise structural form this Islamic future will take, though there is the clear implication that some supra-national bloc will emerge.

Yet there is little to suggest that this kind of alternative is emerging. First, none of the present Islamic institutions is specifically committed to the supersession of the nation-state. The most important of them, the Organization of the Islamic Conference (OIC), refers in its charter to the 'rapprochement and solidarity between Islamic peoples' (Preamble), but does not go beyond provision for the 'co-operation' of member states, and specifically enshrines as basic principles 'non-interference in the domestic affairs of member States' and 'respect of the sovereignty, independence and territorial integrity of each member State' (Article II). Even if members wished to change the charter and advance a form of union, already the short history of the OIC testifies to the kinds of serious problems that would weigh against them.

In fact, there have been four sets of problems. First, there is the most fundamental and ever constant problem of identity, of what is Islamic. There has seemed little in common, for example, between the Tunisian interpretation of Islam and the Moroccan one, or between the Senegalese and Omanian ones, or, for that matter, between the Turkish interpretation and everyone else's. Second, there has been a problem of orientation in world politics. For example, the Algerians have generally given higher priority to the Non-Aligned Movement whereas the Libyans have tended to do just the reverse, stressing the Islamic movement's primacy. There has also been some disagreement over the attitude to be taken towards the two superpowers, particularly as the Soviet invasion of Afghanistan has made it seem that Third World associations can no longer be automatically and exclusively anti-American in tone. Third, there is sometimes a problem in formulating policies towards 'Islamic' issues, such as supporting Muslim separatists in the Philippines. In this case, Libya has agitated for a strong commitment but Malaysia fears antagonizing a fellow member of the Association of South East Asian Nations. In the early days there had also been disputes between the more radical and more conservative members over the extent of support for the Palestine Liberation Organization, and between the Arab and non-Arab members over the maintenance of diplomatic ties with Israel. Fourth, there is the problem of co-operation that arises from basic and serious political differences between the members. Egyptian and Syrian enmity cannot but help filter into OIC deliberations, and, certainly, the split between Iraq and Iran and their supporters has had an adverse impact on the organization's effectiveness.

In addition to these problems of institutional development, there is a second reason why it is unlikely that a supra-national Islamic bloc is about to emerge. It is, simply, that most Muslim thinkers have moved towards accepting the reality of the nation-state. While the conservative or traditionalist critic may argue that this acceptance is due to distorted education or confused values, the fact remains that culture changes occur even within Islamic civilization, and when they do it is hard, if not impossible, to distinguish old indigenous ideas from new exogenous ones. This process of acculturation is consequential precisely because it muddies the conceptual waters, making almost everything indistinct and thus almost anything unoffensive.

The primary agent of change was the invasion virtually everywhere by the nineteenth century of Western powers and the ensuing first-hand experience of defeat at the hands of non-believers. It was a profound shock to the Muslim world-view, sufficient to cause many to wonder about the viability of Islam in this strange technological world and about the strength of the conqueror's liberal ideas. Some, aping the Europeans, became secularists, but there was an influential number who reaffirmed the continued relevance of Islam as they reconsidered the meaning of basic principles. These, whom we generally call modernists, stressed the obligation in Islam to use reason rather than to rely on blind faith, to emphasize independent judgement in changing circumstances rather than blind imitation of ancient prescriptions. Within this guided creativity they came to terms with the idea of the nation-state, although largely and admittedly because they had to, without, however, losing the longing for greater community. After all, the Koran both teaches that God 'made you into nations and tribes so that you may know each other',[10] and commands 'be not divided among yourselves'.[11] For most modernists the latter has become an injunction towards solidarity (*tadamun*) rather than union (*ittihad*); striving towards this is the way to mitigate the harsher edge of the perennial reality of pluralism of which the international system is merely the current expression.

The present turbulent period is a complex one, however. In particular, we cannot so easily lose sight of those Muslims mentioned earlier who think the modernists have damaged Islam and who regard the end of the national experience as both inevitable and desirable. It is hard to gauge attitudes, and it is just possible that the numbers holding this view are growing during the present revival. But there are complicating factors to take into account. The situation has been so confused that it is often very difficult on this issue to separate modernists from traditionalists; indeed, one cannot assume that all traditionalists, those who generally want to put the basics of the faith at the centre of contemporary life, share the same view. All Muslims today stand on shifted ground, bringing modernists and traditionalists closer together; even someone like Khomeiny, despite his occasional appeals to broader unity, acts and sounds the national leader most of the time. Moreover, it is not clear that even those who criticize nationalism are espousing the same thing. Are they talking about one all-embracing state, or a number of Islamic states, or, in a less structured and more vague way, an Islamic order?[12] What, at any rate, would satisfy the constitutional requirements of any Islamic state?

For the foreseeable future, therefore, it is likely that most Muslims will not agree on much other than that they must change the nation-state as they have known it. Whatever the ultimate goal, most seem to be arguing more for the reformulation of the nation-state than for its replacement. It may well be that even most of the traditionalists with an interest in these matters have made their accommodation with the nation-state out of either the conviction that it is not wrong, the logic of the anti-colonial struggle, the impact of political socialization, or simply inertia. In this sense, it is probably the case that most concerned Muslims are wanting to deliver their politics of institutions and procedures that were copied from the European and American examples and that they are not attacking the concept of the nation-state itself. The question of Islamicizing is really inwardly rather than outwardly directed; it is a matter of social justice rather than of systemic restructuring.

The Rules of the Game

Even if we can concede that most Muslim intellectuals are not proposing the *umma* as a realistic alternative for the foreseeable future, we may still wonder whether Muslim states are comfortable participants in the current international order. There has long been doubt that they are because of the legacy of what can be called the Islamic theory of international relations.[13]

Abbasid jurists articulated what became the standard Islamic view of a bifurcated world. The division is between the land of unbelievers (*dar al-harb*) and the land of believers (*dar al-Islam*); the former is the realm of war and the latter of peace. Some scholars also think that there is an intermediary realm of lands at peace with the Islamic world (*dar al-sulh*); but by and large the Islamic medieval grand view is of a straightforward division, with the Islamic world inexorably expanding to the eventual obliteration of the other. Expansion is to come through a combination of inspiring, persuading, helping, and fighting non-Muslims.

There is thus an obligation to fight at times those who persist in unbelief, but the idea of *jihad* is not the simple equivalent of crusade or holy war. Deriving from the word for 'striving', *jihad* takes two forms. The 'greater' *jihad* involves the doing of good and avoiding of evil, the fulfilling of God's ethical injunctions, whereas only the 'lesser' *jihad* involves the fighting of unbelievers. As well, there has always been both a defensive and aggressive side to the lesser *jihad*. The Koran speaks of the need to fight those who are attacking,[14] but also commends Muslims to 'fight until there is no more tumult or oppression'.[15] In addition, while it is true that the *jihad* is sometimes to be directed against 'people of the Book' (*ahl al-kitab*), principally Jews and Christians, it is also and perhaps with greater fervour to be applied against polytheists, apostates, and dissenters. Fighting non-Muslim monotheists is not inevitable, for they can be spared if they pay a tax to the Islamic community and agree to abide by discriminatory regulations; in this case, they become *dhimmis*, or protected people.

Although the goal of Islam is transcendent peace,[16] there is also provision for the temporal kind, even a peace of sorts when Muslims have not eliminated the *dar al-harb*. The last is possible when Muslims seek to stop hostilities because they are at a temporary disadvantage, as they did in the early days of Meccan-Medinan fighting to secure the Hudaybiyya Treaty. They may also enter into a temporary peace when their adversaries sue for peace,[17] but there is no clear guidance as to how long this interruption in the fighting is to last. There is controversy as to whether Islam provides for neutrality,[18] but some have pointed to a *de facto* law of neutralization emerging from the special treatment which was accorded to Ethiopia, Cyprus, and Nubia.[19]

The established thought, then, only faintly approximates to the contemporary theory of international order, for there is no clear provision for a system of non-sectarian territorial demarcations, the equality of all political units, and international peace as the pre-eminent norm. Are we to conclude that Muslims, weighed down by their own intellectual baggage, are incapable of finding their way through the labyrinth of modern international relations? This is the conclusion of many who feel that Muslims who say otherwise are, to change the metaphor, merely reciting the oath of club membership without paying the dues: 'these sweeping assertions about Islam recognising the equality of all mankind and the reciprocality in inter-state relations amount to no more than gratuitous and non-committal slogans'.[20] But this conclusion is unfair for two reasons.

First, it over-estimates the role which culture plays in formulating the views and acts of statesmen. Muslim statesmen, like all statesmen, are guided more by the cold calculation of national interests than by the passionate commitment to ideological values. There are issues, like the law of the sea, on which Islam offers no instruction and thus exercises no claim on the leaders' minds. But even when Islam does have putative relevance, such as in the attitude towards Communist states, Muslim leaders invariably go about determining their business as everyone else does. Force of circumstances – that is to say, operating in the post-Westphalian order – impels Muslims to get along by going along. There is little reason to doubt their ability to do so because of their intellectual heritage, or to conclude that they are any less sincere in their professions than any national leader who talks about commitment to equality and reciprocity in international relations. The case of the hostage-taking of American diplomats in Iran was a matter of revolutionary politics rather than of Islamic guidance.

Second, the suggestion that Muslims do not play by the same rules of the game is unfair because it under-estimates the adaptability of cultures. As most Muslims have come to terms with the idea of the nation-state, most (who care) have also come to accept the concepts undergirding modern international law. Of course, they have had to adapt to minimize the conflict between what they do and what they believe, but they have also shown, contrary to what is often thought, that they can change with relative ease. They have done so through a process over time by which they have found or asserted natural connections between international legal ideas and Koranic values. *Pacta sunt servanda* is thus a version of the Islamic obligation to honour contracts. Sometimes they have made metaphoric connections: if *rebus sic stantibus* is not exactly the same as the broad Islamic principle of fairness in business dealings, then it is at least *like* it and hence acceptable. As well they have come to accept an idea such as peaceful co-existence because they believe that the peace which the classical sources talk about is so obviously timeless and alive that it could not fail to incorporate the present-day standard; what might be a contrived comparison to the outsider often simply seems a natural equivalence to the believer. It is not the case, then, that Muslim leaders reject out of hand most of the principles of the contemporary international order as either offensively alien or ideologically impure; rather, they have internalized them.

But this is not to say that Muslims accept every part of the contemporary order or that Islam has nothing to say about revising it. Many Muslim states have difficulty in subscribing to the emerging law of human rights and particularly object to the provisions of the Universal Declaration of Human Rights and subsequent documents which fail to take into account Islamic sensitivity about the role of women and the freedom to change religion. The language of inalienable rights in these matters disturbs Muslims who believe that the only unassailable rights are God's and, at any rate, that his teaching on women and the sanctity of the faith is at once more binding and more satisfying than any article of an international covenant. Islam, they also feel, can be morally instructive in the search for a juster international economic order since it combines respect for private property with commitment to the welfare of all citizens.[21] Some feel that Islam has a key role to play as well in the creation of a new, universal community,[22] but this positive contribution like the destabilizing one remains to be seen. In the meantime, Islam moves relatively easily with the prevailing order.

21

THE SOVIET UNION AND THE THIRD WORLD: FROM ANTI-IMPERIALISM TO COUNTER-IMPERIALISM[1]

Richard Löwenthal

Tsarist Russia, while a recognized Great Power within the old European system, had been both its most eastern and its most 'backward' member; and Russian Slavophil thinkers, in arguing against their 'Westernizing' opponents, had often stressed what they saw as their country's intermediate position between Europe and Asia – in a cultural as well as a geographical sense. From the other end of the political and intellectual spectrum, Leon Trotsky had once remarked that 'we had in our midst both London and India.'[2] It may thus appear natural that the Russian revolution of 1905, as much as the Japanese victory over the tsarist regime that preceded it, became a stimulating factor for the outbreak of nationalist and modernizing revolutions in Persia in 1906, in Turkey in 1908, and in China in 1910, as well as for the beginnings of Indian nationalism.

Lenin had early conceived the idea that those new national revolutionary movements of Asia, even though he regarded them as 'bourgeois democratic' revolutions, could become allies of the Russian and European proletariat in its struggle against the ruling classes of the established Great Powers. In his famous book on *Imperialism as the Highest Stage of Capitalism*, written during the First World War, he pointed to the common enemy of this future alliance – the capitalist monopolies of Europe and the United States, based on an interpenetration of industry and banking, and the governments serving their interests not only by holding down the workers at home, but by enabling their capitalists to exploit the colonial and semi-colonial peoples and repeatedly fighting wars to extend the sphere for such exploitation. It followed that the victory of the proletarian revolution in Europe and Russia would also sound the death-knell of colonialism.

When the Bolsheviks seized power in Russia, they at once announced their intention to grant self-determination to the oppressed nationalities, including the non-European and less developed ones, and to renounce the quasi-colonial privileges resulting from the 'unequal treaties' the Tsars had concluded with China. Under the fresh impression of this signal – and before the former promise had been somewhat devalued by the Soviets' military reconquest of Georgia, and the latter by their effort to retain Russian rights on the Eastern Chinese railway – the Second Congress of the Communist International in July 1920 adopted the two sets of theses on the 'national and colonial question' proposed respectively by Lenin and the Indian M. N. Roy – theses that proclaimed that the national revolutions of the colonial and semi-colonial peoples, even though not of a primarily proletarian character and in Lenin's view at first necessarily taking place under the leadership of the 'national bourgeoisie', could reach their goal of liberation only as part of the proletarian world revolution for which the Communists were fighting. Roy had indeed attempted to reverse the argument, claiming in his original draft that the proletarian revolution could win in the metropolitan countries only after the imperialists had been deprived of their colonial profits by revolutions on the periphery – but that formulation was 'corrected' before his theses were accepted together with Lenin's. In 1920, when hopes for proletarian revolutions were rising with the advance of the Red Army in Poland and the growth of Communist mass movements in several European countries, the role assigned to the barely emerging movements of the colonial allies was still that of a promising auxiliary, however important it might become by its sheer numerical weight.

The new doctrine was at once popularized among the peoples of Russia and some of the neighbouring Asian nations by the Baku 'Congress of the Peoples of the East' in September 1920. Its propaganda had little immediate impact in the countries at which it was aimed. Nevertheless, when the sick Lenin wrote his last published article in March 1923, two years after the introduction of the New Economic Policy and less than one year before his death, hopes for an early revolution of the European proletariat had become so much dimmer that the colonial 'auxiliary' appeared to him as a potentially decisive force: 'In the last analysis,' he now wrote, 'the outcome of the struggle will be determined by the fact that Russia, India, China, etc. account for the overwhelming majority of the population of the globe.'[3]

It will be observed that in those early years, the Bolshevik leaders tended to talk of the 'peoples of the East' and to choose their examples from Asia; and it was indeed there that their propaganda for 'national liberation' made its only major impact in the inter-war years. There was a big independence movement and a small Communist movement in India; there were isolated Communist uprisings in Indonesia and

Indo-China; and there was, above all, the growth of the Kuomintang movement for national unification and independence in China, and the important initial role of its Soviet political and military advisers and of Communist activists in its ranks. The great successes of the Kuomintang's 'Northern Expedition' in 1926/7 and the growth of Communist-controlled mass organizations in its wake led to a revival of the discussion, both among the Chinese Communists and in Moscow, of how long the 'bourgeois' leadership of Chiang Kai-shek could be tolerated and when the Communists would have to break with him – until Chiang himself in April 1927 determined the moment of the break and massacred the Communists. Promptly, Stalin officially declared that Chiang had 'betrayed' the national revolution and gone over to the side of the imperialists; but Chiang proceeded to unify China in his own way, and his success in this was impaired but not prevented by the Communists' guerilla struggle in isolated Soviet areas. Stalin's refusal to recognize that a country could achieve true national independence under non-Communist and indeed anti-Communist leadership was later to lead him into serious errors with regard to other countries. In China, Japan's increasingly aggressive invasion in the thirties and Chiang's inability to call for national armed resistance before July 1937 gave Stalin and the Chinese Communists a second chance to step forward as the true defenders of the Chinese national interest, resulting in the winning of a much broader mass basis by the Communists during the war years and in their ultimate victory in the renewed civil war.

Apart from China, where Communist wartime activity under Mao Tse-tung proceeded largely in independence from Soviet directives, though under the continued guidance of the Leninist doctrine of anti-imperialist struggle, the Soviet impact on the development of colonial and 'semi-colonial' nationalism during the Second World War was remarkably small: from the time of Hitler's attack on Russia in 1941, Stalin was concerned not to weaken his British allies, with the result that the Indian Communists had to support the British decision on India's entry into the war against the opposition of the Indian National Congress. The real wartime growth of a new self-confidence among the colonial peoples of Asia was due in part to the Japanese initial victories over their masters (a number of later national leaders of South East Asian nations started their movements as Japanese collaborators), in part to the growing support for post-war decolonization in Britain and the United States, resulting in policies leading to the early peaceful granting of independence to the Philippines and the Indian sub-continent. The Soviets, apart from their encouragement of Chinese resistance to Japan, had no share in this development; indeed even Ho

Chi Minh's Vietnamese post-war uprising against France – after a vain attempt at negotiation – seems to have been started without a Soviet blessing, at a time when Stalin still hoped to prevent France's post-war alignment with the Anglo-Americans.

It was only when the fronts of the Cold War were fairly clearly drawn in the course of 1947 that the Soviet Union returned to a general anti-imperialist campaign. But now, Stalin's stubborn clinging to the doctrine, adopted twenty years earlier in the context of Chiang Kai-shek's 'betrayal', that a former colonial or semi-colonial country could become 'really' independent only under Communist leadership, involved him during the last years of his life in a sterile conflict with the first new states: he stubbornly denied that they had become 'really' independent and treated men like Nehru and U Nu as 'imperialist stooges' – even in the face of Nehru's persistent effort to mediate in the Korean war and prevent the approach of the American forces to the Chinese border. While Stalin lived, the appearance of the first states of the 'Third World' could thus make no difference to the predominantly pro-Western character of the United Nations.

The real, major impact of Soviet policy on the emerging Third World thus dates from the same period as the existence of the bulk of the new states themselves – the Khrushchev period between 1954 and 1964. It was in 1954, at the time of the Geneva Asian conference on Indo-China and Korea and on the eve of the creation of SEATO by the West, that the new Soviet leadership not only recognized the substantive independence of the new states emerging, with the single exception of North Vietnam, under non-Communist leadership, but perceived its major interest in establishing friendly relations with those states by respecting their neutrality – their will to safeguard their new-won independence by staying out of the conflict between the Western and Soviet blocs. Possibly in part influenced by Chou En-lai, who had appreciated in time the Indian effort to mediate in Korea and was now seeking to make Sino-Indian relations a model of peaceful co-existence, the Khrushchev leadership began a policy of development aid and state visits to Asian neutrals, applauded the Afro-Asian conferences at Bandung at which Chou played such a prominent role, and developed at its twentieth party congress – the congress of Destalinization – the new doctrine of a 'zone of peace', comprising the familiar, Communist 'camp of peace' and the non-Communist, neutral new states. It was a deliberate attempt to replace the Soviet Union's self-isolation from the emerging Third World of Stalin's time by a gradual isolation of the Western bloc, unwittingly made easier by Secretary Dulles's initiatives for the creation of the SEATO alliance and the Baghdad Pact against the main currents of regional opinion, and by the Anglo-French Suez expedition. Within a few years, the position of the emerging Third World had been much strengthened by the growing political and economic competition for its support – for instance, even limited economic aid from the Soviets made it easier for the neutral new states also to obtain larger Western aid without accepting political conditions. Accordingly, the climate in the United Nations had begun to change considerably, even though the pro-Western majority was as yet far from reversed.

The Suez crisis, however, also marked the point at which Khrushchev, going beyond his initial demonstration of a respect for neutrality, began offensively to stimulate and exploit potential conflicts between the new Third World states and the Western powers – from his secret arms deal with Nasser before the expedition to his public threats to Britain and France at a moment when he was sure that it was being called off under American pressure. No longer confined to Asia, such opportunities for the exploitation of post-colonial conflicts between the new states and the West also arose, or seemed to arise, with Kassem's revolution in Iraq in 1958, with the civil strife in the newly independent former Belgian Congo, the later Zaïre, in 1960, and of course with the victory of Fidel Castro's revolution in Cuba and its subsequent radicalization.

However, those post-colonial revolutions created not only opportunities, but also problems for Soviet policy in the Third World. The initial successes of Khrushchev's had been due to a readiness to seek friendly relations with the non-Communist new states as they were, without pushing for internal changes in a Communist direction. Such ideological self-denial was bound to become more difficult for the Soviets now that not only external post-colonial conflict with the Western imperialists, but internal post-colonial revolutions were beginning to arise: the Soviets, who had not started the latter, could hardly ignore them in their Third World policy – all the less since the beginning of the Sino-Soviet conflict produced increasing ideological rivalry for Third World influence between Russia and China in the very same year. By 1959/61, the Soviets thus produced a theory claiming that while a 'socialist revolution', which would require Communist party power, was not yet on the agenda for the new states, their national and democratic revolutions had not been completed with the achievement of political independence: what was needed was both a struggle for *economic* independence from the imperialist powers and their monopolies, and radical 'democratic' reforms at home, including land distribution, the nationalization of some key enterprises, and if possible Communist participation in the government. The way to achieve this was to create 'National Democratic fronts' which would at first be led by popular nationalist leaders, but in which the Communists would be respected partners and would gradually increase their influence in the process of creating a 'national democratic state'. The model for this new strategic concept appears to have been the situation in Indonesia at the time, where Sukarno's radical nationalist government included the Communists as influential coalition partners.

It will be seen that this 'national democratic' strategy was an attempt to work simultaneously for two goals that were not necessarily compatible: the Soviet Union was both to become, or to remain, the friend and *ally* of the Third World states and the *model* for their internal development. By that time, propaganda for the Leninist concept of imperialism had achieved widespread success in the Third World, far beyond the ranks of the believers in other elements of Communist ideology; and many of the new nationalist leaders, who were by no means 'bourgeois democrats', but chiefly intellectuals and officers wielding or desiring dictatorial power, were indeed not only in sympathy with Soviet 'anti-imperialism' but also inclined to admire the Soviet Union as a successful model for catching up with Western modernity. Only that admiration among Third World nationalists was always selective: they were inclined to imitate the principle of state planning in the sense of public decisions on the basic tasks of investment, but not the Soviet type of detailed administrative planning by command or the forced collectivization of agriculture; and many of them admired the single-party system as a means to suppress the struggle between different organized interests and to re-educate the people for disciplined industrial work and all-national loyalty, but not the egalitarian and internationalist elements of Communist ideology.

Within a few years, the Soviet leaders were to discover that these ideas of 'selective imitation' formed an obstacle to the application of their 'national-democratic' concept in most Third World countries: instead of forming coalitions with the Communists, a number of them formed their own nationalist one-party regimes, combining the acceptance of Soviet aid alongside Western aid with the suppression of their Communist parties or the refusal to allow them to be founded at all. Quite a few of those states, particularly in Africa and the Arab world, developed their own mixtures of nationalism with 'socialist' or even Marxist elements, claiming that in their conditions it was superior to orthodox, Moscow-directed Communism. No less surprising to the Soviets, if rather more welcome, was the fact that Fidel Castro, who had gained power with a vague national revolutionary ideology and a loose guerilla organization which merged with the Communist party only after victory, came as a result of his conflict with the United States, his growing dependence on Soviet support, and the lack of trained cadres for the task of reconstruction among his original followers, to declare himself a 'Marxist-Leninist' and to permit the Communists to transform the unified monopoly party accordingly – provided they swore allegiance to him as the *maximo lider*. The dual experience of the difficulty of getting Communists accepted as independent partners by nationalist one-party states, and of the chance of winning over the leader of a ruling nationalist party by loyal co-operation of Communists within its ranks, finally caused Khrushchev in 1963, close to the end of his own tenure as Party leader, to ask some friendly one-party regimes to permit the co-operation of Communists not as representing an independent party, but as individual members of the nationalist ruling party; and this project of what I have called 'licensed infiltration' succeeded for a time in Algeria under Ben Bella, where the Communists strongly influenced the new programme of the FLN adopted after its seizure of power, and to some extent in Nasser's Egypt. However, the majority of African and Arab one-party regimes, however sympathetic to the Soviet Union in other respects, refused to embark on a similar experiment, and those undertaken in Algeria and Egypt were not to last: no other nationalist party leader has been willing to emulate Castro's conversion to 'Marxism-Leninism' under the influence of Communist advisers, and to become correspondingly dependent on the Soviet Union.

By the time Khrushchev was overthrown by the Central Committee of the CPSU in October 1964, the balance-sheet of his bold forays into the Third World was therefore strikingly mixed. On one side, his turn towards co-operation with the emerging Third World had greatly helped the new states to establish themselves as an independent 'third force' in world affairs. Moreover, Soviet prestige and foreign policy influence among the 'non-aligned' community of those states had greatly increased, with the result that the United Nations now showed an anti-Western majority on an increasing number of occasions. On the other hand, the attempt to expand a form of indirect but real Soviet control over a number of such states by means of Communist influence had generally miscarried: as Vietnam remained the only former colony that had achieved independence from colonialism under Communist leadership, so Cuba remained the only regime emerging from an originally non-Communist revolution whose leader and ruling party were converted. On the whole, Soviet diplomacy in the Third World had been remarkably successful, but Communist ideological strategy had failed.

It seems that the new Brezhnev-Kosygin leadership that replaced

Khrushchev became aware of that uneven balance sheet within the first two years of its rule. The striking collapse of some of the most radical and 'revolution-mongering' Third World regimes – Sukarno's downfall after the failed Indonesia coup of 1965 and Kwame Nkrumah's overthrow in Ghana in 1966, later followed by that of Modibo Keita in Mali – must have demonstrated the limited value of ideological ties to Third World regimes. Just so the Chinese foreign policy defeats – in the collapse of the 'Second Afro-Asian conference' at Algiers in 1965, which Peking had hoped to turn into a demonstration of Third World unity against both America and Russia, again in the fate of Sukarno's regime, with which Peking had hoped to found a counter-organization to rival the United Nations, and in Peking's inability to assist Pakistan in its conflict with India and to prevent Moscow from becoming its arbiter in early 1966 – must have convinced the Soviet leaders that they had little reason to worry about Chinese ideological rivalry, so long as their military and economic power was so vastly superior. At the same time, they seem to have felt that Khrushchev's dispersal of Soviet strength in what amounts to a far-flung 'strategy of denial' against the West, trying simultaneously to prevent a consolidation of Western spheres of influence in Central America and Central Africa as well as the Middle East, did not correspond to the real political and military interests of a great continental power like the Soviet Union, which should rather try to stake out contiguous spheres of influence of its own in the regions to the south of its borders – in Central and South Asia and the Middle East.

The first political expressions of this new concept were Kosygin's 1966 call, before the National Assembly in Cairo, for a bloc of 'progressive' Arab states leaning toward the 'socialist camp', and his 1969 proposal for a pact of regional co-operation between the Soviet Union, Afghanistan, Pakistan, India, and Iran. True, the first suggestion of a pro-Soviet bloc in the Middle East clearly over-estimated the Soviets' real power in that region, as the Six Days War showed in 1967; while the second suggestion of an arrangement linking the Soviet Union by a land bridge to both the Indian Ocean and the Persian Gulf neglected the obvious fact of the bitter conflicts separating Pakistan from both its Afghan and its Indian neighbours. But while both political projects remained dreams, a remarkable expansion of Soviet economic ties with both groups of countries took place beginning in 1966: in particular, Soviet economic aid to such by no means 'progressive' states as the CENTO members Pakistan, Iran, and even Turkey reached substantial amounts in this period, at the very time when the total of new Soviet foreign aid was drastically reduced in order to gain time for implementing previous commitments.

The purpose of those overtures was both economic and political. On one side, there was the prospect of long-term compensation agreements between the Soviets and the raw material producers of those adjacent countries, particularly in the fields of oil, gas, and mineral production, based on major Soviet investment to be repaid by delivery of the products at fixed prices: a prospect attractive for the – mostly state-owned – enterprises of the neighbouring countries because of the instability of raw material prices on the world market, and for the Soviets as a chance to create, in the words of Kosygin's report at the twenty-fourth congress of the CPSU in 1971, 'a stable division of labour, counterposed to the system of imperialist exploitation', while at the same time giving the Soviet Union the opportunity 'to satisfy the requirements of its own economy more fully'. On the other hand, there was the Soviet political hope that such an intensification of economic ties with hitherto pro-Western and by no means revolutionary Third World countries like Iran, and to a lesser extent Pakistan and Turkey, which were relatively developed on a largely 'state-capitalist' basis, would permit them gradually to pull those countries into a sphere of Soviet influence – regardless of their internal political and social structure.

The hope was all the stronger because since the first meeting of the 'United Nations Conference on Trade and Development' (UNCTAD) in 1964, there had been widespread Third World complaints about the under-valuation of their raw material exports in an 'unequal exchange' against modern machinery sold by the advanced Western countries, about alleged 'discrimination' against their manufactured exports on Western markets, and about the increasingly onerous burden of their accumulated indebtedness to the West. Was it not obvious that the planned Soviet economy could offer to the Third World countries both more stable conditions for selling their raw materials at fixed prices, and a less crowded (and less choosy) market for their manufactured products? Indeed the year 1971, in which the twenty-fourth congress of the CPSU took place, also saw the adoption of a new 'comprehensive programme' by the Soviet bloc's 'Council for Mutual Economic Aid', with the explicit offer for non-Communist, Third World countries to participate either in the full programme for a division of labour outside the capitalist world market, or in partial schemes for 'regional integration'.

The Soviets apparently were so confident of this 'alternative' to the

Third World's demand for a 'New International Economic Order' that they felt free to declare that the latter was no concern of theirs: the grievances of the Third World against the Western imperialists were, of course, perfectly justified in themselves, but the Soviet Union and its associates, having no share in the guilt of colonialism, could not be accused of either unequal exchange or discrimination against Third World products, but were already offering a perfectly fair deal to the developing countries. Unfortunately, it turned out that the 'socialist world market' was of very limited attractiveness to the Third World since it was both much narrower than the 'capitalist market' and had no convertible currency. At the same time, the Western imperialists after some years of debate began to make real if insufficient efforts to meet the grievances of the Third World on raw material prices, and rather more positive efforts in offering preferential markets to groups of Third World countries – notably in the Lomé agreements initiated by the European Community. Despite the severe economic difficulties created in the West following the oil crisis, by the middle seventies the Soviet argument that only the West had to make economic concessions to the Third World and that the Soviets were not concerned in its plight came to carry less and less conviction in Third World ears.

The Soviet concept of achieving gradually increasing political control of Third World countries in certain selected regions by making them increasingly dependent on economic ties with the Soviet bloc had, in fact, been the starting point of a new imperialist relationship to those countries – the first step in the transition from traditional 'Anti-Imperialism' to a new kind of 'Counter-Imperialism' closer to the traditions of the West. When the concept of an *economic* counter-imperialism failed, because the Soviet bloc's economic basis was too weak for it, the second step was taken to create an increasingly *military* form of Soviet counter-imperialism in order to achieve the political and economic objectives underlying it. This second step found its opportunities in the continuing domestic instabilities of many Third World states; it was facilitated by the general weakening of the Western powers owing to the effect of rising energy costs on their economies, and by the special temporary paralysis of the United States as a consequence of the Vietnam and Watergate crises, which for a number of years made it impossible for a broad consensus to be reached in the leading country of the Western world on effective counteraction to deter military action by the Soviets and their proxies at sensitive points in the Third World.

The result is that after 1975 Soviet intervention in the Third World assumed a new quality. True, the Soviets had always proclaimed that 'peaceful co-existence' in their language did not mean 'ideological co-existence', and in particular did not exclude their support of 'national liberation movements'. But even during Khrushchev's polemics with the Chinese Communists in the early sixties, they had still insisted that it did exclude 'wars between states', even local wars, and might therefore impose limits on the *form* of support given to liberation movements. When, *after* the liberation of Angola from Portuguese colonial rule, civil war developed between a weaker, Communist-controlled liberation movement, the MPLA, and two stronger non-Communist movements, the Soviets openly intervened in that war by transporting Cuban troops to the scene. Since then, similar Soviet-sponsored intervention has taken place in Ethiopia and South Yemen, both much closer to the scene of Soviet strategic interests in the Middle East, and by Vietnamese troops in Cambodia – and finally by the Soviets themselves in Afghanistan: there, a formerly undisturbed sphere of Soviet influence had become the scene of popular uprisings as the result of the imposition, entirely unnecessary even from the viewpoint of rational Soviet interest, of Communist minority rule in 1978 – and the Soviets apparently believed they had to send their troops in order to prevent a neighbouring Third World country from turning hostile to them for the first time in decades. The net effect is that the Soviets have become visible as a ruthless imperial power in large parts of the Third World, and more particularly in the Islamic world.

Of course, the Soviets had been taking military action against the uprisings of weaker nations in the European empire – the East Germans, the Hungarians, the Czechs – for the last thirty years; but that happened to Europeans, and the Third World did not care. Later, with the comparative stabilization of conditions in Europe in the seventies, Russia came to demonstrate its military power on the classical stamping ground of imperialism, in what is now the Third World. When the Chinese Communists after the Soviet invasion of Czechoslovakia in 1968 began to warn the Third World against the 'hegemonism' of the 'new Tsars', there was much shock, also much doubt, but above all astonishment. Later events, and more particularly the invasion of Afghanistan, may make a more lasting difference: the belief in a basic, anti-imperialist affinity between the Russian superpower and the traditional victims of imperialism in the Third World may not survive them.

22

FRANCE: ADJUSTMENT TO CHANGE

Christopher M. Andrew

Decolonization and decline are inextricably interwoven in the British experience. In the French experience they are quite separate. Colonial expansion coincided not with the rise of French power but with its decline. Decolonization, by contrast, was quickly followed by national revival. De Gaulle was surely right to argue that France's role in world affairs was more influential in the mid-1960s, when decolonization was almost complete, than in the early 1950s before decolonization had even begun. France had lost an Empire and found a role.

France, unlike Britain, has decolonized twice. In her eighteenth-century wars with Britain, France lost a great Empire in the New World and India, retaining only a few tattered remnants of her imperial past. Yet France's period of greatest power and prestige in modern history – during the revolutionary and Napoleonic generation – coincided precisely with the period when her Empire was at its most exiguous. And the construction of a great new Empire – the second largest in world history – during the century after Waterloo was accompanied by the steady decline of France's continental power. From Waterloo to Stalingrad the balance of power in Western Europe – that is essentially the balance of power between France and Germany – shifted inexorably from France to Germany. The turning-point was the Franco-Prussian War of 1870: when the two sides, in material terms at least (with nearly identical populations and iron and steel production), were more evenly matched than in any other major conflict of modern times. But during the seventy years of the Third Republic Germany's population doubled while France's did not grow at all. German GNP increased five times while France's failed to double. For about fifteen years after the First World War the reality of French decline was partially concealed first by the *Diktat* of Versailles, then by the illusions of the Locarno honeymoon, finally by the earlier and more devastating impact of the interwar depression in Germany than in France. But by the mid-1930s the extent of French decline had been laid bare. In 1936 Germany's industrial production already exceeded the pre-depression level. France's did not do so for another fifteen years. And as the Rhineland crisis showed,

France had lost the military and political will to resist the rise of Nazi Germany.

Despite the coincidence of imperial advance and metropolitan decline, the supporters of Empire throughout the Third Republic argued consistently that expansion outside Europe was the key to recovery inside Europe. For Ferry and for Gambetta, the two leading imperialists of the early Third Republic, imperial expansion was – in Gambetta's words – the way to 'become a great power once again'. That was how, almost a century later, de Gaulle explained the construction of the modern French Empire: 'Through the colonial epic [our country] had sought consolation for the loss of her far-away possessions in the eighteenth century, then for her defeats in Europe in 1815 and 1870.'[1] France, as a whole, had in reality done nothing of the kind. The supporters of Empire before the First World War, though influential, were very few in number. It was not until the First World War that the idea that the overseas Empire might somehow compensate for the weakness of the metropolis began to show some sign of capturing the popular imagination. During the manpower crises of 1917 and 1918 almost a million soldiers and factory workers provided by the Empire made a deep impression – not least upon their German foes. The public was easily persuaded that, had the shipping been available, the Empire could also have solved the shortages of food and raw materials. Between the wars, however, imperial enthusiasm gave way once more to imperial apathy. The first comprehensive study of the Empire's contribution to the war effort, published in 1927, gloomily concluded: 'The "average Frenchman" readily imagines that the colonies are only good for giving bureaucrats a living and that they weigh heavily on the metropolitan budget.'[2]

The Fall of France in 1940, however, finally accomplished what the First World War had begun: to persuade both people and politicians of the truth of Gambetta's dictum that the Empire offered the means for France to 'become a great power once again'. To Vichy the Empire offered the only hope of national revival, 'the last card France has left to play': 'France by herself in Europe has lost her place on the chessboard of the old continent . . . But thanks to her Empire she retains a chance of counting as one of the great nations.' De Gaulle too sought to rally the French people after defeat in Europe by pointing to the 'immense imperial resources' which remained intact: 'Is our defeat final? No . . . For France is not alone! She is not alone! She has behind her a vast empire.' The same theme recurred after the Liberation. Gaston Monnerville told the first post-war Assembly in 1945: 'Without the Empire, France would today be only a liberated country. Thanks to her

Empire, France is one of the victors.' The French people, wrote Léopold Senghor, had acquired, at last, an imperial consciousness: 'Since 1945 the word "Empire" has acquired an almost magical prestige.'

The mood of imperial enthusiasm which accompanied the founding of the post-war *Union française* quickly died down. Except in time of crisis – and sometimes even in a crisis – colonial debates in parliament were liable to evoke much the same apathetic response as between the wars. During the 1956 parliamentary elections, with the Algerian rebellion already under way, most deputies still made no specific reference to Algeria in their election manifestos. As late as September 1957 the Senate gave agricultural prices higher priority than the war in Algeria. Yet, despite Communist and Cartieriste objections, a majority of Frenchmen probably remained convinced that the African Empire was essential to France's survival as a great power. The discovery in 1956 of what ministers quickly called 'our Saharan oil' at a time when the Suez crisis threatened France's petrol supplies did nothing to diminish that conviction. 'To abandon Algeria', said Jacques Soustelle in 1957, 'is to condemn France to decadence.' Many, even on the Left, agreed. 'Without Africa,' wrote François Mitterrand, 'France will no longer have a history in the twenty-first century.' That widespread conviction was one major obstacle to French acceptance of a new post-imperial world order.[3]

A second major obstacle was ethnocentrism. The French variety of ethnocentrism is quite different from the British. As Maurice Duverger put it in 1955: 'The English would be shocked that a foreigner could have the idea of becoming British. The French are shocked when a foreigner does not have the idea of becoming French.'[4] The universalist pretensions of French civilization have made French intellectual adjustment to 'a global international order' even more difficult than the British. Unlike Britons, who doubted whether foreigners could ever learn British ways, French nationalists have never doubted that the values of French civilization are universal. Jules Michelet apostrophized his country: 'France, glorieuse mère qui n'est pas seulement la nôtre!' Even his revolutionary contemporaries, Blanc and Blanqui, though preaching that the workers of all nations were brothers, also insisted that Paris was the *ville lumière*, the capital of civilization. The French, said Louis Blanc, were 'an inspired nation'. The British, on the other hand, were not: 'The principle of egoism is incarnate in the English people, the principle of devotion in the French people. England has set foot in no country without setting up her counting-houses. France has nowhere passed without leaving the perfume of her spirituality.'[5]

According to the philosophy of 'assimilation' propounded during the

French Revolution, natives fortunate enough to find themselves under French rule were potential Frenchmen destined for full integration into the universal values of French civilization, irrespective of colour, creed, or cultural traditions. By the First World War 'assimilation' had given way to the more flexible concept of 'association' which stressed co-operation between ruler and ruled based on a degree of respect for native customs, beliefs, and social structures. The natives were none the less still destined to absorb the universal values which France alone could teach. Writing for an American audience in 1951, the leading French political scientist André Siegfried explained that the Frenchman 'possesses a certain intellectual radiance, a Latin gift distinguishing him from the Anglo-Saxon': 'This same Frenchman will manifest a greater idealism and universalism in his thought than any other human being. . . .' France possessed a lesson to 'teach the world – a lesson not to be learned from any other country'.[6]

The educated élite of French colonial Africa thus found it far more difficult than its neighbours in British Africa to preserve its cultural identity. Unlike their Anglophone counterparts, Francophone African leaders felt it necessary to recapture their cultural independence before beginning the struggle for political independence. In the 1940s, while Jomo Kenyatta, Kwame Nkrumah, and other Anglophone Africans were formulating political programmes, Senghor, Jacques Rabemananjara (later vice-president of Madagascar), and Aimé Césaire (later deputy for Martinique) concentrated on the cultural programme of *Négritude*. Their priorities were epitomized by Alionne Dioppe's decision to abandon politics in 1947 to campaign for *Négritude* as editor of *Présence africaine*.[7] *Négritude* was born as a defence mechanism against the universalist claims of French culture. As Senghor wrote in 1950: 'I know no people more tyrannical in its love for mankind. It wants bread for all, culture for all, liberty for all; but this liberty, this culture, this bread are to be *French*.' This was true of Left as well as Right of the political spectrum. Senghor wrote to his American biographer in 1963: '. . . The French left-wing . . . is still not decolonised. It secretes a mixture of "Jacobin" spirit and missionary spirit, typically French. This left-wing wants to impose its *maîtres à penser* on us; above all, it refuses to let us think by ourselves.'[8]

Yet Senghor is himself, in part at least, a victim of the French universalism he has often criticized. That is particularly true perhaps of his devotion to the French language: 'Since the heady adventure of the Renaissance the French language has developed along the highway of the universal.' It is difficult to imagine an Anglophone African as captivated by English vowels as Senghor is by French: 'Le jeu harmonieux des voyelles, nombreuses et nuancées: voyelles longues ou brèves, orales ou nasales, ouvertes ou fermées ou moyennes, sans parler des semi-voyelles, des diphtongues ou des triphtongues.' The French language lies at the heart of French ethnocentrism and universalism. In Siegfried's words: 'The French language, famous for its clarity, is a precision instrument . . . Any thought whatsoever, filtered through the French spirit, thereby receives clarity and order. Even more, it acquires universality; it becomes transmissible, like a medium of exchange acceptable everywhere and usable by everyone.'[9] That remarkable belief provides at least a partial explanation for the attempts since the collapse of the French Community to establish *La Francophonie* as a kind of substitute Commonwealth.

Belief in the universal validity of the *mission civilisatrice* helps to explain why France found it even more difficult than Britain to accept as genuine nationalist opposition to her rule. During the First World War the British accomplished what now appears as the astonishing feat of using simultaneously both Arab and Jewish (or Zionist) nationalism for their own imperial purposes. The French failed to take either seriously until it was too late.[10] Even in 1945 most Frenchmen still could not believe that opposition to the French presence in Syria proceeded from the Syrians themselves. According to an opinion poll 65 per cent of the French people held Britain responsible for the Syrian unrest and only 3 per cent considered France herself to blame. According to another poll on the troubles in Indo-China, 36 per cent of the public blamed Japan, 12 per cent the British, 9 per cent the Chinese, 6 per cent the Americans, and only 5 per cent the French. Even the Communist Party denounced those who demanded independence as 'the conscious or unconscious agents of another imperialism'. Since principled opposition to the universal values of French civilization was, by definition, impossible, vast conspiracy theories were required to explain nationalist opposition to French rule. But the nature of the conspiracy changed. In 1945 the Arab League was regarded as a British puppet. Ten years later it had become the tool of Soviet imperialism. Even liberal intellectuals like Camus persuaded themselves that Algerian independence was a snare and a delusion: that it would lead not to real independence but to subjugation by a rival imperialism.[11]

A third obstacle to French acceptance of a post-imperial world came from the vested interests of the *colons*, overwhelmingly concentrated in North Africa and especially in Algeria. Most *colons* paid no more than lip-service – if, indeed, even lip-service – to the universalist claims of the civilizing mission. The great French proconsul, Marshal Lyautey, denounced the *colon* outlook in 1918 as 'every bit as bad as the *Boche*, with the same belief in inferior races whose destiny is to be exploited'.[12] For the next generation the settler lobby in Algeria successfully emasculated all metropolitan attempts at serious reform. A century after the Algiers expedition of 1830 no more than 2,500 Algerian Muslims had become French citizens. Jules Roy was brought up in Algeria, like most of his contemporaries, in the belief that 'the Arabs belonged to a different race, one inferior to my own'. He later confessed that as a colonel in the Algerian War, 'It came as a great surprise to realise – little by little – that the *figuiers* were men like ourselves. . . .' Despite the contradiction between *colon* racism and the universalist claims of French civilization, the Algerian settlers possessed one argument of great emotional power which bound them to the metropolis. That argument was summed up in General Salan's claim, 'The Mediterranean crosses France as the Seine crosses Paris.' Between the wars the myth grew up, officially sanctioned in the schoolbooks of the Third Republic, of France as the 'new Rome', established on the southern as well as the northern shores of the Mediterranean Sea. Even for metropolitan Frenchmen who had accepted the loss of Indo-China, the decolonization of Algeria still appeared at the fall of the Fourth Republic in 1958 as an unacceptable sacrifice largely because they did not consider it would be decolonization at all. Algeria was not a colony but a part of France herself. For the socialist leader Guy Mollet as for the radical prime minister Mendès-France, 'France without Algeria would be France no longer.'[13]

And yet, astonishingly, only four years later Algeria was lost and French decolonization was virtually complete. At the beginning of the 1960s France made a quite extraordinarily rapid adjustment to the emergence of the new world order. The colonial consensus – the belief that Algeria and its African hinterland remained vital to France's survival as a great power, a consensus vital to de Gaulle's return to power in 1958 – had disapeared by 1962. In July 1962 a majority of 90 per cent voted at a referendum to accept the Evian agreement with the FLN.

The speed with which Frenchmen accepted the end of Empire was due first and foremost to defeat – or at least the impossibility of victory – in Algeria. But it has three other explanations also. The first is de Gaulle. Within four years de Gaulle had created the first truly stable system of government for a century: a system which most Frenchmen evidently considered vastly preferable to the political musical chairs of the Third and Fourth Republics. And while working a political revolution at home, de Gaulle's diplomacy had simultaneously persuaded Frenchmen that France's influence in the world would survive the end of Empire. As de Gaulle boasts in his memoirs: '. . . The same newssheets and broadcasts which, before 1958, scarcely mentioned France except sometimes to commiserate with her, now pay unceasing attention to her. What she says and what she does, notably in the person of her Chief of State, the position attributed to him, his supposed intentions – these give rise to innumerable commentaries which may be either bitter and ironic or else trusting and laudatory, but are never indifferent.'[14]

Secondly, the end of Empire – though traumatic – did not bring with it, as in Britain, a national crisis of identity. For France, unlike Britain, the imperial experience impinged only fleetingly on national life. Most Frenchmen only began to attach importance to the Empire as they began to lose it. The final drama of *Algérie française* did not last long enough to erase the long tradition of imperial apathy which preceded it. France, unlike Britain, has always seen her vital interests overwhelmingly in continental terms. And with the end of Empire France, unlike Britain, possessed a continental identity to which to return.

Thirdly, the Algerian War coincided with the first serious intellectual attack on French ethnocentrism. Decolonization forced at least some French intellectuals to question the universality of French values. The most influential was the anthropologist, Claude Lévi-Strauss, who launched a sustained assault on Western ethnocentrism, beginning with *Race et histoire* in 1952 and culminating ten years later in *La Pensée sauvage*. Though that assault predated the Algerian War it first became really influential during it. There remains something typically French in Lévi-Strauss's restless search for what is universal in *l'esprit humain*, though in reaction to the universalist claims of French culture he may be guilty of idealizing primitive societies instead. In Edmund Leach's view 'he conceives of primitive peoples as "reduced models" of what is essential in all mankind, but the resulting Rousseau-like noble savages inhabit a world very far removed from the dirt and squalor which is the field anthropologist's normal stamping ground.' The challenge to the civilizing mission is none the less profound.[15]

France's rapid adjústment to a new world order in the early 1960s was, inevitably, incomplete. The French representative to the United Nations claimed in 1964: 'There are few traditions that are so much a part of the history of my country as the concept of equality between the races. . . . Everywhere that French laws and mores are the rule, there is no discrimination. It has not even been forbidden because it is not necessary to do so.' In reality, the short-term consequence of decolonization was probably to increase racial discrimination in France herself. Until the 1960s blacks in France were few in number, came largely from educated élites, and – like Senghor – mixed easily with the cosmopolitan society of the Left Bank. Mass immigration of blacks to bidonvilles and menial jobs began only in the 1960s. Algerian immigration increased more rapidly still, from 200,000 before the Algerian War to 845,000 by 1974. According to an opinion poll in 1966, 65 per cent of Parisians had 'a racist attitude towards Arabs'. Recognition that racial prejudice – hitherto denied – actually existed marked none the less a significant step in France's adjustment to a new world order. A bill to outlaw discrimination in housing and employment was debated almost yearly from 1959 onwards. For thirteen years it was voted down on the traditional grounds that racism in France did not exist. In 1972 the bill became law.[16]

At a diplomatic level also France's sudden adjustment to a post-imperial order was inevitably incomplete. De Gaulle's relations with Francophone African leaders retained a neo-feudal character, conducted through personal diplomacy and the secretary-general at the Elysée, Jacques Foccart, rather than through the Quai d'Orsay. De Gaulle's meetings with African leaders had about them an air of almost regal condescension. He notes with satisfaction in *Mémoires d'espoir*: 'Step by step, without failing to solicit and to follow our advice, the young governments assumed their responsibilities.' One African leader, however, presumed to show ingratitude. De Gaulle's dismissal of Sekou Touré's complaints was splendidly disdainful: 'I reply clearly and firmly that France has done much for Guinea; that there is striking evidence of this – for example, the fact that the orator I have just heard spoke in very good French . . . "[France] is indifferent to your retrospective reproaches. . . . She lived for a very long time without Guinea in the past. She will live for a very long time yet if she is separated from her." '[17] Even more remarkable than de Gaulle's imperial manner was the willingness of Francophone African leaders to defer to it. All knew that de Gaulle was trading with Rhodesia and selling arms to South Africa. None dared criticize him for it. The climax to the neo-feudalism of de Gaulle's Black African policy came at his funeral. While the leaders of East and West had to be content with the requiem mass in Paris, the African heads of state were admitted to the graveside at Colombey-les-deux-églises where, amid scenes of great emotion, they were received by Madame de Gaulle.

During the 1970s there was a slow crumbling of the Gaullist neo-feudalism, though Pompidou and Giscard d'Estaing were to preserve some elements of it. Pompidou reinstated Foccart after his sacking by Poher in the interregnum after de Gaulle's resignation. Foccart had eventually to go after one 'action directe' too many, but Giscard appointed his former deputy, René Journiac, in his place. And both

Pompidou and Giscard maintained de Gaulle's ceremonial interchange of state visits, even aiding, abetting – and indirectly financing – the imperial fantasies of the Emperor Bokassa. African leaders had none the less lost much of the deference of the 1960s. In 1977 Giscard was finally forced by African pressure to announce the end of arms sales to South Africa.

In at least three ways, however, France still exerts a quasi-imperial influence in post-imperial Africa. The first is economic. The states of Francophone Black Africa share a common currency invalid in international exchanges except after conversion into the French franc. And while other foreign investors have found Francophone Africa difficult to penetrate, French investors – particularly, in recent years, mining interests – have been welcomed. The doctrine of *Eurafrique*, fashionable during the Giscard years, was a reworking of a colonialist programme of the 1930s. But to the traditional elements of European expertise and African resources, the up-dated programme of the later 1970s had added Arab money. France retains a powerful military as well as economic presence in Black Africa. She has military bases in Senegal, Ivory Coast, and Gabon, and military agreements with all Francophone states save Mali and Guinea. During the later 1970s she intervened in Chad, Mauretania, Zaïre, and the Central African Empire (or Republic).[18]

Last but not least, France retains an impressive cultural presence in Francophone Africa. 'Above all, for us', writes Senghor, '*la Francophonie est culture.*'[19] Approximately 60 per cent of the 100,000 foreign students in French universities come from former colonies. The expansion of the French language remains, according to Xavier Deniau, formerly Giscard's minister for overseas territories, 'a crucial element of foreign policy'.[20] The end of Empire has modified but not suppressed France's sense of her civilizing mission. French national prestige still requires the export of French culture. That is the main reason perhaps why de Gaulle and his successors could never bring themselves to be as stern with Algeria as with Guinea. Even after Algerian nationalization of French oil companies in 1971, Chaban-Delmas (then prime minister) could not bring himself to suspend French aid, since 'the role played there by our language in developing the thinking and training of men is too essential for our co-operation to be ended'.[21] In Senghor's words, 'What would the greatness of France amount to if her language and her culture did not shine over the five continents – this language and this culture to which we are passionately attached and on which we are counting to awaken and enrich our traditional civilisations?' Yet Senghor also once remarked: '*Cultural imperialism*, we too often forget, *is the most dangerous form of colonialism*.'[22] At a cultural level something of France's traditional Middle Kingdom complex survived decolonization.

At the 1981 elections the Socialists promised to complete France's adjustment to the post-imperial world order and inaugurate a new era in Franco-African relations based on co-operation in economic development rather than on military aid, which they criticized for fostering 'internal tensions'. As the first Socialist President of the Fifth Republic, however, Mitterrand had the arduous task of trying to move away from Giscard's neo-paternalism while at the same time seeking to reassure Africa's Francophone leaders that they could continue to 'rely on us'. Half-way through its five year term the Left-wing coalition government, deeply embroiled in military operations in Chad as well as peace-keeping in Lebanon, still found it difficult to reconcile those two objectives.

Part IV

The New International Society

23

A NEW INTERNATIONAL DISORDER

Elie Kedourie

Before 1914 world politics was very much the politics of European states. Relations among these states were fairly stable in their character, and their nature could be grasped and understood with the help of two organizing ideas. These organizing ideas were not imposed by students of international relations. They derived naturally, so to speak, from the way in which European states had come to conduct themselves toward one another. Nor were these organizing ideas simply theoretical concepts. They were also practical rules of thumb with which men of affairs were familiar, and by which they thought it prudent to be guided.

These two organizing ideas were, on the one hand, that of the balance of power, and, on the other, that of the concert of Europe. The notion of the balance of power meant that the security of each individual state, as well as the general peace, could best be preserved if the power and ambition of any state or combination of states could be counterbalanced or checkmated by a rival combination. About the operation of the balance there was of course nothing automatic. To establish and maintain a balance, which was as much worldwide as it was European, required acumen, boldness, cool heads, and moderation. Because the necessary wisdom and the requisite political skills were not always available, because miscalculations could always happen, the balance would sometimes overbalance and war would ensue. To end a war in a manner such that the balance could be re-established required as much skill and wisdom as to keep an existing balance in being. The outbreak of war in 1914 proved the most serious failure in balance-of-power politics in modern European history, and the so-called settlement which followed in 1918–19 was likewise the most serious failure to re-establish a balance – a failure whose consequences have proved infinitely ruinous for Europe and the world.

Underlying the notion of the balance of power is the other organizing idea, that of a concert of European states. The idea is no doubt more complex, less clear-cut, and certainly less amenable to use as a rule of thumb than that of the balance of power. This other idea assumes and expresses the consciousness of a common civilization, common political attitudes, and a common language of international politics. The idea is no doubt met most frequently in the nineteenth century, but this is not to say that it appeared suddenly during this period. The society of states it took for granted, the body of international law that articulated the assumptions and norms according to which such a society could function and endure, were in the making from the time of Grotius in the seventeenth century, and even before. We might say that a *locus classicus* where the system can be seen operating most clearly is the period in the eighteenth century lying between the settlement of the War of the Spanish Succession (1714) and the outbreak of the Revolution in France – a period the international relations of which are magisterially described and analysed in the first volume of Albert Sorel's *Europe and the French Revolution.*

The French Revolution posed a grave challenge to the European society of states and the assumptions on which it rested. The revolutionary ideology dismissed both balance and concert, and strove for hegemony and doctrinal uniformity. The threat was formidable and the triumph of the new order seemed at times inevitable and irresistible. But after a long struggle the threat of French hegemony was at last averted. The authors of the settlement which followed wished to look upon it as a restoration of the pre-1789 world. This of course it could not be, but it remains true that the dominant outlook within the European society of states up to 1914 accepted and took for granted the organizing ideas just described, which the French Revolution had attempted to sweep away.

The balance of power was destroyed during the war of 1914, and the Versailles settlement which followed, instead of re-establishing this balance, put the seal on its irremediable destruction. This was clearly seen when, less than fifteen years after Versailles, Germany under the Nazis embarked on an expansionist policy, and no combination of powers could be put together to act as a deterrent. At the heart of the Versailles settlement there was, it is true, an organizing idea which might look similar to that of the concert of Europe. The League of Nations was regarded as a kind of worldwide concert all of whose members accepted a commitment to act collectively against any disturber of the peace, thus making a balance of power – objected to by reason of its alleged amorality and cynicism, and its supposed tendency to encourage and justify armed conflict – superfluous. But involved in the idea of the League was an element at least as subversive of stability and peace as the Rights of Man had proved to be after 1789. This element, which was at the centre of the League covenant, was that of national self-determination.

The idea of national self-determination assumes quite simply that the world is composed of separate, identifiable 'nations', and claims that these nations are, as such, each entitled to form a sovereign state. Since, manifestly, the world is not what this theory assumes it to be, to make reality conform to the theory must involve endless upheaval and disorder. For one thing, it is by no means easy indisputably to identify these 'nations'; for another, to upset all existing arrangements in order to make national self-determination the sole and overriding aim of all political action is a recipe for perpetual war. National self-determination is thus a principle of disorder, not of order. This was clearly seen when German self-determination involved the destruction in turn of Austria, Czechoslovakia, and Poland – states which, ironically enough, had shortly before themselves been set up in the name of national self-determination.

The war of 1914 also led to the destruction of the old order in Russia and the foundation of the Soviet Union. This too introduced a potent source of disorder in international relations. Bolshevik doctrine in external affairs may quite accurately be summed up by Lenin's dictum about domestic politics: *Kto Kogo*? – 'who [will defeat] whom?' The doctrine of class struggle which this dictum encapsulates is the simple and barbaric one that politics is nothing more than a constant and deadly struggle for absolute and complete domination. Like the principle of national self-determination, that of the class struggle is incompatible with the notion of a balance of power, since balance means precisely that no single interest or principle can assume sole or overriding importance. The ideas of national self-determination and class struggle are also incompatible with the existence of a society of states whose members, irrespective of their own varied political and social arrangements, are and recognize themselves to be part of a more or less coherent international order. It is, incidentally, quite arresting – and ominous – that nuclear weapons, and the concept of a balance of terror associated with them, should so accurately mirror Lenin's maxim. For does not the balance of terror seem the concept most fitted to international relations disordered and subverted by the sway of these totalitarian principles?

World War II, which started as a European war, ended the centrality of Europe in world politics. But the much wider, and eventually world-wide, political stage saw, in the following decades, in an even more accentuated and acute form, the same systematic disorder in international relations which had already become manifest at the end of World War I. The United Nations, even more than the League, was incompatible with international order and stability. It is true that no particularly new organizing ideas or principles were associated with the United Nations. However, by 1945, the Bolsheviks and their doctrine had attained a respectability and influence which they simply did not have in 1918. But instead of seeking to counterbalance Soviet power and influence, Roosevelt worked relentlessly to diminish his Western allies and dismember their empires. There is no indication in recent studies such as Christopher Thorne's *Allies of a Kind* or William Roger Louis's *Imperialism at Bay* that Roosevelt or other US policymakers considered the consequences of doing away so completely with elements which might have helped to counter ambitions by their very nature relentless and limitless. Nor is there evidence that any thought was given to the way the new worldwide society of states was to operate.

An incident typifying the policy and its illusions was the manner in which US agents were instructed to welcome and encourage Ho Chi-minh in the innocent belief that here was another George Washington rising against arbitrary and despotic rule. What is so conspicuous by its absence at the time of Yalta was any awareness by the most powerful country in the world that here was a hinge of fate; that the international disorder which World War I and the ensuing settlement created was now threatening to spread more widely and becoming well-nigh impossible to extirpate. In an earlier crisis Edmund Burke saw clearly that here was no ordinary conflict, that what was being contended with was a formidable armed doctrine. No Burke now appeared. We had instead the Atlantic Charter – toothless pieties facing the armed doctrines of Bolshevism and nationalism.

Since 1945, increasingly so with the passage of years, these doctrines, destructive of international order, have secured a firmer purchase over international life. In the Third World, so-called, the two doctrines have combined in a powerful amalgam which is today the most widespread and the most attractive in Asia, Africa, and Latin America. This hybrid doctrine joins the Marxist emphasis on class warfare with the nationalist vision of a humanity divided into separate nations each one of whom has a claim to full and unfettered sovereignty. This doctrine, the most recent proponents of which are Frantz Fanon and his imitator Colonel Quadhdhafi, divides the world into 'northern', rich, exploiting nations and 'southern', poor, exploited nations. The true class struggle, the only one of any consequence in this view, is the struggle between these two groups of nations, not between proletariat and capitalists in an industrialized society.

One corollary of this analysis is the demand for a New Economic Order, so prevalent today, and voiced in so many quarters from UNCTAD to the Non-Aligned Movement and the Brandt Commission.

The demand for a New Economic Order really signifies that a massive transfer of resources from Western countries to the poor countries of the so-called South shall take place. The demand is justified by a variety of arguments among which loom large allegations about colonialism and neocolonialist exploitation resting on Marxist-Leninist assumptions of whose character the Western advocates of a massive transfer do not always seem aware.

The majority of states now in the United Nations loudly and self-righteously propound these demands. These states, or most of them, attained sovereign status in the period after 1945, as a result of the destruction or self-liquidation of the European empires. They are what Michael Oakeshott has called imitation states. They are formally sovereign, but their rulers labour under strong feelings of insecurity generated by their lack of legitimacy. The product of fake elections or military *coups d'état*, their unrestrained power does not rest on the loyalty of those whom they rule, and they lack the strength and self-confidence which accrues to those who can speak on behalf of a well-established body politic.

Hence these states, where private interests are wholly at the mercy of the rulers, and the public interest entirely what the rulers decree, are condemned to instability and civil commotions, which become cumulative, and progressively more aggravated. Hand in hand with this condition goes an ideological style of politics. Plans and blueprints, ambitious and arbitrary, in the absence of constitutional restraints are pursued by the rulers for the time being, only to be changed or scrapped at the rulers' whim, or as their fortunes dictate. Egypt under Nasser, Syria and Iraq under the Baath, Tanzania under Nyerere are leading examples of this state of affairs.

From the mid-1950s onward, the international disorder which was now endemic in the world – and of which the United Nations may be considered the symptom and the symbol – spread rapidly throughout Africa. 'Decolonization' suddenly became the settled policy of the British, the French, and the Belgians, a policy precipitately and thoroughly applied whatever the costs and the consequences. The policy was, by and large, the outcome of a unilateral decision taken by the metropolitan authorities, rather than a response to some overwhelming or irresistible pressure exerted by the African populations. The decision was based on a judgement about the worth to the metropolitan countries of administering these colonies. It was taken in the light of assumptions about the future tendencies of world politics, of the world balance of power, and of the manner in which this balance –

military as well as political – would be affected by the metropolitan countries relinquishing control over Africa.

There was in these judgements a large element of defeatism, complacency, cynicism, and sheer illusion. The defeatism is best exemplified by the stance which French ministers adopted towards Tunisia and Morocco in 1954–6 when, no doubt influenced by events in Indo-China, they hastily dismantled the protectorates in these two countries. The complacency may be illustrated by Harold Macmillan's well-known 'wind of change' speech, in which the British prime minister unveiled to the world the shape of things to come. If, to pursue his own metaphor, navigation consisted in drifting with the wind, few ships would manage to reach a safe haven. In any case, was there really a 'wind of change', or was it that the words and actions of metropolitan governments were raising a whirlwind – which would undoubtedly engulf their unfortunate African wards, but also damage their own strategic stance *vis-à-vis* the Soviet Union?

Neither African welfare nor the geo-political consequence of abandoning Africa seems to have been given much weight. This may have represented intellectual failure – akin to that which led civil servants in the Foreign Office to press for British withdrawal from Aden and the Persian Gulf in 1968–70 – but it was also the expression of a cynicism which was the ugly obverse of the complacency. De Gaulle may be said to illustrate this cynicism at its ugliest. Having decided that *l'Afrique est foutue et l'Algérie avec*, that these territories were not worth two cents, de Gaulle had no scruple in liquidating French rule abruptly and totally. In the case of Algeria, the abandonment was particularly scandalous. De Gaulle had come to power in 1958, the beneficiary of a *coup d'état*, as the one figure able and willing to maintain the French presence in Algeria. By 1960, the war against the FLN had been won on the ground. But by 1962 he had so manoeuvered as to abandon a territory and its inhabitants who had been under French rule for over a century, causing in the process large numbers of his fellow citizens to be massacred by the new rulers or to become penniless refugees.

De Gaulle chose to act as he did because he looked on Algeria and the African territories as an embarrassment which hindered him in his pursuit of super-power status. He clearly did not think that giving up control, say, of Algerian oil, or of the naval base at Oran, or of other territories inland would damage French military or economic interests. A mere two decades later his miscalculation is patent.

But if Western political leaders no longer harbour de Gaulle's haughty and disdainful illusions, there is still rife among them a cynicism, to be sure not as ruthless as that which de Gaulle was pleased to flaunt, but rather more soft-spoken and comfortable, snickering, shoulder-shrugging, and low-minded. This outlook is admirably captured in an article by Peregrine Worsthorne which appeared in the *Daily Telegraph* of London on 10 September 1979 – the first day of the conference which encompassed the transformation of Rhodesia into Zimbabwe:

The prospects of post-colonial Africa and Asia are beginning to look hideously ominous. For the time being the prevailing Western view is that this does not matter.

Our statesmen and businessmen like to think that Third World raw materials, on which Western prosperity vitally depends, will always be available under whatever political and social system prevails in those parts – short of Russian domination. I have even heard it argued, by a senior Conservative Minister no less, . . . that the more degraded the political and social system, the easier it will be to extract the precious oil and minerals, since trade nowadays follows, not the flag, but the bribe. According to this view it does not matter a damn – the word is well chosen – who governs Africa or Asia. The more corrupt the regime, the better Britain's interests will be served. That is the new *Realpolitik*, disguised under the pretty mask of racial equality.

The policy of 'decolonization' led to the setting up of European-style parliamentary regimes, the workings of which necessarily fell into the hands of European-educated Africans who speedily found themselves in a position both despotic and precarious. Despotic, because European-style government, whatever the paper checks and balances, quickly becomes transformed into an engine of oppression, all the more efficient for being endowed with European-style bureaucratic devices through which the life and livelihood of the ruled can be interfered with and controlled capriciously and minutely. But despotic as their powers are, the new rulers have, and are aware they have, a very precarious tenure. This is because there is little or no relation between the formal Western-style institutions of government and the traditional African society of which these new rulers, by some kind of magic, suddenly find themselves in control. This traditional society was a fragmented one, in which tribal loyalties and preferences ruled supreme. These attitudes naturally lead to the 'corruption' which is the generally recognized hallmark of the new states. But the idea of corruption is intelligible only where it is believed that government is and must be a government of laws, that public office is not a piece of property, and that the public interest cannot be a respecter of persons. A society in which these notions have no hold is one in which the idea of corruption is unintelligible. All this is to say that between the norms and the institutions of the 'decolonized' states and their social realities, between the form and the content, there is great contradiction and very dangerous tension.

In order to escape this tension which threatens their powers, the new rulers have recourse to ideological mobilization. They think to bind together in this way the body politic, to imbue it with the cohesiveness and solidarity on which the European-style institutions they operate are predicated. These ideologies are also derived from Europe, and they are the very same ones which have introduced instability and precariousness in the international order, namely, nationalism and Marxism-Leninism in one of its many varieties.

'Decolonization' has thus created an unstable and explosive situation in Africa where tribalism is at odds with European institutions of government, and where an ideological style of politics, instead of assuaging this conflict, serves to exacerbate it. Thus, the newly-created states find themselves endowed with frontiers which had been established as a result of European rivalries and compromises. A nationalist ideology predicated on the need for a cohesive, self-contained national entity is, in many places, at odds with the territorial arrangements inherited from the European empires. The civil wars in the Sudan, Nigeria, or Chad, or the war between Somalia and Ethiopia, are striking examples of conflicts which are the outcome of tribal differences now articulated – and exacerbated – by an uncompromising ideology: conflicts all the more savage and destructive now that what is at stake is the control of a state apparatus, and the enormous power such control is seen to confer. 'Decolonized' Africa is a potential minefield of similar conflicts.

'Decolonization', therefore, has not brought peace to Africa, and has probably increased the burden of insecurity and oppression which the African peoples carry. It has not made relations between the West and Africa more friendly or easier to manage. The complacency has proved to be mistaken, and the cynicism cheated of those banausic advantages the cynics profess to prize. Trade may follow the bribe, but even a child will realize that bribery can be no basis either for trade or friendship.

The world balance of power, moreover, has been seriously affected – for the worse, so far as Western interests are concerned. The new conditions have enabled the Soviet Union to manoeuvre, to bargain, to hold out political and military inducements, and thus to establish itself on a continent where Russian power and influence had hitherto been unknown. In large part, the new Soviet position in Africa is the beneficiary of the voluntary Western withdrawal. But the Soviets have not purely and simply occupied vacated ground. They have brought with them an ideological style of politics which, as has been seen, has many attractions in 'decolonized' Africa. The techniques of indoctrination and mass control that go with this style not only prove as welcome as political support and military supplies, but also constitute a point of affinity between what are essentially one-party states which differ only in point of efficiency and ruthlessness, and in which power is checked neither by law nor by scruple.

In recent years it has become fashionable, in the United States and Western Europe, to argue that world politics is no longer centred on the conflict between East and West, that the present challenge for the West lies in attracting the friendship and loyalty of the Third World. Even were the current military balance between East and West what it was ten or twenty years ago, this view would still be mistaken. In point of military or industrial power the Third World is negligible. Most of its states are not allies but clients. And, unfortunately, the reasons described above will necessarily make these unhappy regions, for as far as one can see, turbulent and the prey of a radical and deep-seated disorder. Turbulence can be held at bay or, better still, tamed. But you cannot sit down and smoke the pipe of peace with it, neither can you embrace it in friendship.

24

THE EXPANSION OF INTERNATIONAL SOCIETY: THE CONSEQUENCES FOR THE LAW OF NATIONS

Ian Brownlie

By the time of the first Hague Peace Conference in 1899 there had taken place a consolidation of a single system of international relations. The word 'system' begs a good many questions, of course. In practical terms and for present purposes it implies a more or less common set of forms, procedures, and political techniques for managing transactions and more general relations between states. The quality of the system was no doubt flawed in many ways. A number of political entities, such as Morocco, Egypt, the Somali tribes, and the Khanates of Bukhara and Khiva, were a part of the system by proxy and on conditions set by others. Turkey, China, Japan, and Siam were formal members of the community of states in 1899 but their enjoyment of rights was somewhat precarious. The principle of the legal equality of states had been affirmed by Vattel in his treatise published in 1758,[1] and this provided the formal basis for the development of the system.

Since the turn of the century major developments of the 'system' have taken place and the pattern of independent states is now very extensive and complex. The ambitious purpose of this essay is to sketch the role which the law of nations has played in – or perhaps it should be expressed as the ways in which the law of nations has reflected – the long process of consolidation or cumulative adhesion.

In general terms the role of the law must be seen at two levels (but it is not suggested that the two levels are necessarily distinct). At one level writers offer concepts and criteria relating to international affairs and these concepts and criteria may be either inclusive and 'liberal' or exclusive and 'collegiate'. At another level the legal practice of states and writers (in so far as writers at various periods have relied upon the evidence of state practice) may indicate the extent to which, if at all, the concepts and criteria have substance in the world of action.

In what follows certain intervals or periods are taken in a deliberately impressionist fashion as the convenient vehicle for exposition of the sequence of events and ideas. It is the elements in a long and complex process which matter and not the descriptive bindings used to contain the material.

I. The European States and the Stock of Concepts, 1648 to 1750

Whilst it is absurd to think that everything started in 1648, it is reasonable to assume that by the time of the Treaty of Münster and Peace of Westphalia the 'system' was already in being. A simple test is to note both the extensive political reach of the arrangements of 1648 and the Westphalian phase of state relations and also their long-standing role as important territorial settlements.

It is the current cliché to say that the law of nations has been 'europocentric' in nature. In a long retrospect this is true but only in the sense that *it happened* that a certain group of states were to become politically dominant in the world as a whole. This is a fact and not a qualitative assertion. It could have been the case that the Sultan of Turkey or the Empire of China came to exercise an over-all hegemony. Historically the system of state relations was administered by states the more influential of which were European or Christian in civilization. In any case the use of the term 'European' to apply to the situation prior to 1750 tends to involve some degree of a solecism,[2] and, apart from such categories, the state relations of the seventeenth century were not exclusively 'European' even in modern geographical terms.[3] The 'system' of state relations in this period included the Georgian Kingdoms, the Sultan of Turkey, the Empire of Russia, Algiers, Tunis, Siam, the Republic of Venice, the Khanate of the Krim Tartars, Morocco, and Tripoli.

In the period ending with the middle of the eighteenth century there appears both by way of inheritance and by recent invention a fairly complete stock of concepts bearing upon the inclusiveness or otherwise of the international system. The debates concerning the nature of relations with infidels antedate the Westphalian phase and, it is often forgotten, such debates had their counterparts in the Muslim world. The concept of 'organized states' as opposed to 'pirates' may be seen in the work of Bynkershoek.[4] In this context theory was already familiar with sovereignty and distinctions between princes but had not clearly formulated a test of 'civilization'. The period also witnessed the emergence of the concept of the balance of power.[5]

Historians of international law tend to overstress the significance of theory. In the period 1648 to 1750 there were no substantial limitations in the world of ideas beyond the view that the entities within the system should be 'organized states'. There was no conceptual limitation based upon religion and in practice the question of sovereignty did not appear to hinder the diplomatic activity of a great variety of principalities and other polities. The incorporation of the Ottoman Empire into the diplomacy of the eighteenth century was not thought to signal any revolution of categories.

II. Geographical Expansion and the Continuity of Concepts, 1750 to 1850

In the next century many factual and political limitations on the extension of the 'system' were removed by the process of discovery and colonization. The chief exception to this integration of control and cartography was the area of sub-Saharan Africa. In the world of ideas there was substantial continuity and consequently there were no categorical limitations based upon European civilization or religion.[6] However, in the early nineteenth century the exclusive principles of a public law, 'limited to the civilised and Christian people of Europe or to those of European origin', were emerging in the influential work of Wheaton.[7]

In the practical sphere the system of diplomacy expanded and was adopted by the United States and the successor states of Spanish America without any theoretical questions obtruding. The precise rules of international law and diplomacy were not divided off by cultural lines, and the apparatus of diplomacy was widely understood. Moreover, by the eighteenth century the content of diplomacy and the law of nations was more or less ideologically neutral and orientated to patterns of trade and influence, which were not dependent upon any particular principles other than the pragmatics of competition.

The law of nations was at this period concerned with the basic mechanics of state relations:

(a) the definition of the state and its appendages, such as the territorial sea;
(b) the mechanism of establishing and maintaining diplomatic relations;
(c) the forms of treaty-making;
(d) the law of war and neutrality.

Moral concerns were almost exclusively collateral: for example, there was a freedom to go to war but the law was concerned only with breaches of neutrality.

The only general wrong recognized in the law of nations was piracy and to this was added, eventually, the slave trade. Human rights were not a concern of the law: but they might be the concern of policy, as was the case when a certain muted concern was shown for the treatment of Jews in Imperial Russia. The practical and morally neutral concerns of the law of nations meant that the expansion, the 'exportability', of the system is not a matter for surprise.

It is instructive to study the pattern of treaty-making in the period between 1750 and 1850 and this may be done, by way of sample, by reference to the chronological list contained in the *Index to British Treaties 1101–1968* (HMSO, 1970), edited by Clive Parry and Charity Hopkins. An examination of the list reveals the incidence of Great Britain's 'extra-European' treaty partners as follows: Morocco 1750; Russian Empire 1750; Algiers 1751; Tripoli 1751, Tunis 1751; the Marattas 1756; Nizam of Hyderabad 1759; Mogul Empire 1763; Mysore 1769; United States of America (Treaty of Peace, 1783); Rajah of Nepaul 1792; Rajah of Assam 1793; Muscat 1798; Ottoman Porte 1799; Persia 1801; Kabool 1809; Kandy 1815; Ashantee 1817; King of Madagascar 1817; Perak 1818; Johore 1818; Sheiks of Bahrein 1820; Imaum of Senna (Yemen) 1821; United Provinces of Rio de la Plata 1825; Colombia 1825; King of Siam 1826; Ava (Burma) 1826; Brazil 1826; Mexico 1826; Venezuela 1834; King of the Zulus 1835; King of Bonny 1836; Chile 1839; Haiti 1839; The Confederation of the United Tribes of New Zealand (Treaty of Waitangi with 80 Chiefs) 1840; Texas 1840; Ecuador 1841; King of Shoa 1841; Uruguay 1842; Chief of the Basutos 1843; Sandwich Islands (Hawaiian Islands) 1843; Dahomey 1847; Borneo 1847; Nicaragua 1848; Liberia 1848; Guatemala 1849; Abyssinia 1849; Costa Rica 1849; Dominican Republic 1850; Peru 1850.

The countries have been named on the first occasion of appearance in the *Index* of the selected period. Numerous treaties with small polities and rulers and in the Indian sub-continent, the Persian Gulf, and various parts of west and southern Africa have been omitted. In each case the Treaty concerned must be presumed to involve an acceptance of the capacity of the other Party to enter into such an agreement with Great Britain.

There is good reason to assume that the British pattern of treaty-making was sufficiently representative of the activities of the more important powers of the time.[8] Moreover, to the treaty-making pattern there must be added the slowly extending pattern of permanent diplomatic representation, especially in Asia and Latin America.[9] Another sphere of relations of practical importance was the appointment of consuls and the negotiation of consular conventions. Special missions were sent to the more remote capitals.[10]

III. The Quality of the Expansion of the System of Diplomacy: Some Reservations

It is obvious that the making of treaties and the establishment of diplomatic and consular relations constitute a somewhat provisional basis for the expansion of a system of diplomacy. The fact that Ecuador in 1841 or Dahomey in 1847 concluded a treaty with Great Britain is not much evidence that the entities concerned had the means or the habit of mind necessary for the conduct of international relations according to reasonable criteria of efficiency, legality, and consistency. At the least such observance of forms is evidence of a certain aspiration or readiness to conform. Moreover, such transactions and contacts would sometimes promote the development of technical services and recourse to professional legal advice as a form of necessary diplomatic and political self-defence. In any case it would be unrealistic to set nice standards of professional preparedness and thus to ignore the untidy process by which weak and impoverished polities gradually establish themselves on the international plane. It is a salutary exercise to investigate the quality of legality *within* societies at the same period for purposes of fair comparison.

IV. The Unanswered Question of Locus Standi

It is apparent from the chronicle of British treaty-making in the century beginning in 1750 that the British Crown was willing to make formal arrangements with a great variety of political formations in widely differing contexts. In practical terms the question of delimiting the types of entity which counted was not faced – or rather it was faced only in political practice and not as a question of principle.

In the period up to the middle of the nineteenth century the practice reveals two characteristics. First, there was no regional or cultural limitation on recognition of personality in international relations. Secondly, there was no emphasis placed upon the formal criteria of 'statehood'. The legal doctrine of the time reflected this state of affairs. It followed that the existence, the sovereignty, of a state did not depend upon the recognition of other powers.[11]

By the middle of the nineteenth century and in the decades which followed the doctrine developed new features, to be seen in the works of Wheaton, Phillimore, Hall, and many others. Personality in the new doctrine depended upon recognition by the European States and recognition was not dependent upon any objective legal criteria. Statehood became a more important concept, and was associated with political thinking about 'nations', but in the law of nations the matter of definition was of no real significance: recognition, as the political stamp of approval, appeared to take care of the problem of definition.[12] None the less, in the middle of the nineteenth century and thereafter there was, of course, much speculation on the nature of the state, its purpose and so on. Such a work, which went into numerous editions in German and English, was Bluntschli's *The Theory of the State.*[13]

The change of doctrine interacted with an increase in European cultural chauvinism and racial theories. However, the practice did not undergo a sudden change and the lack of an interest in the formal criteria of statehood entailed a certain liberality. Thus it was not the case that tribal societies were ignored and their lands treated as *territorium nullius*. In this respect there was continuity of doctrine. Thus in Lindley's well-known study *The Acquisition and Government of Backward Territory in International Law,*[14] the view is expressed that:

> As an induction from all these instances . . . it appears that, on the whole, European States, in establishing their dominion over countries inhabited by people in a more or less backward stage of political development, have adopted as the method of such extension, Cession or Conquest, and have not based their rights upon the Occupation of *territorium nullius*.

In this tradition it was perfectly possible to conclude treaties with various types of social structure which had a territorial base: but there had to be some definable and unified social structure. Basutos and Zulus qualified whilst Australian aboriginals and Fuegian Indians did not. Feudal structures clearly qualified and thus vassalage did not necessarily rule out treaty relations. That the land belonging to tribal societies was not *territorium nullius* was affirmed by the International Court in its Advisory Opinion in the *Western Sahara* case.[15]

V. Conservatism in Principle and Flexibility in Practice, 1850 to 1950

In the period 1850–80 concepts developed towards a more exclusive system of diplomacy. Thus Hall[16] wrote that:

> International law consists in certain rules of conduct which modern civilised states regard as being binding on them in their relations with one another with a force comparable in nature and degree to that binding the conscientious person to obey the laws of his country, and which they also regard as being enforceable by appropriate means in case of infringement.

Similarly Oppenheim[17] wrote of the body of rules 'which are considered legally binding by civilised states in their intercourse with each other'. In another passage[18] Oppenheim remarks that 'the civilised states are, with only a few exceptions, Christian states. . .. '

There can be no doubt that the changes of conception had practical results. It has already been noted that the concept of statehood became more significant and, further, that determination of statehood was a question of recognition rather than the objective application of legal criteria.

Whatever the developments in doctrine in the period 1850 to 1880, the influence of the new doctrine should not be overestimated. With some exceptions, even the doctrine of the age of Imperialism did not adopt a rigid and exclusively europocentric concept. Christian and 'civilized' states were preferred, of course, and in the late nineteenth century ancient but weak states such as Ethiopia and Siam were in peril of partition, conquest, and general coercion. None the less, the working model of diplomacy remained flexible. The Law of Nations was not in practice confined either to European states or to states of European culture. China, Japan, Persia, Siam, Ethiopia and Madagascar were drawn into the general system of diplomacy.

The roster of states attending the Hague Peace Conferences is significant. Of the twenty-six states represented at the first Hague Conference of 1899, two were American (the United States and Mexico) and five were in some sense from Asia (China, Japan, Persia, Siam, and Turkey). This type of regional analysis has flaws, of course. Thus it is a matter of taste whether Turkey or Montenegro are placed in one or another grouping. The second Hague Peace Conference of 1907 was attended by forty-four states. This number included the same group from Asia, and sixteen Latin-American Republics, to which may be added Haiti and the Dominican Republic.

The period between 1850 and 1950 is complex and many elements are present. The appearance of a strong and diplomatically active Japan and the general survival of independent Asian states are major features. India and Pakistan were to become independent in 1947. Thus by 1950 the programme of independence for *all* the regions of the world was well established and, by a paradox, the programme was based in part on the principle of self-determination generated in European politics in the years 1789 to 1848, and much invoked in the deliberations at the Paris Peace Conference of 1919 to 1920.

The family of Latin American states developed. Chile, Argentina, and Brazil evolved as sophisticated members of the diplomatic community, with experienced statesmen and professional foreign services.

The debates in the Chilean and Argentine national assemblies on the Boundary Treaty of 1881 evidence a high level of sophistication and a general sensitivity to international experience in matters such as arbitration and neutralization of waterways.

In the era of the League of Nations a number of states appeared for the first time: Afghanistan,[19] Iraq, Hejez-Nejd, Albania,[20] Yemen, Yugoslavia, Czechoslovakia, Irish Free State, Finland, Estonia, Latvia, and Lithuania. Poland was able to recover her independence.

Within the British Empire, the so-called 'old Dominions' were masked somewhat by the relation with London and the 'Inter Se' doctrine. Thus the evolution of a mature apparatus of external affairs in Canada was slow. Canada assumed full responsibility for the negotiation of settlements of international claims only in the decade before the Second World War. Independence in the negotiation and signing of treaties evolved by 1923 and this precedent was to be endorsed at the Imperial Conference of 1926.

In other respects the earlier patterns were repeated during the late nineteenth century. Various rulers in Africa and Asia were treated with on the basis that they possessed legal personality for various practical purposes. Treaties were made with the Basutos, Somalis, and other polities not conforming to European conceptions of statehood. The two paths of extinction of personality continued to be the treaty of cession and conquest. Burma, Madagascar, and other polities from the earlier period ceased to be independent. Treaties of protection would lead in practice either to a quasi-independence like that of Morocco or to a directly imposed colonial regime as in the case of the Somalis.

VI. The Paradox of Colonialism

In the modern period of significant European political expansion a major paradox is present. No doubt the British and others were prepared to make treaties with tribal societies like the Basuto and Somalis. The fact remains that before European penetration such societies were to a degree cut off from participation in international diplomacy. Having been colonized, they became part of the world of general diplomacy – but lost their separate personality. However, and herein lies the paradox, European ideas of nationhood and self-determination were adopted and resulted, eventually, in a programme of statehood, and not a desire for a simple restoration of the traditional *status quo ante*. Colonialism and other external influences provided a very radical element in African and Middle Eastern affairs. The outcome has been that various societies have been brought, however precariously and artificially, into the orthodox system of diplomacy and statehood. This general perspective remains valid in spite of the fact that in certain cases, such as Morocco or Tunisia, there has been a certain political continuity with the period before the transient extra-regional hegemony.

VII. Main Features of the Period 1850 to 1950

In certain respects this period was revolutionary. In respect of the forms and techniques of international law and organization there was a series of radical developments: the appearance of international organizations of states, the creation of a code of the law of war, the development of the procedures of arbitration and conciliation, the setting up of the first standing international court in 1922, the appearance of the first universal organization for the maintenance of peace, and substantial changes in the law relating to the use of force by states as an instrument of national policy.

In spite of these striking developments the general political scene changed but slowly. Apart from the dissolution of the Ottoman Empire and the appearance of some new states in Europe (the Baltic Republics, Finland, and Czechoslovakia, among others), no great political changes took place – although in retrospect the period may be seen as the prelude to a period of rapid decolonization.

The conservative nature of the system of diplomacy in this period stems from a variety of factors. The first of these was the obvious influence of European and American power. The South Americans, for example, could not easily exercise influence. It is symptomatic of the period that South American states (and also China and Japan) were apt to use international law, as it were, for defensive purposes, although this ceased to be true of Japan at a certain stage. Indeed, the strategy generally adopted by China, Japan, and Siam was to learn the 'rules of the game' as quickly as possible. This involved translations of British, French, and American books on international law and the employment of foreign advisers.

Yet another, and very basic, element of conservatism was the fact that the content of the law remained, as before, neutral and relatively unambitious. Inequalities in legal relationships were the result of the use of orthodox forms. Thus the institution of Capitulations did not involve any structural or normative development, and accordingly the abolition of Capitulations was a matter of politics and not of legal and normative development.

However prominent the conservative features of the system at this period, there was some scope for multilateral diplomacy. In other words the small and medium states acting in concert had a certain influence even if this sometimes resulted only in a stalemate. Developments were not in any simple sense europocentric. The small powers had a role in the design of the Permanent Court of International Justice, and the failure of the Hague Codification Conference of 1930 was the result of significant differences of opinion which were not reduced or reconciled by means of bargaining between caucuses, as might happen today. Indeed, the differences were not related to regional politics. In the context of the treatment of aliens, the 'national treatment' principle received support not only from Latin American delegations but also from the smaller states of Europe. However, the potential role of regionalism was revealed by the voting strength of Latin America in the United Nations at its foundation (20 states out of a membership of 51).

VIII. The Period 1950 to 1960

The decade which opened with the Korean War can be seen in retrospect as a period of transition, involving a move from war and 'Cold War' to a more stable period of competition, and witnessing the major onset of decolonization in the years 1955 to 1960. During this process of rearrangement of the political scene the world of international law continued much as before. Certain innovations were made and among these was the creation of the International Law Commission in 1949: thus the defects of the League era in the sphere of codification and the machinery therefore were remedied. In general the legal innovations of the period – or at least those innovations which were successful – may be traced to the 'conservative' states of the Western world, acting either individually or collectively. These innovations were principally the concept of the exclusive rights of the coastal state in the resources of the continental shelf and the development and elaboration of human rights standards as legal standards, a process which was initiated by the Universal Declaration of Human Rights adopted by the General Assembly in 1948. The strength and also the limitations of *bloc* politics operating in the framework of a law-making conference may be seen in the first and second United Nations Conferences on the law of the sea of 1958 and 1960 respectively.

IX. The Period 1960 to 1980

After 1960 what came to be known as the 'Third World' or the 'Group of 77' emerged as a political force to be reckoned with and as a vehicle for radical legal and institutional developments. The Group of 77 was created in 1964 and in late 1980 its membership totalled 122.[21] An associated development was the convening of UNCTAD I in Geneva in 1964. The changes in the composition of the United Nations resulted in Third World initiatives intended to establish new legal concepts or to give legitimacy to existing political concepts. The areas concerned included the principle of self-determination, the concept of permanent sovereignty over natural resources, the 'common heritage of mankind' in respect of the resources of the 'international seabed area', the law relating to the consequences of changes of sovereignty such as decolonization (which lawyers describe as 'state succession'), and the concept of the exclusive economic zone in respect of resources of the marginal sea and the seabed out to a maximum limit of 200 miles from the baselines.

In practice the impact of the multilateral diplomacy of the Group of 77 has varied. On certain fronts, such as decolonization in Africa and concern with racial discrimination, the effects have been considerable. However, the degree of change has been restricted by certain significant countervailing elements. These elements are difficult to quantify individually but in sum they are far from negligible. The first such element is, quite simply, the continuing effectiveness of Western diplomatic influence; and it should not be forgotten that Soviet policies on certain questions are aligned with those of the Western group. In the second place a proportion of the new states have tended to behave conservatively after decolonization, a fact which is not always appreciated and which is not always reflected in the general statements of policy produced by governments. Thirdly, the delegations of Western states have often been able to use technical expertise or diplomatic pressure, or a combination of these, to bring about *coups* in the formulation of key texts. Examples of these may be found in the Geneva Convention on the Territorial Sea and Contiguous Zone of 1958 and in General Assembly Resolution 1803 of 1962 on Permanent Sovereignty over Natural Resources.

There are yet other elements which may be conservative in effect and thus classifiable as countervailing, but are more or less unpredictable in terms of consequences. This may be true of the recent exercises in 'soft law', such as the self-imposition of 'guidelines' for the operations of multinational entities. Similar in character is the open-textured and programmatic drafting of parts of the major Convention on the Law of the Sea produced by the third United Nations Conference on the Law of the Sea in the years 1974 to 1982.

X. The Existing System of Diplomacy: An Account

Four features call for emphasis. The first of these is the unmitigated complexity of state relations. Out of hundreds of examples two may be given. Different versions of the law of the sea apply *in practice* to the relations of different states: there is the pre-1958 customary law, the rules based upon the Geneva Conventions of 1958, and a third version which consists of one or other of these, modified by certain aspects of the Informal Composite Negotiating Text of recent vintage, which have been co-opted by certain states in their actual practice. Again, until 1976 Japan had contracted out of all post-1945 developments in the law of the sea, assuming the role of 'persistent objector'. As a consequence Japanese acceptance of new norms had to be purchased by way of a series of political bargains.

A second feature is the *extent* of the matters now governed either by customary international law or by treaty obligations. This extended accountability of states is to be seen in the fields of human rights, economic relations, and the protection of the environment. The conventional view is that this spread of international law into new fields is inevitable and necessarily beneficial, and yet there are some questions. Until *national* legal systems improve their performance it is naïve to put faith in 'progress by [international] legislation'. Legality and administrative competence are important at both national and international levels of action. In the same connection the very concept of legality has become overstretched in international affairs. Many treaties and other legal instruments are in reality mere transactions. We have reached a stage at which almost every disappointed expectation is liable to be rated as a 'breach of international law'. The consequence is that the 'performance of international law' is assessed in an atmosphere of unreality and objectives are set which would be over-optimistic for any kind of legal system.

A third feature involves first the statement of two hypotheses. Suppose that decolonization (in the classical or conventional sense) has been taken to the end of the agenda and suppose that other hegemonial and usurping relations have been terminated. What problems then remain? The crude but essentially truthful answer is that *all* the structural problems of international relations will remain. The changes of the last decades, important though they have been, have involved no more than the reassembling of the cast of international relations, and various changes in power quotas. The basic causes of disputes and conflicts remain unchanged. The constant insistence on 'advances in technology' is an irrelevance except in the sense that the consequences of disputes and conflicts are increased on an appalling scale which includes nuclear exchange. All the old problems remain. The machinery of peaceful settlement of disputes is more or less in the state in which it was by 1870 or 1900. The question of making new rules of international law by majority consent still collides with the necessity to foster change on the basis of acceptance by dissentient states: and this is also a problem seen in the affairs of federal systems within states.

The final observation is appropriately the most general: state relations have not changed very much in their essence. The raw nationalism and religious bigotry of the new states augurs not only a lack of change in the future but perhaps a pace or two backwards. 'Internationalism' and other phrases are bandied about but not matched by the necessary practical action. The 'expansion of international society' and 'the expansion of international law' have nothing to do with integration or real sophistication in conduct of affairs, and the reality is that there are now more states to quarrel and more questions to quarrel about. The only real issues are crisis management and the peaceful settlement of disputes. Success in crisis management cannot depend on law – although legal forms and devices may be used in structuring and elaborating a solution, at the post-clinical stage so to speak. Greater sophistication in the peaceful settlement of disputes involves greater use of existing legal techniques and machinery. It also requires a more mature approach by the political systems *within states*. The recent conduct of China and Vietnam in approaching legal problems relating to land and maritime boundaries is a depressing example of a style of diplomacy more suited to eighteenth-century Europe. At least Vattel and his contemporaries formulated the principle, which is the structural principle of state relations, of the equality of states. It is international law and the procedures for peaceful settlement which can do much to prevent equality from amounting merely to an anarchy of obdurate nationalisms and theocracies.

25

DIPLOMACY TODAY

Michael Palliser

The diplomacy of developed states, and especially of major powers with many traditions of foreign policy, has often been described in recent years: and I do not propose to retread the published ground. Instead I want to consider how the practice of diplomacy has been affected by the expansion of international society – that is to say, by the addition of new states, particularly in Africa and Asia, and by the greater involvement of all states in the conduct of world affairs.

First, what do we mean by 'diplomacy'? Many definitions have been suggested. But let me, for the sake of convenience, adopt Hedley Bull's: diplomacy is 'the conduct of relations between states and other entities in world politics by official agents and by peaceful means'.[1] A more detailed discussion of diplomacy is given in Chapter 1 of Satow's *Guide to Diplomatic Practice*, the diplomat's bible.[2] But we will do well to remember the fundamental and continuing need for states to communicate through individuals whose authority to speak for the state is undoubted and whose communications can be private.

Changes in technology have vastly improved the security and speed of communication between missions abroad and their governments and encouraged the growth of telegraphic traffic. As a result governments react much more quickly to world events, and they maintain a closer and more constant dialogue with their representatives abroad, and thus with other governments. Rapid transport too has had a dynamic effect. On the one hand it has encouraged a much greater frequency of meetings between government representatives at all levels; in particular the summit meetings discussed below. On the other hand, the demands of contemporary tourism, international business, and easy emigration loom ever larger in the calculations of national interest.

The spread of television and the use of satellites for transmission have increased public awareness of foreign policy issues through the immediacy and depth of coverage of far away events. The growing public demand in the democracies for more open government and ever easier access to government information means that the classic techniques of discreet and secret diplomacy have had to be adapted to cater for more public exposure and critical analysis. Diplomatic activities have to be justified more rapidly, carefully, and honestly than in the past, though more authoritarian governments of countries old and new still maintain greater secrecy.

The extent of technological change and the growth of multilateral diplomacy have encouraged the question whether diplomatic missions in traditional forms are any longer necessary to fulfil the indispensable functions of communication between states and between them and other recognized political entities. Recent developments also require us to ask first whether traditional diplomatic missions can still properly fulfil this role. It is worth examining the value and the practicality of present forms of diplomacy in the light of the recent spate of murders, kidnappings, and hostage-taking in the diplomatic world. Diplomacy has been well described as one of the most dangerous of professions, and the institutions of diplomacy have been said to be in urgent need for review by the international community. The whole system of diplomatic representation has been described as being 'under siege'.

The trend is indeed disturbing and the dangers and inconveniences real; but they are far from new and the recent upsurge does not necessarily mean that the institutions of diplomacy are at fault. In most parts of the world the basic diplomatic conventions are observed – at least in form. This is as true of most of the developing world as of the West. Three British Embassies for example were recently burnt down in a dozen years, but such attacks have not been confined to the developing world, and it was in Western Europe that two British Ambassadors were murdered. While there is little doubt that some governments are occasionally less vigilant in preventing – they may even connive at – attacks by mobs on the Embassies of foreign powers who are considered in some way to have offended them, apologies, protection, and offers of compensation tend to be promptly given.

The great shock caused by the holding of hostages in Iran arose not only from the act itself, but from the unprecedented rejection of normal diplomatic behaviour implied by the support given to the students by the Iranian authorities. This major breach by a constituted government of an international convention generally regarded as necessary for the effective conduct of diplomacy was deplored by the Security Council at the United Nations, which was unanimous in calling for the release of the hostages; and the International Court of Justice made an order for their release. Terrorist acts should not be allowed to induce the belief that a code of practice which has been developed over centuries, and which for the most part works well, is in imminent danger of collapse. The Heads of State and Government of the seven major industrial nations meeting in Venice in June 1980 affirmed their determination to deter and combat terrorist acts, condemning vigorously the taking of hostages and the seizure of diplomatic premises and personnel. These sentiments are generally shared by the international community, new and old states alike. If minimum conditions of safety cannot be guaranteed, missions may have to be withdrawn. El Salvador has furnished a recent example of conditions where the cost of ensuring the security of the diplomatic mission outweighed in the eyes of several governments the advantages of keeping the post in existence. But so far this has rarely seemed the right course of action.

When serious attacks on embassies or diplomats occur, a natural reaction is to demand that diplomatic relations be broken, and a failure to do this may be held to imply that the state concerned does not take the breach seriously. But while the breaking of diplomatic relations may be an unequivocal sign of its displeasure, a government must be concerned with the protection of its citizens, property, and investments in the foreign country and its trade, all of which are rendered more difficult if the mission is withdrawn. In the most serious cases, a break in relations may be inevitable. Some Third World governments also break relations with other states as a symbolic gesture of protest at their policies. However, governments normally prefer to maintain at least nominal relations and contact; either through an accredited mission of their own, albeit much reduced, or through the good offices of a protecting power or through representation from a neighbouring capital. These expedients are adopted in order to preserve a channel of communication and to make it easier to restore full working relations when conditions improve. Not to break relations does not mean that an offence is condoned – any more than the maintenance of a permanent mission means that the politics of a particular foreign government are endorsed.

It is sometimes alleged that the 1961 Vienna Convention on Diplomatic Relations – the basic agreement which re-codified those rules – recent though it is, is nevertheless unfair to those newly independent states which had no part in its drafting, and that it is inappropriate to developing countries because it is based on Western practice and ideals. A very wide spread of countries with different interests participated in the negotiation of the Convention which was itself based on customary law and on practice. The inviolability of envoys is intimately connected with their ability to act as effective channels of communication and can be traced back to 'time immemorial'. It was the practice in primitive societies, though the beginnings of modern practice date from medieval times. It is furthermore of the essence of the rules that they are reciprocal – the sending state has obligations as well as privileges and immunities, and the roles of the receiving and sending states are reversed in the other country. The benefits of the Convention should apply equally to both states. Most newly independent countries appear to recognize this by subscribing to the Convention and conforming to the norms of diplomatic practice. Some forty states signed the Vienna Convention when it was opened for signature in 1961. Not surprisingly in view of the date not many were newly independent, though a good few could claim to be members of the Third World. Now ratifications and accessions have reached nearly 140 including most African and Asian states. This is not surprising. Reciprocity implies equality of treatment and the somewhat stately forms of diplomatic protocol have an evident value as a shock-absorber in times of crisis, as well as marking the dignity and respect which the new states are naturally anxious to establish as their due.

As the diplomatic corps has grown, the special status of diplomats and their immunities has also been questioned as being too widespread and, perhaps, out of place in more egalitarian societies. What cause special irritation to the general public are the ostentatious, though essentially trivial, abuses of privilege, e.g. illegal parking. But as Satow puts it, immunities and privileges allow Ambassadors and their staffs 'to act independently of any local pressures in negotiations, to represent a foreign state under protection from attack or harrassment, to speak freely to their own governments and they are thus essential to the conduct of relations between independent sovereign states'.[3] Immunity has to be general. There can be no exception for certain sorts of offence, whether car parking or espionage, since the definition of the crime would be in the hands of the receiving state and the possibility of abuse too great. Diplomatic immunity does not, of course, mean that the diplomat can transgress the host country's laws with impunity. He may be subject to disciplinary measures by his own service and for serious crimes he may be liable under the law of his own state. But, if he transgresses, the only penalty open to the offended state – and this is spelt out in the Vienna Convention itself – is expulsion as *persona non grata*.

Somehow there continues to be in some sense a 'historic commonality' of all diplomats, irrespective of their country of origin. They are engaged in a continuous dialogue and negotiations not only with host governments but also with each other; they all have an interest in access to the government to which they are accredited, and in general freedom of movement. These requirements of the profession are as important to diplomats as the inviolabilities of their persons and their embassies, and all diplomats have a common interest in maintaining them.

But let us look at the role of the diplomat himself in the changed and expanded environment in which he is operating.

The United Nations is the best illustration of the expansion of international society. It had 51 members in 1945. By 1959 it had 81. During the next decade nearly fifty more states joined, mainly from Africa, so that by 1970 there were 127 members and by 1981 there were 157. The states of Africa and Asia now make up more than half the UN membership. The expansion of the membership has emphasized the great disparity in size, in military, economic, and political power, and in experience in foreign relations between the members; in spite of which there is fundamental equality in voting power in the Assembly to which the smaller states attach greater importance. For the West the changed distribution of voting strength seems inadequately related to the realities of power. For the new states, the existing procedures, notably relating to the Security Council, seem weighted against them.

The United Nations continues to show itself an unexpectedly durable and vigorous collective institution. Its various organs have shown considerable adaptability in dealing with an expanding range of problems, and have proved empirically useful in a number of unforeseen ways. It has grown numerically as a result of the admission of many new members, and also functionally in answer to their needs. This responsiveness to changing practical requirements is what makes the organization valuable to its member states.

The presence of such a large proportion of newly independent states has tended to focus attention on certain issues of particular concern to them, e.g. anti-colonialism, apartheid, or racial discrimination. The gaining of independence by a majority of former colonial possessions of established powers has focused attention on those dependent territories which still remain. The continued existence of dependent territories has resulted in criticism from the non-West and, on occasion, in diplomatic difficulties between the colonial power and other states which may consider themselves to have some claim to the territory. There may be conflict between the desires of the non-West to see colonies gaining independence and those of the peoples directly concerned. And decolonization of 'mini-states' creates further problems by leading to the formation of a number that are often scarcely capable of assuming the responsibilities traditionally expected of member states of international society.

For understandable reasons many newly independent states have preferred to distance themselves from East and West and find common ground in the Non-Aligned Movement, and have started 'regional' groups which have grown as international society has expanded. Many have established a permanent secretariat. There is by no means unanimity of view among their members on important questions. But the newly independent states share a common sympathy with 'liberation movements', whether or not they acquired their own independence by force. They tend to favour the recognition of groups which claim to be representatives of the people of a colonial or other territory without fulfilling the normal criteria for a recognized government. The PLO is recognized by many as 'the sole representative of the Palestinian people' and has been granted observer status at the UN; and other liberation movements have had similar or more privileged status accorded to them at Non-Aligned conferences in international fora. This general attitude of newly independent states today corresponds to that of the newly independent republics of the Americas early in the nineteenth century.

The newly independent states have played a specially important role in economic negotiations, finding an identity of interest as developing countries. This finds expression in the so-called Group of 77 – which now in fact numbers over 120 and which acts as a pressure group to oblige developed countries to share their economic wealth and the 'management of the world economy'. The success of OPEC in determining oil prices has encouraged developing countries to try to achieve greater influence on marketing and stabilization of export earnings for the commodities they produce. This has led to a number of attempts to resolve by multilateral diplomatic action differences between the developing and developed worlds in what has become known as the North-South dialogue. The importance of this dialogue has been emphasized in the report of the Brandt Commission; and for some it has become the primary purpose of the United Nations.

The functioning of G77 as a pressure group is illustrated in the United Nations Conference on Trade and Development (UNCTAD) which the developing countries tend to regard as their organization – contrasting it with OECD, GATT, or the IMF which they feel to be dominated by the developed countries. In UNCTAD there tends to be a politicization of what developed countries see as technical issues (as happens also in the specialized agencies of the United Nations). There is a clear difference of approach between the developing and developed states. The former tend to argue about matters of principle, e.g. the restructuring of the world economic order, while developed states argue that a new order can only be brought into practice by detailed changes in the individual institutions, agreements, trading, and financing arrangements which make up the current system. Developing countries see these systems as creations of the older and Western states, and change as an imperative of the new world order. A rather similar phenomenon is to be found in UNESCO where the developing states have been working for a new world information order, which would help them to assert government control over the media.

There is a great disparity between voting power and economic strength in UNCTAD, and resolutions carried only by the votes of developing countries are unlikely to have much practical effect. And G77 is a very heterogeneous group which arrives at a negotiating position only after much debate; positions, once agreed, are difficult to change, leading to greater inflexibility in negotiations. The solidarity of G77 increases pressure on the developed countries, the so-called Group B, to maintain their own solidarity. The process of reaching consensus through contact groups, in the absence of a truly intermediary role on the part of the Secretariat, is very time-consuming and labour-intensive, as are, of course, the negotiations within the groups themselves. But it is this *search for consensus* which is the prevailing trend in most multilateral fora where voting rules are not too deeply entrenched.

Negotiations in UNCTAD or in a large-scale specialized conference, with more than 150 members, such as the United Nations Law of the Sea Conference (UNLOSC) are of particular interest because the size of the Conference and the complexity of the issues have required the development of new diplomatic techniques. UNLOSC in particular has made extensive use of informal negotiating groups and has sought to reach consensus on issues by using informal texts drafted by Chairmen of groups and committees.

In multilateral conferences the groups which evolve may often reflect regional organizations which have grown in number as international society has increased in size. As an example we may quote the Organization of African Unity (OAU) which was formed very early in the process of decolonization; its charter covers the promotion of unity in Africa, co-operation, and defence as well as the eradication of colonialism. Other examples are the Association of South East Asian Nations (ASEAN) formed in 1967 with primarily economic motives, and the Caribbean Common Market (CARICOM) formed in 1973. The Organization of American States has been in existence since before the turn of the century, but the sixties and seventies saw the formation of a number of regional economic organizations in Latin America (the Latin America Free Trade Organization, the Central American Common Market, the Andean Group, and the Sistema Economico Latino-americano).

There are comparable European organizations, many of which like the OECD, the Council of Europe, and NATO grew out of the needs of war-time and the exigencies of post-war economic reconstruction and defence. But the intensive European experience of consultation on economic and defence matters is reflected in the way in which the Europeans, on both sides of the Iron Curtain, increasingly seek to act in concert with their partners and allies in political matters. To take the members of the European Community for example, the practice of political co-operation, which proved so effective in the Conference on Security and Co-operation in Europe, was progressively extended in the actions of the Ten at the UN or in reacting to events around the world. And on matters governed by the Treaty of Rome, the member states find themselves more and more frequently represented in multilateral negotiations by the Presidency (the government of the presiding member of the Community, an office which rotates every six months) and/or the Commission. The intensive co-ordination meetings which are thus required behind the scenes are a fresh challenge to European diplomats, though they parallel the nature of the negotiating process at the heart of the European Community in Brussels.

Regional organizations often have Secretariats and Secretaries-General who may be accorded diplomatic status and become important diplomatic figures in their own right. Their constitution may make provision for Assemblies, Councils of Ministers, and Heads of Government meetings, thus enabling another form of multilateral diplomacy. It is often within these regional frameworks, which provide an answer to the unwieldy size of a global society of over 150 states, that the habit of consultation at the highest level has developed.

The Commonwealth in its modern form shares some of the characteristics of a regional organization (and indeed some of its members hold regional meetings). It has changed markedly as international society has grown, from a few countries with a shared British background to a diverse group of more than forty-five members, sharing historical links with Britain from their colonial past but with most of them participating also in the Non-Aligned Movement or one of the regional groupings such as the OAU or ASEAN. The Commonwealth has a permanent secretariat with a Secretary-General who plays an influential role in Commonwealth affairs.

Another tendency which has been fostered by the development of regional organizations is the increasing frequency of personal meetings of Heads of State or government known as 'summit diplomacy'. The practice is of course not new; European and Indian history in particular are full of celebrated meetings of rulers. But the ease of modern communication has nowadays made it almost a commonplace, and since it is eminently newsworthy there is a danger that too much is expected of it. It undoubtedly has its place in modern diplomacy, for it permits the government leaders ultimately responsible for decision to learn at first hand the views of their opposite members, and the problems which their own preferred courses of action may cause for leaders in other countries whose support and goodwill they need. Leaders of new and Third World states in particular like to see and hear for themselves, and to strike personal bargains and establish a personal relationship with other heads of govenment. But if the meetings are not carefully prepared, they become sterile. By themselves they will rarely produce solutions; but the personal education of heads of government is valuable, and a coherent statement of joint purpose which may emerge from a summit carries authority.

The expansion of international society has certainly had its effect in the world of multilateral diplomacy. It is here that change has been most manifest. Negotiation has always been a classic diplomatic skill and in big conferences or international bodies the art of negotiation remains an essential lubricant of world affairs. But the new 'group' techniques evolved at the UN, in UNLOSC or UNCTAD are likely to be further developed in future. The need to reach consensus and the subsequent search for 'something for everybody' or 'equal dissatisfaction' may result in the preparation of texts which are deliberately ambiguous. But even these can be constructive.

The complexity of the system and the process of negotiation in large international conferences is in some ways more akin to domestic politics than to traditional foreign policy because the negotiations may involve many highly technical questions, the outcome of which may be of great significance for particular sectors of domestic economies. Experts from the relevant domestic sectors are necessarily directly involved in the negotiations; and governments therefore increasingly assign officials from other ministries or departments to them. Some governments, especially those without developed and long-standing diplomatic services, often resort to parallel contacts outside diplomatic channels, such as businessmen, distinguished visitors, and journalists. There has also been an inevitable growth of diplomacy by telephone. This often leads to the lack of a single co-ordinated voice of a government in the international dialogue, and to the exporting of bureaucratic infighting and disagreement between departments of a government. An important role therefore remains to be played by the professional diplomats who know the international institutions concerned and how to negotiate with them, and who are aware of the need to ensure that their government speaks with a single co-ordinated voice. In many countries Ministries of Foreign Affairs perform a co-ordinating role at home in order to ensure that the foreign policy implications of individual domestic decisions are kept in mind and to prevent an uneconomic expansion of foreign policy staffs in domestic Ministries. Such negotiating fora therefore require adaptation by diplomats to new frameworks of negotiation, while at the same time underlining the continuity of the basic diplomatic skills.

On the other hand the technicality of the issues often places special burdens on diplomats from smaller countries, especially many of the newly independent ones. It may be impossible for their capitals to keep abreast of developments or to form a view on every issue. A great deal of discretion will rest with the leader of the delegation who may well have the opportunity to influence the policy of his group or the latitude to follow group consensus.

Though the view is sometimes expressed that improved communications, faster travel, and the growth of multilateral diplomacy make the traditional forms of bilateral diplomacy irrelevant in modern conditions – even 'as obsolete as the sailing vessel' – yet missions in, or accredited to, capitals survive and proliferate. No modern state considers it feasible to handle its external relations solely through the United Nations or one or other of the regional groupings.

There are of course good practical arguments in favour of bilateral missions. They normally carry out consular, commercial, information, and other functions which only the most extreme critics would argue could be dispensed with entirely. These might be tackled in other ways, but they are an inherent part of the essentially political function of such missions.

There is also some tendency to argue that sufficient information is available from the media to make the role of missions abroad in reporting political events unnecessary. But media reporting is necessarily selective and mainly concerned with 'news'. Coverage of many countries in the media, even in newspapers of record, may be sparse or non-existent, and reliance on media reports alone would leave important gaps in knowledge. Moreover, the governments of many new states distrust the news media, which they regard as under the control of developed countries. Virtually all governments feel the need for informed comments from their own man on the spot, based on local knowledge and confidential high-level contacts, in order to achieve a balanced view of local events.

Governments also need to have this informed advice applied and made relevant to the practical prosecution of a government's interests. For instance as domestic economies everywhere come increasingly under the control of governments, international traders have to do more business with governments (now often the largest buyers and sellers, and sometimes virtually the only ones). Businessmen, therefore, need more help from their own government, and from its agencies in foreign countries – that is, its resident diplomatic and consular officials – in their commercial negotiations with foreign governments. Local knowledge, both of the country and of the state of bilateral relations, commercial, consular, and political, will also help a Head of Mission to influence the form and content of instructions he may receive from home. There is room for argument about the right amount of political reporting by an Embassy and what resources should be devoted to it. But the answer has to be based on judgement, rather than on quantitative analysis.

The majority of governments, old and new, clearly accept the continuing need to maintain missions overseas. The result is that as the number of independent states has grown to more than 160, states with worldwide interests have felt a parallel need to increase the number of their missions overseas. The Plowden Committee in 1964 saw a need for Britain to maintain a wide spread of representation abroad, and a British Government report in 1978 saw a 'greater not a lesser need for effective overseas representation'. The number of British missions abroad accredited to capitals has expanded to more than 150, though they include twenty-six capitals in which we have no resident mission. Most of our European partners have similarly increased their number of overseas posts over the past decade. This expansion has put a great strain on staff and financial resources. Although English or French is adopted by many of the newly independent states as a vehicular national language and by nearly all as a medium for external relations, resources have to be devoted to training in a wide range of local languages to ensure that the diplomats sent abroad are able to understand the countries they work in rather than relying on second-hand (and often government-inspired) impressions.

In the British Diplomatic Service the need to create and maintain a larger network of missions with limited resources has led to a reduction in the size of many embassies and to the establishment in some cases of very small missions with the minimum of facilities and only two or three home-based staff. Financial pressures have led to the closure of a number of subordinate posts. But it has been felt more important to maintain representation in as many countries as possible even at the expense of sacrificing many traditional consulates. Multiple missions set up by several states together have not so far been thought practical.

Obviously only the richer countries with worldwide interests can maintain missions in even a majority of the states with which they have diplomatic relations. Where direct representation is not possible frequent resort is made to multiple accreditation. Alternatively, states can communicate through their Ambassadors in a third country capital or at the United Nations. They may also use the good offices of a friendly state. The smallest states, especially those which are newly independent, and thus have the additional task of setting up diplomatic services from scratch, have to restrict the exchange of missions to a very few states, or even a single one, where they have a major interest, normally the major powers or neighbouring states. When they do establish missions they face many practical problems. A few are experimenting with accrediting a senior official, resident in his own capital, as a roving Ambassador to the half-dozen or so states or organizations with which they need links.

In the past the title and rank of Ambassador was granted only to those envoys accredited to the so-called Greater Powers but this distinction became difficult to maintain in the twentieth century. Even as late as 1949 however, twenty-seven of Britain's sixty-five overseas missions were Legations headed by Ministers; but the trend, already evident, to abolish such distinctions was hastened by the arrival of the newly independent states. Nowadays relations are almost invariably established at the ambassadorial level (even if the individual concerned may rank only with or below a Minister in a larger embassy). National pride and the concept of the equality of sovereign states has, in an expanding society, helped to bring about this significant change in earlier practice.

The increase in the number of embassies and Ambassadors in major capitals coupled with changes in social habits, which have caused the dropping of much of the protocol of the past, means that the average Ambassador cannot expect to achieve the status or trappings of great men of the past. As one amongst many he must be content to do much of his business with officials in the Foreign Ministry rather than with the Minister himself. The ambassadorial uniform has become less common as monarchies have disappeared and has never been adopted by the majority of new states. On the other hand some representatives of the newly independent states wear their own national dress on formal occasions. The spread of embassies to all parts of the globe, some of which are distinctly turbulent, means that many Ambassadors live distinctly uncomfortable lives and may be more familiar with the trappings of security than of splendour.

In their relations with colleagues, in entertaining and social life generally diplomats have had to adapt, often very willingly, to the changes in the social climate of the times. Etiquette – and guides to it – is still necessary because, as Talleyrand said, "*elle simplifie la vie*"; but many of the rituals – for example the exchange of visiting cards – have been largely dropped and not only because the expansion of the size of the Diplomatic Corps often makes such exchanges impracticable. Entertaining has become more informal; this trend has been fostered by the rising costs of accommodation which forces diplomats to live in the suburbs, and the difficulty in obtaining, or the cost of, domestic servants. In many of the newly independent countries climate makes formal entertaining uncomfortable and diplomats readily adapt their style of entertainment to conform to local taste and custom, since it is the local people that they wish to attract to their houses.

However, whatever changes a Head of Mission may accept in his lifestyle, he remains, to some extent, a person apart to be treated with special respect and due observance of essential protocol as a mark of regard between the government of the state in which he resides and that of the state which he represents. It is significant that new states are at least as punctilious about the treatment of their Ambassadors as long-established ones. As an Ambassador's essential function is to speak for his government, the ceremony of the presentation of credentials retains its formality and symbolism wherever he may be, for it is by this that he establishes his authenticity.

There has, however, been perhaps less change in the essential features of the work of an overseas mission, and a description written thirty years ago rings true today. Changes in technology have removed some of the drudgery, and changing social habits many of the distinctions between diplomats and others. The balance in a mission's work depends on local circumstances and is regularly assessed. Over the years, in the British service at least, increasing emphasis has been placed on commercial rather than more traditional diplomatic work. Information work, almost unknown before the war as a distinct specialization, developed to its peak in the 1960s and has since been on the decline.

A new development which followed upon the independence of an increasing number of generally poorer non-Western countries has been the appearance of aid work as an integral part of the responsibility of the mission of a developed country. The diplomacy of many newly independent countries is mainly concerned with economic problems – commerce, aid, and development. These subjects can form up to four-fifths of a developing country's activities in Western capitals and in multilateral organizations; and the major part of a Western mission's activities in a developing country. This is a new pattern of work: fifty years ago aid and development, to the extent that they existed, hardly counted as 'diplomatic' tasks.

Multilateral organizations reflect and magnify the economic aspects of contemporary bilateral diplomacy. This is true not only of economic organizations like the International Monetary Fund but also of primarily political ones like the General Assembly of the United Nations. Issues such as the use of the seabed and a New International Economic Order are usually highly politicized, and are dealt with simultaneously by a number of international bodies as well as entering into bilateral exchanges. These are the two sides of the political/economic coin. The discussion of them requires new skills. These skills involve, in the case of developed countries: familiarity with the new subjects, which are often technical as well as political; the exposition of them and of the government's view on them to other governments; keeping those less developed governments for which the developed state concerned feels a special responsibility abreast of new developments and proposals; and representation of the interests of such countries at international meetings where they may not be represented.

In British Missions in 'foreign' (as opposed to Commonwealth) countries, the erstwhile separate diplomatic, consular, and commercial services were amalgamated as a result of the Eden reforms in 1943, that is to say, well before the rapid expansion of international society began. In the missions of many other states commercial services still remain distinct. The significant change to British diplomatic machinery as a result of that expansion (which is in itself the result of the gaining of independence by many former colonies) was the breakdown of the distinction between the various 'external' British services, which were amalgamated from the mid 1960s. The Colonial Office was merged with the Commonwealth Relations Office in 1966 and a joint Foreign and Commonwealth Office emerged in 1968. The bringing together of foreign, colonial, and Commonwealth affairs under one roof marked a formal recognition by us in Britain of the change in international society.

I would draw the following general conclusions.

The significance which states attach to bilateral diplomacy has, on the whole, not diminished. The main effect of the expansion of international society has been to increase the number of missions and the range of environments in which they operate. This change, coupled with improvements in communications, has led to a vast increase in information flowing into the foreign Ministries. The speed with which decisions now have to be reached, combined with the growing pressure for open government, has had a significant effect upon the operation of these Ministries. But although the formalities associated with diplomatic life have been somewhat relaxed, the fundamentals remain much the same. In particular the principles enshrined in the 1961 Vienna Convention have been very widely subscribed. In short, the nature of a diplomat's task is not fundamentally different whether he is serving in an ancient capital of Europe or that of a newly independent state, and a diplomat transferred from one to the other is likely to take his habits of work with him. The overseas missions of newly independent states have tended so far to follow the practices established in the capitals in which they are situated. The rare exceptions, such as the Libyan experiment with people's bureaux, tend to prove the rule, though they may be a foretaste of changes to come.

It is in the still-growing field of multilateral diplomacy, and particularly in large-scale negotiations on complex economic and technical issues, that the changes are most noticeable. Here the impact of new states has been significant for both the content and pattern of negotiation. For example, the doctrine of the sovereign equality of states has clashed with the reality of inequalities of power. Should decisions emerge from consensus or from 'weighted' voting? In parallel with this has grown a wealth of pressure groups, based on regional or political or economic communities of interest, through which individual states seek to marshal support for their views and exert pressure on the international community as a whole: the Non-Aligned Movement, the Group of 77, the Commonwealth, the Organization of African Unity, and the European Community are good examples.

These changes of course reflect the fact that the scope of international negotiation has been enlarged. The international allocation of resources – energy, raw materials, technology etc. – their security of supply, relations with the countries that possess them (and sometimes the denial of them to offenders), these are the issues that now compete for attention in international discussion with more traditional political matters. Indeed, in most cases, handling of them is as much a question of politics as of economics for Western governments. In consequence those governments are finding themselves impelled to adopt governmental positions on issues which they might otherwise prefer to leave to free enterprise and market forces. At a time when most aspects of daily life, political as well as economic, are a matter of governmental involvement in many of the new states of the world, the older ones need an instrument for the conduct of their relations which takes account of this development and is adapted to it; while newer ones usually find that negotiations with other governments and with international organizations are vital to their well-being and even to their survival as independent states. But the fundamental nature of and the need for diplomacy remain unchanged.

26

THE INTERNATIONAL ORDER IN A MULTICULTURAL WORLD

Adda Bozeman

I

International history richly documents the thesis that political systems are transient expedients on the surface of civilization, and that the destiny of each linguistically and morally unified community depends ultimately upon the survival of certain primary structuring ideas around which successive generations have coalesced and which thus symbolize the society's continuity. This cultural substratum of norm-setting beliefs and linguistic guidelines for thought spawns, supports, or ejects a given society's political system, just as it also determines the general cast of its religions, art styles, social structures, and dispositions to the outside world. In short, then, a culture is all of a piece and careful study is required before one can assess and adequately deal with the political systems of the day.

Next, the inhabited world has been multicultural from the beginning, if only because different languages have brought forth different processes of thought-formation and different types of basic norms and ideas. For example, India and China were able to preserve their identities throughout millennia and despite the heavy incidence of political turbulence, natural disasters, and widespread poverty, because they held fast to a life-sustaining confidence in the perennial harmony and order of the cosmic universe.

According to the intricate metaphysics of Hindus, Buddhists, and Jains, all things, including humans, come into being as aspects of a single world manifestation. The phenomena of past and future, time and space, life and death are not problematical here since they are perceived to be mere elements of this one great transcendent form of which every part is in accord with all. Further, and for the same reason, no particular importance adheres in biography or ideas of the self. The aim of existence for a believing Hindu is rather to carry out the caste role assigned him at birth so that selfless performance of dharma may assure maintenance of cosmic harmony.

Hindu India's stamina throughout its long and troubled history is in large measure a function of the caste system. By providing Indians with religious, moral, and social security, it endowed them with a collective identity that could remain intact despite centuries of alien rule. The logic of these structural norms stipulates further that non-Hindus have to be perceived as outsiders. True, resident groups of Muslims and Christians were casted in later times in terms of their particular occupations. Yet no one not associated with Hinduism could be born a brahman, a kshatria, or a sudra; nor could he hope to gain spiritual merit so as to be able to participate in those cycles of reincarnation that would bring him nearer to nirvana and release from life. Above all, perhaps, no one not a Hindu could come close to finding meaning in Sanscrit and such sacred texts as the Laws of Mani or the Mahabharata – texts which transmit and illustrate all basic Hindu norms and values, and which continue to be mandatory as well as cherished literature for modern Indians in all walks of life.

The pivot in traditional China's normative order as it had prevailed on all levels of thought and society until the mid-twentieth century was belief in the unchanging demands of the heavenly order and determination to maintain this harmony by strict control of human behaviour. The main ordering agency was the Confucian family system with its carefully graded relationships, each subject to its own set of unalterable rights, responsibilities, and attitudes, and all held in place by the head of the family, the chief of the clan, the elders of the village, or the superior of the guild. The human being in this culture realm was thus primarily an aspect of the family or other association to which he belonged, a small segment in the intricate web of human relationships that made up society and civilization. The logic of the Chinese world-view therefore required total stress on the person's moral obligations to others; it did not even allow for the conception of individual liberties.

The administration of China was modelled upon that of the natural Confucian family. Conceived as the Middle Kingdom and the abode of civilization writ large rather than as a territorially bounded state, China was deemed to constitute a family of nations. Ruled by the Father Emperor in accordance with Heaven's Mandate, it too consisted of elder and younger sons – all inferior peoples in the sinocentric universe, yet each subject to tutelage through force and persuasion and endowed with special tasks, privileges, and tribute assessments.

In explaining the cast of mind responsible for this entire scheme of multi-levelled, yet organically linked interactions, sinologists point out that all Chinese thinking is essentially 'relational thinking'. Influenced by language which lacks the subject-predicate pattern in sentence structure, the Chinese did not develop the law of identity in logic or the concept of substance in philosophy.[1]

The systems of thought, norms, and values which sustained China and India for millennia as continuing civilizations were radically different from each other in most respects. However, they converged on this: both focused on society viewed as a complex of diverse groups and both stood for preservation of that which was; but neither recognized the individual human being as an autonomous person and the ultimate source of thought. Neither was therefore hospitable to innovation.

Similar factors combined to favour the integrity on the one hand of other literate cultures in the Orient – among them those of Japan, Cambodia, Burma, and the Semitic West Asian realms of the Islamized Arab and Arabized peoples and the Jews; and on the other, of all non-literate societies – among them those in black Africa. The cultural map of that continent as completed by modern linguists and anthropologists now shows more than one thousand small communities, each different from the other, yet all participating in a common heritage marked by the absence of writing and the perfection of compensatory carriers of thought. Here, where human communication required the physical presence of 'the other', language evolved as a mode of action rather than as an instrument for reflection or a mirror of reflected thought. This circumstance sets definite limits upon the elaboration of theories, systems, generalizations, and the kind of ideas that underlie, for example, Indian metaphysics and European jurisprudence.

Dependence on orality also implies constraints on the control of space. The viable African community thus simply had to be the small linguistically, ethnically, and morally unified community in which each human being was, above all, a representative of the family, absolutely dependent on his 'umbilicals' (Noni Jabavu's phrase). In the logic of such a basic set-up, other people must be perceived as outsiders, subject to distrust, enmity, and scapegoating as well as to attack and enslavement. Greater unions of ethnically distinct groups evolved in all parts of the continent, usually through conquest; however, most succumbed to fragmentation after the conqueror's death, being too conflicted to endure. Security and order were closely identified with the small folk society. Yet nothing in black Africa's millennial history suggests that peace was included in this constellation of values and norms. The records indicate rather that conflict was accepted on all levels of existence and that violence and war, whether in the form of regicide, succession wars, civil wars, raids, or full-fledged intertribal wars, were endemic everywhere.

The major sustaining conceptions that distinguish Europe's literate civilization are wholly different from, in important respects even contrary to, those identified with all other literate and non-literate cultures. Foremost amongst them is the idea of individuation. This principle, which is rooted in the linguistic and intellectual heritage of Greece and Rome, was to remain the guiding force in Western approaches to the arts, sciences, and letters as well as to religion, ethics, politics, and law. The primary concern in each of these contexts was not the age-set, the family, an economic class or a caste, not 'man, the father', 'man, the sudra', or 'man, the umbilical', but the individual human being viewed here as the exclusive source of thought and the carrier of rights as well as obligations. This is as apparent in such literary forms as the tragedy and the novel as it is in systems of law and government. The English common law certainly differs significantly from the Roman civil law, but both normative orders converge on the commitment to identify the essence of law in counterpoint to other norm-engendering schemes such as nature, religion, or reliance on sheer force; to cast human associations, including those of the state and the church, in reliable legal moulds; and to emancipate the individual from the group by defining his status not only as an autonomous person but also as a citizen of his state or city.

Numerous instruments and agencies evolved in the course of European and American history for the purpose of assuring these objectives, among them constitutions and bills of rights. What is noteworthy today about all these norms and models is the fact that they constitute severely abbreviated renditions of the general code of ruling values and beliefs. Just as one has to know that dharma is the basic theme in traditional Indian life and thought before one can appreciate the fact that the Indian Kingdom, being the patrimony of the warrior caste, is rightly associated with the commitment to wage war, so must one know that the typically European idea of a 'law of nature' could not have evolved before 'law' as such had been carefully set apart from 'nature'. Likewise, such phrases as 'the rights of man' or 'the dignity of man' are meaningless unless one remembers that 'man the individual' had been carefully detached from such indeterminate generic references as 'mankind' or 'humanity'. And conversely, it is clear that only this European view of the human being allows for meaningful universalization. Lastly, individualism stands for inventiveness, and inventiveness makes for intentional development. In counterpoint to all other cultures that of the West has therefore long been identified with risk, discovery, and change. Indeed, and as suggested by Robert Redfield, it may be said to have invented progress and reform.[2]

II

In the absence of a common language, a common pool of memories, and shared ways of thinking, reasoning, and communicating, it is hard to fathom a 'world culture' (or for that matter a 'world history'), at least if one takes ideas seriously. The evidence points instead to a plurality of frames of reference. Neither of these statements implies that cultures are static or destined to endure for ever. Nor do they suggest that cultures do not interact, or that one set of concepts and institutions cannot be deeply influenced from without. We thus learn from the history of the eastern Mediterranean region that classical Greece was closely linked to Egypt and Persia by commercial, intellectual, and diplomatic relations, but that even after Alexander and his successors merged all three realms into a single Macedonian states system, each of them none the less continued to retain its cultural identity.

Studies of trade between Ming China and Japan during the fourteenth to sixteenth centuries enlarge on this motif. Each of these East Asian societies was committed to the promotion of commerce. Yet this convergence proved irrelevant because the Chinese and Japanese understandings of the very idea of trade were incompatible. For the Chinese, trade was just an annoying aspect of the tribute system which they wanted to restrict. They valued the periodic Japanese missions mainly as symbolic confirmations of Japan's willingness to pay tribute. For the Japanese, by contrast, trade was the *raison d'être* of tributary relations – a Chinese conception they viewed as utterly humiliating and undesirable.[3] Trade, then, in no way narrowed the culture gap, despite attempts by Zen Buddhist élites to mediate the conflict between these conflicting persuasions. In fact the tone of Japan's diplomatic correspondence suggests strongly that Buddhism – one of the world's great religions which addresses mankind as a whole – was made to cede to Shinto, a specifically Japanese order of norms and values.[4] And the Buddhist message was similarly blunted, adapted, or nationalized in Sino-Indian relations when the faith was carried from India to China,[5] and in India's relations with Southern Asia.[6]

The diffusion of Buddhism, then, did not conduce to 'world culture' or world unity, and neither did that of Christianity or Islam, also universal creeds. Statistics indicate, to be sure, that *x* million people profess to being Christians or Muslims. Observations and scholarly literature, however, provide uncontestable evidence first, that the meaning of each of these religions differs significantly from region to region; and second, that the difference is in each case an expression of a given people's earlier beliefs and values.

However tolerant in accommodating deviations, the faithful in the Arabian heartland of Islam are thus definitely at odds with certain Iranian or Turkish renditions of their faith, and find much that is entirely alien to them in the beliefs and practices of, for example, the American Black Muslims or Islamic communities in Negro Africa. As J. P. Trimingham remarks in his analysis of the resilience of Bantu culture, whereas in the Near East peasant beliefs were thoroughly Islamized, in Africa the parallel elements bear the mark of their African origins. Here, he notes, where the traditional world remains real, religious life rests on a double structure, namely the animistic substratum and the Islamic superstructure.[7] And the records of Christianization tell of parallel transformations. Indeed, and as evidenced in the last centuries by relations between Russia and most of Eastern Europe, there is a culturally and strategically important line separating communities Christianized by Rome from those Christianized by Constantinople. Russia's control over the former – whether tsarist or Marxist-Leninist – has therefore invariably led to revolts and thus to regional instability, since the fundamental sustaining ideas of these two cultures are discordant in their essentials. The continuing turbulence in that area of the world, officially sanctioned as it were by the post-Second World War agreements of Yalta and Helsinki, may therefore in considerable measure be ascribed to the West's misperceptions of cultural realities.[8]

Secular theories and ideologies undergo similar transpositions in their passage from one thought world to another. This was as true of eighteenth-century European interpretations of Confucianism and twentieth-century American understandings of Indian metaphysics as it was of medieval Arab/Islamic attempts to find formulations of classical Greeek philosophy that would be compatible with their own traditional truths, and of nineteenth-century Chinese decisions to accept the Occidental law of nations as a useful aid in planning China's border defence while disallowing its validity as a code.[9]

In short, then, ideas are not transferable in their authenticity, however adept and dedicated the translators.[10] This does not mean, of course, that cultures and conceptual orders (like nations in this respect) cannot be smashed deliberately by armed force or coercive manipulations of thought and its expression.

III

The world is a manifold of political systems as it is a manifold of cultures. One culture realm may consist of diverse politically separate units as evidenced by traditional India where numerous warring kingdoms were coexisting in the morally unified Hindu order; by black Africa where ethnically and politically distinct societies are usually hostile to each other while yet complying with the same basic values; by the Islamic Middle East where relations between different caliphates, sultanates, empires, and states have been marked by endemic strife even as all contending parties are at one in acknowledging the principles implicit in the Dar al-Islam; and by the medieval Holy Roman Empire and the modern European states system whose separate provinces were similarly engaged in adversary politics while at the same time standing for Europe's unity of thought and experience. Conversely, of course, it needs to be stressed – especially in the light of the inquiries pursued by the present book – that one and the same political system may comprise a variety of culturally unique fields of thought and experience. Since this was and continues to be true of most empires and international organizations, it is necessary for academic as well as practical political reasons to assess the cultural factor in each case and to monitor its changes over time. In fact, useful comparisons of empires and other multicultural political orders simply cannot be conducted unless one lifts the cover of such generalizing modern trade terms as 'empire', 'imperialism', 'expansion', 'order', 'state', 'law', 'bureaucracy', 'élite', etc. so as to examine the underlying realities. Only then, it is here suggested, can one proceed to ask: 'What was new about the European Empires?' and 'in which if any ways did the reactions of dependent peoples to European administrations differ from those registered by dependent peoples in other, i.e. non-European empires?'

Empires are legion in history. Among those associated with the Orient and parts of Africa one thinks of the Assyrian, the Egyptian, the Chinese, the Mongolian, the Persian, the Turkish, and the Arab imperial systems. In the Americas several expansionist, well-organized Indian imperialisms come to mind, while Europe is identified with the Macedonian, Roman, and later Byzantine empires. All these designs have been carefully studied, assessed, and compared, and it is thus possible to draw attention to some indisputable conclusions.[11] One is that all great non-Western orders, with the possible exception of Achaemenid Persia, have always been despotisms; the other indicates that they were tax-taking not legislating empires, and that they did not interfere much in the customs of the communities they ruled if only because they insisted on preserving rigid lines of discrimination between themselves as imperial establishments and all others. Furthermore, none of the Orient's vast political conglomerates could accommodate the image of man as an individual representative of the human species. Cognitive thought about 'humanity' or 'mankind' was therefore not developed there, and a 'world order' regulated by universally valid norms could not be fathomed. Administrative policies thus aimed exclusively at securing the self-view and interest of the dominant imperial power.

This could be said also of the empires built by European nations, for each of them was permeated by convictions of its own supremacy. The world view, however, informing the Occidental designs was at all times markedly different in the sense that it did not screen out the possibility of recognizing the essential, purely human factor under the trappings of attributes assigning inferiority to certain classes of people. Defeat and spoliation were brought to countless nations in the wake of European conquests, in both classical and modern times. Yet, and in stark contrast to the expansionist thrusts carried out throughout the millennia in the Orient, those originating in the Occident were challenged and at times redeemed in the very homeland of the culture because they were found to violate moral norms to which universal and hence superior validity was assigned.

The millennial Roman Empire was a legislating empire.[12] In that capacity it could introduce the idea of *humanitas* into liberal arts education as the major goal of intellectual aspiration, if only because Roman thinking was decisively guided by Latin (see *supra* this chapter). Further, it could fashion law and jurisprudence as systems of objectively valid concepts around which men of various origins could rally, and finally, it could institute reforms that altered local customs.

This particular heritage was reinforced in Europe by the New Testament which is addressed to everyman everywhere and has been consistently interpreted as a severely demanding moral code that commits believers to aid their fellow-men – regardless of whether they are friends or foes. Dispositions such as these were activated by the expansion of Europe after the great voyages of discovery and the ensuing establishment of empires in America and parts of Africa and Asia. They thus help explain why European history is so rich in biographies of the kind exemplified in the sixteenth century by the Spanish Dominican Bartolomé de Las Casas and in the nineteenth century by David Livingstone, the Scottish missionary and explorer, and why the records are replete with projects to improve the lot of mankind as well as with successful reforms in the actual administration of culturally alien peoples – concerns not dominant in any non-Western empire.

The pacing of these revisionist endeavours was quickened during the twentieth century throughout the world's non-self-governing areas in response to the following developments:

The spread on one hand of universalist values, on the other of nationalist movements – both Western in inception.
The occurrence of two prolonged world wars which had particularly weakening effects upon the European nations.
The rise to prominence in world affairs of the United States which is conditioned by its history to think of liberty, equality, and opportunity as the birthrights of men everywhere and which is inclined therefore to overlook cultural differences.
The creation, after each of the two wars, of international organizations which were structured in accordance with Euro-American models of constitutional federalism and related Occidental norms and values.
The effective propagation of Marxism-Leninism, notably of its combat ideology and its doctrine that 'imperialism' is associated exclusively with the capitalist states of Europe and America and that all colonial peoples, led by the international communist party, must rise against these oppressors.

These factors combined to provide the auspices under which one European state after the other proceeded to dissolve its empire and to grant political independence to its former dependencies – an unprecedented set of decisions in the long history of empire which continues today in the annals of the Communist empires of the Soviet Union, China, and North Vietnam.

IV

The response of the non-Western nations to these developments in international affairs have been greatly various, and the same holds naturally for the impact of the responses upon world society. No assessment can therefore be definitive, least of all one that is supposed to aim at generalization and brevity. The present limited attempt addresses the following questions:

(1) Which aspects of Western civilization have proved to be generally attractive, perhaps even irresistible?
How were they understood and transposed in non-Western societies by indigenous policy-making élites, and what can be said in this regard about their mediating function?
(2) Which are the critical concepts and institutions – the ones, namely, that were taken for granted in the modern West as incontestably universal norms, but that were misunderstood or dropped altogether by recipient nations?

(3) How does Westernization relate to modernization, and what can one say about the effect of these and related processes upon 'system' and 'order' in world politics?

It seems to have been generally recognized by all élites in the non-European world that Europe's civilization could be made to speak to everyman. Contrary to their own essentially closed conceptual schemes, the intruding alien was an open invitation to explore the unknown, question that which exists, arrive at new truths, aim for intellectual freedom, and thus participate in the universe of learning – a phenomenon openly acknowledged only in the Occident.

The main agency providing access to this life-style was education, and Europe offered it in an entirely new key. Symbolized in later phases of Westernization by the university and its maze of interconnected disciplines as well as by medical schools, law schools, learned societies, and in modern times by education-minded philanthropies, it has been the irresistible magnet drawing aspiring members of local élites into close relationships first with Europe and later with North America. However, none of these institutionalized inter-cultural encounters could have occurred, it is here suggested, had it not been for the orientation towards learning that was exemplified in the Orient as well as later in Africa by an altogether unique type of human being, the self-directed individual European whose commitment to learn about foreign lands and peoples was basically personal and voluntary, far exceeding the needs of the colonial administration in whose service he usually stood.

One looks in vain for such public-spirited élites in earlier Asian imperialisms. There are those today who maintain that English rule in India, as for that matter all Western imperialism, was in no way different from former exploitation. What is being overlooked by them are two incontestable facts. First, it was the European élite which reconstructed India's history, art, and architecture; rediscovered India's languages, religions, and sacred texts; and identified the region's legal, social, and political traditions in their full complexity, even as it worked out the compromises between local customs and English common law, equity, and constitutionalism that were essential if India were ever to exist as a unified nation. Second, the West, personified in such men as Sir William Jones, called forth Indian nationalism by giving this fragmented land a new sense of its own old cultural values and achievements.[13]

Parallel developments in the propagation of learning, political consciousness, and élite-formation were set in motion in the ancient literate cultures of South East Asia and the Middle East as well as in hundreds of non-literate communities in black Africa where even the indispensable infrastructure for intellectual and political emancipation – namely writing – had to be implanted from without by the West's colonial administrators.

Westernized élites obviously differed from country to country and from epoch to epoch. Yet all stood on the margins of two cultures: they could not belong to the foreign civilizations that attracted them intellectually, and they were no longer comfortable in their own traditional society where they were a very small minority, alienated from the majority. The ambivalence of this position was probably least unsettling in the early period of Europeanization during which these marginal men could participate in heady intercultural dialogues, carried by optimism about the future of their nation and unburdened by the responsibilities implicit in the actual administration of their own, now split society. All this changed completely with the attainment of statehood when they themselves were required to govern in accordance with Occidental norms and systems upon whose introduction they had originally insisted.

From the mid-twentieth century onwards it thus became apparent that the Westernized élites were not able to Westernize the basic beliefs and values of their nations; that unity and order could not be maintained in the new Asian and African states through reliance on imported Occidental institutions and standards of behaviour, and that nationalism was being identified increasingly with commitments to traditional culture. Frustration soon led to doubt and disenchantment about the worth of European precepts and models. Unrelieved by self-criticism, or other analytical reflections, these sentiments grew into suspicion and resentment until the West as a whole was being imagined in many lands as a false prophet or a mischievous sorcerer who had led his apprentices astray deliberately.

The Europeanized reformist élites gradually lost power and influence in this changed social and psychological context. In some societies they became recessive minorities as leadership passed to countrymen who were more closely attuned to prevalent local ways of thought and expectations. In others they changed course by turning against the alien civilization that had awakened them – an option that was facilitated by the effective propagation of Marxism-Leninism.

The main explanation for the atractiveness of this new ideology was the circumstance that it was conceived as an assault upon the West's main sustaining values and norms. In denying the force of ideas and of individual inventiveness, Marxist doctrines of materialism, economic determinism, the primacy of economic classes, and the inevitability of class conflicts thus had the effect of explicitly exonerating non-Western élites from responsibility for failures in administration while sanctioning the perception of the West as a historically near-defunct power-complex which is guilty by fiat of theory for all that turns out wrongly in their societies.

A second but related attraction of Marxism is the reductionist view of the European political order, specifically of 'the state' and 'law', norms that are put down there as mere power manifestations of the economically dominant class. A third, psychologically perhaps decisive appeal is the open invitation to indulge in righteous hatred of the West and to fight the capitalist oppressor so as to help redeem history's promise of freedom and power for the exploited working classes of the worlds.

Leninism – which is not of the West – transposes some of these propositions and supersedes others. The following theses seem to impress themselves most readily upon the sets of mind of non-Western political élites.

The identification of imperialism with the export of capital, in conjunction with the view that twentieth-century imperialism is the highest stage of capitalism, makes it possible to forget the long inconvenient records of all non-Western empires; to disregard as irrelevant the dissolution of all former European empires as well as the creation, in the twentieth century, of numerous new Communist and non-Western empires; and to indict the United States for the sin of subscribing to the capitalist free enterprise system (with the proviso, however, that the latter must be used as the main source of economic aid and needed export of capital to non-Western states).

The Leninist notion that the economically backward nations have joined the West's proletarian class and are in fact today the 'Chosen People' in virtue of the imperialist exploitation of their economic conditions gives pride of status where before there had been frustration and uneasiness.[14]

Another tenet, the admission that the revolutionary struggle of classes and nations is of uncertain duration and may well be permanent is also emotionally satisfying because it puts the emphasis on the dynamics of political action including fighting, not on the tedious task of peaceful consolidation and development. Indeed, and as six decades of Communist economics have shown, consumer economics and thus consumer development in general are near-irrelevant in Communist societies, be they states or non-state bodies.

These norms have been and continue to be made concrete in a variety of political systems. In the formerly non-Communist societies of Eastern

Europe, Afghanistan, and Tibet communization was accomplished by superior military forces in the service of the Soviet Union and China, both established Marxist-Leninist states. Elsewhere, however, élites have been subscribing voluntarily to the new ideology. This trend is observable particularly in those African, Asian, and Latin American states in which traditional pre-Western patterns of political organization also focus on despotism. To the extent, then, to which the new non-Western élites accommodate Communist precepts by choice, they may well find some anchorage, however shallow, in their own old order of values.

Marxism-Leninism also swept the Occidental intellectual establishments. But the impact of Communism upon Occidental minds had effects on Western civilization that were the reverse of those imprinted upon non-Western cultures by their Marxist-Leninist élites, most of whom were invigorated by their affiliation with Communist beliefs. Scores of Europeans and Americans, by contrast, were taught and willingly learnt – that their Western way of life was all wrong: democracy was depicted as sham, law as too flawed by inequities to merit either respect or reform, and economic norms as mere camouflage for the wanton exploitation of non-Western groups of peoples. In short, they were led to refute, not re-confirm their heritage. Further, and following basic Communist understandings of history and politics, the West's new Marxist élites acceded readily to the Leninist definition of imperialism. The sum total of these commitments explains why they were prepared to help dismantle their own civilization.

The touchstone in this sentimentalist, yet politically effective revolt is guilt. This theme is more highly developed in Christianity than in any other religion and it is nowhere as strenuously professed as in the United States. Here it merges with strong strains of a deeply rooted anti-imperialism and with a peculiar form of economic determinism according to which all underdeveloped people can become 'developed' given opportunity and assistance. Traditionally internalized on levels of biography, the guilt complex is so wantonly socialized and politicized today as to constitute a major element in the conduct of the West's foreign relations.

V

It is questionable in the context of the foregoing analysis whether the cultural and political relations between Western and non-Western societies[15] are adequately summarized by such captions as 'The Revolt of the Third World against Western Dominance' and 'The Anti-

Colonial Revolution'. For one thing, the processes and interactions covered by these terms are too complex, ambiguous, and protracted to justify references to 'revolt' and 'revolution', all the more so as few colonial peoples had to struggle hard to attain independence. For another, we learn from the multifarious records of responses to the West's challenge that resentment mingles almost everywhere with admiration as well as with frustration and self-doubt. Also, we know of numerous, perhaps particularly talented Asian peoples, from the Japanese to the Turks, who retained their composure in encountering the West because they chose to borrow only those attributes of the alien civilization that could be integrated successfully into their established value-systems and political orders.

The majority of non-Western and non-Communist states – those which were independent to begin with and those which had been non-self-governing territories or trusteeships under Western administrations – have not accepted certain crucial European norms. The most important among these relate to constitutional law, penal law, and the whole complex of ideas that sustain the cause of self-determination and development and that makes it mandatory to think of the individual as an autonomous person and a citizen, endowed with rights as well as responsibilities. And since the post-1945 framework for the conduct of relations between states has come to rest on precisely these now embattled Occidental norms, one may also doubt whether 'the state' is still a shared experience or reference and whether we can count on the existence of an organically unified system of states.

One of the main shared themes in the non-Western realms here surveyed is the reaffirmation of traditional religious beliefs as ultimate norm-setting principles of identity in politics and culture. Shinto and Buddhism serve this function in Japan, one of the most creative of all 'borrowing' nations whose élites have long known how to shape attractive ideas, be they Chinese, European, or American, so that they would not break the form or denature the irreducible essence of that which calls itself Japan.[16] Throughout the twentieth century, surely one of the most severely trying periods in their history, the Japanese could thus assure stability in law and government by adapting select precepts of Occidental law codes and constitutions to their own tested and revered imperial institutions and traditions.[17]

Public order in the vast, ethnically and linguistically fractured new Indian nation is also being upheld by institutions of secular law and constitutional democracy that are of Occidental derivation. However, each organ of India's modern administration – and therewith the very cause of the unified state – is severely challenged today by orthodox

Hinduism and the human dispositions it engenders.[18] The resuscitation of the traditional faith has thus brought a revival of caste consciousness and related social norms that conflict sharply with India's modern systems of constitutional and criminal laws. Two sets of incidents illustrated this collision in 1980/1: the blinding of suspected criminals in some of India's states, and the mass demonstrations of women in Delhi asking for the right to widow-burning, a Hindu practice officially outlawed by the British in 1829. The impact on contemporary international society of an India that is becoming increasingly conscious of its own traditions is discussed in Chapter 21.

The resurgence of religiosity is nowhere as pronounced as in the Islamic world. It is particularly intense in the Middle East where the faith originated and where relations with the Christian West have been close and in conflict from the seventh century AD onward. The history of these interactions has never ceased to puzzle the thoughtful among Arab and Arabized élites. To recover the lost dynamic which had brought victory over Christianity, self-confidence, power, and prestige has thus been the standing challenge in modern times. And since the glory of the past is forever associated with Islam, it is the road back to the Koran that is being fervently sought not only in the Near East but throughout the commonwealth of *c.*600 million believers.[19] This means, *mutatis mutandi*, a near total refutation of the West's Promethean civilization which earlier generations had accepted as the most promising source of guidelines for the recovery of success in history.

The moods and dispositions here in play are fundamentally alien and therefore not readily intelligible to Euro-American journalists, scholars, and diplomats. And the cause of comprehension is not served by the practice of indulging in stereotyped distinctions between 'conservatives' and 'radicals' or 'left-wing' and 'right-wing' factions, since the meaning of such appellations is seldom if ever spelled out even in the West. At any rate, and as Bernard Lewis reminded us a few years ago,[20] this language simply does not explain political phenomena in the Muslim world. So-called conservative states such as Saudi Arabia and Pakistan are thus found to be at one with so-called radical states, for instance Iran, Syria, and Libya, when it comes to citing the Koran as the ultimate reference. This sacred text provides the mortar for the unity of the most disparate communities.

Further, opposites converge today in the judgement that Euro-American principles of constitutional and criminal law, notably those bearing on the status of the individual, are not only irrelevant but also nefarious for the well-being of Islamic societies – a conclusion that has been in the works from mid-nineteenth century onwards. As Albert

Hourani notes in a thought-provoking chapter,[21] the alien laws, not being rooted in deep convictions and old customs, were simply not accepted by the people as the necessary regulative principles of society. More importantly, they led to deep – and as we now know lasting – confusions in political thought. The central problem in the new context has thus been not how to preserve the law and make the community virtuous, but how to preserve the community and make it strong by generating dynamism and a common will.

Comparisons of Islamic states and their respective orientations to existing international orders or systems should therefore be made in different terms. It is thus the singular distinction of Saudi Arabia that it chose not to emulate Western norms of constitutional and criminal law. For this made it possible to fashion a relationship of mutual trust between the governing royal house, the religious authorities, and the public without undermining commonly shared traditions of justice. This is no longer the case in most other Islamic states, albeit for different reasons. For example, Shi'ite Iran, a prestige nation in the eyes of contemporaries from antiquity onwards, seemed to have fused Achaemenid, Islamic, and Western elements of statecraft so successfully that it could 'modernize' to the satisfaction even of Western critics. This proved to be an illusion. For nowhere in the Middle East has the return to Islamic orthodoxy been as decisive and ferocious as here, and in few, if any, states has it created such havoc in normative references to the state, government, and law.[22]

What different groups of liberal supporters of the Ayatollah Khomeiny's leadership and opponents of the Shah ignored – and that both in Iran and the West – is the confluence of Achaemenid and Islamic thought on the general Oriental belief that despotism is the only reliable form of government and that man the individual is simply not endowed with inalienable rights to liberty.

In modern Syria, Iraq, and South Yemen, meanwhile, government became lawless and capricious after early Marxist-Leninist 'waves of socialism' had swept aside indigenous traditions as well as Western reforms, thus creating the vacuum that invites the dynamics of personalized will. And this is the condition also to which the former desert kingdom of Libya was reduced after Colonel Muammar el-Qaddafi's *coup d'état*.

Nowhere has the reaffirmation of traditional norms and values been as sustained and deliberate in the last decade as in black Africa. In fact, developments on all planes of thought and behaviour and the testimony of representative Africans lead to the conclusion that African realities today are not convincingly covered by Western concepts and words.

Further, they leave one doubtful whether any important traditional belief or institution has ever been seriously Westernized – and this even though Europeans succeeded in revolutionizing the very premisses of thought and communication by introducing writing to hundreds of different African speech communities. This astounding accomplishment in intercultural relations – and it has not yet received the appreciation it deserves – seems to be experienced merely as a technical facility in modern Africa.

Dr T. Adeoye Lambo, has closely analysed the conflict between traditions and modernism that is disturbing African minds in our times. He notes[23] that Africans have a merely ritualistic admiration for western civilization, and that it is problematic, to say the least, whether norms and standards can be introduced from without, or whether it is possible to assure a smooth interaction between traditional values and the demands of economic and social growth. The traditional faith in the magic power of certain symbols to produce certain results explains why it was customary in periods of tribal distress – e.g. during a famine, drought, or epidemic – to offer expiatory sacrifices. Officially detribalized Africans have not only reverted to this practice under the stress of modern problems, Lambo notes, but have cast it in new and more savage or malignant forms. Further, we learn from this and numerous other observers of the present scene, that the prevalence of magico-religious beliefs including witchcraft is as widespread among urban Western-educated Africans as among tradition-oriented non-Westernized Africans.

The recorded work of professional élites strongly reflects this bent of mind. Whereas African jurists showed a pronounced concern for the disjunction between customary and European legal orders in pre-independence times, later generations became progressively more relaxed in the search for acceptable syncretisms. It was thus only with the greatest reluctance that Sir Samuel Lewis, a barrister from Sierra Leone, had concluded in one of his reports that one might have to recognize bona fide cannibalism, abandon the jury system in the light of tribal conflicts, and compromise the standards of English law in many other ways. Judge K. Azina-Nartey of Ghana, and of Lincoln's Inn in London, saw no difficulties several decades later during the trial of a hunter charged with the manslaughter of a fellow hunter in admitting 'the wonderful evidence of the mother of the deceased that she killed her son by changing him into that animal which lured the accused to shoot. . . '.[24]

Black Africa's states and governments are in a class by themselves also because the very idea of the state is eclipsed by the reality of enduring commitments to kinship and tribal groups. And since relations between the state's ethnic components are marked by mistrust and usually by hostility, national unity remains an elusive goal. (A notable exception is Somalia.) Further, all of the fifty or so black African polities are either authoritarian or totalitarian despotisms, with some of them run on Communist lines. Power is almost everywhere held by one man who is usually identified as the representative of one ethnic party. Yet government is almost by definition unstable since rivals are always bent on dislodging the incumbent either by intrigue or assassination. Violence bred by lawlessness, fear, and mistrust thus marks human relations in all segments of society. Indeed, events as chronicled in post-independence times show that most African states are easily reduced to fields of violence by military coups, civil wars, guerilla wars, inter-tribal combat, and inter-state wars.

The human and material cost of these approaches to politics continues to be prodigious. Energies formerly invested in assuring adequate food supplies and in combating incipient drought are critically sapped. Farm output is lagging everywhere, with the result that Africa's peasant economies are pronounced stagnant or repressive, not developing. Starvation is chronic in many regions, and famines have been sweeping the land relentlessly. Most importantly, the spiritual and physical resources of Africa's talented peoples are being critically drained away. These are the circumstances in which whole communities engage in flight to escape starvation, tyranny, and war, leaving the continent awash with millions of hapless refugees.

VI

To sum up, an international system is as solid as the concepts that combine to compose it. Such concepts are solid if they are equally meaningful in the different local orders that are encompassed by the international system. We do not have such a globally meaningful system because the world society consists today as it did before the nineteenth century of a plurality of diverse political systems, each an outgrowth of culture-specific concepts.

Some of these non-western realms were linked to the Occident and to each other between the mid-nineteenth and the mid-twentieth century in an international order, which European governments had designed and administered in preceding centuries under the title 'the modern states system', and in which member states were juridically equal, and both willing and able to maintain what Europeans called 'standards of civilized behaviour' within their boundaries. The internationalization of this design seemed successful before *c.*1945, but has proved illusory thereafter. A survey of the world society at the end of this century permits the conclusion that the core concept of the system, namely 'the state', is critically embattled everywhere. In some regions, notably in Africa and the Middle East, it has resulted in altogether reductive versions. In others it has degenerated into a protective cover for the dissemination of contra-state ideologies. Internationally relevant decision-making emanates increasingly from scattered, often dissimulated command posts of liberation fronts, terrorist brigades, provisional governments or international communist parties. All of these operate across state boundaries and none is recognized in international law as an equivalent of the state.

The integrity of the concept 'state' is critically impaired also because it is applied to political establishments that are too different to be comparable or equal in terms of either international law or power politics. The term thus covers today new types of multinational empires, such as those of the Soviet Union and of communist China and Vietnam, where strategic and ideological doctrines of expansion insist that existing boundaries are provisional only since the proper limits of jurisdiction have not yet been reached. It also covers Muslim regimes which reject the western concept of a community of states in favour of traditional Islamic concepts described earlier in this book. At the same time the word 'state' continues to be the unchallenged appellation also for nations whose independence has been cancelled through conquest or military occupation. The Soviet Union's satellites are thus not classified as protectorates or dominions in the manner customary, for example, in the former British Empire. Rather, each ranks as a sovereign state and therefore rates a full vote under charter provisions of the UN and other international agencies, even though it was officially deprived of its sovereignty in domestic and foreign affairs by the Brezhnev Doctrine (1968) and a re-enforcing sequel enunciated by Brezhnev in the wake of the Soviet invasion of Afghanistan.

In the West, meanwhile, attributes once firmly assigned to the state have been transferred gradually on the one hand to 'government', on the other to 'the world society', even though both were traditionally perceived in the West as derivatives of the state. A complex process of decomposing the European system has thus been going on for quite some time, without much attention being paid to it by the Occident's scholarly and political elites.

These developments have had adverse effects on international law – the leading European reference for the conduct of relations between states without which 'international order' could not even have been imagined in the West. Loosened from the context of Euro-American jurisprudence, history, and ethics, and associated instead with a new free-wheeling ideology that proclaims unsubstantiated human rights for everyone, the law of nations is now conscripted to serve the cause of political rhetoric and tactics. More importantly, it no longer provides unifying guidelines for thinking about war and peace. This is so partly because 'the rights of war and peace' have ceased to issue from definitions of the state, but mainly because there simply is no consensus in today's multicultural world on the essential meanings of war and peace. Furthermore, as indicated in earlier sections of this paper, war-affirming theories and traditions predominate in non-western and communist societies, thus eclipsing the new pacifism that has been sweeping the West in recent times.

The conjunction of these factors explains why today's world can be perceived as a conglomerate of different conflict systems or different theatres of war, some localized, others contiguous and interdependent. The term 'international war' thus no longer refers exclusively to violent conflicts between states. Rather it now stands also for a broad spectrum of armed belligerence within the state, ranging from sporadic urban guerilla activities to full-fledged revolutionary uprisings and civil wars, many of them initiated or kept going by foreign principals. This interpenetration of the domestic and foreign environments has had the foreseeable effect of effacing altogether the conventionally accepted lines of separation between legitimate and illegitimate force. Indeed, it puts in question established Western distinctions between peace and war.

The de-westernization or de-establishment of the norms and institutions that together had sustained the short-lived global international order constitutes a major challenge for European and American diplomacy. For where the distinction between war and peace is blurred; where values supportive of hostility and warfare outweigh those related to co-operation and peace; and where international relations are conceived, in principle, as conflict relations between adversaries, there diplomacy must follow suit. Comparative studies of modern and traditional statecraft indicate that this is the case in most non-western and all communist societies today. This means that occidental diplomacy must henceforth be prepared to function again, as it did before the nineteenth century, in a world that has no common culture and no overarching political order, and that is no longer prepared to abide by western standards of international conduct.

27

UNITY AND DIVERSITY IN WORLD CULTURE

Ronald Dore

Why does culture matter to the student of international order? In what sense does the prospect that the world might be getting more culturally homogeneous (Westernized, modernized) have implications for the possibilities of sustaining an international order?

In at least three possible senses. First, there is the view that 'a' culture is 'all of a piece', is shaped by 'certain primary structuring ideas' which determine the 'general cast' of the religions, art styles, social structures, and political systems (including relations with outsiders) which that culture can spontaneously create, or can enduringly tolerate if it happens that they are imposed from outside. According to this view, Chinese or Hindu or Islamic culture are each *in their substantive content* incapable of integration within a system of international order which has grown out of a different, Judaeo-Greco-Roman culture. The obstacles are at two levels.

First, at a purely cognitive level, there is not always enough similarity between cultures in their basic ways of conceptualizing the world (especially in their ways of conceptualizing the area of social relations embodied in such Western concepts as 'contract', 'law', 'responsibility', etc.) to make possible the minimum level of effective communication necessary to sustain an international order.

Secondly, different cultures embody different value-systems and moral injunctions. Other cultures do not place the same relative valuations on order, peace, national (or ethnic, or regional, or ecclesiastical) self-assertion, neighbourly co-operation and so forth, as each other or as the West does.

The third sense in which cultural differences affect the possibility of international order has, unlike the other two, nothing much to do with the *substantive content* of cultures. The rules of order in a society of states – that agreements should be obeyed, that envoys should be immune, etc. – rest on some sort of perception of the inevitability of continuing intercourse, some sense that the society of states requires moral commitment to certain basic rules because it is a community and there is no alternative to that community continuing to exist – neither the alternative of withdrawal of self, nor that of elimination by genocide of other. The society of states, that is to say, requires the existence of some sort of moral community, some degree of Kantian reciprocity and ability to take the role of the other which at minimum rules out the contemplation of genocide – at the very least it requires some such sense of community among those who act on behalf of states, and, if order is to be enduring, potentially also among the populations they represent. The sort of 'fellow feeling', the sense that the other person is of one's 'own kind', necessary for that minimal sense of moral community can be inhibited by a variety of things – most clearly, perhaps, by the fact that people have different skin colours or facial bone structures, but also by the perception that they have different tastes and faiths and values and table manners – different cultures. Greater similarity in these respects, therefore, on whatever substantive pattern the convergence takes place, enhances the possibilities of fellow-feeling, and hence the observance of the rules which sustain international order.

For handy reference we might call these three postulated mechanisms the cognitive dissonance mechanism, the value-clash mechanism, and the fellow-feeling mechanism. My first point is that the fellow-feeling mechanism is the most important of the three.

Cognitive Dissonance

Let us look at the cognitive dissonance mechanism first. Most of the supposed examples of the working of this mechanism turn out on examination to be something else. Take, for example, the supposed difference between Americans and Japanese with respect to the notion of 'contract'. To be sure, mistaken *expectations* of other people's behaviour (a form of cognition, certainly) are a potent source of conflict – as the story of almost any British strike shows, and international affairs perhaps more acutely. But they do not necessarily depend on misunderstandings of each other's concepts. Such well-known differences in behaviour as that between Americans and Japanese with respect to contracts are well known and discounted for. Japanese *expect* Americans to behave like Shylocks. They *understand* that 'contract' means something different from *keiyaku* – only too well.

And the identity of understanding is even more complete with respect to international contracts – treaties. The sophisticated apprehension of the meaning of 'law', 'contract', 'treaty' is in any society a minority accomplishment. There is much to be said for the view that the international system is a relatively autonomous one which socializes its own participants, whether they be Nigerian diplomats or Argentinian, and rarely encounters cognitive obstacles to the absorption of its basic terms of discourse.

It is certainly in terms of that universal conceptual currency, not in terms of concepts unique to their shared Confucian culture, that China and Japan have conducted their bilateral diplomatic relations in the course of this century. A recent study of how 'the inscrutable have negotiated with the inscrutable' over the last thirty years (Ogura, 1979) makes this clear. The special features are primarily a matter of occasional use of claims to a 'special relationship' analogous to that used in Anglo-American relations. That is to say, fellow-feeling mechanisms, not cognitive dissonance/sonance mechanisms, are involved.

Incompatible Values

As for the second mechanism, the value-clash mechanism, clearly differences in the dominant value priorities of states can exacerbate conflicts between them. In principle it need not. Provided there is no cognitive dissonance, provided the difference in values is clear, it can be taken account of as merely affecting the weightings of each side in conflicts of interest the resolution of which by orderly processes of compromise is what international order is all about. The fact that State A values a particular good (e.g. freedom from the constraint on national economic decision-making of the influential presence of foreign corporations) more than State B, does not make conflict unresolvable; if the difference is appreciated State B can form an accurate perception of the compensating price it would have to pay in order to get State A to make a concession to one of its multinationals. Conflicts are exacerbated, or created, by differences in values when the difference is not accurately perceived – as when successive British Governments failed to appreciate either the strength of Argentine nationalism or the extent to which the claim to the Falklands was a central expression of it. It may also be exacerbated or created when the difference is perceived, but the values of the other side are denounced as 'unreasonable' – as when, at the opening of Japan, the Western powers declared that the value Japan's rulers placed on their seclusion served only unreasonably to deprive the Japanese people of the benefits of international trade. Hitherto, as in that case, claims that another state's value priorities were unreasonable have usually been used simply as justification for the challenging state's self-interest. Lately, however, with the emergence of embryo notions of a world community, states have begun urging their own values on others for moral rather than self-interested reasons – as in the brief American concern with human rights or the attempts to urge the Japanese to abjure the wickedness of catching whales.

Another special case of the substantive nature of values leading to conflict is when the value-system of a particular state gives great weight to war activities themselves as one of the highest manifestations of the State's existence. As the appeasement policies of the 1930s showed, it would have been hard for any peace-loving state whatever its accurate perception of the values of Hitler's Germany and its forebearance from denouncing them as unreasonable, to avoid conflict leading to war.

So conflicts of values obviously do make the maintenance of a peaceful international order more difficult. In fact, the very distinction between 'interests' and 'values' is spurious. An interest is not an interest until it concerns something which is valued. And even dyed-in-the-wool militarism as a value can be translated into an 'interest' in gaining opportunities for warlike self-expression – which is why Weber used to talk about 'ideal and material interests' and economists talk about 'psychic income'. What is really at issue here is the distinction not between values and interests, but between *universal* values/interests like territory or opportunities for trade (one can safely assume that for all states the more of them the better) and *idiosyncratic* values/interests which some states have and others do not depending on their 'culture'.

What has to be guarded against, however, is the assumption that this culture is an implastic unity, that the interest-defining values relevant to international behaviour are the expression of some deep-rooted all-of-a-piece culture. The difference in the value priorities relevant to international behaviour of Helmut Schmidt's Germany and Hitler's Germany should be enough to undermine that notion.

Nor are the core values of a society necessarily best deduced from its admired scriptures. Someone setting out for Teheran might, indeed, gain some insight if not exactly from the Koran, at least from what Khomeini says about, or quotes from, it. But if his interest is, indeed, in states like Iran whose domestic and foreign policies are avowedly derived from some traditional faith claimed to be *peculiar to* the nation (or a sectional group of brother nations), states whose foreign policy stance is indeed often deliberately inimical to the acceptance of any universal system of international order, he will probably gain even greater insights by reading, instead, in the general sociology of nationalism and nativist reactions. It is, indeed, true that societies differ greatly in the degree of their secularization and that the principles of traditional religions like Islam or modern religions like Marxism are more likely in some societies than in others to have an effect on foreign policies – if only the effect of providing justifications for nationalist self-assertion.

But even in such societies it generally *is* a matter of action being provided with justification, rather than of action being dictated by the central moral imperatives, by the internal logic, of the religious tradition. All the large (literate) religious traditions in question are extremely diverse. Japan, in the twelfth and thirteenth centuries alone, spawned one version of Buddhism very similar to evangelical Christianity and another very similar to militant Islam. The available inventory is generally large – even Marxism is already a house with many mansions – and which items are drawn from stock is very much a discretionary matter.

Discretionary, but not arbitrary. In the last century, whether in the form of the Mahdis, the Boxers, Shinto patriots, Ghandians, or modern Islamic fundamentalists, the point being made by the revivalists is generally a nationalist point (Matossian, 1958). The attribution of value to a traditional religion is a claim to parity of respect asserted against 'dominant other' nations, and often, simultaneously and more proximately, against a local ruling class which has embraced the values and life-styles of those dominant other nations. The tradition to be reasserted can be crafted out of the available inventory to provide the maximum dimensions of differentiation from the oppressors. Thus Gellner, describing the variety of traditional Islam in terms of an austere Great Tradition and a more indulgent superstitious Little Tradition notes that it is from the former that the urbanizing or urban-aspiring revivalists draw their new Islamic fundamentalism, because 'it does a triple job. It defines them against the foreigner. It defines them . . . against a Westernized and envied elite, and it . . . defines them against their own rural past of which they are openly ashamed' (Gellner, 1980, p. 199). Just as, one might say, the castelessness of Ghandism allowed its followers to assert the virtues of rural simplicity while disavowing those elements of traditional rurality of which – under Western influence – they no longer approved.

So let us grant some causal force to the overt *doctrinal* traditions of formal religious faiths – just as it makes some difference to the shape of the pantomime horse whether there are fat men or thin men inside. And perhaps one should grant even more force to the less overt, less avowed subtleties of culturally-determined patterns of interpersonal relations and the way they work through to the value priorities of states. For example, the considerable concern in Japan's foreign policy with the international reputation of the country, is surely very largely the product of a century's struggle to gain recognition as an equal member of the white-skinned club of Great Powers, but it is also, probably, a reflection of the fact that Japan has traditionally been, and to some extent remains, a hierarchical society in which people more often show a concern to establish who ranks above or below whom than they do in more egalitarian countries. But the motive force (to strain the metaphor a bit further, the pay-off which persuades both fat men and thin men to get into the pantomime horse) remains interests defined by *universal* values – the resentful urge to correct one's nation's perceived deprivations of prestige, power, income, territory, or economic opportunity which has always formed the issue between status quo and non-status quo powers.

Those who doubt this, particularly those whose doubts rest on the perception that much of the Third World, once Europeanized by imperial masters, has partly reverted to idiosyncratic traditional cultures and thereby become less accessible to the appeals of an order based on Western civilization, should look at Tucker's examination of the collective claims of the Third World to a redistributive New Economic Order (Tucker, 1977). The arguments of 'the new political sensibility' (which he is concerned to scotch) are all couched in terms wholly familiar from the claims of, or on behalf of, the poor and underprivileged *within* Western societies (even the 'reparations' argument is used in the case of American blacks). They are arguments appealing to principles of morality familiar within Western civilization. The only novelty – extending those principles 'beyond the confines of the state' – is a novelty which owes nothing to any non-Western culture: Boulding, Myrdal, MacNamara, and the other authors of the authoritative statements of this novel principle whom Tucker quotes are not noted as exponents of any traditional non-Western culture.

FELLOW-FEELING

Finally we come to the third, the 'fellow-feeling' mechanism. The main questions to be asked are: first, how genuinely important is it; secondly, are there reasons to think that the cultural bases for fellow-feeling are increasing, or decreasing?

There are many who would answer the first question with a firm: 'of minimal importance'. Thus Morgenthau:

> Let us suppose that American and Russian education and culture could be brought to the same level of excellence or completely amalgamated, and that

Russians would take to Mark Twain as Americans would take to Gogol. If that were the case, the problem of who should control Central Europe would still stand between the United States and the Soviet Union as it does today. (Morgenthau, 1966, p. 505.)

I would beg to differ. Quite apart from the ambiguities of the phrase 'control Central Europe', and the fact that there have been times when there was an influential view in both Moscow and Washington that the two powers had a *shared* interest in not encouraging any Warsaw Pact state to think it could swing to NATO, or vice versa, there is surely plenty of evidence that an increase in fellow-feeling does enhance the propensity to perceive shared interests, and lessen the tendency to exacerbate conflicts of interest by attributing malevolence or moral turpitude to opponents. No French observer would deny that as a result of this fellow-feeling, there is something of a special relationship between the United States and the United Kingdom. No Japanese observer would deny that there is equally something special in the relation between the US and all European countries that is not present in relations between the US and Japan – and they might well ascribe to that difference the fact that Europe makes such a conflictual thing about its trade deficit with Japan, but not about its equally large deficit with the US. Similarly, most Japanese would agree that the phrase which resounds in the speeches of friendship delegations – the Japanese and Chinese 'are of the same culture, the same stock' – has some meaning, even if it is difficult to specify how much it has meant in terms of concrete concessions rather than in demands for symbolic assertions of solidarity (as in the famous dispute over the anti-hegemony clause in the Treaty of Friendship).

All that is contended is that it *would* make a difference to the possibilities of international order if 'people in Maine should feel the same degree of responsibility toward the people of Japan or Chile or Indo-China as they feel towards California' – a sense of responsibility for which 'fellow-feeling' is an obvious precondition. This proposition is equally accepted by Boulding who thinks that state of affairs desirable and even possible, and by Tucker who would find it abhorrent if he were not convinced of its impossibility (Tucker, 1977). It would, of course, be naïve to attribute the fact that there has been no civil war between Maine and California while the US *has* been engaged in major wars with Japan and Indo-China to differences in degree of fellow-feeling. The system of order which regulates conflicts of interests between Maine and California is one enforced by the whole apparatus of a federal state with a well-honed constitution, a system of justice, and a monopoly (or near-monopoly) of violence. But the development of those federal institutions, as any historian of the US would affirm, did depend on the existence, the cultivation, and the appeal to fellow-feeling as well as shared material interest. And it is to the same dialectical feedback between strengthening institutions and strengthening fellow-feeling that optimists must look for prospects of the establishment of world order.

But fellow-feeling between whom? Most importantly, clearly, between those who formulate foreign policies. One has to make a distinction, as Bull does, between those directly involved in state-to-state contacts, who participate in a diplomatic society and are inducted into a world diplomatic culture, and the larger urban élite within whom they interact and inter-marry and from whom come the interest-group pressures on their policies. Diplomats can be over-ruled and rapidly replaced (more especially where bureaucratic traditions are shallow). Hence the possibilities of fellow-feeling between these wider urban élites of the world becomes important if one is thinking of building *sustained* commitment to the conventions of an international order. Beyond them lie the men on the Clapham omnibus: the extent to which the stretch of *their* sympathies counts varies, of course, from country to country, depending on whether they are indeed men who ride on omnibuses and read daily newspapers, or men who think themselves lucky to ride on a bullock cart and wouldn't know what to do with a newspaper if they had one, and depending also, of course, on the extent to which the political system is such as to allow the popular sentiments to have an effect on policy.

These answers to the 'fellow-feeling between whom?' question become important as soon as we begin to address ourselves to the second question, the possibility of an increasing volume and more widespread distribution of fellow-feeling in the world. Hitherto, in the guise of enunciating a single proposition, I have covertly been using two, viz:

1. Increased fellow-feeling between state representatives in a society of states, and between the national groups of their compatriots who influence or control them, increases the likelihood that they will have some moral commitment to the rules of order established in that international society and subordinate the pursuit of national interests in conflicts with other states to those rules.
2. Ego is more likely to experience fellow-feeling towards alter the more he perceives him to be similar to himself (if I may phrase the matter in the jargon of the psychologists who have provided evidence for this proposition – though they would add the qualification: up to the

point at which the similarity becomes close enough to evoke the eery discomfort of the doppelganger echo effect) (Snyder and Fromkin, 1980).

All one needs now as a preliminary to asking the important question about change in the modern world is a third proposition:

3. People are more likely to perceive similarities between themselves and others (a) the more similar they in fact are, (b) the more they have a chance to observe each other, and (c) the less actual contact is preceded by the absorption of hostile stereotypes of each other.

INCREASING CULTURAL HOMOGENEITY?

There are two kinds of arguments in support of the view that similarity is increasing. The first is the popular assumption about cultural diffusion – about the Westernization, Americanization, coca-colanization, etc. of the world. The second is a family of arguments of a social evolutionary kind about the unfolding logic of industrialism. Let us take the more complex second family of arguments first.

They come in many versions, from the more obviously ethnocentric argument that 'moral progress (i.e. *their* becoming more like us) follows material progress', to more subtle arguments to the effect that the material interest which nations have in adopting the principles of scientific rationality in matters of technology or business accounting so firmly roots those principles in the society – in the first place in the schools – that they are diffused to politics, to law and administration (leading to the universal growth of bureaucracy), to family life (leading to family planning, etc.) to religion (leading to a decline in superstition), and so on. At the same time the growing division of labour with economic development, increased specialization in ever more sophisticated occupations, greater spatial and social mobility, all lead to greater individuation and an expansion of individual choice, the growth of the nuclear family, the weakening of community ties, egalitarianism, the switch from particularistic to universalistic norms, from principles of ascription to those of achievement, etc.

Convergence of cultures occurs, in other words, because (broadly speaking) there is only one way of organizing societies to make an industrial system work efficiently, and all societies do want to get an efficient industrial system.

These versions of the convergence theory were most influential in the late 1950s and early 1960s when it was possible to argue that the Japanese, poor souls, were not very efficient industrially because they somehow could not get their societies organized according to the best principles of individualism and scientific rationality in the way that Americans did. (C. Kerr *et al.*, 1962, was one of the more influential exponents of the view.) It is rather awkward for the thesis that, while still failing to organize themselves properly, the Japanese have perversely managed to achieve a considerable level of industrial efficiency.

But if hopes of increasing similarity arising from the inner logic of industrialism must be tempered, there are also the diffusion processes at work. These proceed at two levels. First there is the direct spread of fashions and tastes, of architectural styles and wallpaper patterns, of pop songs and Kentucky Fried Chicken, along established commercial channels; the spread of religions by missionaries, of ideologies of self-determination or racial equality through academic and political congresses and by tired journalists who find it easier to purloin ideas by translation from a foreign journal than to think of something new. Secondly, diffusion takes place through the directly imitative transplant of institutions, usually from countries considered more, to countries considered less, advanced – the implantations of bureaucratic systems of civil service organization, of school and health systems, are examples. These institutions shape the behaviour, the aspirations and sensibilities of those who are involved in them as surely as do those of industrialism itself, and in ways which probably, on balance, make for greater similarity with people in the countries where those institutions first evolved.

There is, indeed, some empirical evidence to show that increasing similarity of outlooks and values does result from these processes. A study of urban workers in six developing countries sought to measure the extent to which they held a set of attitudes and values (stressing individual choice and responsibility, belief in rationality and the possibility of controlling one's fate, etc.) which were labelled by that question-begging term 'modern'. Their responses showed clearly a greater incidence of these modern attitudes the longer the exposure to schools, to factories, and to urban living (Inkeles and Smith, 1974).

These advances in similarity are still limited: British, Chinese, and Pakistani factory workers may all live in nuclear families, have educational ambitions for their children, limit their families, and plan household expenditures, but still behave very differently towards their wives or their foremen or their politicians. Nevertheless they *are* advances in similarity stretching to social strata beyond the middle class élites, if not yet very far into the rural hinterlands where the bulk of the population of some states lives.

For these real advances in similarity to affect perceptions of similarity, and hence fellow-feeling, the second of the conditions in proposition 3 must be fulfilled – viz., increasing contact. That the density of such contacts is in fact increasing is clear enough. Inkeles uses a variety of statistics to prove the point – for university students overseas, for volumes of foreign mail, telephone calls, tourist travel, world trade, overseas investment, and the number of non-governmental international organizations (increasing in the early seventies at 5 per cent p. a.). And to physical movements must be added the worldwide exchange of television films. That factory workers are less affected than middle classes is obvious, but then they are, as argued above, less important to the argument about cultural homogeneity, fellow-feeling, and world order.

Transnational Contacts

One particular form of international contact relates to the earlier argument about industrialization and individuation as well as to the distinction, as Bull draws it, between a 'society of states' and 'world society'.

One version of the view that we are moving towards a world society is what Pettman calls the structuralist view of the world as a global capitalist system in which divisions between states are seen as ('ultimately'?) of lesser consequence than divisions between classes (Pettman, 1979). There may, indeed, be rare manifestations of global working class solidarity – Swedish workers, perhaps the world's most internationally travelled workers, have been known to strike in support of the Brazilian employees of their Swedish multinational – but the chances of growing cultural homogeneity and an emerging sense of solidarity are probably somewhat greater in the international capitalist bourgeoisie.

But greater still (since international capitalists are often competing directly with each other) are the chances of such cross-frontier solidarity among professional groups. The arguments go as follows.

One universal feature of the transformations of industrialization and modernization is a switch from family production in hereditary lines of business to wage/salary employment in *chosen* occupations. The extent to which this opportunity, even necessity, for choice promotes individualism may vary (in Japan, as is well known, it does so much less than in Britain). But everyhere it leads to some increase in individuation, some increase in the exercise of choice and in the degree to which people are committed to the choices they have made. Men and women who *choose* their loyalties are more likely to define their identity in terms of their chosen occupation, more likely to be self-consciously committed to a religious or ethnic group.

And this, together with the increase in communications and travel leads to some transnationalization of inter-personal allegiances: people who are musicians to their fingertips may feel a greater sense of brotherhood with foreign musicians than with tone deaf fellow-countrymen. Frontier-crossing ties of community of this type can develop among physicists, boy scouts, Orientalist scholars, Jews, tennis players, engineers, and bird-watchers.

These allegiances can lead, for example, to an intensified concern of UK musicians for USSR musical dissidents. Multiple pressures from musicians, writers, Jews, Baptists, etc., can prompt the US government to make human rights representations to the USSR which can lead to Helsinki agreements, and some continuing pressure to reinforce them.

The underlying process is arguably a movement towards a world society, a frontier-eroding process inimical to the institutionalization of a society of states. Yet the effective expression of this process is in inter-state agreements, and the society of states is also strengthened by the increase in the scope and diversity of the binding ties of international agreements, and by the strengthening pressures within the states to see that agreements are kept. The distinction between movement towards a world society and movement towards a society of states is a useful one, but (*pace* Bull, 1979) the two trends can be complementary rather than contradictory.

The Constituents of Culture

So far in this argument I have left the concept of 'cultural similarities' unexamined. It can, perhaps, remain that way to be understood at a common sense level. If we are concerned with the stretch of sympathy, the degree of fellow-feeling which provides the impulse occasionally to try to see the world from the other person's point of view, which prompts the diffusion of positive rather than negative stereotypes of foreign counterparts, and the willingness to take risks in, say, disarmament agreements, gambling on the other side's good faith and thereby building relations of trust, then almost any kind of similarity can contribute to it: similarity in material and artistic and intellectual culture – shared tastes for blue jeans, Polish films, hamburgers, or

Japanese pottery, the shared appreciation of engineering skills or sportsmanship on the soccer field – can be as important as deeper and more private matters like religious faiths or moral principles.

The 'world culture' which is emerging as the common elements of middle-class life-styles in Washington and Moscow, Havana and Caracas, Dakar and Tokyo, may indeed be a rather superficial matter of parallel tastes and snob values in cars or domestic architecture, classical music, or patent medicines; similar concerns about children's education and lung cancer; a similar familiarity with the Hilton Hotel coffee-shop culture of muzak and orange juice, discos and cheesecloth blouses.

But that does not necessarily reduce its importance for the diffusion of fellow-feeling. And there seems no reason to doubt that the increasing density of communications (slower though that proces may be in the recent years of economic stagnation than in the previous three decades) is leading to an increasing similarity of these urban middle-class cultures – an increasing fleshing out of a skeletal 'world culture', and its diffusion to larger numbers of people.

Inhibitors

Except where explicit obstacles are interposed to hinder this 'natural' process. One can include Moscow and Havana in a list of 'world culture' capitals, as I did above, a little more easily that one can include Peking. All countries which call themselves Communist try to limit the penetration of this 'world culture' to some degree, but the Chinese more strenuously, more publicly, and more self-consciously than most for reasons which tell us something about the nature of the phenomenon. It is not just a matter of the rejection of symbols of bourgeois ideology: there is nothing more intrinsically bourgeois about blue jeans than about dachas. It has a lot to do, also, with the nativist reaction in have-not countries which was mentioned earlier as prompting, and shaping the form of, the revival of traditional religions. When Islamic fundamentalists in Iran burn down night clubs and insist that their women veil their faces, they are not only expressing religious convictions but also the resentments bred of the deprivations of have-not status.

In poor societies, world culture, especially the material aspect of it, is a luxury culture, predominantly enjoyed by those who hold power and their friends. They are the objects of envy. This envy becomes significant when the anti-government opposition tries, as oppositions naturally do, to use nationalism against its opponents and accuse them of allowing rich and powerful countries to exploit and slight the nation with impunity. Perhaps, borrowing the paradigms of the dependency theorists, the opposition will brand the ruling group as a comprador bourgeoisie clasped in a profitable symbiotic embrace with foreign capital – an embrace which they seek to justify as a means to economic development, not understanding what sins they commit by defining development as a process of (servile) imitation of the West. Such a nationalist appeal finds it only too easy to mobilize the envy just referred to. To say that the out-of-reach grapes are immoral and forbidden is even more satisfying than claiming that they are sour. So the ruling class can be denounced for its mistaken objectives, for its lack of proper national pride in accepting subordination to foreigners, *and* for betraying the national culture by whoring after Western fads and fancies – pop music, female emancipation, eating cow meat, foreign religions, or whatever shows the most heinous contrast with local traditions.

There is a very particular twist to the process just described which can, if I may be forgiven the jargon, be called the 'second-generation indigenization phenomenon'. This brings the split between the adherents and the denouncers of Western values and life-styles into the élite groups themselves – between older and younger generations. The phenomenon can be observed in ex-colonial societies, but also in societies like Japan in the last century or China after 1949, or even, perhaps, Quebec after the Second World War, which are suddenly opened to catching-up 'modernization'. The first 'modernizer' or 'post-independence' generation has often received its training in foreign (Western) universities in a Western cosmopolitan language. Partly because they first go abroad as impressionable teenagers, their absorption of Western values and life-styles may well be profound – far more than the superficial veneer which, after a couple of decades' experience as a sergeant in a British African regiment, made Idi Amin a half plausible president of a modern state.

But the far more numerous second generation get their intellectual training at home in the new universities which the first generation have set up. They get their Western culture at second hand, and only a fraction of them get abroad, the majority for postgraduate study in their twenties when they are no longer plastically impressionable. At first the universities may use a metropolitan language (as is still the case in Singapore, in some universities or some faculties in India and Sri Lanka, and in French West Africa). At that stage the written-word contact is still first hand, and only the verbal, personal intercourse, life-style transmission is second hand. But soon the demand for mass university education forces a switch to teaching in the native language: knowledge is indigenized by means of translations – usually of limited range and of poor quality. The new universities provide a much more diluted contact with metropolitan world culture. Their products are likely to resent the superior sophistication of the older generation – who are also likely to be seen as blocking their chances of promotion in the hierarchies of the modern sector organizations into which they are recruited (or into which, as graduate unemployment increases, they *fail* to get recruited). Their proneness to succumb to the appeals of nativist opposition movements is naturally enhanced. In Japan, as the second home-trained generation gained power, this process resulted, by the early decades of this century, in a situation in which the graduates of Western universities were severely *dis*advantaged in the competition for jobs in the bureaucracy and leading modern sector organizations. The diplomatic élite of the mid-century was arguably a good deal less cosmopolitan than its counterparts at the beginning of the century. But the underlying processes of absorption of world culture have continued through the medium of Japanese-language education. It takes longer than direct foreign study and metropolitan-language transmission, but is more far reaching, and lasting in its effects.

The reactions just discussed can have a *general* effect in inhibiting the spread of world culture. They have a particular and acute effect on the diplomatic representatives of non-Western countries – the people whose ability to generate fellow-feeling with their opposite numbers has the most direct effect on the chances of creating and sustaining some kind of commitment to the rules of a world order. Their situation makes them peculiarly liable to schizophrenia. While being, by and large, the members of their country most likely to have absorbed, and to have a personal taste for, world culture, they paradoxically have the strongest motives for disavowing it – for two reasons. First, being most often in contact with foreigners they are most vulnerable to the charge of betraying the national interest and national culture. If the British Foreign Office smarts under the charge that it was almost traitorously willing the see the 'Argie' point of view over the Falklands, its travails are as nothing compared to those of Chinese diplomats during the Cultural Revolution who were forced to prove their Mao-loving Chineseness and hatred for the corrupt culture of the West in all sorts of humiliating ways.

The second reason is more complicated. The whole culture of diplomatic intercourse, of bilateral talks, international conferences, nobbling in the lobbies, and partying in the reception rooms – the arts of chairmanship, of cocktail party charm and conference rhetoric, of knowing when to be incisive and when to bore the time away, of judging what will count as a joke and what as an insult – is all part of a world culture as Western in its origins as apple pie. Diplomats from non-Western countries are often not very good at it. This can be for two reasons: first, because they have often had to start learning this kind of social intercourse in adulthood and then with limited chance of practice solely in professional contexts, whereas their opposite numbers have often been learning those, or highly cognate social skills, from childhood – in their middle class Western families as well as in schools. Secondly, doing all these things well requires confidence, especially in the crucial early stages, and it is much easier to develop that confidence if you start with the halo of the representative of a top nation than if you represent a nation low down in the prestige scale. The delegate from Ecuador, coming straight from his Swiss school and seigneurial holidays on his hacienda, soon known to the diplomatic hostesses as that charming Dr Oliviera, may suffer from the second disability, but never, at all, from the first. For the Japanese delegate the second gives fewer problems, but the first, compounded by sheer language-fluency difficulties, is likely to disadvantage him for all his professional life. For the Indonesian or the Malian delegate, both disabilities can bite with equal force. He may well have reason to feel ill at ease.

As a result two things can happen, both inhibitive of fellow-feeling. Sensing that he does not cut much of a figure by the values of that small specialist bit of world (Western) culture in which he is engaged, he may reject those values and the values of the whole world culture of which it is a part. Secondly since his contacts with his opposite numbers do not advance far in intimacy, since he does not get beyond being 'that boring Malian chap' (to be approached by such conversational gambits as 'would it be raining in your country at this time of year'), he is in effect treated in terms of his national identity rather than as a person in his own right. And that means that his national identity *does* become a more salient part of his personal sense of identity: in that context he is a Malian first, and the individual Dr Mbanka second. As such, every slight to his nation *is* a personal slight to himself. In New York, perhaps, he suddenly discovers for the first time what the xenophobia of the opposition's nativist nationalism was all about. So he may withdraw, start insisting on wearing national costume, using interpreters, and keeping his socializing to the formal minimum – and have as little sense of belonging to a world community linked by ties of fellow-feeling as a fully clothed Martian suddenly precipitated into the middle of a human nudist colony.

World Culture: Western Culture

So when one says that, *other things being equal*, an increasing density of communication should ensure an increasing basis for fellow-feeling between the nations, or at least the middle classes, or at the very least the diplomats of the world, one has to acknowledge that some of the things that may not be equal can be very important indeed.

It will be noted, however, that all the inhibiting factors listed above spring from the fact that the emergent 'world culture' is perceived as Western culture. And by and large that perception is correct: the addition of a few 'exotic' elements – Chinese cooking, vodka, soul music, the fad for Japanese quality circles in American business schools, the incorporation of Zen Buddhism and Indian Art into the catalogue of things the man of taste should appreciate, make a very small contribution to that stock of what it is that the middle class culture of Tokyo, Bonn, Dakar, etc. have in common. But the Western character of that shared culture only matters – in all the ways just described – because the Western nations identified as having a proprietary claim to that culture are clustered around the top of the international power/prestige hierarchy and seen as exercising unfair domination over the others.

When that ceases to be the case – when, say, the Japanese or the Chinese or the Koreans perfect the first cheap and effective ABM system and secure military as well as economic dominance, when it is the Tokyo or the Peking autumn collections that dominate the fashion magazines, and the computers churn out more translations from Japanese into English than vice-versa, and Japanese or Chinese universities become the goal of the world's ambitious youth – then that situation will change. World culture will still be basically Western culture. Many post-Confucian elements may be absorbed: geisha parties might replace cocktail parties at the UN and there may be more talk of benevolence and less of justice in the rhetoric. But the modes of international law and conference procedure, the *idea* of autumn collections and annual art shows, the shape of the novel and the structure and functioning of universities will still be Western in origin. But if the Western nations have been clearly demoted from their position at the top of the power/prestige hierarchy that will not matter so much. The blockages to the steady diffusion of world culture which arise from the various manifestations of the nativist reactions described above will be dissolved – not least the very important blockages to be found at present in the nations of the Sinic culture area themselves. So, in the long term, the prospects of the structure of a world order receiving reinforcement from the binding ties of a world culture might improve. The more immediate problem is to prevent the chain reactions set off by somebody's anti-Western nativism from embroiling the super-powers into a conflict which blows up the world's chance of having that long a term.

CONCLUSION

The Editors

We began this survey of the development of our present international system with the world as it was on the eve of European expansion, about the year 1500. That world was composed of a number of regional international systems, each rooted in a particular cultural tradition: one of them Christian and European, three Islamic or at least dominated by Muslims, and one centred upon China. There were marginal contacts between neighbouring systems, notably in the fields of trade, war, and religion, but these contacts did not amount to a single integrated international system, let alone a single universal international society with agreed rules and institutions. They were conducted according to the elementary precepts for human intercourse which members of different, developed civilizations have been able to utilize to define and regulate intermittent contacts. Beyond this area of developed civilizations lay the extensive still pre-literate regions of the globe.

In Part I we saw how, in the course of the next four centuries, this scene was transformed by the expansion of the Europeans over the rest of the globe. In Europe itself they fused the Western and Northern European systems into one, in which the Ottoman Empire was an active military and economic participant; and within this system they developed an elaborate and distinctive society of European states, based not on the hegemonial or suzerain-state principle, but on mutual acceptance of one another's independence and preservation of a balance of power. In the Americas, South Africa, and Australasia they established colonies of settlement which in due course became independent states. In Asia they pushed forward in competition with one another, until by the end of the eighteenth century the mercantile and colonial European powers and many west, south, and south-east Asian powers formed together a loose Eurasian system of economic and strategic ties. Finally, in the course of the nineteenth century, the European settlers came to extend their penetration over the whole of the rest of the globe, most notably Africa, and directly or indirectly to establish domination over it.

It is notable that before the nineteenth century, the more inclusive international system and society that was taking shape as the consequence of the process of expansion was not founded, either in theory or in practice, upon European claims to superior or exclusive rights, at least in relation to other developed political communities. The Spanish conquest of the Indies was indeed justified on theological premisses (challenged at the time by Vitoria), which denied its victims rights of political independence, but this took place before the idea of a secular system of inter-state relations had matured in Europe. The European powers before the nineteenth century had not entered into treaty or diplomatic relations with China and Japan, but this was more the consequence of Chinese and Japanese attitudes than of European ones. There was indeed, from the mid-seventeenth to the early nineteenth centuries, a waning sense of the special unity or intimacy of Christian states, and a waxing idea of the unity and intimacy of European ones, but this did not prove incompatible with the growth of treaty and diplomatic relations with many non-Christian and non-European powers on a basis of equality and mutual respect.

In the course of the nineteenth century this changed. As the gap in power grew between European societies and others, the Europeans extended direct rule over much of the rest of the planet and, while tolerating the continued political independence of some Asian and African states, denied them full rights in an international society whose criteria of membership they laid down. An element of cultural chauvinism and racial self-consciousness came to occupy a more prominent place in the attitudes of Europeans, who now came to think of themselves as superior not only to 'savage' or pre-literate peoples, but also to peoples of other than European civilization. The ability of the Europeans to determine events in other continents was limited not only by the capacity of other peoples to resist, but also by rivalries among the Europeans themselves: they did not face the outside world, as the hellenizing Greeks and the Latin Crusaders had done, in a posture of unity. But a cardinal feature of this first, global international system in which European expansion had resulted in the nineteenth century was that it was dominated by the European states, who had come to conceive themselves as forming an exclusive club enjoying rights superior to those of other political communities.

Part II showed how, in this era of European dominance, the club became less exclusive as various categories of non-European states were deemed to have graduated to membership. The process began with the achievement of independence by Europe's colonies of settlement in North and South America. These first 'new states' extended the geographical circle of membership of international society, whilst also fashioning a new rhetoric of national independence, non-alignment, and 'continentalism', which was to have later imitators; but because they were Christian and European in culture their presence in the club did not imply any basic challenge to the rules of membership. Nor, perhaps, did the admission of Haiti and Liberia, which in the view of some governments had taken place by the middle of the nineteenth century, on the ground that their populations, although black, were Christian.

A change was clearly taking place in the rules, however, when at the end of the Crimean War the Ottoman Empire – not only non-European in culture and race, but the historic enemy of Christendom – was declared to be admitted to the public law and concert of Europe; when later in the century China, Japan, Siam, and Persia entered into diplomatic relations with European powers, and took their places at the Hague Conferences of 1899 and 1907; and when after the First World War Ethiopia, even if after a close debate, was admitted to membership of the League of Nations.

What became clear as a consequence of this entry of non-European states into international society, registered in practice by the growth of diplomatic and treaty relations, and in theory by the writings of international lawyers, was that the 'standard of civilization' laid down by the European powers was not a permanently exclusive test of admission, but one which other than European states could and did pass. Japan, indeed, not merely became a full member of international society but by its alliance with Great Britain and victory over Russia acquired the status of a great power.

No doubt the 'standard of civilization' which the European powers used initially to deny equal status to others was often a cloak for their own aggresion, but it is a shallow view which treats it as nothing more. The standards of international conduct which the European powers observed in relation to one another could not in fact be met by those Asian and African states that were unable to provide domestic law and order, administrative integrity, protection of the rights of foreign citizens, or the fulfilment of contracts. The need for Asian and African countries to meet the 'standard of civilization' demanded by the Europeans, moreover, came to be recognized in these countries themselves, as domestic reforms were undertaken in many of these countries, often at the urging of the Europeans, to close the gap. If the eventual removal of 'extraterritoriality' regimes and other signs of inferior status showed that a system of European privilege had been brought to an end, it also reflected the fact that the Asian and African states concerned had reformed themselves domestically in such a way that in respect of their capacity to fulfil international obligations the gap between themselves and the European states had been closed.

But the international society into which these non-European states had sought and gained entry, although it was in principle universal, was still dominated by the Europeans, even as late as the Second World War. Much of Asia and nearly all of Africa and Oceania comprised colonial dependencies of the European empires. With the partial exception of Japan and Turkey, those Asian and African states that had retained their formal independence were in a position not only of practical but also of legal inferiority and subordination to European powers. The very conception of the entry of non-European states into international society, conceived as a process whereby candidates were accepted by the original members, prepared and finally deemed to have graduated, took for granted a world directorate of European states.

Part III described the rise of the coalition of Asian, African, and Latin American states and movements that transformed this European-dominated international society after the Second World War. The latter conflict left the European colonial powers exhausted and the United States and the Soviet Union, both committed to an anti-colonialist position, as the sole great powers, but they also, as quasi-European states and products of the historic process of European expansion, became the targets of Asian and African attempts to bring about a redistribution of power within the system. The anti-colonial revolution tripled the number of independent states in the world and created a new international system in which the European states were a small minority. Through the Afro-Asian movement, the Non-Aligned Movement, the Organization of African Unity, the Group of 77, and other bodies, and making use of the UN, in which they could now command easy majorities, the non-European states set about changing the international order that had been created by the Europeans so as to remove the elements of discrimination and special privilege which they held to be so conspicuous within it.

They accelerated the pace of decolonization or national liberation, and brought about a new legal and moral climate in world affairs in which colonial rule, and by extension rule by settler minorities, came to be regarded as illegitimate. They found a new target in neo-colonialism, the domination of ex-colonial and other weak countries by indirect means. They upheld the equality of races, especially in relation to the white supremacist governments of southern Africa. They formulated demands for economic justice as between rich and poor nations, culminating in their proposal in 1974 for a New International Economic Order. They found a new field of endeavour in the idea of cultural liberation, the repudiation not merely of the political and economic, but of the intellectual or spiritual suzerainty of the West, against which the resurgence of Islam, among other manifestations of this movement, served as a dramatic protest. They propagated a Third World ideology or world view, derived partly from Leninism, that served to explain the history of relations between European and non-European peoples in terms acceptable to themselves. This ideology had a deep impact on the way in which world affairs were perceived not only in Third World and Soviet bloc countries but in the Western countries also.

The transformation of the position of the non-European or non-Western peoples in the post-1945 era was not the work of Third World movements alone. The right of all nations to self-determination, the right of all states equally to sovereignty, racial equality, the duty of rich nations to assist poor, were all ideas present, or at least implicit, in the liberal political tradition of the Western countries, and indeed it was the impact of this tradition on the political beliefs of Western-educated leaders of Asian and African countries that was a major cause, along with Marxist-Leninist influences, of their struggle against the old order.

Nor could it be said, after three decades during which this struggle has been waged, that the old ascendancy of Europe, together with its American and Russian extensions, has been brought to an end. The United States and the Soviet Union remain the predominant military powers; Western Europe has experienced an economic and, to a lesser extent, a political recovery; North America and Western Europe, together with Japan, are predominant in the world economy; the rhetoric of the Third World coalition itself continues to proclaim that the dominance of the world by the rich, industrialized powers of the northern hemisphere continues unabated.

Nevertheless, the rise of the Third World, together with broader historical processes at work, has brought to an end the European-dominated international society of the late nineteenth and early twentieth centuries. There has been a vast change in the legal and moral climate in which relations between the mainly white, industrialized, and culturally European or Western countries conduct their relations with the rest of the world. There has been a considerable shift in political, economic, and even in military power away from the former and towards the latter, who are now clearly subjects and not merely objects in the international political process. A new international political order, in which the interests of the non-Western majority of states and peoples are reflected, is already in some measure constructed.

In Part IV we have considered the implications of the expansion of international society for international order at the present time. It is possible to argue that the emergence of a universal or inclusive system of states, and the collapse of European dominance in the present century, have contributed to a grave weakening of the structure of international society. Certainly, a number of features of the international society of today support this conclusion.

Although the period since the Second World War has witnessed an immense growth of international law, diplomatic representation, and international organization, it is clear that the member states of the universal international society of the late twentieth century are less united by a sense of a common interest in a framework of rules and institutions governing their relations with one another than were the European powers of the period from the end of the Napoleonic Wars to the First World War. This is especially so if we consider the extent to which the member states of international society recognize the most basic of all rules of international relations, the rules of coexistence, which enable them to recognize one another's rights to exist, and live in peace.

One basic feature of the present international order is that much of the world is under the sway of states that are not states in the strict sense, but only by courtesy. They are governments or regimes, and exercise power over persons and control over territory, but they do not possess authority, as distinct from mere power; they do not possess enduring legal and administrative structures, capable of outlasting the individuals who wield power at any one time; still less do they reflect respect for constitutions or acceptance of the rule of law. It would be absurd to maintain that all Asian and African states were of this nature, or to overlook the role played by governments of this sort in the history of Europe and its colonies of settlement. But we do have to recognize that it is no more than a pious fiction that the 160 or so governments of which international society is at present composed are not merely equal in their sovereign rights (no one pretends that they are equal in population, wealth, or power) but all alike in their character as states. A number of Asian and African states are more like the nascent states or quasi-states that existed in Europe before the age of Richelieu than they are like the modern Western and Soviet bloc states of today. They still share some of the characteristics that led European statesmen in the last century to conclude that they could not be brought into international society because they were not capable of entering into the kinds of relationship that European states had with one another. The presence of these pseudo-states or quasi-states within the international society of today, whether we regard it as good or bad, inevitable or avoidable, makes for a weakening of cohesion.

Another feature which we must note is that over large areas of the world, where during the era of European dominance the prevailing states were able to coexist with one another, today this coexistence has given place to endemic conflict or a state of war. The struggle waged by the anti-colonial movements against colonial rule involved not merely the claim that it was morally unjust but also a denial of the sovereign legal rights of colonial powers in their colonial territories. As the struggle developed, it came also to involve authorization of the use of force against colonial rule, and forcible intervention in support of national liberation; colonial rule, moreover, came to be extended by some to embrace the rule of settler or immigrant communities, to be applied to territories whose populations indicated a wish to remain connected with metropolitan powers, to be invoked in support of annexationist demands over neighbouring territories, or even to cover the case of so-called 'internal colonialism', where no question of alien rule was involved.

These examples of the breakdown of a prior coexistence arise out of the challenge delivered by the anti-colonial states to the established international order. We have also to note the extent to which coexistence has not proved possible among the anti-colonial or Third World states themselves, where in a number of cases it is obstructed by conceptions of international relations that are not compatible with the mutual acceptance by states of one another's sovereign rights. One thinks here of the long-standing conflict between Israel, by origin an anti-colonial or national liberationist settler state, and its Arab neighbours; the endemic conflicts among Arab states themselves, complicated by a pan-Arabist sentiment which challenges the legitimacy of territorial divisions among Arab states; the influence of Islamic fundamentalism and solidarism, which in strict interpretation implies that coexistence among Muslim states is not necessary because it can be transcended, and that coexistence with non-Muslims is not possible; the long hostility between India and Pakistan, that has replaced the coexistence that once prevailed between Hindu and Muslim communities in the days of British rule; the clash of China and Vietnam in South-East Asia, complicated not only by socialist or proletarian solidarism, which asserts that conflicts between peoples that have experienced proletarian revolutions are not possible, but also by a heritage in both China and Vietnam of thinking about international relations in terms of the relations of a suzerain state to its vassals.

We have also to note that militant Third World demands have persistently raised doubts in Western minds as to whether Third World countries were merely seeking a reform of the rules and institutions of international society, or were likely to repudiate them altogether in their relations both with outside parties and with one another. Certainly, at some points in the course of the last thirty years a great gap has been apparent between Western and some Third World understandings of such basic rules as the sanctity of treaties, the rule prohibiting force except in self-defence, the duty to compensate in connection with nationalization of foreign property, the immunity of envoys, the meaning of the principle of national self-determination or national liberation, the status of resolutions of the UN General Assembly, and the criteria for determining legality in international conduct. In the course of the 1970s, in particular, the clash between Western and Third World positions over the question of national liberation, the demand for a new international economic order, and the distinction between technical and political functions of the UN Specialized Agencies saw a hardening of positions on both sides and a clear erosion of the areas of consensus.

Finally, the cultural heterogeneity of the global international society of today is evidently a factor making against consensus about its underlying rules and institutions. The former European-dominated international society presupposed a Latin and Christian culture from which its rules and institutions derived and with the help of which they were reinforced. Today, the cultures of Asia, Africa, and Oceania are reasserting themselves and making their impact on relations among states, which can no longer presuppose a European or Western cultural base. In the early decades of the post-1945 period, as new Asian and African states took their place in international society and old ones asserted their rights more forcefully, there was a widespread impression that the cultural homogeneity of the international order had not been fundamentally breached because the new states were ruled by Western-educated groups, who spoke the language either of Western liberalism or (less commonly) of Western Marxism; because Western culture was widely thought to be destined to triumph throughout the world as a whole; and because these non-European states were still basically weak and in the position of suppliants.

More recently, however, the Western-educated leaders of the Asian and African countries have come to be challenged by the representatives of indigenous cultures. It has become evident that Western culture has not in fact had any easy triumph over non-Western traditions of behaviour, which have reasserted themselves vigorously in many parts of the world, the resurgence of Islamic consciousness being only the most striking example. And the acquisition of a substantial degree of political, economic, or military power by a number of non-Western countries has liberated them from the need they once felt to pay cultural deference to their Western tutors and mentors, and led them to adopt more strident and self-assertive postures which have served to make more clear how great the gap is in basic values between themselves and the Western countries. The fact that the international society of today has outgrown its original cultural base is, in the view of some students of international order at the present time, a basic source of weakness.

But in our view it would be wrong to conclude that as a consequence of the challenge to European dominance in the present century, the international society of the present time is in a state of disintegration. For one thing, it is important not to exaggerate the degree of cohesion that existed in the old, European-dominated system, which in the first half of this century gave rise to war and human catastrophe on a scale far exceeding anything that has taken place since it went into demise – not, moreover, because of any impact of the outside world upon it, but because of the inability of the European powers to manage adequately their own relations with one another.

For another thing, we have to remember that the anarchy or disorder that plays so large a role in the global international system of the present time is by no means to be ascribed solely, or perhaps even mainly, to the presence within it of new Asian and African states, or to their attempts to change the rules by which it operates in their favour. The source of the anarchy and disorder is in large measure to be found in factors that would be having their effect on the Western, industrialized world, even if it had not had to cope with the problem of adjusting itself to a resurgent Third World: the ideological divisions arising out of the Russian Revolution, the terrible legacy of the two World Wars, the tensions arising out of rapid technological, economic, and social change, the impact of nuclear weapons.

It might be thought evidence of the underlying strength and adaptability of the international society created by the Europeans that it has been able to absorb such a vast accretion of new members, interests, values, and preoccupations, without giving rise either to any clear sign that its rules and institutions are collapsing under the strain, or that the new states have repudiated them. Indeed, the most striking feature of the global international society of today is the extent to which the states of Asia and Africa have embraced such basic elements of European international society as the sovereign state, the rules of international law, the procedures and conventions of diplomacy and international organization. In all these areas they have sought to reshape existing rules and institutions, to eliminate discrimination against themselves and to assert their own interests forcefully, but all this has been against the background of the strong interests they have perceived in accepting the rules and institutions, not only because of their need to make use of them in their relations with the erstwhile dominant powers, but also because they cannot do without them in their relations with one another.

It is significant that the leaders and governments of the new states and of those which recovered their independence have demanded that the most distinctive feature of the European states system, namely the sovereignty and juridicial equality of all member states, large and small, should be maintained and reinforced. They want those modifications of the rules and institutions of European international society which are necessary to remove discrimination and accord them what they consider their rightful say in the conduct of international affairs. They attach importance to the formalities of diplomatic recognition and to membership of omnilateral international organizations such as the United Nations. In particular, Third World governments insist on the originally Western premiss that the stronger members of society have an obligation to protect the weaker, rather than licence to exploit or oppress them. In what is known as the North-South dialogue they have demanded the extension of the concept of collective security from its original Wilsonian military guarantee into a demand for collective economic security, on the very realistic ground that political independence is not enough to achieve sovereignty and that the economically powerful states also have an obligation to guarantee economic standards which a weak state cannot provide unaided. Third World governments also maintain with great firmness the European doctrine that neither collective security nor financial aid nor any other guarantee or arrangement gives the stronger powers any right to interfere in the domestic relations between the new governments and their subjects. They reject any idea of a directorate or concert of great powers entitled to 'lay down the law'. They manifest little if any wish to revert to the hegemonial or suzerain systems of states which prevailed outside Europe before the era of its expansion. In short, Third World governments do not want to replace the society of sovereign states but rather to improve their own positions within that society. This attachment to juridically equal sovereignty is encouraging to those who welcome continuity with the European system, and disappointing to those who hoped that functional or other pressures would lead to the obsolescence of the sovereign state as the basic unit of international society.

Nor are we able to regard the multicultural nature of the global international society of today as inimical to its working. The history of relations among political communities different from one another in culture, about which a good deal has been said in this book, suggests that perceived common interest will often lead to the improvization of the rules even in the absence of a common culture that already contains them. Cultures, moreover, are not indestructible, and there are few societies in the world today whose cultural complexion can be described except in terms of plurality and change. International legal, diplomatic, and administrative institutions, moreover, clearly do rest upon a cosmopolitan culture of modernity, to which the leading elements of all contemporary societies belong even if the masses of the people often do not.

It is indeed the case that the global international society of today is without the moral and cultural cohesion that underlay the European international society for almost a century after 1815. But even in the international history of Europe, that degree of cohesion was unusual: it was preceded, just as it was followed by deep ideological schisms and general war. It is a cardinal fact about our present world, and one that affords some hope for the preservation of international order within it, that the international society which was forged in Europe in the same centuries in which Europe extended its sway over the rest of the globe, has not disappeared now that Europe's sway has ended, but has been embraced by the non-European majority of states and peoples as the basis of their own approach to international relations. If there are dangers that the new majority of states, as they seek to reform international society to take account of their own interests, might strain its rules and institutions to breaking point, so are there dangers that the European or Western minority might fail to see that it is only by adjustments to change that the international society they created can remain viable.

NOTES

Chapter 1. European International Society and the Outside World

1. Eric Christiansen, *The Northern Crusades. The Baltic and the Catholic Frontier 1100–1525* (London, 1980), pp. 250–1.
2. *Henry V*, IV, 3.
3. C. H. Alexandrowicz, *An Introduction to the History of International Law in the East Indies* (Oxford, 1967).
4. A. H. L. Heeren, *Manual of the History of the European States-System and its Colonies* (F. P. Gottingen, 1809; English translation, London, 1834), vol. i, p. vii.

Chapter 2. The Military Factor in European Expansion

* Since this chapter was written Professor V. G. Kiernan has published his *European Empires from Conquest to Collapse 1815–1960* (London, 1982), which elaborates many of the points made below.

1. Peter Padfield, *The Tide of Empires: Decisive Naval Campaigns in the Rise of the West*, vol. i (London, 1979), p. 7.
2. J. H. Parry, *The Spanish Seaborne Empire* (London, 1966), pp. 95–6.
3. Sir Percival Griffiths, *The British Impact on India* (London, 1952), p. 57.
4. Sir John Fortescue, *History of the British Army*, vol. ii (London, 1899), p. 132.
5. Ibid., p. 183.
6. J. P. Lawford, *The British Army in India* (London, 1970), p. 212.
7. Griffiths, op. cit., p. 79.
8. R. G. Pierce, *Russian Central Asia 1867–1917* (Berkeley, 1960), p. 19.
9. Ibid., p. 44.
10. This phase has been brilliantly dealt with by Daniel R. Headrick in 'The Tools of Imperialism: Technology and the Expansion of European Colonial Empire in the Nineteenth Century', *Journal of Modern History*, li (June, 1979); an article that came to my attention only after this paper had been drafted.
11. G. S. Graham, *The China Station* (Oxford, 1978), p. 147.
12. Loc. cit.
13. Ibid., p. 399.
14. Quoted by Phillip Ziegler in *Omdurman* (London, 1973), p. 134.

Chapter 3. Europe in the World Economy

1. C. Cipolla, *Guns, Sails and Empires* (1965), p. 137.
2. P. K. O'Brien, 'European Economic Development', in *Economic History Review*, vol. xxxv, no. 1 (Feb. 1982), p. 7.
3. I. Wallerstein, *The Modern World System* (1974); A. G. Frank, *World Accumulation, 1492–1789* (1978); S. Amin, *Accumulation on a World Scale* (1974); A. Emmanuel, *Unequal Exchange* (1972).
4. P. Bairoch, *Commerce extérieur et développement économique de l'Europe au xixe siècle* (1976).

5. Frank, *World Accumulation*, p. 44.
6. F. Braudel and F. Spooner, 'Prices in Europe from 1450 to 1750', in E. Rich and C. Wilson, eds., *Cambridge Economic History of Europe*, iv (Cambridge, 1967), 446.
7. I. Wallerstein, *The Modern World System* (New York, 1974), p. 333.

Chapter 4. Russia and the European States System

1. Quoted in Geoffrey Parker, *Europe in Crisis 1598–1648* (London, 1979), p. 14.
2. Quoted in H. Summer, *Survey of Russian History* (London, 1944), p. 260.
3. S. M. Solovev, *History of Russia* (Petersburg, no date), vol. xvii, chapter iii.
4. James Billington, *The Icon and the Axe* (London, 1966).
5. G. F. Kennan, *Russia and the West under Lenin and Stalin* (London, 1961), p. 190.

Chapter 5. Spain and the Indies

1. Miguel León-Portilla (ed.), *The Broken Spears, The Aztec Account of the Conquest of Mexico* (London, 1962), p. 16.
2. Huamán Poma, *Letter to a King*, ed. Christopher Dilke (London, 1978), p. 108.
3. C. Jane, *Select Documents illustrating the Four Voyages of Columbus*, i (London, Hakluyt Society, Series II, LXV, 1930), p. 2.
4. H. Cortés, *Letters from Mexico*, trans. A. R. Pagden (London, 1972), p. 36.
5. Jane, p. lxxii.
6. J. H. Elliott, *The Old World and the New, 1492–1650* (Cambridge, 1970), pp. 81, 101.
7. Francisco de Vitoria, *De Indis*, ii, 3rd title.
8. O. Gierke, *Political Theories of the Middle Age*, trans. F. Maitland (Cambridge, 1900), pp. 19, 126 n.56.
9. M. F. de Navarrete, *Colección de los Viajes y Discubrimientos que hicieron por mar los españoles*, new edn. (Buenos Aires, 1945), ii. 40–8.
10. *Apparatus in quinque Decretalium Gregorianum Libros*, iii., 34, 8; *Summa Aurea Super Titulis Decretalium*, i, de Treuga et Pace, v, de Saracenis.
11. Francisco de Vitoria, ii, 2nd title, and notes to this in modern editions.
12. W. H. Prescott, *The Conquest of Peru*, vol. iii (New York, 1847), p. 5.
13. *The Spanish Colonie or Brief Chronicle of the Acts and Gestes of the Spaniardes in the West Indies*, trans. M.M.S. (London, 1583, a translation of the *Brevísima Relación*, 1540), fo. C.
14. Francisco de Vitoria, iii, 1st title.

Chapter 6. British and Russian Relations with Asian Governments

1. Robert K. Sakai, 'The Ryukyu (Liu-chiu) Islands as a Fief of Satsuma', in John K. Fairbank (ed.), *The Chinese World Order* (Cambridge, Mass., 1968).
2. *Hansard*, 3rd ser., vol. lxxll, col. 443–4.
3. Oliver B. Pollak, *Empires in Collision: Anglo-Burmese Relations in the Mid-Nineteenth Century* (Westport, Conn., 1979), pp. 76–7, 163–4, 183.
4. For Kelly's theory, which seems to me far more useful in historical explanation than Freudian or behaviourist psychology, see George A. Kelly, *The Psychology of Personal Constructs*, 2 vols. (New York, 1955), and D. Bannister and F. Fransella, *Inquiring Man: The Psychology of Personal Constructs* 2nd edn., (London, 1980).
5. Asad Husain, *British India's Relations with the Kingdom of Nepal, 1857–1947* (London, 1970), pp. 51–111 discusses Jung Bahadur's policy and the differences between Nepal's position and that of other south Asian states in relation to Britain.

6. Cf. Jung Bahadur's remark in 1864: 'I know very well the advantages that would accrue to Nepal for a few years if we were to open the country to British officers and merchants, but even supposing that we were to double our revenue for ten or twenty years, what good would that do us? At the end of that time, you would, probably, take our country.' Quoted by Mridula Abrol, *British Relations with Frontier States, 1863–1875* (New Delhi, 1974), p. 54.

Chapter 7. European States and African Political Communities

1. On the former, see especially Lucy Mair, *African Kingdoms* (Oxford, 1977). On the latter, see M. Fortes and E. Evans-Pritchard, *African Political Systems* (Oxford, 1940); and J. Middleton and D. Tait, ed., *Tribes Without Rulers* (London, 1958).
2. See Roland Oliver, ed., *The Dawn of African History* (Oxford, 1961), p. 40.
3. On the kingdom of Kongo see Jan Vansina, *Kingdoms of the Savannah* (Madison, 1966).
4. See Roger D. Masters, 'World Politics as a Primitive Political System', *World Politics* vol. xvi, no. 4 (July 1964); and Hedley Bull, *The Anarchical Society. A Study of Order in World Politics* (London, 1977), pp. 59–65.
5. See especially Ragner Numelin, *The Beginnings of Diplomacy. A Sociological Study of Inter-Tribal and International Relations* (Oxford, 1950).
6. See Robert S. Smith, 'Peace and Palaver: International Relations in Pre-colonial West Africa', *Journal of African History*, vol. xiv, no. 4 (1973); and *Warfare and Diplomacy in Pre-colonial West Africa* (London, 1976). See also A. J. G. M. Sanders, *International Jurisprudence in African Context* (Durban, 1979).
7. The text is given in Sir Edward Hertslet, *The Map of Africa by Treaty* (London, 1896), vol. i.
8. Ibid., p. 27.
9. See, for example, S. E. Crowe, *The Berlin West Africa Conference 1884*–5 (London, 1942).
10. See M. F. Lindley, *The Acquisition and Government of Backward Territory in International Law* (London, 1926); and C. H. Alexandrowicz, *The European-African Confrontation* (Leiden, 1973).
11. See Saadia Touval, 'Treaties, Borders and the Partition of Africa', *Journal of African History* vol. vii, no. 2 (1966).
12. On Shaka's mission see E. A. Ritter, *Shaka Zulu* (Harmondsworth, 1978).
13. See especially T. Ranger, 'Connexions between Primary Resistance Movements and Modern Mass Nationalism in East and Central Africa', *Journal of African History* vol. ix, nos. 3 and 4 (1968); and 'African Reactions' in L. H. Gann and P. Duignan, ed., *Colonialism in Africa 1870–1960* (Cambridge, 1969).

Chapter 10. The Ottoman Empire and the European States System

1. On the issues of state, government, and law in Islam, *jihad*, Ottoman perceptions and attitudes towards Europe, etc., see T. Naff, 'Introduction: The Central Administration, the Provinces, and External Relations', and 'Ottoman Diplomatic Relations with Europe in the Eighteenth Century: Patterns and Trends', in T. Naff and R. Owen, eds., *Studies in Eighteenth Century Islamic History* (Carbondale, Ill. and London, 1977), pp. 3–14, 75–87; 'Towards a Muslim Theory of History', *Islam and Power*, ed. A. Cudsi and A. E. Hillal Dessouki (London, 1981); 'Reform and the

Conduct of Ottoman Diplomacy in the Reign of Selim III', *Journal of the American Oriental Society*, no. 83 (1963), pp. 295–315.

2. On the reigns of Mehmet II, Bayezit II, and Selim I, see Halil Inalcik, 'Mehmed II', *Islam Ansiklopedisi* (Istanbul and Ankara, 1940 to date), vii. 506–35 (hereafter *IA*); *Fatih Devri uzerinde tetkikler ve vesikalar* (Ankara, 1954); *The Ottoman Empire* (New York, 1973), pp. 23–40; Selahettin Tansel, *Sultan II. Bayezid'in Siyasi Hayati* (Istanbul, 1966); I. H. Uzuncarsili, 'II. Bayezid', *IA*, ii. 392–8; V. J. Parry, 'Bayezid II', *EI*[2] i. 1119–21; S. N. Fisher, *The Foreign Relations of Turkey 1481–1512* (Urbana, Ill., 1948); Sinasi Altindag, 'Selim I', *IA*, x. 423–34; S. Tansel, *Yavuz Sultan Selim* (Ankara, 1969); V. J. Parry, 'The Ottoman Empire (1481–1520)', *New Cambridge Modern History* (Cambridge, 1957), i. 395–410; G. W. F. Stripling, *The Ottoman Turks and the Arabs, 1511–1574* (Urbana, Ill., 1942 and 1968); on Suleyman the Magnificent see M. Tayyip Gokbilgin, 'Suleyman I', *IA*, xi. 99–155; H. Inalcik, 'The Heyday and Decline of the Ottoman Empire', *Cambridge History of Islam* (Cambridge, 1970), i. 324–53; and *Ottoman Empire*, pp. 31–40; on the agreement of 1536 see Inalcik, ibid., p. 228; Ismail Soysal, 'Turk-Fransiz diplomasi munasebetlerinin ilk devresi', *Tarih Dergisi*, iii (1953), 63–94; J. C. Hurewitz, *The Middle East and North Africa, A Documentary Record* (New Haven and London, 1975), i. 1–5. On the contemporary European view of the Ottomans, Richard Knolles, *The general historie of the Turkes* (London, 1603), cited also in B. Lewis, *The Muslim Discovery of Europe* (New York and London, 1982), p. 32; on the influence of the Ottomans on the Reformation, see S. A. Fisher-Galati, *Ottoman Imperialism and German Protestantism, 1521–1555* (Cambridge, Mass., 1959); Max Kortepeter, *Ottoman Imperialism during the Reformation* (New York, 1972), pp. 126–36, 215–44; R. S. Schwoebel, *The Shadow of the Crescent: The Renaissance Image of the Turk, 1453–1517* (New York, 1967); on the Islamic and European frontiers in the Mediterranean during the 16th century, see F. Braudel, *The Mediterranean and the Mediterranean World in the Age of Philip II*, 2 vols. (New York and London, 1972), and (as a corrective) A. Hess, *The Forgotten Frontier* (Chicago and London, 1978). See also O. Okyar, 'Ottoman Economic Growth During the 16th Century', *Turkiye'nin Sosyal ve Ekonomik Tarihi (1071–1920)* (Ankara, 1980), pp. 111–16.
3. Very good summary treatments of the reigns of the sultans of the seventeenth century can be found under the appropriate headings in *IA* i. 164–5; v. 880–5; viii. 625–47, 692–700; ix. 443–8; vii. 547–57; xi. 155–70; see also Paul Rycaut, *Present State of the Ottoman Empire* (London, 1668; Arno reprint, New York, 1971), esp. pp. 75–96; A. N. Kurat, 'The Retreat of the Turks 1683–1730', *New Cambridge Modern History*, vi. 608–47; A. H. De Groot, *The Ottoman Empire and the Dutch Republic, 1610–1630* (Leiden, 1978), pp. 106 ff. and 190–231; R. A. Abou El-Haj, 'Ottoman Diplomacy at Karlowitz', *Journal of the American Oriental Society* lxxxvii (1967), 498–512; B. Lewis, *Islam in History* (New York, 1973), pp. 199–216 and *idem*, 'Ottoman Observers of Ottoman Decline', *Islamic Studies* i (1962), 71–87.
4. A. K. Kurat, *Prut Seferi ve Barisi*, 2 vols. (Ankara, 1951), i. 74, 76–7, 136, 139–42, 287; ii. 517, 634; M. L. Shay, *The Ottoman Empire from 1720 to 1734* (Urbana, Ill., 1944), pp. 93 ff., 142–6; H. Inalcik, 'Reisulkuttab', *IA*, ix. 671–82; N. Itzkowitz, 'Eighteenth Century Ottoman Realities', *Studia Islamica*, xvi. (1962), 73–94; T. Naff, 'Reform and Diplomacy', *JAOS* lxxxiii (1963), 295–315; A. W. Fisher, *The Russian Annexation of the Crimea, 1772–1783* (Cambridge, 1970), pp. 19–28; Destari Salih Efendi, *Tarih*, ed. B. S. Baykal (Ankara, 1962), pp. 1–48; I. H. Uzuncarsili, *Osmanli Tarihi*, vol. iv, pt. 1 (Ankara, 1956), pp. 255 ff.; pt. 2, p. 266; Hurewitz, *Middle East*, i. 92–101; B. Lewis, *Muslim Discovery*, pp. 61–3.

5. T. Naff, 'Reform and Diplomacy', pp. 295 ff.; Inalcik, 'Imtiyazat', *EI*[2]; *Muahedat Mecmuasi*, 5 vols. (Istanbul, 1877–80), especially the concessions of 1774, 1779, and 1783, iii. 275–84; Ahmet Cevdet Pasha, *Cevdet Tarihi*, Tertib-i Cedid, 12 vols. (Istanbul, 1884–5), ii. 135, 144, iii. 125–7, vi. 129–30, 253–7; N. Sousa, *The Capitulatory Regime of Turkey* (Baltimore, 1933), pp. 15–42, 70–7, 93–100; Charles Issawi, ed., *The Economic History of the Middle East*, pp. 30–7, 46–59; T. Naff, 'Ottoman Relations with Europe', *Studies*, pp. 93–103; N. Berkes, *The Development of Secularism in Turkey* (Montreal, 1964), pp. 51–85.
6. On Ahmed Resmi see *Hulusat-up Itibar* (Istanbul, 1899), pp. 75–6; Unat, *Osmanli Sefirleri ve Sefaretnameleri* (Ankara, 1968), pp. 102–5; *IA*, 'Ahmed Resmi', p. 268; on Selim III's diplomacy and reforms, T. Naff, 'Reform and Diplomacy', *JAOS*, pp. 295 ff. and idem, 'Ottoman Relations with Europe', *Studies*, pp. 102–7; S. Shaw, *Between Old and New: The Ottoman Empire under Sultan Selim III, 1789–1807* (Cambridge, Mass., 1971), pp. 71–210; M. S. Anderson, *The Eastern Question, 1774–1923* (London and New York, 1966), pp. 1–40; the Tri-Partite Treaty of 1799 and Amiens 1802, Hurewitz, *Middle East*, i. 126–33, 140–1, 154–5; Ahmed Asim, *Asim Tarihi*, 2 vols. (Istanbul, 1871), i. 67–70, ii. 237–59; Cevdet, *Tarihi*, vii. 304–11 ff.
7. Hurewitz, *Middle East*, 275. On Mahmud II's reign, Cevdet, *Tarihi*, x. 200 ff.; I. H. Danismend, *Iyhali Osmanli Tarihi Kronolojisi*, 4 vols. (Istanbul, 1961), iv. 93–120; B. Lewis, *The Emergence of Modern Turkey* (London and New York, 2nd edn., 1968), pp. 75–103; N. Berkes, *Secularism*, pp. 89–135; on the Greek War of Independence, Mahmud's rivalry with Muhammad Ali, and the rivalry of the European powers through the Crimean War, see *Anderson, Eastern Question*, pp. 53–148; on Muhammad Ali see P. J. Vatikiotis, *The Modern History of Egypt* (New York, 1969), pp. 49–125; for the Turkish perspective, see S. Shaw, *History of the Ottoman Empire and Modern Turkey*, 2 vols. (Cambridge, Mass., 1977), ii. 1–83; Danismend, *Kronoloji*, iv. 120–83; on the economic background see Issawi, *Economic History*, pp. 17–90; on Hunkyar Iskelesi, the Convention of 1840 and Self-Denying Protocol, and the Treaty of Paris 1856, as well as documents relevant to the diplomatic manoeuvres of the European powers 1833–56, see Hurewitz, *Middle East*, pp. 252–319.
8. Ibid. 275.

CHAPTER 11. CHINA'S ENTRY INTO INTERNATIONAL SOCIETY

1. See Hedley Bull, *The Anarchical Society. A Study of Order in World Politics* (London, 1977), pp. 9–16.
2. C. H. Alexandrowicz, *The European-African Confrontation* (Leiden, 1973), p. 5.
3. Immanuel C. Y. Hsu, *China's Entrance into the Family of Nations* (Cambridge, Mass., 1960), p. 3.
4. Hsin-Pao Chang, *Commissioner Lin and the Opium War* (Cambridge, Mass., 1970), p. ix.
5. Ssu-yu Teng, *Chang Hsi and the Treaty of Nanking* (Chicago, 1944), p. v.
6. Chang, *Commissioner Lin and the Opium War*, p. 40.
7. H. B. Morse, *The International Relations of the Chinese Empire* (London, 1910), i. 299.
8. Ibid.
9. Masataka Banno, *China and the West 1858–1861* (Cambridge, Mass., 1964), p. 10.
10. Some of the parameters of this process are examined in John K. Fairbank, 'Synarchy Under the Treaties', in *Chinese Thought and Institutions*, ed. John K. Fairbank (Chicago, 1957) and Rhoads Murphey, 'The Treaty Ports and

China's Modernization', in *The Chinese City Between Two Worlds*, ed. Mark Elvin and G. William Skinner, (Stanford, Calif., 1974).
11. Successive treaty texts can be compared in Godfrey E. P. Hertslet, ed., *Hertslet's China Treaties*, 3rd edn. (London, 1908), 2 vols.
12. John Carter Vincent, *The Extraterritorial System in China*, Harvard East Asian Monographs No. 30 (Cambridge, Mass., 1970), p. 2.
13. Jerome Ch'en, 'Historical Background', in *Modern China's Search for A Political Form*, ed. Jack Gray (London, Oxford University Press under the auspices of the Royal Institute of International Affairs, 1969), p. 12.
14. Banno, *China and the West*, p. 1.
15. Ibid., p. 243.
16. Mary C. Wright, *The Last Stand of Chinese Conservatism* (Stanford, Calif., 1957), p. 231.
17. Jerome A. Cohen and Hungdah Chiu, *People's China and International Law* (New Jersey, 1974), i. 12.
18. *Important Documents Relating to China's Revolution, 1912* (Shanghai, 1912), pp. 67–8 cited in Hungdah Chiu, 'Comparison of the Nationalist and Communist Chinese Views of Unequal Treaties', in *China's Practice of International Law*, Harvard Studies in East Asian Law 6, ed. Jerome A. Cohen (Cambridge, Mass., 1972), p. 244.
19. Sun Yat-sen, *The Three Principles of the People* (San Min Chu I), trans. Frank W. Price (Taipei, Taiwan, n.d.), p. i.
20. Fariborz Nozari, *Unequal Treaties in International Law* (Stockholm, 1971), p. 112.

Chapter 12. Japan's Entry into International Society

1. *Tsūkō-ichiran*, (Tokyo, 1912), vol. 1, preface, p. 1.
2. Hidetaka Nakamura, *Nissen-kankei-shi no Kenkyu*, 3 vols. (Tokyo, 1969), vol. iii, chapters 3 and 8.
3. Ibid., pp. 302–3.
4. Eishō Miyagi, *Ryūkyū no Rekishi* (Tokyo, 1977), pp. 94 ff.
5. Nakamura, op. cit., vol. iii, p. 540.
6. John Stephan, *The Kuril Islands* (Oxford, 1974), pp. 52 ff.
7. Kiyoshi Tabohashi, *Kindai Nihon Gaikoku-kankei-shi*, rev. edn. (Tokyo, 1943, reprinted 1976), chapter 13.
8. Sakuzō Yoshino, 'Waga-kuni Kindaishi ni okeru Seiji-ishiki no Hassei', in his *Sūfu to Naikaku* (Tokyo, 1950), pp. 85–6.
9. On the Iwakura Mission, see W. G. Beasley, *The Modern History of Japan*, 2nd edn. (London, 1967), pp. 113–14.
10. Note Harris's effort to teach basic principles of international trade to the Bakufu administrators. See Toshio Ueda, 'Nihon no Kaikoku to Chūgoku', in *Kokusaihō Gaikō Zassi* vol. xlix (1950), nos. 2, 4, and 5, pp. 347 ff., esp. p. 355; p. 471.
11. See Tabohashi, op. cit., p. 631.
12. Takashi Ishii, *Nihon Kaikoku-shi* (Tokyo, 1972), pp. 230 and 276–7. Tabohashi, op. cit., p. 630.
13. Yoshino, op. cit.
14. J. Shinobu, 'Vicissitudes of International Law in the Modern History of Japan', in *Kokusaihō Gaikō Zassi*, vol. l (1951), no. 1, pp. 217 ff.
15. Michiari Uete, 'Taigaikan no Tenkai', in Bunsō Hashikawa and Sannosuke Matsumoto, *Kindai Nihon Seiji Shisōshi*, 2 vols. (Tokyo, 1971), vol. i, pp. 33–74, esp. p. 36.
16. Shinkichi Etō, *Kindai Chūgoko Seijishi Kenkyu* (Tokyo, 1968), pp. 235 ff.

17. Ueda, op. cit., pp. 129 ff. and 474 ff.
18. Martin Wright, *Power Politics*, ed. Hedley Bull and Carsten Holbraad (Leicester, 1978), p. 46.

Chapter 13. The Era of the Madates System and the Non-European World

1. Quoted by David Hunter Miller, 'The Origins of the Mandates System', *Foreign Affairs* (Jan. 1928), p. 277.
2. See *Foreign Relations of the United States: The Paris Peace Conference 1919*, vol. ii.
3. Imperial War Cabinet Minutes, 20 Dec. 1918, CAB 23/42. All CAB., PREM, CO, and FO references are to documents at the Public Record Office, London.
4. *Foreign Relations: Paris Peace Conference 1919*, iii. 750.
5. *Parliamentary Debates* (Commons), 14 June 1921, c. 266.
6. W. K. Hancock and Jean van der Poel, eds., *Selections from the Smuts Papers* (4 vols., Cambridge, 1966), iv. 55–6.
7. Eastern Committee Minutes, 5 Dec. 1918, CAB. 27/24.
8. 16 Aug. 1941.
9. Moyne to Amery, 26 Aug. 1941, CO 323/1858/9057.
10. Memorandum entitled 'Constitutional Future of the British Empire', enclosed in Eastwood to Martin, 1 Sept. 1941, PREM 4/42/9.
11. 'The First World War in African History', *Journal of African History* vol. ix, no. 2 (1968), pp. 337–8.
12. See Elie Kedourie, *In the Anglo-Arab Labyrinth* (Cambridge, 1976).
13. Quoted by Christopher Sykes, *Crossroads to Israel* (London, 1965), p. 57.
14. *Parliamentary Debates* (Commons), 22 May 1939, c. 2006.
15. Richard Meinertzhagen, *Middle East Diary* (London, 1959), pp. 17–18.
16. Ibid.
17. Elizabeth Monroe, *Britain's Moment in the Middle East 1914–1956* (London, 1963), p. 89.
18. JP (46), 27, 18 Feb. 1946; minutes in CO 537–1842–45 and FO 371/52572.
19. *Parliamentary Debates* (Commons), 22 May 1939, c. 2035.
20. Minute by Amery, 2 Feb. 1920, CO 649/21.
21. Memorandum by the General Staff, 22 Dec. 1920, CAB 24/117.
22. Imperial War Cabinet Minutes, 20 Dec. 1918, CAB. 23/42.
23. See Memorandum by Smuts, 'The Italian Colonies, and British Interests in the Mediterranean-Red Sea Route', 25 Sept. 1945, CP (45) 189, CAB 129/2.
24. This is one of the main themes of James B. Crowley, *Japan's Quest for Autonomy* (Princeton, 1966).
25. As recorded in Alston to Curzon, no. 33, 23 Jan. 1920, *Documents on British Foreign Policy*, First Series, vol. vi, no. 695.
26. Memorandum by Wellesley, 20 Oct. 1921, FO 371/6660.

Chapter 15. The Emergence of the Third World

1. See 'What is the Third World?', *Third World Foundation monographs* (London, 1981).
2. See John T. Marcus, *Neutralism and Nationalism in France* (New York, 1958) and Peter Lyon, 'Neutrality and the emergence of the concept of neutralism', *Review of Politics* (Apr. 1960).
3. The first mention of the Non-Aligned 'movement' in an official meeting seems to have been at the Preparatory Committee of Non-Aligned Countries meeting in

Kabul, Afghanistan, in May 1973. See O. Jankowitsch and K. P. Sauvant (eds.), *The Third World Without Superpowers. The Collected Documents of the Non-Aligned Countries* (New York, 1978), ii. 530. The NAM and/or the Group of 77 today are often rather too easily identified with 'the Third World', though 'the Third World' is a much more metaphorical term and has no distinctive institutional embodiments of its own as have the NAM and the G77.

4. See Peter Lyon, *Neutralism* (Leicester, 1963), esp. chapter 6; see also G. H. Jansen, *Afro-Asia and Non-Alignment* (London, 1966) and Robert A. Mortimer, *The Third World Coalition in International Politics* (New York, 1980).
5. For the Cairo conference of October 1964 see Peter Lyon, 'Non-alignment and the Cairo Conference', *Peace News* Oct. 1964; and for an elaboration of this theme of viewing Non-Alignment from its Summit Conferences see Peter Lyon, 'Non-Alignment at the Summits. From Belgrade 1961 to Havana 1979. A Perspective View', *The Indian Journal of Political Science* vol. xli, no. 1 (Mar. 1980).
6. See Mortimer (1980), esp. chapter 3; also Peter Lyon and Carol Geldart, 'The Group of 77: a Perspective View', *International Affairs*, winter 1980–1.
7. There is still, so far as I know, no serious analysis of this conference, though much of its documentation is available in volume 4 of Jankowitsch and Sauvant (eds.), mentioned at note 3 above.
8. See Peter Willetts, *The Non-Aligned in Havana. Documents of the Sixth Summit Conference and an Analysis of their significance for the Global Political System* (London, 1980).

Chapter 16. Racial Equality

1. I am grateful to Mr Dan Keohane for his comments on an earlier version of this chapter.
2. Lothrop Stoddard, *The Rising Tide of Colour* (London, 1922), p. 5.
3. Ibid., p. 300.
4. Ibid., pp. 169–70 and 198.
5. A. P. Thornton, *The Imperial Idea and Its Enemies* (London, 1959), pp. 73–6.
6. Quoted in ibid., p. 82.
7. See Christopher Thorne, *Allies of a Kind: The U.S., Great Britain and the War Against Japan 1941–1945* (London, 1978), pp. 8 and 356.
8. Stoddard, *Rising Tide, passim.*
9. An Asian observer has the First World War collapsing rather than merely undermining the European's conviction of their superiority (although he excepts Churchill from this generalization). K. M. Pannikar, *Asia and Western Dominance* (London, 1953), p. 265.
10. Stoddard, *Rising Tide*, pp. 173–9 and 207–9.
11. Hugh Tinker says that when the terms 'racialist' and 'racialism' entered the English language between the two world wars, they were applied to those who sought to upset white dominance. *Race, Conflict and the International Order* (London, 1977), pp. 131–2. How the terms are more commonly associated either with any doctrine asserting the superiority of one race over others, or with the particular doctrine of white superiority.
12. Arthur de Gobineau, *The Inequality of Human Races*, transl. Adrian Collins (London, 1915), pp. 205–7.
13. Benjamin Kidd, *Social Evolution*, 3rd edn. (London, 1902), pp. 31, 43, 47, 278, and 329.
14. Sir Charles Dilke, *Greater Britain* (London, 1870), p. 88.

15. Frank B. Livingstone quoted in M. Banton and J. Harwood, *The Race Concept* (London, 1975), pp. 56–7.
16. From UNESCO's Moscow Declaration on Race cited in John Rex, *Race Relations in Sociological Theory* (London, 1970), pp. 2–4.
17. See L. C. Dunn, 'Race and Biology', in Leo Kuper, ed., *Race, Science and Society* (New York, 1975), p. 41.
18. Ralph Korngold, *Citizen Toussaint* (London, 1945), p. 32.
19. Ibid., p. 171.
20. *The Cambridge History of the British Empire*, vol. ii (Cambridge, 1940), p. 202.
21. Ibid., p. 200.
22. Ibid., p. 91.
23. Quoted in Korngold, *Citizen Toussaint*, pp. 147–8.
24. Quoted in ibid., p. 7.
25. Winwood Reade, quoted in V. G. Kiernan, *The Lords of Human Kind* (London, 1969), p. 280.
26. Kiernan, *Lords of Human Kind*, p. 180; Edward Said, *Orientalism* (London, 1978), p. 38.
27. Panikkar, *Asia and Western Dominance*, pp. 206–8.
28. Kiernan, *Lords of Human Kind*, p. 156.
29. See Harold Nicolson, *Peacemaking 1919* (London, 1933), pp. 145–6.
30. Thorne, *Allies of a Kind*, p. 4.
31. The tenacity of notions of western superiority in war is illustrated in Michael Herr's book on Vietnam. 'The belief that one Marine was better than ten Slopes saw Marine squads fed in against known NVA platoons, platoons against companies, and on and on, until whole batallions found themselves pinned down and cut off. That belief was undying . . .' (*Dispatches* (London, 1978), p. 86).
32. Thorne, *Allies of a Kind*, pp. 7–10, 727–8.
33. Ibid., p. 730.
34. Jerome Ch'en, *China and the West* (London, 1979), pp. 44 and 46.
35. Ibid., p. 45.
36. Ibid.
37. Ibid., p. 58.
38. Dilke, *Greater Britain*, p. 192.
39. Ibid., p. 190.
40. Russell Ward, *Australia* (Sydney, 1969), p. 121.
41. Dilke, *Greater Britain*, pp. 339–40.
42. Richard Jebb, *The Empire in Eclipse* (London, 1926), p. 334.
43. Ibid., p. 335.
44. Panikkar, *Asia and Western Dominance*, pp. 149–62.
45. Kiernan, *Lords of Human Kind*, pp. 42–5.
46. See Louis L. Connell, *Kipling in India* (London, 1966), p. 5.
47. Jawarharlal Nehru, *An Autobiography* (London, 1936), p. 417.
48. Ibid., p. 419. Nehru also quotes Gandhi in this non-racial vein. The point about the British was their foreignness not their race. Ibid., p. 533.
49. See James S. Coleman, *Nigeria: Background to Nationalism* (Berkeley and Los Angeles, 1958), p. 97.
50. Quoted in Bernard Porter, *Critics of Empire* (London, 1968), p. 20.
51. Speech to the House of Commons, 13 June 1910.
52. Porter, *Critics*, pp. 151–4.
53. Ibid., p. 181.

54. *The Cambridge History of the British Empire* vol. viii. (Cambridge, 1963), pp. 262–5, 281–2.
55. *CHBE*, vol. iii (Cambridge, 1967), p. 371.
56. *CHBE*, iii. 374–5.
57. Speech to the House of Commons, 16 August 1909.
58. *CHBE*, iii. 374–5.
59. Ibid.
60. Panikkar, *Asia and Western Dominance*, pp. 494–5.
61. See *CHBE*, ii. 191–2; Jebb, *The Empire in Eclipse, passim.*
62. *CHBE*, iii. 348.
63. Kiernan, *The Lords of Human Kind*, p. 55.
64. Frantz Fanon, *The Wretched of the Earth*, (Harmondsworth, 1967), pp. 170–1.
65. Coleman, *Nigeria*, p. 107.
66. Ali Mazrui, *Towards a Pax Africana* (Chicago, 1967), chaps. 1 and 2.
67. Mazrui, *Africa's International Relations* (London, 1977), chap. 1.

Chapter 17. China and the International Order

1. For full text see *A Documentary History of Chinese Communism* ed. Brandt, Schwartz, and Fairbank (Harvard, 1952), pp. 449–61. The italicized sentence was edited out of later Peking editions of Mao's works, for diplomatic reasons.
2. Khrushchev's memoirs provide a glimpse of this period, and make it clear that Stalin did not exempt Mao from his usual paranoiac suspicion. The Chinese Communist Party as a whole had grievances against the Soviet Party going back at least to the Shanghai blood-bath of 1927, which was largely occasioned by following Soviet advice. For an account covering the period to 1973, see Alfred O. Low, *The Sino-Soviet Dispute* (Brunswick, N.J. 1976). See also N. S. Khrushchev, *Khrushchev Remembers: the last testament* (ed. Talbott, 1974).
3. According to an interview given by the then Defence Minister, Chen Yi, *Evening Standard*, 31 May 1966.
4. Lin Piao, *Long Live the Victory of the People's War*. Full text is reprinted in Samuel B. Griffith, *Peking and People's Wars* (London, 1966): '. . . The Khrushchev revisionists have come to the rescue of US imperialism just when it is most panic-stricken and helpless in its efforts to cope with people's war. Working hand in glove with the US imperialists, they are doing their utmost to spread all kinds of arguments against people's war and, where ever they can they are scheming to undermine it by overt or covert means. . . .'
5. A fuller account of official attitudes to Lin Piao may be found in Philip Bridgham, 'The Fall of Lin Piao', *China Quarterly*, July–Sept. 1973.
6. *White House Years* (London, 1979), pp. 163f.
7. Report to the 10th Congress of the Chinese Communist Party (Peking, 1973).
8. *Renmin Ribao*, 1 Nov. 1977.
9. *Houngi*, Oct. 1978.
10. Hu Yuabang (General Secretary of the Communist Party) to the Japanese Minister, *Xinhua*, 3 Dec. 1980.
11. Michael Loewe, *Imperial China: The Historical Background to the Modern Age* (New York, 1963).

Chapter 18. India and the International Order – Retreat from Idealism

1. K. M. Panikkar, *Asia and Western Dominance* (London, 1953).
2. Ibid., p. 11.
3. See H. Bull, *The Anarchical Society* (London, 1977), for a comprehensive treatment of this theme. The anarchical society is inevitably an unequal society. Professor Bull identifies as one of the main features of the anarchical society, i.e. society without government, 'the politically competent groups may legitimately use force in defence of their rights, while individuals and groups other than these must look to the privileged, politically competent groups for protection, rather than resort to force themselves' (p. 62).
4. For a survey of India's foreign policy, see Charles H. Heimsath and Surjit Mansingh, *A Diplomatic History of Modern India* (New Delhi, 1971); also Bimal Prasad (ed.), *India's Foreign Policy* (New Delhi, 1979).
5. Jawaharlal Nehru, *India and the World* (London, 1936), p. 23.
6. S. Gopal (ed.), *Jawaharal Nehru, an Anthology* (Delhi, 1980), p. 346.
7. Nehru, *India and the World*, p. 46.
8. Ibid., p. 178.
9. Ibid., p. 177.
10. Henry Kissinger, *The White House Years* (London, 1979), p. 845.
11. J. Nehru, *Independence and After* (New Delhi, 1949), p. 241.
12. Tibor Mende, *Conversations with Nehru* (London, 1956), p. 98.
13. Nehru, *Independence and After*, p. 257.
14. For the text of the India-China Agreement on Trade and Intercourse between Tibet region of China and India, dated 29 April 1954, see *Foreign Policy of India, Text of Documents 1947–1964* (New Delhi, 1966), pp. 198–206.
15. *Jawaharlal Nehru's Speeches, 1953–1957* (Delhi, 1958), pp. 262–3.
16. Nehru, *Independence and After*, pp. 274–8.
17. *Jawaharlal Nehru's Speeches, 1953–1957*, pp. 329–31; see also J. D. P. Miller, *The Commonwealth: Survey of Commonwealth Affairs, 1953–1969* (London, 1974), pp. 42–3.
18. See Michael Lipton and John Finn, *The Erosion of a Relationship, India and Britain since 1960* (London, 1975).
19. See Stephen N. Hay, *Asian Ideas of East and West* (Cambridge, Mass., 1970), for a comprehensive discussion of Indian ideas of Asia and Europe, first developed by Ravindranath Tagore and later taken up by Nehru and Radhakrishnan. The contrasting images of Asia as peaceful and Europe as dynamic and violent and oppressive were popular in India till about the mid-fifties.
20. Gopal, *Jawaharlal Nehru, an Anthologj*, p. 361.
21. See Nehru's speech at the 11th session of the Institute of Pacific Relations, Lucknow, October 1950, in *Jawaharlal Nehru's Speeches, 1949–1953* (Delhi, 1954), p. 160.
22. Gopal, *Jawaharlal Nehru, an Anthology*, p. 399.
23. Mende, *Conversations with Nehru*, p. 138.
24. See J. Bandyopadhyaya, 'The Non-Aligned Movement and International Relations', *India Quarterly*, Apr.–June 1977, pp. 137–64.
25. *Jawaharlal Nehru's Speeches, 1957–1963* (Delhi, 1964), p. 317.
26. T. Ramakrishna Reddy, *India's Policy in the United Nations* (Rutherford, New Jersey, 1968), pp. 24–5.
27. *Jawaharlal Nehru's Speeches, 1949–1953*, pp. 348–9.

28. Gopal, *Jawaharlal Nehru*, vol. ii, 1947–1956 (London, 1979), p. 288.
29. Michael Brecher, *India and World Politics, Krishna Menon's View of the World* (London, 1968), p. 133.
30. For the text of the Simla Agreement concluded between India and Pakistan in July 1972, see *Asian Recorder*, vol. xviii, no. 29 (1973), p. 10876.
31. Nehru, *Independence and After*, p. 278; Mende, *Conversations with Nehru*, p. 76.
32. See Onkar Marwah, 'India's Military Power and Policy', in O. Marwah and J. D. Pollack (eds.), *Military Power and Policy in Asian States: China, India, Japan* (Boulder, Colorado, 1980), p. 129.
33. *Jawaharlal Nehru's Speeches, 1963–1964* (Delhi, 1968), p. 190.
34. The Constituent Assembly of India (Legislative), *Debates*, vol. v (1984), p. 3,334.
35. *Jawaharlal Nehru's Speeches, 1953–1957*, p. 257.
36. Michael Mandelbaum, *The Nuclear Question: The United States and Nuclear Weapons, 1946–1976* (Cambridge, 1979), pp. 193–4.
37. Ashok Kapur, *International Nuclear Proliferation, Multilateral Diplomacy and Regional Aspects* (New York/London, 1979), p. 10.
38. Ibid.
39. M. Rajan Menon, 'The Military and Security Dimensions of Indo-Soviet Relations', in Robert H. Donaldson (ed.), *The Soviet Union and the Third World* (London, 1981), p. 237.
40. Indira Gandhi, *India – Speeches and Reminiscences* (London, 1975), p. 137.

Chapter 19. Africa Entrapped

1. For a fuller treatment of this subject see p. 319.
2. Basil Davidson, *The African Genius* (Boston, 1969), pp. 211–12.
3. A. S. Kanya-Forstner, 'Mali-Tukulor', in Michael Crowder (ed.), *West African Resistance* (New York, 1971), p. 53.
4. Crowder, *West African Resistance*, p. 15.
5. Crowder, *West African Resistance*, p. 15.
6. Aimé Césaire, *Return to My Native Land* (Paris, 1939).
7. Colin Leys, *Underdevelopment in Kenya: The Political Economy of Neo-Colonialism* (London, 1975).
8. F. Engels, 'Russia and the Social Revolution', *Volksstaat* (Leipzig, 21 Apr. 1875).

Chapter 20. Islam in the International Order

1. Daniel Pipes, ' "This World is Political!!" The Islamic Revival of the Seventies', *Orbis*, xxiv (Spring 1980), 9–41.
2. V. S. Naipaul, *Among the Believers: An Islamic Journey* (London, 1981), p. 285.
3. James Finn, 'Secular Discontents', *Worldview*, vol. 24, no. 3 (Mar. 1981), pp. 5–8.
4. Daniel Bell, *The Cultural Contradictions of Capitalism* (London, 1976), p. 170.
5. Dante L. Germino and others have done extensive work on this notion. See, for example, Germino, *Political Philosophy and the Open Society* (Baton Rouge, 1982).
6. See Mohammad Kamal Hassan, 'Contemporary Muslim Religio-Political Thought in Indonesia: the Response to 'New Order Modernisation'' ' (unpublished Ph.D. thesis, Columbia University, 1975).
7. Alexandre Bennigsen, 'Muslim Religious Establishment and Muslim Religion in Soviet Union', unpublished paper presented to the Foreign and Commonwealth Office Seminar on Soviet Central Asia, London (9–10 Apr. 1982), p. 12.
8. For example, see Koran, iii. 106; viii. 47.

9. Kalim Siddiqui, *Beyond the Muslim Nation-States* (London, 1980), pp. 10–11.
10. Koran, xlix. 13.
11. Ibid. iii. 103.
12. See G. H. Jansen, *Militant Islam* (London, 1979), esp. pp. 172–87.
13. For example, see Bernard Lewis, *The Middle East and the West* (New York, 1964), pp. 115–40; also, Adda Bozeman, *The Future of Law in a Multicultural World* (Princeton, 1979), pp. 50–85.
14. Koran, ii. 190.
15. Ibid. ii. 193.
16. Ibid. xiv. 23.
17. Ibid. viii. 61.
18. Much of the dispute centres about the interpretation in the Koran of iv. 90.
19. See Majid Khadduri, *War and Peace in the Law of Islam*, (Baltimore, 1955), pp. 251–67.
20. Rudolph Peters, *Islam and Colonialism: The Doctrine of Jihad in Modern History* (The Hague, 1979), p. 140.
21. See *Islam and a New International Economic Order: The Social Dimension* (Geneva, 1980).
22. See, for example, Marcel A. Boisard, *L'Humanisme de l'Islam* (Paris, 1979).

CHAPTER 21. THE SOVIET UNION AND THE THIRD WORLD

1. Some of the ideas underlying this essay were earlier developed in my book *Model or Ally. The Communist Powers and the Developing Countries* – particularly in the Introduction and the Epilogue.
2. Quoted from the Russian edition of Trotsky's Collected Works (*Sochineniya*, xii. 104) in E. H. Carr, *The Bolshevik Revolution*, vol. iii (London, 1953), p. 231, n. 1.
3. Lenin, 'Better Fewer but Better' (Mar. 1923), *Collected Works* (English edn., Moscow, 1966), p. 500.

CHAPTER 22. FRANCE: ADJUSTMENT TO CHANGE

1. Charles de Gaulle, *Mémoires d'espoir*, vol. i (Paris, 1970), p. 41.
2. C. M. Andrew and A. S. Kanya-Forstner, *France Overseas: The First World War and the Climax of French Imperial Expansion* (London, 1981).
3. C.-R. Ageron, *France coloniale ou parti colonial?* (Paris, 1978), chap. 8; R. Girardet, *L'Idée coloniale en France de 1871 à 1962* (Paris, 1972), chaps. 10, 11; X. Yacono, *Les étapes de la décolonisation française* (Paris, 1971), chaps. 4, 6. Tony Smith, *The French Stake in Algeria, 1945–1962* (London, 1978), chaps 2, 7; C. M. Andrew and A. S. Kanya-Forstner, *France Overseas*, chap. 10. In 1956 all Communist and all Poujadist deputies used identical party manifestos. The Communists mentioned Algeria: The Poujadists did not. Of the remaining deputies only 29 per cent made specific reference to Algeria (Christopher Harrison, 'French Political Attitudes to the Algerian War: the Election Manifestoes of 1956 and 1958', dissertation for Part II of the 1980 Cambridge University Historical Tripos.)
4. Cited by P. C. Sorum, *Intellectuals and Decolonisation in France* (Chapel Hill, N.C., 1977), p. 211.
5. A. Loubère, 'Les Idées de Louis Blanc sur le nationalisme, le colonialisme et la guerre', *Revue d'histoire moderne et contemporaine*, vol. iv (1957), pp. 50 ff.
6. A. Siegfried, 'Approaches to an Understanding of Modern France', in E. M. Earle (ed.), *Modern France* (Princeton, 1951), pp. 6, 15.

7. Davidson Nicol, 'Alionne Diop and the African Renaissance', *African Affairs*, vol. lxxviii, no. 310 (Jan. 1979), pp. 3–4.
8. Léopold Senghor, *Liberté* (Paris, 1964–77), i. 98; J. L. Hymans, *Léopold Sédar Senghor. An Intellectual Biography* (Edinburgh, 1971), p. 263.
9. Senghor, *Liberté*, iii. 187, 84; Siegfried, 'Approaches', p. 15; Sorum, *Intellectuals*, p. 211.
10. Andrew and Kanya-Forstner, *France Overseas*, *passim*.
11. Sorum, *Intellectuals*, pp. 35, 44, 78.
12. Ageron, *France coloniale*, p. 214.
13. A. Horne, *A Savage War of Peace*, paperback edn. (London, 1979), pp. 55, 545; Andrew and Kanya-Forstner, *France Overseas*, chaps. 9, 10.
14. De Gaulle, *Mémoires d'espoir*, i. 218.
15. Sorum, *Intellectuals*, pp. 224 ff.; E. Leach, *Lévi-Strauss*, rev. edn. (London, 1974), p. 18. According to a recent opinion poll, Lévi-Strauss is the most influential living French intellectual. According to the same poll, the only living politician widely regarded as an influential intellectual is Senghor. *Encounter*, Aug. 1981, p. 29.
16. W. B. Cohen, *The French Encounter with Africans* (Bloomington, Ind., 1980), pp. 248–9; *idem*, 'Legacy of Empire: The Algerian Connection', *Journal of Contemporary History*, vol. xv (1980).
17. De Gaulle, *Mémoires d'espoir*, i. 69, 60.
18. A. Rondos, 'France/Africa. A Widening Role', *Africa Report*, Sept.–Oct. 1979; C.-R. Ageron, 'L'Idée d'Eurafrique et le débat franco-allemand dans L'Entre-deux-guerres', *Revue d'histoire moderne et contemporaine*, vol. xxii (1975).
19. Senghor, *Liberté*, iii. 80.
20. Cohen, 'Legacy of Empire', pp. 118–9.
21. *Africa Contemporary Record*, 1971–2, section C, p. 88.
22. Senghor, *Liberté*, ii. 210; i. 282.

CHAPTER 24. THE LAW OF NATIONS

1. *Le Droit des gens*, introduction, para. 18.
2. See Denys Hay, *Europe: the Emergence of an Idea* (1957), pp. 117–25, and for a more thorough set of references, Parker, *The Geographical Journal*, cxxvi (1960), 278–97.
3. There was debate about the status of Poland, Lithuania, and Russia.
4. *Quaestionum Juris Publici Libri Duo* (1737), chap. xvii.
5. See Anderson, in Ragnhild Hatton and M. S. Anderson (eds.), *Studies in Diplomatic History* (1970), pp. 183–98.
6. See the successful and influential work of Vattel, *Le Droit des gens* (1758), preface and introduction.
7. Wheaton, *Elements of International Law* (1866 edn.), Part I, paragraphs 10, 11, 12, and 13. The passages in the original edition of 1836 are similar, but rather less dogmatic in tone. Cf. Ward, *An Enquiry into the Foundation and History of the Law of Nations in Europe*, 2 vols. (London, 1795), chap iv.
8. See further Martens, *Cours diplomatique ou tableau des relations extérieures des puissances de l'Europe* (1801); Alexandrowicz, *British Year Book of International Law* vol. xxxvii (1961), p. 506 at pp. 510–12.
9. See D. B. Horn, *The British Diplomatic Service 1689–1789* (Oxford, 1961); Alexandrowicz, *An Introduction to the History of the Law of Nations in the East Indies* (Oxford, 1967), pp. 185–223; Parry (ed.), *British Digest of International Law*, vii. 570–1.
10. Michael Symes, *An Account of an Embassy to the Kingdom of Ava* (London, 1800).

11. See Saalfeld, in a work published in 1833, and see generally Alexandrowicz, *British Year Book of International Law* vol. xxxiv (1958), pp. 176–98 (Saalfeld is cited at p. 189).
12. See Hall, *International Law*, 5th edn. (1904), Part II, chap. 1.
13. 3rd edn. (Oxford, 1901).
14. (London, 1926), at p. 43; and see also p. 20.
15. ICJ Reports, 1975, p. 12 at p. 39 (para. 80). The date in issue was 1884 but the principle was already established by then.
16. *International Law* 4th edn. (1895), p. 1.
17. *International Law*, 1st edn. (1905), i. 3.
18. Ibid., p. 10.
19. This was not a new appearance in all respects.
20. Independence began precariously in July 1913.
21. Sauvant, *The Group of 77* (New York, 1981).

CHAPTER 25. DIPLOMACY TODAY

1. Hedley Bull, *The Anarchical Society. A Study of Order in World Politics* (London, 1977), p. 163.
2. Sir Ernest Satow, *A Guide to Diplomatic Practice*, 5th edn. (London, 1979), p. 3.
3. Ibid., p. 107.

CHAPTER 26. THE INTERNATIONAL ORDER IN A MULTICULTURAL WORLD

1. See Yu-Kuang Chu, 'The Chinese Language', in John Meskill, ed., *An Introduction to Chinese Civilization* (New York, 1973), pp. 601 ff. and notes 20–3 for citations of other authorities.
2. *The Primitive World and Its Transformations* (Ithaca, New York, 1953; repr. 1958), p. 111.
3. See Wang Yi-T'ung, *Official Relations between China and Japan 1368–1549*, Harvard-Yenching Institute Studies IX, (Cambridge, Mass., 1953), pp. 3, 39, 53 in particular.
4. There is considerable evidence of a revival of Shintoism in present-day Japan, notably in dispositions towards government. While it is fashionable today to allude to this Asian state as 'an honourable Western nation' on the ground of its spectacular technical achievements in finance, industry, and trade, such references are off the mark when one examines Japanese modes of decision-making and negotiation in precisely these areas of evdeavour.
5. For a discussion of this matter see Bozeman, *Politics and Culture in International History* (Princeton, 1960), pp. 146–61.
6. See Bozeman, *The Future of Law in a Multicultural World* (Princeton, 1971), pp. 21, 121–39.
7. See *History of Islam in West Africa* (London, 1962; repr. 1963), pp. 232 ff.; and *Islam in East Africa, Report of a Survey Undertaken in 1961* (London, 1962), pp. 31 ff., 43 ff.
8. In this context it is undeniable also that Peter the Great's efforts to 'Westernize' Russia were bound to lead to wholesale ejections of grafts that simply could not, and did not, 'take'.
9. See Bozeman, 'On the Relevance of Hugo Grotius and *De Jure Belli ac Pacis* for our Times', *Grotiana*, i. 65–124; and p. 79 for bibliographical references to this matter.
10. See Bozeman, 'Do Educational and Cultural Exchanges Have Political

Relevance?', in *Exchange*, A Publication of the U.S. Advisory Commission on International Educational and Cultural Affairs, Fall 1969, vol. v, no. 2, pp. 7 ff.

11. It is not in the purview of this paper to discuss these records in depth.
12. Sir Henry Maine, *Lectures on the Early History of Institutions* (New York, 1888), Lecture XI, pp. 329 ff. Maine says this on the Hindu law: 'There is no reason to suppose that philosophical theory had any serious influence on the jurisprudence of the Hindoos. . . . I believe that none of the remarkable philosophical theories which the genius of the Race produced are founded on a conception of the individual as distinct from that of the group in which he is born.'

    Some of my thoughts in this section are more fully developed in 'On the Relevance of Hugo Grotius and *De Jure Belli Ac Pacis for Our Times*', pp. 68 ff.
13. See David C. Gordon, *Self-Determination and History in the Third World* (New York, 1917), p. 61 for this reference to K. M. Pannikar, *Asia and Western Dominance: A Survey of the Vasco de Gama Epoch of Asian History 1498–1945* (New York, n.d.), pp. 492–3.
14. For a full analysis of this psychological tangle see Alfred G. Meyer, *Leninism* (New York, 1963), pp. 257 ff.
15. I am using the terms 'Western' and 'non-Western' because they relay well the essence of the themes with which this paper deals. By contrast, I avoid 'Third World' and 'Fourth World' because the implications of these references are quite unclear. The same holds in my view for contrasts or comparisons between 'Rich' and 'Poor', 'Developed', 'Less Developed', and 'Underdeveloped' nations and between 'North' and 'South'.
16. One of several reasons for omitting South and Central America from this survey of the multicultural world is the difficulty of identifying cultural traits that are incontestably common to the states in the hemisphere as a whole or in some of its major regions. A richly suggestive evocation of certain constant themes is Gabriel Garcia Marquez's novel *One Hundred Years of Solitude* (New York, 1970). Affinities between Indo-Iberian societies no doubt exists, but these states as all other American states including the United States originated in rather recent times as racially and culturally syncretic organisms. In regard to the Iberian factor it may be relevant to bear in mind that the conquerors and settlers of the 15th and 16th century were carriers also of Arab/Islamic traditions. After all, the Spanish discovery of America coincided with the final Spanish defeat of Arab and Arabized peoples that had controlled much of Spain for *c*.500 years. Analogies between the political systems of the Middle East and Latin America – and these are readily discernible – may stem from this historical circumstance.
17. This Japanese achievement is described in more detail in Chapters 13 and 20.
18. See *supra*.
19. Exception must be made in this respect for the Islamic provinces of the Soviet Union.
20. See his 'The Return of Islam', in *Commentary*, Jan. 1976.
21. See Albert Hourani, *A Vision of History* (Beirut, 1961), pp. 151 ff. For additional illustrations see Bozeman, *The Future of Law in a Multicultural World*, pp. 50–85, esp. notes 12, 30, 51.
22. See Bozeman, 'Iran: U.S. Foreign Policy and the Tradition of Persian Statecraft', *ORBIS, A Journal of World Affairs*, Summer 1979, pp. 387–402, for a commentary on this revolution.
23. 'The African Mind in Contemporary Conflict', The Jacques Parisot Foundation Lecture, 1971, *WHO Chronicle*, vol. xxv, no. 8 (Aug. 1971), pp. 343–53.

24. *The Daily Graphic* (Ghana), 18 Aug. 1977. For other cases illustrative of the ease with which killings are legally accommodated, especially when it is possible to link them to witchcraft, sorcery, dream evidence, and the confounding of identities, see Paul Brietzke, 'The Chilobwe Murders Trial', in *African Studies Review*, vol. xvii, no. 2 (Sept. 1974), pp. 361–81; James R. Hooker, 'Tradition and Traditional Courts: Malawi's Experiment in Law', American Universities Field Staff, *Fieldstaff Reports*, vol. xv, no. 3 (Mar. 1971), pp. 1 ff.; and Bozeman, *Conflict in Africa: Concepts and Realities*, Part VI, 'The Role of Intermediaries and the Settlement of Disputes', pp. 227–303. On the role of magic in military operations see John Michael Lee, *African Armies and Civil Order*, Studies in International Security, (London, 1969), and Kenneth W. Grundy, *Guerrilla Struggle in Africa; An Analysis and Preview* (New York, 1971).

Chapter 27. Unity and Diversity in a Multicultural World

References

H. Bull, 1979: 'Human Rights and World Politics', in R. Pettman, *Moral Claims in World Affairs* (London).
E. A. Gellner, 1980: 'State and Revolution in Islam', *Millennium*, vol. viii, no. 3 (winter 1979–80).
A. Inkeles and D. H. Smith, 1974: *Becoming Modern* (Cambridge, Mass.).
C. Kerr *et al.*, 1962: *Industrialism and Industrial Man*, Clark Kerr, J. T. Dunlop, F. H. Harbison, C. A. Myers (London).
M. Matossian, 1958: 'Ideologies of Delayed Industrialization'. *Economic Development and Cultural Change*, vol. vi, no. 3 (Apr. 1958).
H. J. Morgenthau, 1966: *Politics Among Nations*, 4th edn. (New York).
K. Ogura, 1979: 'How the "Inscrutable" Negotiate With the "Inscrutable": Chinese negotiating tactics vis-a-vis the Japanese', *China Quarterly*, Sept. 1979, pp. 529–55.
R. Pettman, 1979: *State and Class: A Sociology of International Relations* (London).
R. W. Tucker, 1977: *The Inequality of Nations* (New York).

INDEX